MW00830983

OTHER BOOKS BY MARIO GIAMMETTI

*Genesis Story*
Gammalibri, Milan, 1988
*Genesis Discografia 1968/1993*
Kaos Edizioni, Milan, 1994
*Peter Gabriel – Il trasformista*
Arcana, Padua, 1999
*Genesis – Il fiume del costante cambiamento*
Editori Riuniti, Rome, 2004
*Phil Collins – The Singing Drummer (Genesis Files Vol. 1)*
Edizioni Segno, Tavagnacco, 2005
*Steve Hackett – The Defector (Genesis Files Vol. 2)*
Edizioni Segno, Tavagnacco, 2005
*Tony Banks – Man Of Spells (Genesis Files Vol. 3)*
Edizioni Segno, Tavagnacco, 2006
*Anthony Phillips – The Exile (Genesis Files Vol. 4)*
Edizioni Segno, Tavagnacco, 2008
*Musical Box: Le canzoni dei Genesis dalla A alla Z*
Arcana, Rome, 2010
*Mike Rutherford – Silent Runner (Genesis Files Vol. 5)*
Edizioni Segno, Tavagnacco, 2011
*Genesis – Gli anni Prog*
Giunti, Florence, 2013
*Ray Wilson – Gypsy (Genesis Files Vol. 6)*
Edizioni Segno, Tavagnacco, 2014
*Genesis – Gli anni Prog (second edition)*
Giunti, Florence, 2015
*Peter Gabriel – Not One Of Us (Genesis Files Vol. 7)*
Edizioni Segno, Tavagnacco, 2016
*Genesis – Tutti gli album tutte le canzoni*
Il Castello Editore, Cornaredo, 2020
*Genesis – 1975 to 2021: The Phil Collins Years*
Kingmaker, Great Britain, 2021

MARIO GIAMMETTI

# GENESIS

## 1967 to 1975

*The Peter Gabriel Years*

KINGMAKER

*To my son, Simone*

First published in Italy as Genesis: Gli Anni Prog in 2013 by Mario Giammetti

www.giunti.it

Editing: Studio Angelo Ramella, Novara

KINGMAKER PUBLISHING
First published in Great Britain by Kingmaker Publishing Limited in 2020

www.kingmakerpublishing.com



Translated into English by J.M. Octavia Brown

Printed in Great Britain by
Biddles Books Limited, King's Lynn, Norfolk

# Contents

## A NOTE ON THE SOURCES

All of the quotes from members of Genesis included in this book are taken from interviews given to Mario Giammetti and Mike Kaufman.
The Mike Kaufman interviews were conducted in October 2007 at The Peninsula Chicago Hotel, Chicago (Banks, Collins and Rutherford) and at Sarm Studios, London (Gabriel, Hackett and Phillips).
All of the quotes from non-band members involved in the Genesis story are taken from interviews given exclusively to Mario Giammetti.

The record listening sessions with members of Genesis and Mario Giammetti took place at:

- Steve Hackett's house, Twickenham, 27 January 2008 (with Steve Hackett – SELLING ENGLAND BY THE POUND);
- B&B Domus Traiani, Benevento 13 March 2011 (with Steve Hackett – FOXTROT);
- Englewood Studios, London, 7 May 2011 (with Anthony Phillips – FROM GENESIS TO REVELATION AND TRESPASS);
- The Farm Studios, Chiddingfold, 10 May 2011 (with Tony Banks – THE LAMB LIES DOWN ON BROADWAY);
- MAP Studios, Twickenham, 1 December 2011 (with Steve Hackett – NURSERY CRYME).

The remaining dialogue used in this book from members and associates of the band comes from interviews given to Mario Giammetti which have previously been partially published as follows:

- John Alexander: e-mail interview, 13 May 2015 ( "John Alexander: Mr. Bad Example" in Dusk, Issue no. 80, July 2015)
- Tony Banks: telephone interviews, 1 October 2009 ("Nei meandri della memoria" in Dusk, Issue no. 63, November 2009) and 16 February 2012 ("Six not simply shrouded pieces" in Dusk, Issue no. 70, April 2012)
- Mick Barnard: telephone interview, 3 December 2001 ("Looking For Someone" in Dusk, Issue no. 38, February 2002)
- Ronnie Caryl: telephone interview, 27 February 2002 ("Come Talk To Me" in Dusk, Issue no. 39, June 2002)
- Steve Hackett: telephone interview, 7 February 2008 ("I colori della chitarra" in Dusk, Issue no. 58, March 2008)
- David Hitchcock: Fasano, 1 June 2015 ("In the land of grey and foxes – Intervista esclusiva a David Hitchcock" in Dusk, Issue no. 80, July 2015)
- Jonathan King: e-mail interview, 11 April 2014 ("Magic JK and four humble boys – Intervista esclusiva a Jonathan King" in Dusk, Issue no. 77, July 2014)
- Richard Macphail: telephone interview, 12 May 2005 ("Il sesto Genesis" in Dusk, Issue no. 50, August 2005)
- John Mayhew: London, 28 May 2006 ("Working Class Hero" in Dusk, Issue no. 53, July 2006)
- Anthony Phillips: London, 25 February 2007 ("Anthony Phillips – The Exile", Edizioni Segno, September 2008)
- John Silver: London, 7 May 2011 ("Lo Stan Kenton del punk" in Dusk, Issue no. 69, December 2011)
- Chris Stewart: telephone interview, 6 July 2000 ("Intervista esclusiva a Chris Stewart" in Dusk, Issue no. 33, September 2000)

## PHOTOGRAPHIC REFERENCES

© David Gahr / Getty Images p. 98;
© Roberto Masotti pp. 175, 178-179, 180, 183, 192-193, 196, 206.

The author also thanks for the images provided:

John Alexander Archive p. 20-21, 106; Tony Banks Archive p. 61; Mick Barnard Archive p. 80; David Chadwick / David Thomas Archive p. 27; Len Fifield Archive p. 34; June Leaney Archive pp. 130-131; Silvio Amenduni pp. 37; Maurizio Contardi pp. 118, 119; Jonathan Dann p. 22; Ernesto De Pascale p. 105; Ada Donnarumma p. 70; Salvatore Intragna p. 75; Natale Nitti pp. 152, 153; Willi Rupp pp. 144, 145, 150, 159, 189; James Stokes pp. 184, 194, 198, 201, 202, 212, 216, 217, 227, 239; Lino Vairetti pp. 90, 188; Angéla Vicedomini pp. 14-15, 32.

The publisher declares itself available to regulate any expectations
for those images whose source could not be found.

# Foreword by Tony Banks

*It goes without saying that when we made our first recording together back in the school holidays in 1967, before we were even called Genesis, that we had no idea the band would continue in one form or another for the next forty years or so, or indeed any books would be written about us. This book on the early period coming from an Italian pen is apt, as Italy was among the first countries to enjoy Genesis. Many line-up changes have occurred in the band's history, most in the era covered here; that Mike and I are the only ones to remain from the beginning was not predictable, given we hardly knew each other before that first recording. The most difficult departure at this stage for the band to deal with was that of Anthony Phillips. We were still pretty much unknown and he was probably the main reason the group existed in the first place, being the keenest to go professional. However the later additions of Steve and particularly Phil made us into a much better playing band, which made it much easier for us to continue.*

*This book deals with the period up to the departure of Peter, which although a big moment in our history was easier for us than the departure of Ant because we had by then some sort of a following. We knew while we were touring* THE LAMB LIES DOWN ON BROADWAY *that he wanted to leave, so we had time to prepare. The only problem was to find a singer! Looking back on these earlier albums the two that stand out for me are* FOXTROT *and* SELLING ENGLAND BY THE POUND. *The first album,* FROM GENESIS TO REVELATION, *feels like it was made by a different group, the next two have some great moments on them particularly* Stagnation, The Musical Box *and* The Fountain of Salmacis, *but were a little less consistent. It was during this period that we first played Italy, which soon became a favourite destination. The audience there seemed more receptive to our more elaborate stories, chord sequences and time signatures. Also there was the food and the weather. We were playing there to crowds numbering in the thousands while we were still struggling to fill small venues back in England. Some songs were heard for the first time in Italy as well, for example* Watcher of the Skies, *which we played on one tour before we had recorded it. I remember one gig in Sienna at the Palasport where we started the show with* Watcher, *the introduction sounded fantastic in this huge echoey room, but as soon as the drums came in the whole thing just descended into a chaotic mess where I am afraid it remained until the end of the show. Unfortunately later, after a bit of crowd trouble in Milan and Rome, we were not able to play in Italy for a few years, but it always had a special place in our hearts for being the first country to really take to us.*

**ACKNOWLEDGEMENTS**

The author wishes to thank:

- Tony Banks, Steve Hackett and Anthony Phillips for listening to Genesis albums and sharing their memories with him exclusively for this book;
- Mike Kaufman for full use of his interviews which provide details that would otherwise never have come to light;
- George German for his essential contribution to piecing together the list of concerts and memorabilia (concert tickets, posters, flyers);
- Paul Davis and Stephen Tonna Lowell for having transcribed hours of interviews;
- Massimo Satta for having translated hours of interviews;
- Jonathan Dann for clarifications on the most obscure part of Genesis' live history (1969/70);
- Alessandro Borri, Alessandro Bosi, Aleardo Cecchi, Giorgio Coslovich, Elio Ministeri, Roberto Paganin, Mino Profumo, Volker Warncke and Marco Zatterin for helping to throw light onto some of the uncertain live dates;
- John Alexander, Silvio Amenduni, Maurizio Contardi, Ernesto De Pascale, Ada Donnarumma, Salvatore Intragna, June Leaney, Natale Nitti, Willi Rupp, James Stokes, Lino Vairetti and Angéla Vicedomini for the photographs;
- Massimo Natali and Pier Tintori for the Swiss contacts;
- Valerio Cester, Marcello Cirese and Diego Zanti for the memorabilia;
- Octavia Brown for her peerless work on translating this book from Italian into English;
- Nick Shilton and Greg Spawton for helping to make the English publication happen, with additional thanks to Greg for his work as editor for the English text;
- Dr Geoff Parks for proof-reading the English text;
- Nick Clabburn, Jo Greenwood, Jo Hackett and Carol Willis – *you know why!!*

# Introduction

In all probability, had they found someone else willing to perform their songs, the lives of these four young boys would have taken a completely different turn. Who knows, maybe they would have enjoyed successful careers in the financial or legal sectors, living up to the legitimate expectations of parents who, in order to give them a head start in life, had sent them off to one of the most prestigious public schools in the UK. Although able to write songs, Peter Gabriel, Tony Banks, Anthony Phillips and Mike Rutherford had only basic levels of skill on their chosen instruments, but unfortunately (and thank goodness!) no-one was interested in their still very naive melodies and sixth-form lyrics. As a result, they decided to play the songs themselves. And therein lies the start of it all.

England in the mid-1960s was already a cultural hotbed. And all of these influences, duly mixed, were making their way into four young receptive minds: the perfect pop produced by The Beatles, the impetuous beat of The Kinks, the driving blues-rock of The Rolling Stones, the folk of Fairport Convention and the symphonic soundscapes offered by The Moody Blues and Procol Harum. Later on King Crimson would make their appearance on the scene and, yet again, everything would change.

Genesis are considered one of the forerunners of progressive rock and are usually cited alongside bands such as Yes and other successful groups of the period. However, if truth be told, although each one of those progressive bands had its own individuality, Genesis' uniqueness shines like a star in the multifaceted galaxy of rock: less convoluted than Crimson, less prolix than Emerson, Lake & Palmer, less pretentious than Yes, less hypertechnical than Gentle Giant and less menacing than Van Der Graaf Generator, Genesis limited themselves to taking their extraordinary songwriting skills into the world of progressive rock (those same skills would later see them achieve international pop stardom throughout the 1980s – but that's another story which will be told in a separate book). In other words, Genesis never sought to do anything other than stick to their initial intentions of writing good songs. The fact that they then mastered their instruments to the point of becoming a reference point for other musicians is secondary to their overall importance as a band. After all, with the exception of Phil Collins who joined the band on drums in 1970, there were no super-virtuoso musicians like Emerson or Howe in their line-up. No other band has ever had quite so much songwriting talent and marked individuality in its ranks, something which could go on to produce equally prestigious solo careers. Phil Collins and Peter Gabriel are among the biggest names of pop and rock music of all time; Rutherford's band, Mike &

The Mechanics, has sold over 10 million records; Steve Hackett is still filling venues around the world with his concerts based on a mix of old and new material; while Anthony Phillips and Tony Banks, despite never having reached the heights of success as solo artists, have had long and fascinating musical careers. But, again, that's another story.

The song, and therefore the melody, represents the essential ingredient of Genesis' style. To this mix we should add the classical-symphonic ambitions (never in poor taste) of Banks and Hackett, the extraordinary revolutionary style of the 12-string guitar arrangements pioneered by Phillips and Rutherford, and the voice and charisma of two incredible frontmen: which other band can boast two lead singers like Gabriel and Collins in the same line-up? In the early years of their history, the band underwent an extraordinary metamorphosis. After their tentative steps of From Genesis To Revelation, Genesis released Trespass, an album which is almost unique in the history of rock, an enchanting fresco of romantic folk rock. After the 1971/73 triptych, Nursery Cryme / Foxtrot / Selling England By The Pound, arguably unbeatable in the field of progressive rock, Genesis showed themselves ready to face a completely new challenge with The Lamb Lies Down On Broadway, a controversial album which, in some ways, can even be considered a precursor of punk rock, and which may have been, who knows, the start of a whole new series of great albums if Gabriel (essential to the equilibrium of the band at this stage) had not decided to leave.

So, yet another book on Genesis? What is there left to say? The only solution was to let the band itself help write this one. The author steers the book, acting as the glue holding together the scattered and sometimes tangled tales of Banks, Collins, Gabriel, Hackett, Phillips and Rutherford, allowing himself, chapter by chapter, to tell the story of the band, to offer his critique on each of the albums and to report on the live performances associated with the album releases. In addition, there is a list of Genesis concerts compiled in collaboration with the American collector, George German and, for this new English-language edition of the book, with Alessandro Borri. In those far off days, when the band was anything but famous, no-one thought to keep a record of all their live dates, so perfection in this regard is difficult to achieve. Nevertheless, by integrating new research and sifting out the inaccuracies found even in some of the fundamental starting points, such as the *Genesis - The Movement* website and the books *Genesis Revisited* by Alan Hewitt, *Play Me My Song* by Paul Russell and the self-produced *Old Memories ...* by Luca Alberici, I believe that the list presented in this book is the most reliable to date.

I feel it is essential to underline that the dialogue provided by the members of Genesis, making up the heart of this book, is all (without exception) previously unpublished material and is taken mainly from two sets of interviews: those given to the English journalist, Michael Kaufman before the 5.1 remixed albums were released in 2008 (only a part of which was used in the video interviews connected with the releases) and the listening sessions which I had the good fortune and honour to conduct with some of the band members, record by record. The latter was the key which opened the door onto the previously unknown perspectives of the writers and performers of these albums. Their listening to them with me (sometimes for the first time in decades) just for the purpose of this book, provides us with an exclusive new insight as they dwell on details which every enthusiast can then verify in person thanks to the timing indicated in the text (note: the timings refer to the remastered editions except for From Genesis To Revelation which refers to the standard CD version).

The result is therefore a brand new take on the music and evolution of Genesis during that extraordinarily creative period between 1967 and 1975. Despite the obvious and unavoidable repetitions, even the most knowledgeable fan will be able to tap into a wealth of information which has never previously surfaced, including the hint of discord seemingly buried under decades of dust but which every now and then resurfaces, albeit tempered by their oh so British aplomb.

This book was originally published in Italian and I am delighted that we are now able to make an English language version of the book available for the first time.

Mario Giammetti

# From Genesis To Revelation

(Decca, 1969)

***Where The Sour Turns To Sweet / In The Beginning / Fireside Song / The Serpent / Am I Very Wrong? / In The Wilderness /// The Conqueror / In Hiding / One Day / Window / In Limbo / Silent Sun / A Place To Call My Own***

- **Release date: 7 March 1969**
- **Recorded at Regent Sounds Studios, Soho, London in 1968 by Brian Roberts and Tom Allom**
- **Producer: Jonathan King**

- **Peter Gabriel: lead vocals, flute, tambourine**
- **Anthony Phillips: electric and acoustic guitars, vocals**
- **Anthony Banks: keyboards, acoustic guitar, vocals**
- **Michael Rutherford: acoustic guitars, bass guitar, vocals**
- **John Silver: drums, percussion (except on *Silent Sun*)**
- **Chris Stewart: drums on *Silent Sun* (not credited on the original release)**
- **David Thomas: backing vocals (not credited on the original release)**
- **Arthur Greenslade: string arrangements**
- **Lou Warburton: brass arrangements**

## THE MAKING OF

"The Battle of France is over. The Battle of Britain is about to begin." With these words, on 18 June 1940, Prime Minister, Winston Churchill, confirmed that Britain's policy of stubborn resistance and of "blood, toil, tears and sweat" was to continue. Following the defeat of France, Hitler's Nazi Germany was convinced Great Britain was on the verge of seeking a peace agreement. But Churchill's indignant refusal, relying on British patriotism, meant Germany was forced to plan an invasion by sea. "Operation Sea Lion" (*Unternehmen Seelöwe*), as it was called, envisaged launching several attacks from the French coast – but Great Britain was anything but unprepared. The RAF brilliantly succeeded in maintaining control over the English Channel, forcing Hitler to abandon his invasion plans indefinitely.

Around this time, 22-year-old Edwin Phillips, one of many young men called up to serve King and Country, was part of a small group of soldiers undertaking reconnaissance in Dunkirk. Many of his comrades were killed and he was hit in the leg by a bullet. Luckily for him the bullet went straight through leaving him injured but still able to walk (albeit with a little help), so when British and Allied troops were evacuated, he was able to get away, unlike the less fortunate non-walking wounded who had to be left behind.

Just a few months earlier, while waiting to be called up, Phillips, like so many soldiers at that time, had married. Knowing that once they reached the front there was a strong chance of never making it back home, it became common practice for soldiers to marry their sweethearts. Marriage became a desperate attempt to cling onto life, enjoying every last remnant of freedom, trying to imagine a happy future on their return after the war was won.

But when World War II finally ended and Edwin Phillips came home, many, too many things had changed, and not even baby Anne, born while her father was at the front, was enough to hold the young family together. Shortly afterwards Edwin met another woman, much younger than himself, whom he married in March 1951. On 23 December that same year, she gave birth to a son, Anthony Edwin Phillips, in a hospital in Putney, South London.

Anthony Phillips' story isn't very different to that of the friends he would meet during his adolescence who together would change their lives and make a part of rock history.

After all, those born at the dawn of the '50s were all post-war children, a generation brought up with the greatest of fears dictated not only by the conflict itself but also by considerations which up until then had never been put into focus, such as the level of collective folly sick ideologies like Nazism could reach, or the worrying advances in technology which could also be applied to weapons of mass destruction. And yet, in post-war England the desire to start again prevailed, a barely suppressed yearning to get back to living, after so much fear, death and destruction, and to rebuild the foundations of a decent life.

Putting the war behind him, Edwin Phillips became the archetypal middle-class Englishman, absorbed in his work to which he dedicated all of his time in order to ensure the well-being of his family. Anthony Phillips: "My father worked in the City. He was a very successful banker and later on in life he moved on from having the one job to what we call diversifying: he became chairman of a number of big companies, like Higgs & Hill, a

Charterhouse School, the place where Genesis was formed.

construction company, and Friends Provident, an insurance company. He did really well. He was a very successful man." (1)

His wife, Pauline, on the other hand, took care of the home. Phillips: "Nowadays all the roles have changed, everyone shares things. In those days it was quite unusual for a woman to work. The man went to work and the mother looked after the kids; men did nothing in the house at all. None of my father's friends had wives who worked." (1)

It was fairly common practice, among better-off families, to send their children to public schools, where they believed they would benefit from a superior education and be better prepared for later life. In a generation still getting over the traumas of war, there was little time for fuss and affection and children got used to looking after themselves from a very early age.

Phillips: "When I was eight years old, I got sent to boarding school. These schools often started originally because you had a lot of people in the forces. During the British Empire you had people in India and all over the world, and they wanted to have somewhere for their children to stay and be educated. It wasn't because parents didn't want their children at home; they thought this was where you got the best education and that it made you tough, made you a man. So you were sent away to this place and you didn't see your parents for three or four weeks which was pretty frightening actually." (1)

The situation was made even more unpleasant due to the pupil-teacher relationship. Phillips: "1960 wasn't that long after the war which ended in 1945. Some teachers had been in the war and some of them had bits missing. Some of them would get you by the hair if you didn't understand something right away. I was very unhappy to start with. You didn't see your parents very much so it drove a wedge between you and them. It was a real shock for an eight-year-old boy who had never been away from home, but after two or three years it was OK. You couldn't really tell your parents you weren't happy, because you didn't want them to go and talk to the school. You had to be a man, you had to be tough." (1)

Crawford Rutherford was also a military man. A captain in the Royal Navy, he was constantly moving up and down the country taking his family, including the young Michael John Cloete Crawford Rutherford, with him. Born on 2 October 1950, at the age of seven and a half, Mike was sent to the Leas Preparatory School in Hoylake on the Wirral peninsula, Cheshire. Here, due to the distance, he would rarely see his parents.

Anthony George Banks, born on 27 March 1950, was sent to the Boarzell Tutorial College, in Hurst Green, East Sussex, before moving to Hastings.

Tony Banks: "In this country we have public schools as opposed to private schools, that require an entrance exam to get in. My father, John, taught a number of subjects to 13-year-old boys, the ones who had failed to get in the first time round, so that they could get into the school of their choice, such as Eton. Basically he was teaching rich kids how to get into those schools. But he had already retired from doing that by the time we moved to Hastings. He just wanted to move to a smaller house and he was a chicken farmer for a while after that." (2)

Peter Brian Gabriel, born 13 February 1950, had a slightly different childhood. His father, Ralph, whose family had run a profitable timber business, excelled in the field of science (graduating in Electronic Engineering, he even played a part in some important inventions, including the first fibre-optic cable television system). He had moved into the countryside where he first sent Peter to an independent school in Woking (Cable House) and then to the St. Andrew's School for Boys from where he could cycle home every weekend.

Anthony, Mike, Tony, Peter. Four boys whose paths were set to cross, between September 1963 and April 1965, at Charterhouse, the austere public school, just a few miles from the centre of Godalming, Surrey. A place where teachers were very authoritarian and where life in a boarding school forced them to deal with a reality not only marked by a lack of family affection, but also one of bullying from some teachers and older boys.

Fellow Charterhouse student, Christopher Stewart (born in Crawley, 27 March 1951), who soon began to work with the four friends says: "I detested public school. I hated the people, I hated the routine, I hated the very idea of college. I went back there a couple of years ago and, to be honest, I thought it was an amazing place, but the set-up just wasn't right for me. It didn't do me any harm, if anything it made me a better person, but I hated it. It was just like you read and see in the film *If* (1968); it was like something out of the

was replaced by Mick Colman. Anthony was also in another band outside Charterhouse, Spoken Word, which in 1966 recorded a cover of *Evening* by Jimmy Whiterspoon on acetate with the following line-up: David Thomas (vocals), Ronnie Gunn (piano), Jeremy Ensor (bass guitar), David Chadwick (guitar) and Peter Gabriel (drums).

1800s." (3)

Two things kept the boys afloat: sport and music. Sport gave them the chance to vent their growing angst through competition, whilst music let their minds wander and open up to art.

And so this is the educational and socio-cultural context that gave birth to the legend we call Genesis. It was in the classrooms of Charterhouse that the idea of a band began to form in the minds of the four young friends. The most precocious, musically speaking, was the youngest: guitar-player Anthony Phillips, Ant to his friends. The curiously named Rivers Job (Anthony's friend since St. Edmund's Preparatory School in Hindhead) played bass, whilst singer Richard Macphail and drummer Rob Tyrell both came from Charterhouse. Together with Mike Rutherford on rhythm guitar, the five formed a band called Anon, short for Anonymous. Despite being just 13 years old, Ant was already writing simple songs which Anon alternated with covers of classic rock songs, particularly by The Rolling Stones.

As with any young band, Anon went through numerous line-up changes. When Rutherford's housemaster banned him from playing guitar, he

In the meantime, Gabriel had also become great friends with Tony Banks in another wing of Charterhouse. The two used to fight over the only piano available in the school until they eventually came to a compromise: Tony on keyboards and Peter on vocals.

These young musicians all came together in the summer of '66 when Anon's lead singer, Richard Macphail, organised an end-of-year concert at Charterhouse. The programme for the 'Beat Club Concert' included three bands, the most important of which was, of course, Anon, which featured the following line-up: Phillips, Macphail, Job, Tyrell and Colman. Rutherford, who in the meantime had managed to get his guitar ban lifted by his housemaster, played with Climax, while the third band, Garden Wall, featured Banks and Gabriel, drummer Chris Stewart and trumpeter Johnny Trapman (with the help of Phillips and Job for the actual stage performance as they didn't have a guitarist or bass player).

Shortly after the 'Beat Club Concert', Anon (with a reinstated Mike Rutherford in the place of Colman) recorded the track *Pennsylvania Flickhouse* at the Tony Pike Studio in Putney, which was

CD released by the German Genesis Fan Club in 2011, featuring the 1966 recording of *Pennsylvania Flickhouse* by Anon.

printed on six acetate discs, one for each member of the band and one for sound engineer and friend, Brian Roberts. This gem (a beat piece similar in style to The Rolling Stones) would see the light of day in November 2011 on a CD single issued to celebrate the twentieth anniversary of the Genesis fan club in Germany.

At the end of the year, however, both Macphail and Job left Charterhouse and consequently the band. For a while Anon continued as a three-piece with Mike switching to bass guitar and lead vocals. After a last concert by the trio in December 1966, Anon finally called it a day.

During the 1966 Christmas holidays, Ant and Mike found themselves writing songs together at Mike's grandmother's house and here they planned to cut a demo in Brian Robert's studio. This was the first step in one of the most amazing musical adventures in the history of Rock. A dream called Genesis.

It was April 1967 when Brian Roberts opened up his studio doors to Anthony and Mike, ready to record three brand new songs (*Try A Little Sadness, Listen On Five* and *That's Me*) along with two other songs from Anon's old repertoire (*Don't Want You Back* and *Patricia*). They decided they wanted to add some piano to the recordings and asked Tony Banks of Garden Wall for help. Tony brought Peter Gabriel along with him and, in exchange for playing piano, asked to record a demo of the song *She Is Beautiful*, which he had written with Gabriel. As Peter had a far better voice than Ant (who in the meantime had taken over from Mike on lead vocals), the young Peter Gabriel ended up singing on all the songs and playing drums on the instrumental track *Patricia*.

A school friend called Jonathan Alexander handed the demo tape over to record producer (and Charterhouse alumnus) Jonathan King. Alexander: "It fell to me to give it to Jonathan King when he visited the school whilst the others stayed out of the way. I wasn't convinced he would listen to it, especially when I told him that it was basically a band with no name yet." (4)

Although only 20 years old and still a student at university, King had achieved considerable success in the music business and was a minor celebrity at Charterhouse. King: "I had just had a huge No.1 hit - *Everyone's Gone To The Moon* - and instead of following it up with another vocal release I went into the studio with a Cambridge group, Hedgehoppers Anonymous. They couldn't play so I used all session men. I wanted to become a record producer - being a "pop star" was more a hobby, my interest was producing. I'd written a song called *It's Good News Week* and produced them singing it instead of myself. Not only did I have my first hit as a producer with it but I made loads more money. Going back in triumph [to Charterhouse] in my little Austin Healey Sprite car, this lad gave me the tape and said "this is the school group. They don't have a name". Driving back I listened to the tape and loved Peter's voice. I decided to produce them by the time I got home in London." (5)

King called Peter Gabriel and asked the band to give him something else to listen to.

King: "It was quite hard getting through to Peter. One phone in each house. 60 boys. There were a dozen houses in the school. I'd been in Daviesites. They were in Duckites, the nickname for Girdlestoneites - I think because Mr Girdle-

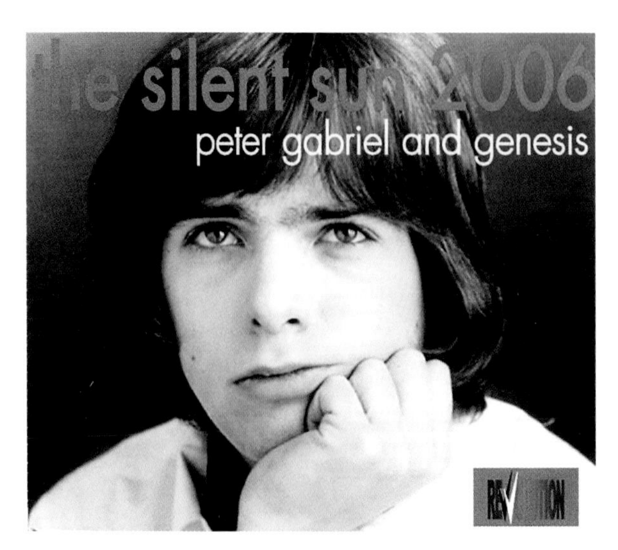


Jonathan King re-issue of *Silent Sun* on a CD single in 2006, accredited to 'Peter Gabriel and Genesis ' and featuring additional (and intrusive) overdubs of drums.

stone, the original housemaster, walked like a duck. So I had to phone and ask whoever answered to fetch Peter. I think two or three boys said "yes" then just hung up - couldn't be bothered. Eventually I got Peter." (5)

In the summer of '67, the four musicians recorded a second demo at Regent Sounds Studios in London with four songs, two of which were newer versions of those recorded just a few months earlier: *She Is Beautiful, Try A Little Sadness, Image Blown Out* and *Where The Sour Turns To Sweet.*

Peter Gabriel: "I was 17 in 1967, an amazing year to be entering adulthood. I'd sneak out from school and go down to the Electric Garden in Covent Garden, a sort of basement club. You'd see all these oil projections on the wall, all this psychedelia really and that was just the Indica Gallery. There was just so much going on, IT and Oz magazines... There was this cultural explosion happening and this sense that youth, for the very first time, was taking over the world. Every barrier was being smashed down and we, in our small, little isolated cell, definitely felt connected to that, I think me probably more than everybody else. This sense of trying to do things in a new way, in a different way was very important. You had all sorts of groups working to explore things. On the folk side there was Fairport Convention and Family. Then you had The Beatles, obviously, and lots of different influences and there was still a core of black music. I had a passion for soul music while Tony, Mike and I all liked English Blues, although they more than I." (6)

Back in Regent Sounds Studios, in the autumn of '67, a third demo was recorded with eight new songs (*The Mystery Of The Flannan Isle Lighthouse, Hidden In The World Of Dawn, Hair On The Arms And Legs, Sea Bee, Barnaby's Adventure, From Shapes To Shadows, Lost In A Drawer, Fourteen Years Too Long)* which, however, proved not to be to Jonathan King's liking.

Gabriel: "From the beginning, we set out as songwriters and were quite happy to be writing what were effectively pop songs. But I think there was always a yearning inside us to explore, to push the boundaries and mix styles and so we started to get a little more adventurous. We were rehearsing and building an identity and a sound but for Jonathan King and our publisher, Joe Roncoroni, it got too out of mainstream, too left field." (6)

King: "They weren't very good instrumentally. Just learning. Very ambitious but self indulgent. Lots of long solos that went out of tune, rambled, were boring and unstructured. I made them cut the length, sharpen up, tighten the tunes and lyrics, not play things they weren't able to play yet. They needed to learn and develop." (5)

Phillips: "Ironically, in the very early days we used to write verse-chorus songs. After Jonathan King signed us, we used to do these kind of five minute epics with lots of sections, but he would

London 1968, promotional photograph for Decca Records. In the front row Anthony Phillips and Chris Stewart. Seated, Tony Banks and Mike Rutherford. Standing, Peter Gabriel.

talk about hit singles, which is fair enough, he wanted to make money out of us, so we wrote *Silent Sun*." (7)

Disappointed by the lack of enthusiasm shown for their marked creative growth, Peter and Tony deliberately wrote *Silent Sun* in order (as the band remembers) to emulate the Bee Gees, one of King's favourite groups.

King: "The Bee Gees thing has grown out of the reality. The album I actually gave them was Crosby, Stills and Young. Simple, acoustic songs meant they had to strip down the sound, stay in tune, not try to play things they couldn't yet play. That was the reason I wanted softer pop stuff. And I loved *The Silent Sun*. It showed off Peter's voice at his best." (5)

In fact, King must be mistaken in this matter as the first Crosby, Stills and Nash (not Crosby, Stills and Young) album was only released in May 1969. The first international release by the Bee Gees was in 1967, so it may be that the band's account is correct.

In any case, the plan had worked: the producer liked the song and managed to get the band signed to Decca Records (the same label as The Rolling Stones!).

Needing a drummer, Genesis brought in Chris Stewart, one of Peter and Tony's Garden Wall bandmates, and together they recorded *Silent Sun* and a song by Phillips, *That's Me*, for a single released in February 1968, which, however, failed to arouse any real interest. The same went for their second 45, released in May with two more songs written by Gabriel and Banks, *A Winter's Tale* and *One-Eyed Hound*.

In the midst of all of this, in March to be precise, Genesis found time to record another demo at Central Sound in London which featured the tracks *Hey!*, *I'm Here*, *2:30 Park Time* and *There Was A Movement*.

In the meantime, King had decided the band needed to be put to the test with a full album. So, in the summer of '68, after recording three more tracks in Roberts' studio in Chiswick, (*Everywhere Is Here*, *You've Got To Be Perfect* and *Humanity*), Genesis went into Regent Sounds Studios and

Genesis at Send Barns in late 1967/early 1968.

Chris Stewart photographed in London on May 1, 1998. After the music stopped, Stewart moved to Andalusia where he became an internationally renowned writer. His first book, *Driving Over Lemons*, has been translated into ten languages.

recorded a total of 12 songs, most of which were to end up, in revised versions, on the debut album: *One Day, In The Beginning, Image Blown Out, The Magic Of Time, In The Wilderness, Am I Very Wrong?, In Limbo, Wandering, Fireside Song, A Place To Call My Own, Visions Of Angels, Where The Sour Turns To Sweet.*

For this recording, alongside Gabriel, Banks, Phillips and Rutherford, the band line-up included new drummer, Jonathan "John" Silver (born in Oxford, 22 February 1949), who took over from Stewart, who had been fired by Jonathan King.

Chris Stewart (now a successful author): "King didn't like me and I didn't like him. King threw me out, which was actually the right thing to do, mainly because I wasn't a great drummer, but also because he wanted us to go professional and we started working like a real band. I was still at school though and there was no way my parents were going to let me leave. Making a record was the most exciting thing that could have happened to me. I was 15 or 16 and I went from school to a recording studio in London in the 1960s! In the end, of course, I was really upset. You start dreaming of becoming a rock star and then, all of a sudden, it's gone... That said, I wasn't upset for long because they gave me 300 pounds, which at that time was a massive amount of money." [3]

When Genesis entered the recording studio in the summer of '68, they had a number of weeks behind them spent composing new songs in their homes, left empty by their parents away on holiday.

Phillips: "Some of the songs (*Where The Sour Turns To Sweet, She Is Beautiful, The Serpent, One Day*) were written earlier. We started off at John Silver's house in Oxford, then went to David Thomas' house [a friend and supporter of the band] and then my parents' house. There wouldn't have been that much time because we broke up from school at the end of June, so we probably had just a couple of weeks, maybe ten days, at each at those places. We did some demos at Brian Roberts' house. That was tragic because then he moved and left all those tapes in the attic and somebody threw them away. Which is a pity because somewhere he had a whole lot of Genesis demos. I wonder what they sounded like. It would have been fascinating to have heard those demos." [7]

Banks: "The original intention was that other people would do the songs we wrote but, when no-one else wanted to do them, we modified them a bit so they fit this kind of broad concept we had and we recorded them just after we left school. They were very simple songs, we never played live or anything. I played mainly piano on the album." [6]

Phillips: "I suppose you could analyse From Genesis To Revelation as being a piano-based album,

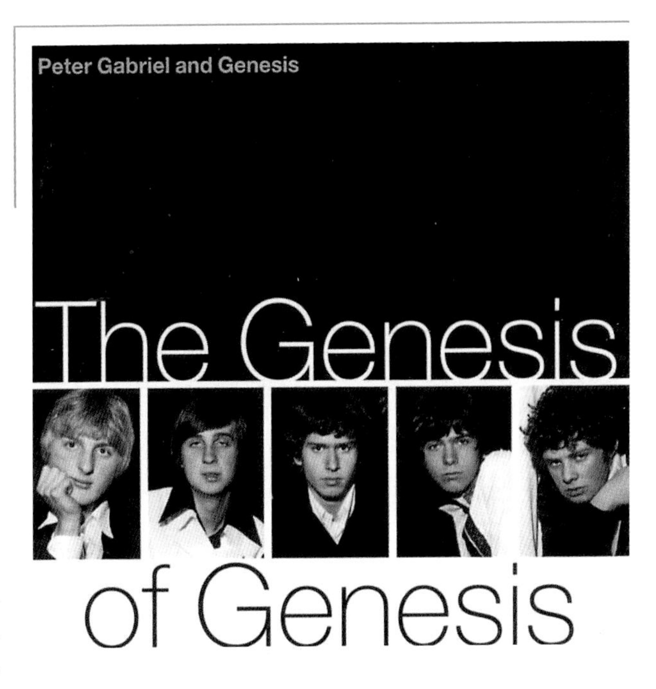


Another re-issue from Jonathan King in 2006, again incorrectly attributed to 'Peter Gabriel and Genesis'.

because Tony obviously played piano and interpreted Peter's stuff on piano. Mike and I were very much on the sidelines although I wrote more." [6]

Rutherford: "My parents, bless them, were supportive. I'm sure they were hoping it wouldn't last. However, in all fairness, in those days parents had no idea you could have a career making pop music, it hadn't really been seen. So in a sense, I think they were very good and very brave in supporting me." [6]

In the end 12 songs were selected, which together with *Silent Sun* (in the version recorded a few months earlier with Chris Stewart) made a total of 13 tracks in all. In other words, quite a few songs were left out, including the first version of *Going Out To Get You*, a song which would be resurrected, along with a number of others, years later to be included in the Genesis Archive 1967–75 box set (released 22 June 1998).

Phillips: "*The Magic Of Time*, *Build Me A Mountain* and *Visions Of Angels* were going to be on the album but got left off. *Visions Of Angels* just didn't work out at all. There was another song from the same time *Everywhere Is Here*; that was pretty but the demo never survived. I don't know why *Build Me A Mountain* got left off. I thought it was quite good." [7]

## THE ALBUM

From Genesis To Revelation was recorded in the summer of 1968, an extraordinarily volatile year punctuated by dramatic political events (in the space of just two months, between April and June, both Martin Luther King and Robert Kennedy were assassinated) and by marked cultural unrest (which culminated in the "May '68" uprising in France). But the young and budding Genesis showed no signs of being part of that incredible period of social ferment. On the contrary, while the hippy philosophy managed to survive on the album in a few images tightly linked to the desire for spiritual communion, as in the opening track, *Where The Sour Turns to Sweet*, most of the lyrics put together by Gabriel and the band address the birth of the world as a tribute to the band's name. Genesis is, after all, the first book in the Bible describing Creation, Original Sin and the Flood in its opening chapters. Without pushing the boundaries too far, Genesis put together, and not without a certain measure of chaos, a number of scholastic and religious reminiscences. *In The Beginning*, for example, uses naive imagery to describe the moment when 'an ocean of motion' creates the land 'scattering mountains all around', while *The Serpent* uses the biblical reference of the reptilian tempter to outline the creation of man and

The promotional demo of *The Silent Sun,* made available by Decca on 2nd February 1968.

woman, which then finds its sublimation in the concluding *A Place To Call My Own*, sung from the point of a view of a child being born.

Not everything on the album is strictly linked to the biblical concept: *Am I Very Wrong?* cites the "happiness machine" (taken from the novel by American sci-fi writer, Ray Bradbury), whereas in other places themes touch on the predatory ambitions of man (*The Conqueror*) and the admiring contemplation of nature (*In Hiding*), reserving a special place, of course, to the topic of love (*One Day, Silent Sun*).

Musically speaking, however, Genesis found themselves blown out of the water by some of the biggest names in rock history who were, at that time, churning out one masterpiece after another on both sides of the Atlantic. Over in America, Simon & Garfunkel released not only the soundtrack to The Graduate but also their fourth studio album, Bookends, The Velvet Underground brought out White Light / White Heat, Frank Zappa - We're Only In It For The Money, Joni Mitchell - Song To A Seagull, The Doors - Waiting For The Sun and The Grateful Dead - Anthem Of The Sun.

And Europe responded with just as much creative fervour: Pink Floyd had brought in David Gilmour to replace Syd Barrett on guitar for the album A Saucerful Of Secrets. But Genesis were particularly interested in the bands that inspired them most. The Beatles, approaching their inevitable demise, released the double White Album, while The Moody Blues and Procol Harum both brought out their second albums (respectively In Search Of The Lost Chord and Shine On Brightly). And just as Genesis were heading into the recording studio, Family also appeared on the scene, bringing out their debut album (Music In A Doll's House) along with Jethro Tull (This Was) and Traffic who released their self-titled second album.

In 1968 Buffalo Springfield split up as did The Yardbirds, which gave us the New Yardbirds, a band which would soon change its name to Led Zeppelin. And the bands Yes and Black Sabbath also formed in 1968.

Released into the very midst of this extraordinary music scene, From Genesis To Revelation fared the best it could, which was very little. The writing on the album leaves a lot to be desired. The more prolific song-writing pair, Banks and Gabriel, wrote more than half of the songs, the rest coming from Anthony Phillips (with a small contribution from Mike Rutherford). There were a few minor and occasional reciprocal incursions between the two composing pairs, but for the most part they worked separately. The songs inevitably reveal, first and foremost, a heavy Beatles influence, as

well as some slightly more structured compositions along the lines of Procol Harum and The Moody Blues. The latter had just had a massive hit with *Nights In White Satin*, enriched with a symphonic arrangement.

This may be why Jonathan King was convinced that the songs needed dressing up with some orchestral parts as opposed to them being left as otherwise simple songs, primarily performed on piano accompanied by some acoustic rhythm guitars and soft drumming. The budget, however, was not one with which miracles could be worked: in fact, the limited number of audio tracks available made it necessary to make an initial mix of the band's tracks, the sound of which is therefore not only compressed but also reduced to mono, in order to leave enough space for the strings and brass arrangements. Despite having an excellent pedigree (including collaborations with Cat Stevens and Diana Ross and as an arranger of both the *Goldfinger* theme tune for the Bond film of the same name and the legendary erotic song *Je T'aime*), conductor Arthur Greenslade failed to get any of the compositions off the ground. If anything, he actually managed to smother whatever musical promise the album may have held, and Lou Warburton's brass sections only made matters worse.

The production was also below par. The crystal quality of Gabriel's voice clearly stands out, as do the albeit restrained contributions on piano from Banks, but Phillips and Rutherford on the other hand, despite some tasteful acoustic guitar playing, remain decidedly in the shade, with only the occasional foray on lead guitar by Ant and some evanescent bass work from Mike.

In other words, not the greatest of debuts, although it has to be said there were more than just a few mitigating factors, such as Jonathan King's excessive interference, the unacceptable time lapse between the recording and release and, above all, the very young age of the band members.

## THE SONGS

### WHERE THE SOUR TURNS TO SWEET

Phillips: "This was more a Gabriel and Banks song. We tended to write in pairs, maybe a bit more so later on. Early on, Gabriel and Banks did most of the writing. They probably wrote most of this album. Mike didn't write much. I had a few guitar riffs. This is one of the early ones." [7]

Starting off with finger clicking and a three-chord piano riff, the song which opens the debut album of the very young Genesis immediately reveals the quality of Gabriel's voice with its intense timbre and soul feel. The musical accompaniment, built around soft acoustic rhythm gui-

Photograph taken in 1968. From the left: David Thomas, John Silver, Mike Rutherford, Peter Gabriel, Anthony Phillips.

Promotional copy of *The Silent Sun* made available on the Parrot label and distributed in America by London Records.

tar and dominated by Tony Banks on piano, flows over a base of maracas and tambourines.

Genesis had previously recorded another version of this song which was supposed to be released as a single (something which never happened) with another song, the hypothetical B-side, called *From the Bottom of A Well*.

Phillips: "Jonathan King led us to do that just after we signed a publishing contract, with the idea of making a single. At Advision Studios. Probably August 1967. I remember I wore my kaftan from Tangier and Jonathan King said: "Oh you're such a flower child." No-one's ever come across that recording. I don't know whether Advision exists anymore but it's possible that they might have tapes there. It's worth trying to find out. If the studio doesn't exist, you'll have to find out where the tapes went. Jonathan King might have them." [7]

At the end of the song, electronic sounds link the first track to the following one. The linking pieces of music, which act as bridges between the songs, feature on almost the whole album, maybe to reinforce the idea of it being a concept.

Phillips: "The links were mainly hymns that we all loved. Funnily enough, Charterhouse asked me to write a piece of music for the school's fourth centenary. They asked Peter and Tony to write something too, but they probably weren't interested." [7]

## IN THE BEGINNING

The introduction to the second track is well and truly in the territory of psychedelia.

Phillips: "That's very '60s that sound. It's like something from *Doctor Who*. I've no idea what made that noise at the beginning but this song was based on a guitar riff of mine." [7]

An insistent bass riff overlying the dialogue between rhythm guitar, piano and percussion is the foundation supporting Gabriel's voice, whereas at the end of each verse a psychedelic electric guitar riff by Phillips stands out.

Phillips: "I used just fuzz I think, maybe a bit of wah wah pedal, but I didn't use guitar phasing. There weren't any phase pedals back then, it was tape phasing [Phasing is a technique whereby two instruments record the same part but slightly out of sync, creating a pleasant effect], where you put your hands on the tape to slow it down and cause that 'shhhh' sound. Nowadays you can go in the shop and buy any kind of pedal for any effect. It was a very ambitious song, where we were tracing history. It was really over the top actually." [7]

## FIRESIDE SONG

Here the linking piece is a sombre piano solo by Tony.

Phillips: "This is a choral hymn that we used to sing in church by someone called Herbert Howells. We loved his music." [7]

The song, on the other hand, based on acoustic rhythm guitar and strings, stands out for Gabriel's soft vocal performance, supported in the chorus by Ant.

Phillips: "We sound very upper class here. People always joked about this one. But it's a very nice song. It was mainly Tony's song and we added a bit. The one thing you really notice is how badly the guitar is recorded because it's all plectrum. Whereas on the next album, TRESPASS, I had my own sound and I insisted on how I recorded. I even had a big argument with Robin Cable, the engineer, because he said it didn't sound like a 12-string. Everyone used to use a 12-string like a percussion instrument, like a washboard. And what you hear is 'kshh kshh kshh' as opposed to the notes. If you record the microphone on the soundboard you just pick up the plectrum. If you take the mic further away it gets the whole sound. And they [the sound engineers] were always putting it too close and I'd always be pushing it away when they weren't looking." [7]

## THE SERPENT

After a psychedelic link (with percussion and acid guitars playing a riff which would be used again years later in *Twilight Alehouse*), *The Serpent* turns out to be a remake of the first song ever written by Banks & Gabriel, *She is Beautiful*, with a joint electric guitar and bass riff and Bank's organ enveloping Gabriel's voice with a rhythm 'n' blues feel.

Phillips: "This is the song Jonathan King signed us for. Also because, to be honest, the others were all rubbish. I'm not sure about the backing harmonies there. This is very much a Gabriel & Banks song." [7]

## AM I VERY WRONG?

After another piano intro ("another hymn," explains Phillips, "but I'm not sure who this one

is by. We weren't particularly religious, we just liked the hymns and tunes") [7] the song is divided into two sections; in the first part, the voice is intense and Gabriel lays the vocals softly over the acoustic guitars and strings, whereas in the chorus the lead vocals seem to disappear, leaving room for his companions' voices, Ant's in particular.

Phillips: "I don't know if Peter is singing in the chorus or not. Our friend, David Thomas was also singing here. He did a lot of the backing harmonies. He sang a lot. He probably should have been paid some money actually, but nobody was paid anything at the time. We stayed at his flat. That's where everybody lived during that summer. There was one night, I don't remember why, when seventeen people stayed in that two-bedroomed flat and John Silver slept in the bath. I think it was when the album was finished. This song is quite Beatle-ish. It works quite well. It's quite an odd song really because the chorus is completely different. The song is in a very minor key, kind of desolate, quite sultry while the chorus is very jolly." [7]

## IN THE WILDERNESS

This track is a ballad mainly for piano and voice, with a little bass, which gains body during the chorus preceded by catchy strings with enjoyable rhythm guitar and drums.

Phillips: "This is mainly mine. Peter obviously did the vocals. A lot of friends used to like it, they used to call it *Raindrops* and asked us why it wasn't a single. It's quite commercial and catchy, isn't it? This could have been a single." [7]

The band have never been happy with the orchestral overdubs imposed by King.

Phillips: "Back then, to add the strings it meant reducing everything else to mono, so the whole album sounded very weak. We had no control." [7]

## THE CONQUEROR

Flipping the album over to Side Two, conceptual continuity is provided by the electric guitar picking up from the track which ended Side One, *In The Wilderness*. *The Conqueror*, with its triumphant tones, emphasised by Gabriel's rich voice (and the harmonies of the others), is based on a riff made up of five low notes on the piano, with the beat provided by the acoustic guitars, drums and tambourines.

Phillips: "We used a lot of tambourine in those days. It was a very 60s thing, all this tambourine, but we didn't all play it. Probably Pete and maybe I had a go. I couldn't stay in time though. But

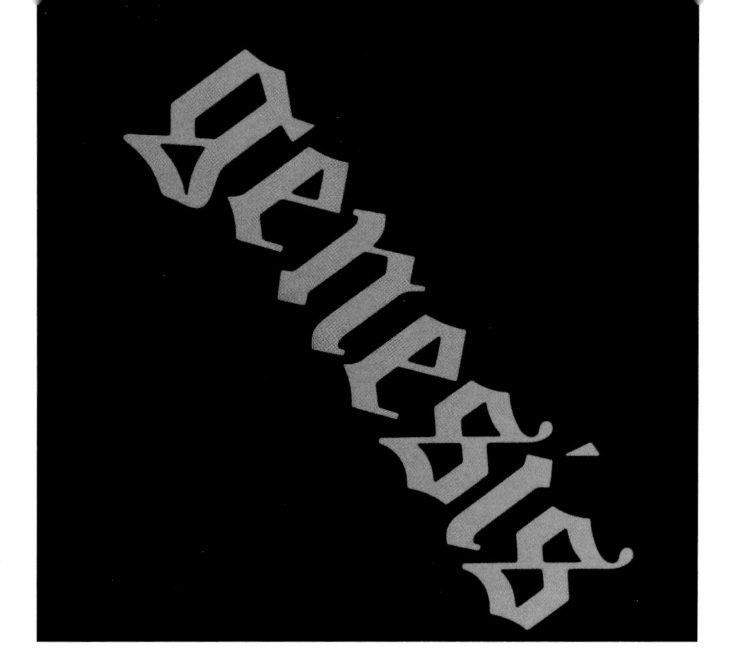


mostly it was John Silver. I hadn't heard this song for a long time. This was very much a Peter and Tony song. The guitar sounds better, there's not a lot of plectrum. This is a bit more like Dylan, especially that vocal line; quite monotone, all around a few notes. You could imagine Dylan doing this in a completely different way. Slower. A bit rougher. Shall we get Dylan to do a cover of it? Bob Dylan sings Genesis? I don't think it will happen somehow." (7)

Whilst Bob Dylan singing Genesis may seem unlikely, *The Conqueror* has recently received acclaim from an even more improbable source, Noel Gallagher of Oasis. Gallagher's song *If Love is the Law* (which featured on Noel Gallagher's High Flying Birds 2017 album, Who Built The Moon) was heavily influenced by *The Conqueror*. Interviewed by Steve Lamacq on BBC Radio 6, Gallagher said: "There are at least six great songs on that first Genesis album."

## IN HIDING

Previously called *Patricia*, in the instrumental version recorded for the first demo by the still-to-be-called Genesis, this song is all Ant, his first ever composition.

Phillips: "My first crush on a girl. I was 13. It had a lot of versions before it ended up on the album. It kept appearing as this and appearing as that. I made some attempts to write lyrics for it but they were all bad." (7)

The atypical structure of the song starts with the chorus sung by Gabriel and Phillips over the acoustic guitars with a waltz time signature. The verses, on the other hand, are sung only by Gabriel with the support of the orchestra.

Phillips: "I don't remember these strings. I realise I've hardly ever listened to this one [since it was recorded]. The strings are not too bad but they could have been better. This is quite commercial. This could have been a single. It's certainly a lot better than some of the things that were hits back then. I like Peter's voice here. His voice is really good. I mean, of course, it's good later, but I don't remember it being this good back then." (7)

*In Hiding* is one of the two songs which, shortly after the album was recorded in November 1968, Ant, Mike, Peter and Tony mimed to in the BBC studios for Brian Roberts, who, as part of a training course, was required to film a short piece to illustrate what he had learned. Phillips: "He was working as a trainee cameraman up at Evesham. We went up there and did a couple of songs to help him. It was also an experience for us." (7)

Unfortunately, the tape was probably recycled; to date it has never been found.

## ONE DAY

Distant acoustic guitars supported by strings give way to the piano which leads the instrumental part of the song. In the chorus Gabriel's

Decca label re-issue from 1974, with a new title of In The Beginning and new cover art.

voice is boosted by solemn harmonies, the drums and even the brass section conducted by Lou Warburton.

Phillips: "I don't remember that introduction at all. I don't think I ever listened to it, once they put the strings on it. I didn't want to listen to it ever again. I've heard bits of tracks obviously... This is a really good song. I'm not sure about the chorus so much but the verse is very pretty. It was always very flowery and pretty. The arrangements are fine but we couldn't have big strings; it was just one single line which is a bit restricted". (7)

## WINDOW

After another piano intro ("sounds very Chinese!" – Phillips (7)), *Window* features a massive brass section, with an acoustic rhythm guitar and solid vocal performance. Other vocals appear in the chorus as well as strings, with the rhythmic support of the drums in the final fade out.

This song was composed on the roof of David Thomas' house. Phillips: "Mike and I wrote this pretty much together. I'm sure Peter wrote the lyrics. I don't remember that horn. I've not listened to it since. That's really the truth. I always have what I call a two-year rule. When I finish an album, I don't listen to it for two years, then it all sounds OK. In this case it's been forty years though. The rearrangements aren't bad. Now I can see why Jonathan King thought it needed these extra parts. But the problem was the recording at the time which meant [to free up the tracks needed for the orchestra] everything had to go to mono. The 12-string is very bad again, it's very clicky. Pete's voice sounds good." (7)

## IN LIMBO

Starting with another piano intro ("I think that's me playing with Tony", says Phillips (7)), this is a lively song with a brass section again as well as the acoustic guitar. In the chorus you can hear the others harmonising, especially Ant.

Phillips: "I always liked this song. It was written by Tony and Peter. The horns don't work on this though. It is very punchy. When we were doing this track it was powerful. But the backing track sounds really small and the brass is sort of stuck out in the middle of nowhere. There's a terrible trumpet note there, all out of tune [the sustained trumpet note can be heard at 2'42"]. It should have been re-recorded! Something's different on this one. I remember, when we mixed together the brass and strings, we pushed all the backing track over to one side and the horn parts were left in the middle by themselves. That's what seems to be happening on this song; it's more extreme. Anyway, this could have been better." (7)

### SILENT SUN

The piano plays a riff on which the vocals and Chris Stewart's drums (not credited on the original release) come in immediately. In the second verse, Gabriel's voice deliberately emulates that of Robin Gibb, with the addition of other vocal timbres in the choruses while the strings go crazy. Phillips: "This is Jonathan King trying to make us be commercial. I've never liked this song. I find it irritating. He wanted us to have a hit. I understand that but I didn't like it." [7]

### A PLACE TO CALL MY OWN

A song written by Phillips on the piano but played by Banks and sung by Gabriel, with a lovely and heartbreaking melody, which gets cut after just over a minute to leave space for an orchestral conclusion driven by the brass section, the harmonies of the whole group and a bass loop.

Phillips: "This was a five-minute epic that got cut down to just this bit. I had nothing to do with the orchestral part." [7]

## THE ALBUM ARTWORK

A completely black cover. In the top left corner yellow, lower case Gothic lettering spells out: "from genesis to revelation". This is how the band's first album looked, with graphics apparently leading many shops to mistakenly place it in the religious section. Jonathan King confirms that this happened: "Absolutely true. It killed us." [5]

King's choice of cover art was in part due to the ongoing confusion over the legitimacy of the band's name after it was discovered that another band called Genesis already existed in America, whose first album, published in 1968, was ironically called In The Beginning.

Inside the cover, the first words seek to explain the arcane: "The group started as Genesis, biblical centuries ago. But fate intervened, other groups became Genesis and who were we to fight? So we changed our name in America to Revelation. Moments later up came another Revelation. Now we are the group without a name, but we have a record and we want to give it to you, name or not".

And then goes on to say: "Those years between fifteen and twenty. No longer boy or girl, not yet man or woman. Confused by the bright light of age, remembering the hazy mellowness of youth. Years when one tries to go back, forwards, upwards, downwards - never to remain static, at peace in growing up".

The original inner sleeve was decorated with a series of drawings inspired by the Bible: serpents, rain, landscapes, mythological figures.

## EPILOGUE

The album was recorded in August 1968 but only made it into record stores 7 months later in March 1969: an incomprehensible time lapse for an up-and-coming band and for that time in general.

Phillips: "That was down to Jonathan King; he thought about it and thought about it some more and in the end decided that it needed more. Then

John Silver in London, 7 May 2011.

sometime around October or November he decided it needed strings and they got added some time around Christmas or just after. I think we heard it in February and I got a terrible shock: it sounded so different, so strange... So I think he just slept on it, sat on it, thought about it. Probably played it to a few different people who maybe said it needed something extra. So he then had to get somebody to write the orchestral parts, and that would have taken a couple of weeks. So the record wasn't actually finished until the end of August, early September. So he probably spent a couple of months thinking about it, adding the strings and then released it in March. It sold six hundred copies and we virtually knew everyone who bought it." (7)

Despite their first single receiving positive reviews, the lack of sales resulted in Jonathan King and Decca immediately losing interest in the band, and Genesis quickly found themselves without a contract.

Banks: "I went to university for a year, then I sort of took a year off and then another... I think my parents always hoped I'd go back. I felt this was an opportunity [musical] that would only come once. I thought about not doing it and then I thought "I really would miss this, I really, really want to do this, there's a chance...." even if at the time it was an incredibly slim chance." (6)

Gabriel: "John Silver, the drummer after Chris Stewart, a wonderful guy, as is Chris, was very good at encouraging us to develop an individual personality and push the folk thing. I mean, he was a sort of a jazz fan really in lots of ways. He dropped out because of parental pressure and ended up at Cornell University in America. He said afterwards he was hoping he'd get a letter inviting him back, whereas we just thought "okay, that's what he's decided to do, fair enough"." (6)

Phillips: "On listening to the album, I'm pleasantly surprised at how it sounds. The only song I thought sounded rubbish was *In Limbo*, although I like the actual song. But overall it stood up pretty well. I was listening to some Neil Young stuff from the 60s, with Crazy Horse from about '67, '68. I thought his stuff was pretty rough. This album compares very favourably to that. Some of the songs are really nice. The lyrics were a bit early, a bit naive, but Pete's vocals sound very good." (7)

This revised opinion from Phillips is welcomed by Jonathan King: "Good for Ant. I think it's a great album and works tremendously. Still, over 40 years later, it's a delightful, innocent, charming album by very young lads starting out on their careers." (5)

# THE CONCERTS

FROM GENESIS TO REVELATION was released in March 1969 and barely sold over 600 copies. The band members were bitterly disappointed, even more so as Jonathan King had already lost all interest and neither he nor Decca Records believed in them anymore. The following weeks were a time of reflection during which a number of things happened. First and foremost parental interference began to set in. Now that these 18-year-old musicians had had the satisfaction of making a record, their parents were expecting them to go back to studying and prepare for a life more in keeping with their upbringing. In fact, during the months preceding the release of their debut album (which as we have already seen was recorded during the summer of the previous year), Tony Banks had been accepted into Sussex University to read Physics, Mathematics and Philosophy, Mike had moved on to the Farnborough College of Technology and Peter and Ant had decided to carry on and get more 'A' levels (Peter had also been accepted into the London School of Film Technique, now the London Film School).

During this period of despondency, however, the band continued to rehearse hoping they could prove their worth on stage. Thanks to a parental loan of £150, they managed to buy an organ, a bass guitar and an amplifier and rehearsed in their own homes or at friends' houses, including Brian Roberts' grandmother's house (Brian, as you will remember, being the friend who worked in a recording studio).

These sessions gave rise to new inspiration (some of which came together in *The Movement*, a lengthy piece that was never professionally recorded), while songs in the existing repertoire were further perfected. But things were still very much in a state of flux; whilst the most sceptical band members (Banks and Gabriel) had now decided to carry on, matters were suddenly made worse in July, when drummer John Silver decided to leave for good.

John Silver: "There was an institution, part of the British Empire, which encouraged English youngsters to go abroad, be it Australia, Canada, the US, South Africa – anywhere. So I got a grant and I went to Cornell University, a very big Ivy League university in upstate New York. It's a Liberal Arts college and I originally went to the hotel school. I double majored with Economics and did the first two years of an MBA before coming back to England." (8)

The bespectacled drummer left the band with few regrets.

Silver: "We had made an album and in those days that wasn't something you could just go out and do. It was only the result of luck and the connections Jonathan King had in Decca. We rehearsed and so I got to meet famous pop stars. I got to phone my mother and tell her to switch on the radio because my record was going to be aired. These were big moments in life! There was a lot of excitement, the single came out, the album came out. Later I left the band to go to university in America. I remember, there was an important television programme back then called 'The Old Grey Whistle Test' in London; the deal was that if we got on this programme I would stop university, come right back and we'd be in business again. I didn't tell my family the whole story but, basically, that was the important development that never materialized. I tried to

Jonathan Mayhew in 1979.

promote the record in America. I contacted London Records in New York and said: "Hey, I live in New York at the university, this is a fantastic record when is it going to be released?" but nothing. Absolutely nothing. They wrote a very nice letter saying: "Yes, it is very nice but we have no plans to release it." And in those days the mechanics of production and releasing were very different to today. If they said they weren't going to release it, that was that. I had the only copies of the first album in America. So I took a few of these records around the radio stations, again to try and promote the English pop revolution. I told them it was a fantastic record and I did some interviews on the local stations. They played the tracks and again nobody was interested in the material at all. And so I stayed in America and the band eventually got a replacement." [8]

Despite the ongoing confusion, Genesis had no intention of giving up. The first step was to place a 'Drummer Wanted' ad in Melody Maker.

Phillips: "1969 was the summer of many drummers, many adverts, many auditions, people being picked up from stations, "Who's gonna tell him?" and all that sort of stuff. It was absolutely awful because we loved John Silver and he had decided to pack it up and go to university in The States. John Mayhew, on the other hand, was older than us, he was more experienced. He was from a different background and he was very unsure of himself. We tried to do our best to make him feel comfortable, I'm not sure we ever did." [6]

John Mayhew (born in Ipswich, 27 March 1947): "I'd left my telephone number around London.

The telephone rang while I was at work. When I got home my wife said a guy called Mike Rutherford had called from a band named Genesis, and as soon as I heard that name, Genesis, I knew for sure that this was special. Mike phoned back at six o'clock and he was trying to persuade me to join the band because they weren't famous then, they were very small. And so I said: "Yeah, I'll come and audition." I took a train from Woking down to Farnham. I remember I was dressed in black and I had a whole drum kit. I don't know how I did it. It was more baggage than anybody else was carrying. Anyway, they turned up in a taxi and Peter Gabriel was in the back writing lyrics on bits of paper. I looked at the sky and thought, "he's a hard worker". They were all hard workers." [9]

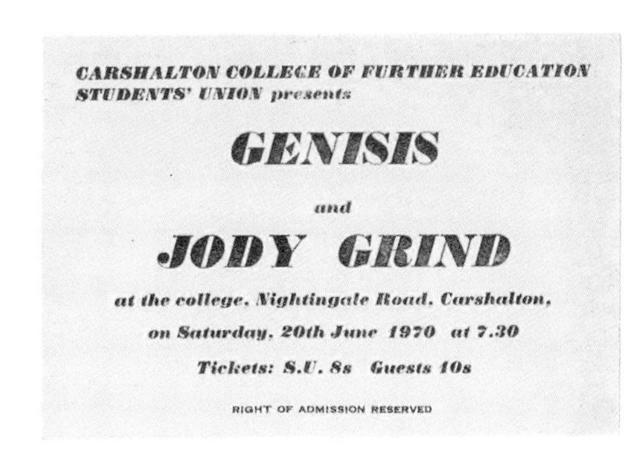


Following the recruitment of John Mayhew on drums, the first step was to record another couple of demos in August 1969: the first in Regent Sound Studios (*White Mountain, Family, Pacidy* and *Going Out To Get You* – only the latter of which ever saw the light of day when it was released as part of the Genesis Archive 1967–75 box set) and the second at the Phillips' family house, Send Barns (*Stagnation, Stranger, The Movement* and *Little Leaf*).

On Monday 22 September, again at Send Barns, the whole band started rehearsing for two weeks. During the middle weekend (27–28 September), Peter, Tony and John went home while Mike and Ant stayed behind to record the demos for a couple of songs. The band rehearsals came to an end on Friday 3 October, making it highly likely that the following day, Saturday 4 October, was the day Genesis made its live debut in the household of the Balme family (Peter Gabriel's neighbours).

One of the Balme children, Anthony, was going to be twenty-one on 27 October, but to date no research has been able to prove with any certainty that Genesis actually played at the Balme home for his birthday and not for a different occasion on this earlier date. The performance (for which the band were paid £25) was an important event, even if it was hardly a roaring success: the numerous guests were more interested in partying and making friends than in listening to a young and unknown band. And yet, the publication of a manuscript in the first edition of Armando Gallo's book 'Genesis - The Evolution Of A Rock Band' sheds a little light on a period about which little is known. The document is a setlist drawn up for the Balme party, written out by Peter Gabriel himself. On the left side of the page, there are 34 songs listed (*Black Sheep, Going Out To Get You, Eastern Magic Boogie, The Serpent, In Limbo, Build Me A Mountain, Digby, Masochistic Man, Crossroads, Stumble, Chobham Chords, Do I Still Figure In Your Life, Sitting On The Top Of The World, Nice, Visions Of Angels, White Mountain, Pacidy, Family,*

*Shepherd, Classic, Wandering, Babies, Let Us Now Make Love, Classic, Window, Grandma, Little Leaf, In Hiding, One Day, Conqueror, Stranger, Silver Song, Epic, Think Again*) while on the right side there is a shortened version of the list with 26 songs divided up into four sets.

The right-hand column (which is headed 'Order') may well have been the concert schedule with three interludes. First set: *In The Beginning, Serpent, Going Out To Get You, Masochistic Man, Stumble, Black Sheep, Visions Of Angels*. Second set: *Build Me A Mountain, In Limbo, Sitting On The Top Of The World, Key To Love, Chobham Chords, Digby, Nice*. Third set: *Little Leaf, Pacidy, Family, White Mountain, Window, Stranger, Babies*. Fourth and last set: *Movement, One Day, Grandma, Let Us Now Make Love, Conqueror.*

Although obviously, there is no way of knowing for sure whether or not these songs were actually played at the Balme family event, the list without doubt represents the repertoire from which early Genesis selected their songs for later concerts. Comparing the two lists written out on the piece of paper, as well as the title *Classic* appearing twice, one notices the nine songs which were left out of the list featuring four-sets compared to the full list of songs on the left-hand side. These songs were probably dropped at the last minute, but there's a chance some of them were actually performed, especially songs like *In Hiding* and *Shepherd*. On the other hand, it is highly likely that the song *Silver Song*, written by Ant and Mike as a tribute to their previous drummer, John Silver, was left out. The pair did, however, go on to record this song (with Phil Collins on drums and vocals) in 1973. This version was finally released in 2008 on a re-issue of The Geese And The Ghost.

A look at the setlist reveals the presence of six songs from the debut album (*In The Beginning, Serpent, In Limbo, Window, One Day, Conqueror*), plus three more recorded in the same period which didn't make it to the tracklist (*Going Out To Get You, Visions Of Angels, Build Me A Mountain*).

Some of these songs would appear on the following album Trespass (the already mentioned *Visions Of Angels* in a completely new version and *White Mountain, Family* and *Nice*, the latter two under the new titles of *Dusk* and *The Knife*), whereas others would only be released years later on Genesis Archive 1967–75 (*Shepherd, Pacidy* and *Let Us Now Make Love*).

The lengthy song *The Movement* has already been mentioned and some covers were destined to be excluded from the setlist immediately after the event (*The Stumble* by Freddie King, *Black Sheep* by the American band SRC, *Key To Love* by John Mayall and *Sitting On The Top Of The World* written by Walter Vinson and Lonnie Chatmon, released in 1930 and later made famous by Cream), which leaves half a dozen tracks still to be discussed, all of which were destined to quickly disappear not only from the setlist but from the history of Genesis as a whole.

A couple of these were the work of Anthony Phillips, such as *Stranger* (which the guitarist went on to release years later and which he says was only ever played at the Balme party) and *Little Leaf*, a song which was actually quite important in the early stages of Genesis' career; predominantly acoustic with Tony Banks starting out on guitar, it was often used as a bridge to the more rhythmic section of the show.

Decca advertising.

Richard Macphail in Orvieto on September 22nd 2007.

Another acoustic song, destined to be discarded as early as the winter of '69 in order to make way for something a little more uptempo, was *Grandma*, whereas *Digby* (also known as *Digby Of The Rambling Lake*) was a song by Tony which he says was partially recycled at a later date.

The rest of the songs were in all likelihood by Peter Gabriel, most definitely *Masochistic Man* and *Babies* and very probably *Chobham Chords*.

Having passed the acid test of their first ever live performance (albeit at a private party) Genesis were all set to put on some real stage shows shortly afterwards. Their first proper concert was on 4 November at the Brunel University London campus in Acton, in west London. Here the band was spotted by the secretary of the Twickenham Technical College who signed them up to support Black Cat Bones on the 15th for the fee of fifty pounds (all of which went on repairing the van after Richard Macphail, driver, friend and general dogsbody, crashed it).

Phillips: "We used to start with *In the Beginning*, including at the first big gig where all the agents came. That time my strings were completely out of tune – it was in that break, 'dah-dah, dah-dah-dah'. I was just turning in panic." (7)

During this period, Genesis often had the difficult task of opening for much better-known artists. On 23 November, at the Kingston Hotel, Piblokto were headlining and bass player Steve Glover asked to borrow Mike's bass. Caught up in his own enthusiasm, Glover broke two of the strings, taking Genesis' already fragile finances almost to breaking point.

The last concert of November, on the 28th, was at the Woolwich Polytechnic. Headliners, Caravan, had cancelled and were replaced by bluesman Jimmy Witherspoon. Genesis, Steve Miller's Delivery and Gunhill were billed as support bands and the evening ended with a striptease.

During this stage in the band's history, they were mainly playing the university circuit around the capital but at long last, in December, they got a couple of gigs on two consecutive nights over 120 miles further north, near Birmingham. On the first night Genesis were expected to entertain the workers of Nettlefolds Ltd., a well-known company which manufactured metal fasteners. Needless to say, they did not go down very well.

However, 1970 got off on a whole new footing, starting with two important dates. On 9 January Genesis were hired by the BBC to write the soundtrack for a documentary on the painter Michael Jackson. Although the documentary was never finished, during this session (which would

Handwritten note from Peter Gabriel to the promoter of the 9th National Jazz Blues and Pop Music Festival (8th to 10th August 1969). Genesis did not perform.

PETER ▬. GABRIEL, DEEP POOL, CHOBHAM, NR. WOKING, SURREY
TELEPHONE: CHOBHAM 8884

We are looking for some work; particularly in the period July 20 – September 20.
If you are interested, we would be very pleased to send you a tape of the L.P.
We would be grateful if you could reply as soon as possible – if at all interested
Peter Gabriel

only surface in 2008 in the GENESIS 1970 - 1975 box set), the band recorded four short pieces from which they would draw heavily in the following months.

On 22 February the band returned to the BBC studios for the radio programme 'Night Ride'. In front of DJ Alec Reid, the band played six songs live in the studio; although, unfortunately, no trace of *Dusk* remains, the other five tracks (*Shepherd, Pacidy, Let Us Now Make Love, Looking For Someone* and *Stagnation*) reappeared as bootlegs in the mid-1990s and, later on, the first three of these were released on GENESIS ARCHIVE 1967–75.

During the first two months of the year, Genesis were still a support act, but for bigger bands if nothing else. In fact, they opened for Roy Harper, Atomic Rooster, T-Rex and Rare Bird amongst others and had their debut on the stage of the legendary Marquee Club in London on 4 February, supporting Keef Hartley.

But things didn't always go to plan. For example, at the private event organised at the Hurlingham Tennis Club in Fulham, Genesis were completely ignored and the 'Wear Your Dreams Festival', where they were scheduled to play alongside big names such as The Doors, Led Zepplin, Frank Zappa, Pink Floyd and The Who (to name just a few) at Crystal Palace on 11 February, was cancelled.

On the 20th, Genesis opened for Free, but the venue was so small that Phillips had to keep moving out of the way for people to go to and from the toilets while he was playing.

The turning point finally arrived after 'Night Ride' when Genesis played two concerts on the same day at the Queen Mary College, London. The first was in a small upstairs room, but the second was on the main stage, an honour Genesis managed to achieve, over the half-dozen or so bands on the bill, thanks to television producer Marcus Bicknell, who was one of the band's first fans. Here, for the first time ever, the audience seemed really interested in what Genesis were doing. Singer-songwriter Nick Drake, who was at the show, was particularly keen on *Let Us Now Make Love*, which he defined as "dangerous".

After the Uxbridge concert on the 27th, where the audience clearly preferred Genesis over the headliners (Fairport Convention), Bicknell resolved to organise a tour of 7 concerts in clubs in and around London from 25 February to 3 March, which was also advertised in Melody Maker.

Alas, the venues didn't always turn out to be very suitable for live events. Often they were

Re-issue from 1993, released by Music Collection International.

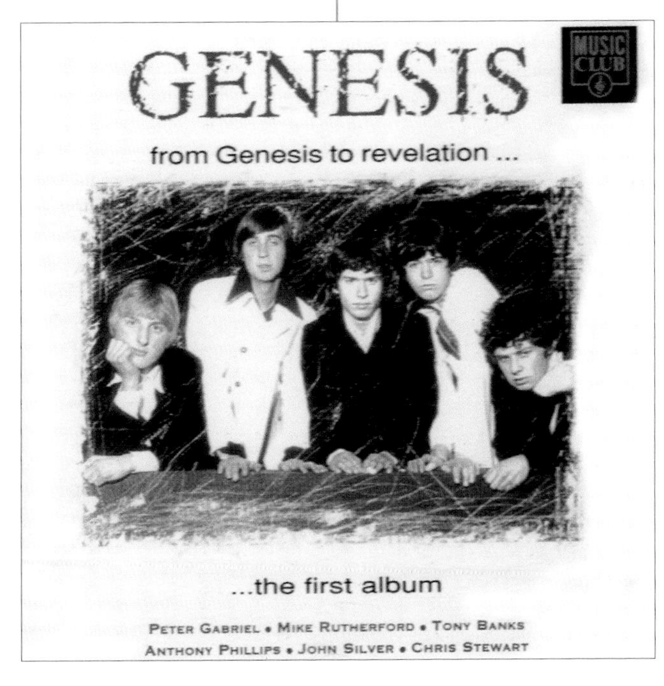


clubs which were so small that, at Blaises on the 26th, for example, while playing *Little Leaf*, Mike accidentally lifted a girl's skirt with his cello bow. The last of these concerts, the one on 3 March, was at Ronnie Scott's, a famous jazz club in the heart of Soho. Genesis performed in the upstairs venue and were so popular that they were confirmed a slot for the next six consecutive Tuesdays. This was the best place to get spotted because record producers, managers and talent scouts were often present, and it mattered very little that there was so much confusion that Gabriel was able to sing a song for which the lyrics had yet to be written called, on the spur of the moment, *I've Been Travelling All Night Long*.

And while they were continuing with their live schedule, which by this point had become rather hectic, Genesis were still desperately trying to obtain a record deal. It was during this period that contact was made with Threshold Records, The Moody Blues' own label, which seemed very interested. Genesis were called into the De Lane Lea Studios in Holborn on 8 March. Here, under the supervision of Moody Blues keyboard player Mike Pinder and record producer Tony Clarke, they spent the whole day and night recording. The band finished at six in the morning and then had to drive all the way to Sunderland, where they had a gig booked for that same day in a rather oddly decorated ballroom where Ant had to play under a plastic palm tree.

Between performances at Ronnie Scott's, Genesis had the chance to play at the Atomic Sunrise Festival at the Roundhouse. This was a week-long festival (9–15 March) with input from Yoko Ono. Anyone who was anyone in the London rock scene was invited. The idea was to combine musical performances with those of the Living Theatre, an American experimental theatre company. The festival bill included some big names such as Hawkwind, Quintessence, Kevin Ayers, Brian Auger and Arthur Brown, to name but a few. On Wednesday 11th, Genesis were billed as openers for David Bowie. Despite all the publicity, the performance didn't get as much attention as it should have.

Gabriel: "There were more performers on the

New Zealand single of
*Where The Sour Turns To Sweet.*

stage than there were in the audience, even though David Bowie and Genesis were both playing on the same night, which was very strange because we were both beginning to get some momentum." (6)

The fact that the concerts, at least in part, were both recorded and filmed (as announced by the press at that time) was only confirmed in 1978 with the American promo disc used by 'Earth News': Peter Gabriel was promoting his second solo album and, during the chat, a snippet of *Twilight Alehouse* from the Roundhouse was aired. Forty-three years later, on 11 and 12 March 2013, the film was finally screened in the Roundhouse, showing the full performance of *The Knife* and *Looking For Someone* in very good quality, albeit without the original sound (to put music to the footage, film director-producer Adrian Everett used the studio version of the first song and the 'Night Ride' radio performance of the second). This film is of great historical value as it is the only footage featuring Genesis with Phillips and Mayhew in the line-up, only a small fragment of which would later appear on the DVD 'Sum of the Parts'.

Despite interest from Island Records in the person of producer Guy Stevens, and after coming close to signing a contract with Threshold Records, Genesis were eventually signed to Charisma Records, the up-and-coming record label founded by Tony Stratton-Smith.

From here onwards the band's rise to fame was slow but sure. One important step was meeting David Stopps, the promoter of the famous Friars Club in Aylesbury, where Genesis played for the first time on 13 April 1970, receiving unprecedented enthusiasm from the audience. This concert marked the beginning of the band's special connection with the Aylesbury audience, and they returned there several times over the following months.

In the following weeks, Genesis increased their number of live appearances, still mainly in the role of support band but increasingly to famous names such as Fairport Convention, Mott The Hoople and Deep Purple. Occasionally, Genesis were themselves supported by artists who went on to achieve a high profile; Nick Drake, for example, opened for Genesis on at least one occasion.

Banks: "In 1970 there were an awful lot of clubs and places where you could just play, supporting some other group, in front of maybe 80-90 people, sometimes less. When we headlined we were sometimes playing to as few as 5 or 6 people. But

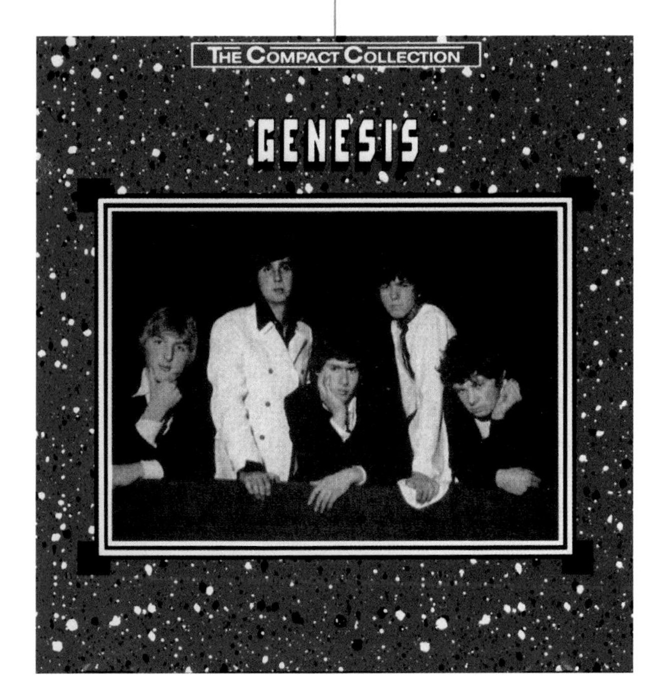


Castle Communications re-issue in 1990 for the series *The Compact Collection.*

you had a chance to learn your craft and you could just about get enough money to keep yourself going." [6]

Phillips: "We felt very junior to the other bands, very, very junior! We really didn't know whether we had anything at all. You'd get one bloke coming down saying he really liked it. I remember somebody coming down saying he was quite knocked out. And we had all these different agents coming to see us. So there were good gigs and bad gigs and we didn't really know what we had. To be honest, we used to look at King Crimson. When we mentioned King Crimson, it was like they'd seen the Messiah and we knew we had to try harder. Someone would bring us all these reviews of Yes by Chris Welch and we'd think, "God we're nowhere". I think we were very unsure of ourselves and what often happens is that you overcompensate. I know we were called snotty-nosed bastards by somebody at Leicester University, but we weren't going around being arrogant." [6]

The constantly evolving setlist changed quite radically as the weeks went by.

Phillips: "Whether it was either wild university gigs on a Friday night or else the Revolution or Blaises clubs filled with arms dealers in shades and stuff, they weren't interested in our poncey kind of acoustic stuff. So all we could do is stamp on them with volume, so a lot of the more sensitive stuff got wiped out. When it came to recording the album [TRESPASS] we were bored stiff of always playing the same thing, we'd been doing it for nine months non-stop and we would have liked to do some different music but there was no question of it. It had got to the point where it was like an orchestra going out and doing the *New World Symphony* every night because hardly a note changed. I was lucky in that I had a solo in *The Knife* where I could change a few notes. I mean it was exciting if the audience were really keen and re-invented it for you, but most of the time they didn't know who we were. You must know the famous time of us playing a gig to just one person where Peter Gabriel just gave up and said: "Any requests?"" [6]

The total lack of any recordings of these concerts unfortunately makes it impossible to surmise as to what the setlists may have been. It is well-known, however, that the first part of the concerts focused on acoustic pieces, dominated by Ant and Mike's 12-string guitar parts, occasionally joined by Banks, with the interesting addition of Rutherford on cello (on *Pacidy* and *Little Leaf*) and Gabriel on accordion.

Phillips: "Peter used to play it on *Stagnation*. That was one of the more bizarre things live. I remember once he put the accordion down during the quiet section but didn't put it down properly so it started playing during the quiet bit by itself, like bagpipes when they've finished." (6)

Some interesting songs to be remembered from this period: *Let Us Now Make Love* (with an electric guitar part played by Tony Banks, filtering Ant's Stratocaster through his Leslie cabinet), *Little Leaf* (Banks would start out on guitar before switching to the organ and sing the song with Rutherford in an attempt to emulate, without success, the harmonies of Simon & Garfunkel), *White Mountain, Twilight Alehouse, Family* (alias *Dusk*) and *Shepherd* (with, for a couple of lines of the lyrics, an exceptionally rare vocal solo by Banks).

As the concert progressed, as already mentioned, the set would become more uptempo: songs like *Digby* and *Jamaican Longboat* disappeared whilst *In The Wilderness* and a harder version of *Limbo* remained, and *Looking For Someone* was rearranged. Phillips: "I can't remember how we played the instrumental part. Live it was pretty powerful but being as we didn't have a piano on the stage, Tony had to do it with the organ." (7)

After *Pacidy*, usually somewhere towards the end of the set, the concerts ended on the heaviest songs of all: *Going Out To Get You* and *Nice* (alias *The Knife*).

In the meantime, Gabriel was getting more confident in his role of frontman. During his earlier shows, he was so shy that a friend of the band, Macphail, had had to introduce the songs for him, but now he was starting to invent surreal stories to tell the audience while the others tuned their 12-string guitars.

In April, however, Anthony started to feel unwell. His poor health caused a slowdown in band activity and, after the concert on 25 April (at Imperial College, London), they took a three-week break so that Ant could go to Cornwall with his parents and convalesce. All the concerts planned for May had to be cancelled, including those for which posters and newspaper ads still exist, such as the one at Ronnie Scott's on the 5th, Canterbury on the 8th (Genesis should have opened for The Who), Twickenham on the 9th, Stockport on the 15th, Guildford on the 16th, Southall on the 23rd and the famous Marquee Club in London on the 24th.

With May behind them, during which the cause of Ant's ill health had been diagnosed as glandular fever, Genesis went back to performing in front of a live audience at the beginning of June with a concert at the Gin Mill Club in Godalming (where they would also rehearse before going into the studio to record TRESPASS).

On 14 June the band finally returned to performing regular live shows, starting at the Marquee. They even played two gigs in one day (27 June), first at the Surrey Free Festival in Guildford in the afternoon (where the band played in a marquee which collapsed right in the middle of their show), then Dalston in the evening.

Unfortunately, Phillip's health didn't seem to be improving and the guitarist started to toy with the idea of leaving the band, something he first mentioned to his long-time friend, Mike Rutherford, after the concert at Kingston Polytechnic on 9 July. The decision to quit was officially announced to the whole band on 18 July at the end of the Haywards Heath concert.

And so it was that Anthony Phillips left Genesis; what few other concerts had been planned were cancelled and a new phase in the history of Genesis was about to begin.

## NOTES

(1) Mario Giammetti's interview with Anthony Phillips, London, 25 February 2007, partially used in the book "Anthony Phillips – The Exile", Edizioni Segno, September 2008

(2) Mario Giammetti's telephone interview with Tony Banks, 16 February 2012, partially published in the article "Six not simply shrouded pieces" in Dusk, Issue no. 70, April 2012

(3) Mario Giammetti's telephone interview with Chris Stewart, 6 July 2000, partially published in the article "Intervista esclusiva a Chris Stewart" in Dusk, Issue no. 33, September 2000

(4) Mario Giammetti's e-mail interview with John Alexander, 13 May 2015, partially published in the article "John Alexander: Mr. Bad Example" in Dusk, Issue no. 80, July 2015

(5) Mario Giammetti's e-mail interview with Jonathan King, 11 April 2014, partially published in the article "Magic JK and four humble boys – Intervista esclusiva a Jonathan King" in Dusk, Issue no. 77, July 2014

(6) Mike Kaufman's Genesis interviews, Chicago / London, October 2007, partially used in the bonus disc accompanying the 2008 remasters

(7) Mario Giammetti listening to 'From Genesis To Revelation' with Anthony Phillips, London, 7 May 2011

(8) Mario Giammetti's interview with John Silver, London, 7 May 2011, partially published in the article "Lo Stan Kenton del punk" in Dusk, Issue no. 69, December 2012

(9) Mario Giammetti's interview with John Mayhew, London, 28 May 2006, partially published in the article "Working Class Hero" in Dusk, Issue no. 53, July 2006

# 1969

## OCTOBER

4 **Chobham** (ENGLAND), Balme Family Residence
*Uncertain date.*
*Dancing party for the Balme family. The first ever Genesis public performance.*

## NOVEMBER

4 **Acton** (ENGLAND), Brunel Bar - Brunel University
*First professional gig.*
15 **Twickenham** (ENGLAND), Twickenham College of Technology
23 **Kingston-upon-Thames** (ENGLAND), Kingston Hotel
28 **Woolwich, London** (ENGLAND), Woolwich Polytechnic

## DECEMBER

6 **Smethwick** (ENGLAND), GKN Sports & Social Club
7 **Cheadle Hulme** (ENGLAND), Adsworth Youth Club
12 **Uxbridge** (ENGLAND), Brunel University

# 1970

## JANUARY

4 **London** (ENGLAND), Haverstock Hill Country Club
9 **London** (ENGLAND), Kensington House Studios
*'Genesis Plays Jackson' sessions. The band played 20 minutes of music live in the BBC studio for a documentary which was never completed*
9 **London** (ENGLAND), Revolution
*Evening Show*
14 **Bognor Regis** (ENGLAND), Bognor Regis School
17 **Watford** (ENGLAND), Watford Technical College
24 **Ewell** (ENGLAND), Technical College
28 **Kingston-upon-Thames** (ENGLAND), Kingston Technical College

## FEBRUARY

4 **London** (ENGLAND), Marquee Club
6 **Fulham** (ENGLAND), City University
7 **Canterbury** (ENGLAND), Blues Playground
*Uncertain date*
8 **Fulham** (ENGLAND), Hurlingham Tennis Club
*Uncertain date*
13 **Uxbridge** (ENGLAND), Technical College
14 **Leicester** (ENGLAND), University of Leicester Students' Union
15 **Kingston-upon-Thames** (ENGLAND), Kingston Hotel
18 **Brighton** (ENGLAND), The Dome
19 **London** (ENGLAND), Marquee Club
20 **London** (ENGLAND), Eel Pie Island Hotel
22 **London** (ENGLAND), Maida Vale BBC Studios
*'Night Ride' session. The band recorded six songs live in the BBC studios. Three of the songs were eventually released on ARCHIVE 1967–75.*
24 **London** (ENGLAND), Queen Mary College Hall
*Uncertain date. Two shows, the former in the afternoon, the latter in the evening.*
25 **London** (ENGLAND), Revolution
26 **London** (ENGLAND), Blaise's
27 **Uxbridge** (ENGLAND), Brunel University
28 **Colchester** (ENGLAND), University of Essex

## MARCH

1 **Southall** (ENGLAND), Farx - The Northcote Arms
2 **Beckenham** (ENGLAND), Mistrale Club
3 **London** (ENGLAND), Ronnie Scott's Club
9 **Sunderland** (ENGLAND), Locarno Ballroom
10 **London** (ENGLAND), Ronnie Scott's Club
11 **London** (ENGLAND), The Roundhouse
*'Atomic Sunrise Festival'*
12 **London** (ENGLAND), Blaises
13 **Fulham** (ENGLAND), Town Hall
*'Chiswick Poly Rag Dance' event*
14 **Watford** (ENGLAND), Watford Technical College
17 **London** (ENGLAND), Ronnie Scott's Club
22 **Southall** (ENGLAND), Farx - The Northcote Arms
24 **London** (ENGLAND), Ronnie Scott's Club
31 **London** (ENGLAND), Ronnie Scott's Club

## APRIL

7 **London** (ENGLAND), Ronnie Scott's Club
9 **Edmonton** (ENGLAND), Cooks Ferry Inn
10 **Twickenham** (ENGLAND), Eel Pie Island Hotel
11 **Chatham** (ENGLAND), Central Hall
12 **Godalming** (ENGLAND), Angel
13 **Aylesbury** (ENGLAND), New Friarage Hall
*Two shows*
14 **London** (ENGLAND), Ronnie Scott's Club
18 **Potters Bar** (ENGLAND), Farx - Elm Court Youth Centre
19 **Camberley** (ENGLAND), One Oak Inn
22 **Barnet** (ENGLAND)
*Venue unknown*
24 **Manchester** (ENGLAND)
*Venue unknown*
25 **London** (ENGLAND), Imperial College
30 **London** (ENGLAND), Blaises

## JUNE

6 **Godalming** (ENGLAND), Gin Mill
*Uncertain date*
14 **London** (ENGLAND), Marquee Club
15 **Aylesbury** (ENGLAND), New Friarage Hall
16 **London** (ENGLAND), Ronnie Scott's Club
18 **London** (ENGLAND), Blaise's
20 **Carshalton** (ENGLAND), Carshalton College
23 **London** (ENGLAND), Ronnie Scott's Club
27 **Guildford** (ENGLAND), University of Surrey
*'Surrey Free Festival'. Afternoon show*
27 **Dalston** (ENGLAND), Hackney Technical College
*Evening show*
28 **Southall** (ENGLAND), Farx - The Northcote Arms
30 **London** (ENGLAND), Ronnie Scott's Club

## JULY

3 **London** (ENGLAND), College For The Distributive Trades
9 **Kingston-upon-Thames** (ENGLAND), Polytechnic Hall
11 **Rickmansworth** (ENGLAND) St. Joan of Arc Catholic School
12 **London** (ENGLAND), Marquee Club
17 **Croydon** (ENGLAND), Star Hotel
18 **Haywards Heath** (ENGLAND), Sussex Hall
*Last concert with Anthony Phillips and John Mayhew.*

# Trespass

(Charisma, 1970)

***Looking For Someone / White Mountain / Visions Of Angels /// Stagnation / Dusk / The Knife***

- **Release date: 23 October 1970**
- **Recorded at Trident Studios, London in July 1970**
- **Engineer: Robin Cable**
- **Producer: John Anthony**
- **Artwork: Paul Whitehead for Cleen Mashine Studio**

- **Peter Gabriel: lead voice, flute, accordion, tambourine, bass drum**
- **Anthony Phillips: acoustic 12-string, lead electric, dulcimer, voices**
- **Anthony Banks: organ, piano, Mellotron, guitar, voices**
- **Michael Rutherford: acoustic 12-string, electric bass, nylon, cello, voices**
- **John Mayhew: drums, percussion, vocals**

## THE MAKING OF

Over two years had passed between the recording of FROM GENESIS TO REVELATION and TRESPASS. A long time by any new band's standards, but for Genesis it was an eternity in terms of style and growth. At the same time, the period was so overwhelmingly hectic that any attempt at pinpointing the watershed moment is purely arbitrary.

We have already mentioned a few decisive events, including the demo with four songs (*Family*, which would evolve into *Dusk, White Mountain, Going Out To Get You* and *Pacidy*) recorded on 20 August 1969 thanks to their friend, Brian Roberts, and the band's stage debut where Genesis incorporated their third drummer, John Mayhew. During their early live shows, the band began to experiment with a new repertoire, gradually abandoning the simple songs to bring in new, more challenging material. The two weeks of rehearsals at Anthony Phillips' home, Send Barns, between 22 September and 3 October 1969, also proved to be of fundamental importance. One day the band received a very welcome visit from Richard Macphail. The former lead singer of Anon had just come back to England after spending a few months away working on a kibbutz. He went to listen to his ex-school mates and was astounded by their unexpected technical and creative progress. Spotting the potential, Richard asked his father if he and his friends could stay at the Macphail weekend-retreat in Wotton, Surrey, a house called Christmas Cottage.

Richard Macphail: "In the summer of 1969 the cottage was broken into and burgled. Even though it was actually quite close to London (an hour's drive from the centre), it was very remote. After the burglary, my mother was nervous about going there and the decision was made to sell it. It was autumn and my father thought it was best to wait until the springtime, when the cottage was at its best. In May, when all the trees are out, it's just wonderful. So essentially it was going to be empty the whole winter and that's why we were able to use it. My father worked for a large baking company and they had vans for delivering bread; he managed to get us one and they got it serviced and painted up. So I was able to provide accommodation and transport and the guys did the rest. I provided food as well, I cook. That's basically how I became their road manager." (1)

The band's retreat to Christmas Cottage lasted six months, through to April 1970, possibly a rather excessive period of time which would take the five young men almost to breaking point. It would, however, have an enormous impact on their future and, from an artistic point of view, it was priceless. It was there, in fact, that Genesis started to reveal its true colours. Shedding the constraints of pop imposed on them when they worked on their immature debut album, they began to create a sound that was to become legendary. But living together 24/7 in a secluded place, far away from any distractions, was enough to put even the most resilient natures to the test.

Gabriel: "We were used to having this passive-aggressive tone to rehearsals and, although Tony and I were best friends, we would often be at loggerheads about the music. He was a lot more nervous back then and not at ease within himself. He would try to hold on to controlling as much as he could, in a lot of ways, and I would always want to push it wide open, you know, let the sunlight in, the rain, and see what grew. Ant and Mike, for the most part, got on pretty well but occasionally I would be battling it out with one of them. Mike tended to avoid confrontation and, in later years, the same could be said of Phil and Steve; Tony and I were the ones most frequently at odds. Without question, we were passionate about creating something great, but I think we were also both awkward buggers, so it was a personality thing as well." (2)

Despite the unavoidable conflicts, Genesis managed to overcome their difficulties and concentrate on the music. During those weeks, the band managed to distil some of their previous concepts and, bursting with inspiration, give greater expression to their songwriting. It's hard to estimate just how much music bounced off the walls of Christmas Cottage, but one thing is certain, the five young men emerged as a new creative force at a totally different level in terms of compositional abilities. The qualitative leap forward, compared to FROM GENESIS TO REVELATION, was quite simply phenomenal.

Rutherford: "In the Christmas Cottage period we just wrote and wrote and wrote for six months. We had sections and long bits and 20-minute songs. It was very formative in how we would go on to operate, forever really. It was a mixture of jamming and bringing things into the band that we'd written as individuals." (2)

Phillips: "When we wrote *Looking For Someone* and *The Knife*, we were very excited because we were charging off into new territory, down roads no-one else had been down. It was kind of exciting to break out of the constraints of the verse-chorus song." (2)

Day after day, Genesis focused on their music, sometimes rehearsing for 11 hours a day. The only moments of distraction involved walks in the surrounding countryside and reading sci-fi novels and books on mythology (which would greatly influence their lyrics). In the meantime, promotional activities were being handled by Macphail and, above all, Peter.

Gabriel: "I was always the one promoting the band. I just realised that this was a pipedream and unless we actually got income, gigs, record deals, this whole thing was going to fall flat on its face. I worked my arse off just trying to sell the band around the place and that was frustrating sometimes for the others as I would be off making phone calls. We tried every week to get agents and promoters, social secretaries, A & R people, everybody... to come down. It was absolutely extraordinary the number of flat tyres and breakdowns that occurred between London and Dorking! Every week there'd be a different excuse from a different person and it was hard to get the live work, I think it's even harder today. Yet you

Label Nippon Phonogram, Japanese print.

learn so much from being in front of an audience, you know. A lot of musicians are dreamers, fantasists, and you create this little world for yourself, but as soon as you stand in front of an audience it's like a big pin that is ready to pop your balloon. And that's actually a useful part of the evolution of music and of a song. Not everything has to appeal to everyone but you have to know when people are feeling it and when you're just missing it. When it's dying."[2]

Putting their music to the test in a live scenario consequently became a crucial factor. In the last quarter of 1969 opportunities to play live were few and far between, but the situation began to improve at the turn of the decade.

On 9 January 1970, the band was called into the BBC studios to create the soundtrack for a film based on the work of painter Michael Jackson, in turn inspired by Fritz Lang's *Metropolis*. Being a silent movie, Genesis were given the task of creating a score to accompany the artist's paintings. To date, it is not clear whether or not the band actually got to see these paintings, which appear to have been of a particularly violent nature. What is known is that the band rushed into the BBC studios in Shepherd's Bush under the guidance of Paul Samwell-Smith (formerly of the Yardbirds and already a successful producer).

The Jackson Tapes (an exceptionally important missing evolutionary link between the band's first two albums) disappeared without trace for over 30 years, and it was believed they were gone for good until a copy surfaced in 2001 (together with some written notes providing indications as to what the music was intended to evoke). The material was finally released in 2008 as part of the bonus disc included in the Genesis 1970 - 1975 box set. In the notes Peter Gabriel puts the poor quality of his vocal performance down to the limited recording time available (just a couple of hours in all), explaining that the vocals on the tape were in any case only intended to act as a guide track. Musically speaking, the band used this opportunity to experiment and test material which, despite being in a different form, was beginning to take shape in rehearsals and live shows. On listening to the tracks which consist of about 15 minutes of previously unreleased material divided under four titles (*Provocation, Frustration, Manipulation* and *Resignation*), it becomes clear that this recording session planted the seeds from which future tracks were destined to grow. *Provocation*, for example, is a combination of the initial organ sequence of *The Fountain Of Salmacis* (which would see the light of day one and a half years later) and what would eventually become the second part of *Looking For Someone*. *Frustration* is, for the most part, an early incarnation of *Anyway* (a song which, in 1974, became part of The Lamb Lies Down On Broadway album) but also includes a short section from a 1967 track, *Hair On The Arms And Legs*. *Manipulation* is an embryonic version of *The Musical Box*, making *Resignation* (which used to go by the title *Peace* in their live shows) the only track to feature completely previously unreleased music (although there is just a hint of a re-use of the opening chords from *The Fountain Of Salmacis*).

Just over a month later, on 22 February 1970, Genesis returned to the BBC studios (this time in Maida Vale) for the radio programme 'Night Ride'. On this occasion the band played six new songs

Poster for the concert in Dunfermline on 22nd November 1970

live in the studio, this time complete with final lyrics and arrangements: *Dusk, Shepherd, Pacidy, Let Us Now Make Love, Looking For Someone, Stagnation*. The difference between these songs and the naivety of their debut album is startling: the songs, albeit pleasant, on FROM GENESIS TO REVELATION were as linear and unpretentious as the new ones were complex and variegated. The growth in musicianship was truly staggering: Gabriel (also playing flute as he had on the Jackson Tapes) revealed a more mature and confident voice; Tony had begun to master the organ, an instrument which now represented a signature sound for the band, replacing the piano; Ant and Mike had the task of weaving brilliant and highly original harmonies on guitar; and, without reaching superlatives, John Mayhew turned out to be a solid drummer.

That same February, thanks to a push from promoter Marcus Bicknell, the band began to pick up the very first signs of real interest from audiences at a series of concerts held in and around the capital. Having finally attracted the attention of various talent scouts, including the producer of Island Records, Guy Stevens, Genesis appeared to be on the brink of signing a contract with Threshold Records, the label founded by The Moody Blues, so much so that their keyboard player, Mike Pinder, invited them to the De Lane Lea studios to record *Looking For Someone*. However, not everything lived up to Banks' expectations; hitting a wrong note on the organ, he ended up arguing with Pinder, who didn't think another take was necessary.

Charisma was still a small label at this time, but it was already considered a rising star of the British record industry. Its artists already included Rare Bird (who had just had a huge hit with *Sympathy*), The Nice, Van Der Graaf Generator, Audience and Lindisfarne. It was producer John Anthony who was so impressed by Genesis that he insisted label boss Tony Stratton-Smith checked them out. For Stratton-Smith it was love at first listen and he signed them to the label, while at the same time prohibiting them from accepting a commission to write the music for a radio theatre production by George MacBeth, entitled *Sunken Gold* (it was the producer of the radio programme 'Night Ride', Reid, who had recommended Genesis to the Scottish poet and producer Michael Mason; the *Sunken Gold* project after initially being shelved, was later picked up and transmitted by the BBC in 1984, featuring music by other artists.) For Stratton-Smith, it was more important for the band to concentrate on new music and the Charisma boss wanted no distractions.

So, schedules were mapped out and Genesis, while waiting to book the recording studio to record their second album, resurrected a song which hadn't made it to the FROM GENESIS TO REVELATION tracklist, *Visions Of Angels* (in a completely new version) plus a few fragments dating back to the Oxford period at Silver's house. The rest of the songs came from the music written in the Macphails' holiday cottage.

When the five young musicians crossed the threshold of Trident Studios in London, the problem as to which songs they should choose for the album did not arise. The amount of studio time they had was very limited, so Genesis were basically forced to select the songs they knew best, the ones they had tried and tested in their live shows.

Phillips: "If we'd had more time, we would have actually gone back to some of the music we'd jettisoned because recorded music is different to live music. The tendency then was to record the music that you were touring with, particularly if it was complex, simply because there wasn't enough time to rehearse anything new. We'd jettisoned all this sort of what you might call more adult progressive music written after From Genesis to Revelation because it'd just died on the road." (2)

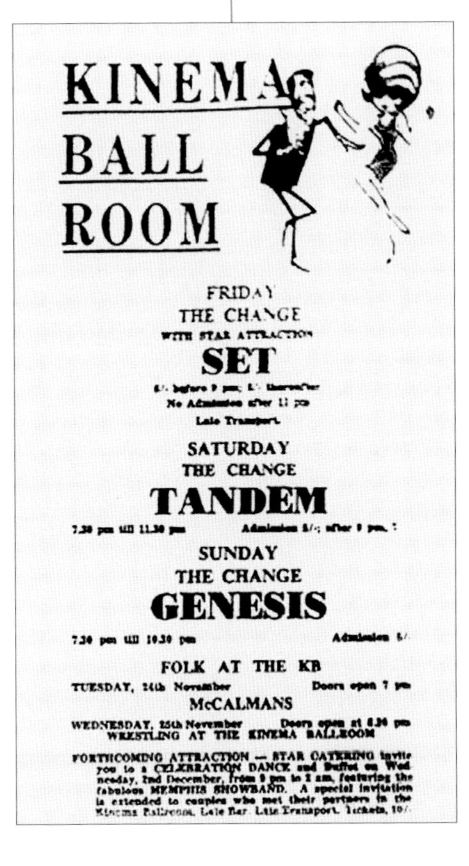


Banks: "We were finding our feet. We were rehearsing in this cottage for a long time, writing all these songs and some of them didn't end up on the album. We were playing live, something we'd never really done, finding out how it went, getting used to playing in front of an audience, how to construct sets and everything, and Trespass was just a selection of songs we had at the time. I mean there were two or three other songs that were good that didn't end up on this record. What we recorded is a bit arbitrary, I think. It was very rushed, you went into the recording studio and had a day or two to do it in." (2)

Phillips: "I seem to recall that we rehearsed and then recorded the main part of it in a few days. Then we had to go off and do some gigs and come back in to do some additional bits. But I think all the main stuff must have been done at one time, because it was too complicated to come back in and set up the mics for the 12-strings and Tony's organ. We knew it all back to front and there wasn't really any time to try out other things. There are some additions of note, extra piano parts from Tony and some extra acoustic guitar in *Looking For Someone* and *Dusk* by Mike. John Anthony added a few effects on the vocals, obviously, because that's where he came into play, getting the right sound. But most of the time it's just as we did it live really, including the drums, in Trident Studios. And quite far apart as well which didn't help. Behind screens and stuff so it was quite difficult to get the vibe of being a group." (3)

John Anthony was the obvious choice for working on the production desk and the results can be heard immediately, despite the limitations in terms of equipment.

Phillips: "Trespass was a slightly more sophisticated recording than From Genesis To Revelation. Eight-track I think it was. I know that John

Anthony wouldn't let anybody drop in. I was able to double track a guitar solo on *The Knife*, which would have been unheard of on the previous album. I remember Mike had a bit of a clash with a guitar at the end of *Stagnation*, about six minutes in. He had to just sit there, listen to the whole track and, of course, by the time it got to his bit he was so nervous that he fluffed it, you know, "start again"." (2)

Rutherford: "You couldn't drop in, so if you made a mistake in a ten-minute song you had to go back to the beginning and play it through till your mistake came again and overdub it. Don't know what that was about, it took forever. John Anthony actually made it a nice atmosphere and I think we overdid it; *Stagnation* is a prime example where Ant and I put on far too many acoustic guitars. I mean so many. Layer after layer of stuff, completely betraying the principle of *"less is more"*. We were just so full of ideas." (2)

Banks: "I remember being quite nervous. You didn't want to make any mistakes because there wasn't the option of going back and repairing and over-dubbing stuff. The whole band went in there and we all played it, and you went on and did a take until you got something that was half-way decent from all of you. Particularly for the drums it was a problem, because that was the one you really couldn't do anything about." (2)

Overdubbing apart, John Anthony proved to be a very collaborative producer.

Phillips: "From Genesis To Revelation was embarked upon in a very naive way but with a huge amount of fun. I think we always felt that we had a lot of say despite Jonathan King obviously being head honcho. With both the first album and Trespass, I don't think we felt that we were not doing what we wanted to do. With Trespass, I don't think we felt emancipated from some sort of odious yoke and this was going to be different because we had John Anthony as producer. For me the recording was kind of pleasant because it wasn't too difficult, we knew exactly what we were going to do. Nice sounds, nice crowd of people, John Anthony was really fun, very humorous and told a lot of bad, bad filthy jokes, and I went through it on auto-pilot. There were no arguments; there'd been so many when we were writing that there was nothing left to argue about really, and I suspect the level of the organ was higher than the guitar or whatever, but John Anthony was in charge of that." (2)

Promotional of *Looking For Someone*.

Gabriel: "TRESPASS was really the first opportunity we had to make a real album where we felt we were in the driving seat. John Anthony was there as a producer and he was a great man for performance and getting the energy. But the style, the arrangements and the approach were all determined by us for the first time." (2)

Phillips: "In terms of writing we were going back to something that was familiar to us, but what was different was doing it in a live context, with the power. By the time we got to record it, John Anthony probably helped to re-invent it for us. A lot of our friends liked the album, but I don't think there was any thought in our minds that we were recording a classic, you know, that in 40 years' time people would still be talking about the solo in *The Knife*." (?)

Rutherford: "You make an album out of the best songs you've got at the time. FROM GENESIS TO REVELATION had material in it that went way back but, with TRESPASS, we were already in the next phase, with songs written between concerts. This is where the process of touring, gigging, recording and writing started. We had some good songs, although they were probably better live than they were on the record." (2)

Even though the songs were developed as a group, the truth of the matter is, each one had a very different story behind the writing.

Banks: "Some of the songs developed out of things that Ant and Mike had written together or Peter and I had written. In particular, *The Knife* was something Peter and I put together, which we then developed in the studio. The same goes for *Looking For Someone*, then obviously things like *Dusk* and *White Mountain* came more from Ant and Mike's side." (2)

Phillips: "Originally it used to be very much a case that Mike and I would write and Peter and Tony would write. Then, during the period at the cottage, where we started doing these longer instrumental pieces, it all got much more mixed up. Mike and I might kick something off with two 12-strings and then Tony would add some organ. Very, very early on, *Stagnation* came from that sort of mixture. Obviously, Pete sorted the lyrical aspect, the vocal lines and flute. So there was a lot more 'cross-fertilization'." (2)

Gabriel: "The writing was still, to some extent, a continuation of where we'd started, in pairs, although some overlapping was beginning to happen. For example, *Looking For Someone* started with things I had begun and in *The Knife* there's one section which Tony did musically, whereas *Dusk* was an Ant thing, as was *Visions of Angels*." (2)

Phillips: "*Dusk* and *White Mountain* were Mike and myself with everyone else mucking in. I think the significant difference was Mike's involvement, because he wrote very little on FROM GENESIS TO REVELATION. He played a bit of bass and told a lot of good jokes, but he didn't do a lot in terms of actual writing." (2)

The instrumentation used also became a lot more complex and, as well as occasional additions and background sounds from Peter on accordion, Ant on dulcimer and Mike on cello, the overall sound was far richer than on the debut album, above all thanks to Peter's flute and Tony's organ.

Phillips: "The flute was part of the music scene, wasn't it? It was used by bands like Traffic and Ian

Label ABC / Impulse, US pressing.

McDonald had blazed a trail with it on the quieter King Crimson numbers, which had a huge influence on us. I think where we were slightly different was that we were using folky sounding instruments but in a slightly more classical way so it sounds a little bit different. We would experiment with these cross chord textures: Mike would be playing one chord and I'd be playing another." (2)

Gabriel: "Tony was extraordinarily possessive about the keyboards. I'd done a bit of flute at school, I always liked the sound, and a little bit of oboe (I was an even worse oboe player, but it made a couple of good noises now and again). Then the bass drum was something physical, visual, that I could kick hard and occasionally it was in time!" (2)

Phillips: "We went through a period of experimentation with the live sound. Tony found the organ difficult. I always remember him referring to it as a box of tricks. A lot of pianists don't like organ: for a start, you've got no light and shade of the touch, and if you're used to that expressiveness it's terribly different, it takes a lot of time. I think he was a bit at sea and, in a sense, lost his power base slightly, and for Peter it was difficult as well. So, whilst they were adapting their writing to the new medium, Mike and I started this two 12-string thing, we just had a period where we wrote more. I think it was easier for us really and that probably explains the folky feel because *Dusk*, *White Mountain* and *Stagnation* were all born out of 12-string guitar stuff, and *Visions Of Angels*, although that was a piano song, it was developed as a guitar-based song for live shows. I remember some guy in the East Grinstead News labelled us 'folk blues mystical'." (2)

Without doubt, the dominant instrumental role of Genesis during this phase was given to the intertwining sounds of Ant's and Mike's 12-string guitars. And this is the instrument which was behind the most stressful moment during the recording session.

Phillips: "Up until then, most 12-strings were recorded as a background instrument that accompanied the song and often they'd put the mic right on the sound hole and you couldn't really hear the notes, you'd just get a very strummy sound. But, of course, the notes were important so I had a set-up where the 12-string went through an old tape recorder, I think called a Bayer Corder. Robin Cable came down and said that it didn't sound like a 12-string to him and I answered: "but it does to me." And that was quite difficult, because Robin Cable was an engineer of high standing. But I had the support of the others because that's how we did it live." (2)

Rutherford: "The album started a bit like our live shows used to in those days. We'd start with a soft song. For half an hour we'd play quiet acoustic music and very often the drummer wouldn't come in till the *Stagnation* bit, which is like 20 minutes into the set. So the album, in a way, reflected that. Part of our operation was an acoustic area. Myself and Ant on guitar, Tony playing piano or organ and Pete playing flute. A lot of our music was acoustic mixed with the heaviness of a song like *The Knife*. In those days there was a lot going on acoustically all around us: Crosby, Stills and Nash, who had a great sound, and Joni Mitchell..., a lot of good artists whom we enjoyed listening to wrote great sounds and acoustic background." (2)

What finally emerged was a record that was unique to the rock scene of those extraordinarily fertile years. Banks: "We didn't think of ourselves as part of any kind of movement. Obviously in the early days our influences were The Beatles, The Beach Boys and The Kinks, but by the time we got to the second album we'd heard groups like Family and the Procol Harum albums, Shine On Brightly and A Salty Dog, as well as Fairport Convention, and the way they were doing things interested us, it just showed slightly different approaches. We weren't trying to write hit songs but to do a little bit more than that. And the idea of having a bit more room to breathe, with songs creeping up to seven or eight minutes, just seemed a lot more exciting to us." (2)

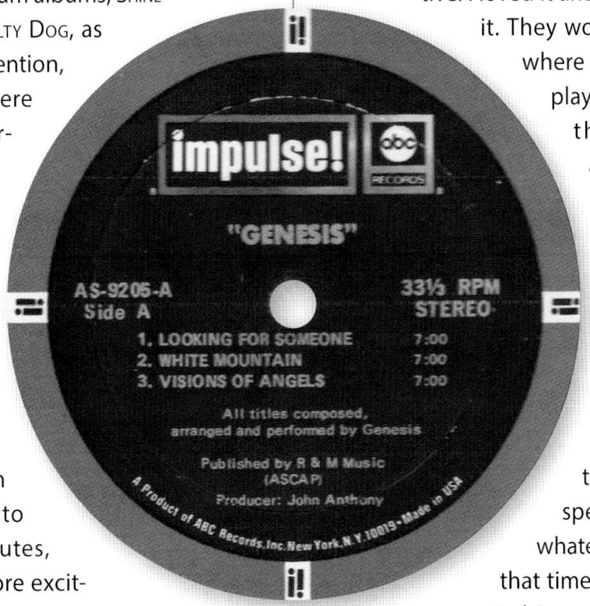

Phillips: "Tony was more from the classical side but loved pop, whereas Peter was probably heading more towards soul. The guys into the heavy stuff were Mike and I because we'd been in the school bands doing The Stones, Kinks and Beatles. We were the ones writing really third rate kind of blues riffs. We were much less sophisticated to start with. What sorted Mike and me out was switching to 12-strings and finding a bit of refinement there. We used to do a song called *Going Out to Get You*, which was in the direction Mike and I wanted to go in, but it's a good thing we didn't early on because we weren't very good at it." (2)

Gabriel: "The folk sound of the album was definitely from Ant and Mike and their 12-string combination, and I think that was really quite innovative. I loved it and I tried to encourage it. They would do these things where one guitar would be playing one chord while the other played another and you would get a composite of the two. The effect gave us a sound that was quite unique. We were always trying to blend our influences. Nowadays that seems nothing special, everyone takes whatever they want, but at that time music was very segregated. I remember sitting in some publisher's office or was it a record company, and they were saying: "No, you can't...you have to decide what you want to be; or you're a folk group, or you're a blues group, or whatever, you can't try and cross all these borders and barriers." And yet I feel that's what I've been doing my entire musical career: whenever someone puts up a barrier, I try and find a way through it. Which I think is the most interesting thing for any creative person. The worst thing you can ever do to an

Advertising for the Charisma Show - Six Shilling Tour, with Van Der Graaf Generator and Lindisfarne.

artist is give them complete freedom because they go right up their arse; they don't know what they're doing, where they're going. However, if you say to an artist, "You can't go here. You definitely can't do that and you mustn't touch this", then they'll start, in their devious way, to get really creative." (2)

While still remaining predominantly acoustic, the new songs also required a more daring rhythmic component than the simple songs on the debut album.

Banks: "On this album we had John Mayhew on drums, who was actually our third drummer, someone we picked up through an ad, and we were slowly getting some cohesion going between the five of us. It was quite difficult for John, I think, because we had all been to public school and behaved a certain way which must have been very irritating to him. We had our own language and we used to fight an awful lot, and we had terrible arguments and shouting matches. I was probably the main instigator." (2)

Gabriel: "John was much more of a professional musician; he'd actually played with real bands of musicians rather than with a bunch of songwriters pretending to be a group. He had different sets of experiences and he worked really hard and was very dedicated and delivered well in some places, but it still felt a bit of a struggle. Ant was the other person who was also drum-sensitive, so he and I sort of overlapped in some of those areas. Between us, we would have a lot of ideas for what the drum parts should do, in much the same way that I think Paul McCartney did with Ringo in The Beatles." (2)

## THE ALBUM

There is little left to discuss: Genesis went into the recording studio, under the guidance of John Anthony, with the specific goal of recording the songs they were routinely playing live at that time. This meant the recording sessions could be completed much more quickly and would stay within the very limited budget, which effectively precluded the band from making overdubs, except for very small parts. The tracklist was basically predefined, the idea being that they would follow the format of their live shows: a soft start getting progressively heavier. The only doubts concerned the final track, the heaviest on the album. Between *Going Out To Get You* and *The Knife*, it would be the latter that finally ended up on the record, whereas fans would only get to hear *Going Out To Get You* many years later in two versions, the original acoustic version (released on GENESIS ARCHIVE 1967–75) and the version that was occasionally played live between 1970 and 1972.

The creative driving force behind TRESPASS was, without a shadow of a doubt, Anthony Phillips. He wrote the song *Visions Of Angels* by himself and *White Mountain* and *Dusk* with Mike. Again with Mike, he created the main structure of *Stagnation* (a song partly sourced from *The Movement*), embracing the input of his bandmates. He also added his touch to the other two tracks on the album, even though these are above all the work of the other writing pair (*Looking For Someone* was mainly written by Peter and *The Knife* by Tony and Peter). Phillips was therefore the undisputed leader of the band at this stage of its

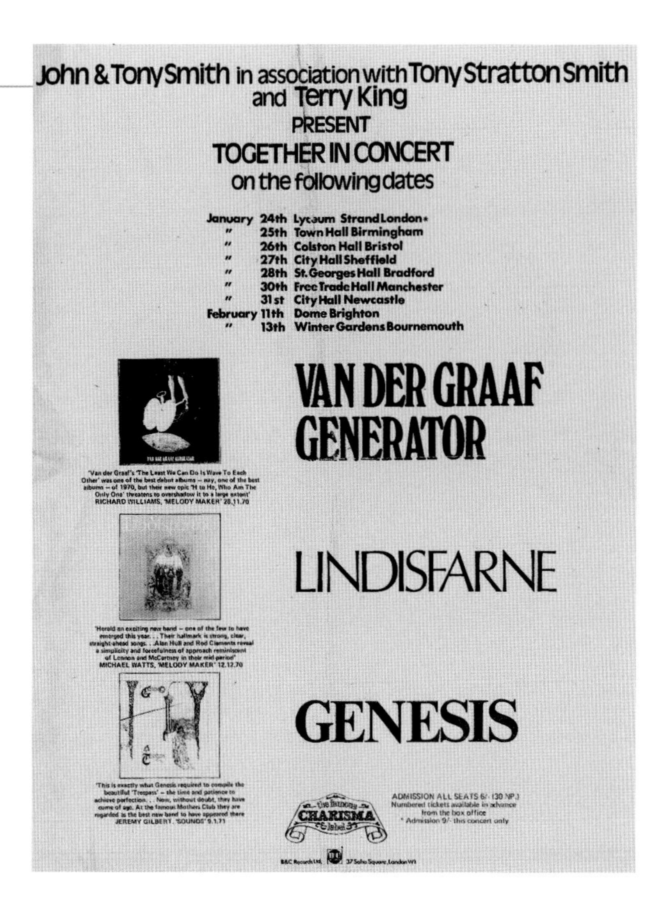


career, with Mike Rutherford acting as his sounding board, providing his consistent contribution on 12-string guitar as well as on bass. The pair represented the core of the band during this period of its history and their tinkling strings make TRESPASS a chapter apart, not just in the group's career, but in the entire history of rock. However, TRESPASS was a record not above drawing its influences from folk music, albeit in a very personal way. At that time, the role of the 12-string acoustic guitar was still linked to simple strumming or the jingle-jangle of Roger McGuinn of The Byrds, but those extraordinary innovators, Phillips and Rutherford, imposed a radical change, also thanks to the use of special tunings and an arpeggio (as opposed to rhythm) playing technique. The multilayer guitar parts (sometimes also including Tony Banks) created a unique and almost ethereal sound in which Tony was the musician paying the price of a personal situation that was yet to be clearly defined. After primarily playing piano on the debut album, Banks was forced to devote most of his time to the organ. With the band relying on their acoustic 12-strings, Genesis' new music no longer required as much piano and the organ still represented a box of tricks for the musician, from which he would gradually learn to extract some of the eeriest of sounds. TRESPASS turned out to be an album of many contrasts: the initial bucolic atmosphere proving deceptive as the songs gradually shift (mainly thanks to the organ) towards more dramatic and dark overtones, with sudden bursts of dynamic emphasis. The songs often start out gently, characterised by a soft sound as if they were draped in silk, but it's as if there is a disturbing, sometimes macabre element lurking just below the surface. The crescendos, the organ arpeggios and the backing vocals filtered with echo are the perfect canvas for lyrics which are much more personal than in the previous album, with literary references to movements such as Surrealism and authors like J.R.R. Tolkien and Lewis Carroll (for the fairy tale themes) and William Blake (for the visionary aspect).

The improvement in musicianship displayed by each member of the band is astonishing: despite remaining primarily an acoustic guitarist, Phillips crafted some convincing electric guitar

# GENESIS, ovvero: POPOESIA

A Thomas S. Eiselberg, uomo ricchissimo, che fu così accorto da spendere ogni suo avere nel seppellirsi molte miglia sotto il suolo. Come unico membro sopravvissuto della razza umana, egli eredita il mondo intero ».

I Genesis sono stati conosciuti solo quest'anno con il loro « Trespass » del '70; ma l'epoca della loro formazione è molto più remota, risalente cioè al '66. In quell'anno, ancora studenti, Tony Banks, Anthony Phillips, Peter Gabriel e Matthew Rutherford incisero alcuni brani da loro stessi composti.

« Speravamo di farci notare per quella che noi ritenevamo fosse una pietra miliare nella storia della musica — ha dichiarato Banks.

« Ciò non avvenne ed il gruppo continuò la sua strada. Assumemmo come batterista Chris Stewart, e definimmo i nostri ruoli, molto confusi fino a quel momento, Peter divenne il cantante, e occasionalmente flautista; Anthony restò chitarrista, Matthew fu spostato al basso ed io mi... limitai all'organo ».

Sostituito il batterista con John Silver, i Genesis incisero in quegli anni ('67-'68) alcuni singoli e un album, in cui già si delineava la loro tematica musicale pur nello stile rockeggiante di allora.

« Ai primi del '69, stanco di un'attività priva di risultati », è sempre Banks a parlare, « Silver abbandonò ed il suo posto fu preso da John Mayhew.

« Con Mayhew gettammo le basi del successivo L.P. e lasciammo la campagna per recarci a Londra in cerca di una nuova casa discografica ».

I cinque furono notati da Tony Stratton-Smith, leader dell'etichetta Charisma, sempre alla ricerca di gruppi d'avanguardia; furono messi a loro disposizione i Trident Studios.

Nacque così Trespass, il cui titolo significa all'incirca «Violazione » o « Offesa ». Poco dopo l'uscita di Trespass si sono separati dal gruppo il chitarrista Phillips ed il batterista Mayhew, subito rimpiazzati da Phil Collins, ex Flaming Jouth, e da Steve Hackett.

Più che la loro biografia, è però la loro opera a parlarci dei Genesis, certo uno dei migliori complessi dell'ultima generazione. Le loro prime incisioni sono assolutamente irreperibili, pertanto, limitandoci all'ultimo album, porremo soprattutto l'accento sui testi.

I sei brani del disco, compo-

I GENESIS COSTITUISCONO UNA DELLE PIU' PROMETTENTI RIVELAZIONI DI QUEST'ANNO SOPRATTUTTO PER LA POETICITA' DEI TESTI CHE ACCOMPAGNANO LE LORO CANZONI. IL LORO ALBUM PIU' IMPORTANTE « TRESPASS », E' UNA DIMOSTRAZIONE LAMPANTE DI COME IL POP POSSA RAGGIUNGERE LIRICITA' NON SOLTANTO MUSICALI

From *Ciao 2001*, 15th December 1971. Genesis achieved significant success in Italy before any other country.

solos (*Looking For Someone*, *The Knife*), while Mike, as well as being Phillips' irreplaceable counterpoint on the 12-string, had gained confidence with the bass, giving an impressive performance on *The Knife*, where he plays a duet with Ant on guitar. Despite not having played any part in the songwriting process, drummer John Mayhew proved to be far more capable than his predecessors, successfully managing to pull off the time changes imposed by his bandmates. As for Peter Gabriel, his voice had acquired not only depth and confidence but above all personality, splendidly and effectively interpreting the main characters and states of mind evoked by the lyrics.

To fully appreciate the uniqueness of a record like TRESPASS, it's worth digressing into the music scene of the period. In the months following the release of FROM GENESIS TO REVELATION (March 1969) a series of events linked to rock music occurred which in some way restyled its characteristics.

In particular, the end of the 'Summer of Love' was marked by a number of serious episodes which not even the great utopia of Woodstock (15–17 August 1969) managed to thwart. That desperate attempt to rekindle the carefree naivety of the hippy dream (which had already suffered a severe blow just a few days earlier with the Bel Air massacre, where a number of Charles Manson's followers had broken into Roman Polanski's villa and murdered the film director's pregnant wife) was given the coup de grace in Altamont on 6 December when a spectator at a Rolling Stones concert was killed by a security guard belonging to the Hell's Angels.

Within the space of just a few months, the illusion of 'peace and love' was smashed to pieces by a rude awakening fuelled by the early deaths of rock stars (on 3 July 1969, Brian Jones of The Rolling Stones instituted what would become known as the '27 Club', later being joined by Jimi Hendrix, Janis Joplin and Jim Morrison). That year also marked the final chapter for the most important band in the history of rock music, when The Beatles played their last live performance on the roof of the Apple Studios on 30 January.

But these were also months of extraordinary creativity. On 22 April 1969, The Who played their rock opera TOMMY live for the first time, and on 24 September Deep Purple performed their CONCERTO FOR GROUP AND ORCHESTRA within the austere walls of the Royal Albert Hall, London.

In 1969 the record market was inundated with album releases from great North American artists such as Bob Dylan (NASHVILLE SKYLINE), Leonard Cohen (SONGS FROM A ROOM), Joni Mitchell (CLOUDS) and outsider Tim Buckley (HAPPY SAD), as well as by bands like The Grateful Dead (AOXOMOXOA), The Doors (THE SOFT PARADE), Creedence Clearwater Revival (WILLY AND THE POOR BOYS), not to mention the self-titled debut albums by Crosby Stills & Nash and The Allman Brothers Band. To this list we can also add the albums by jazz legend Miles Davis (IN A SILENT WAY), Frank Zappa's HOT RATS, and Santana's self-titled debut album.

But, of course, an English band like Genesis were mainly listening to British artists, and while The Kinks released ARTHUR (OR THE DECLINE AND FALL OF THE BRITISH EMPIRE), one of the first concept albums in the history of rock, Pink Floyd brought out the heavily-psychedelic MORE and

Genesis at Newark Abbey in Ripley, September 1969.

UMMAGUMMA. The bands which most heavily influenced Genesis' debut album still represented models to be followed: The Beatles released ABBEY ROAD, The Moody Blues TO OUR CHILDREN'S CHILDREN'S CHILDREN, Procol Harum A SALTY DOG and The Nice released their third album (self-titled). In the meantime new groups had emerged which would have a fundamental role in the coming years: Yes (with their self-titled album) and Jethro Tull (with STAND UP).

So, here we have a list of artists and records which help put the music scenario in which Genesis were writing their second album into perspective, while at the same time giving an insight into the sounds of most bands of the time. However, the cottage retreat period had meant almost total isolation for Genesis, who were more focused on writing their own material than on any models to be followed. But there was just one exception: IN THE COURT OF THE CRIMSON KING by King Crimson. Released on 10 October 1969, the debut album by Fripp, McDonald and their band-mates defined a new genre, progressive rock, and it was about to have an extraordinary impact on the young Genesis, so much so that a copy of the record was quite literally played to destruction at the Macphails' cottage.

In the first months of 1970, however, while Genesis were busy playing live and perfecting their sound, other important events were happening in the rock world. On 10 April, Paul McCartney officially announced the break-up of The Beatles. A few weeks earlier BRIDGE OVER TROUBLED WATER was released, an album which would turn out to be Simon & Garfunkel's last studio record. Many of the North America rock giants, on the other hand, were still very much alive and kicking: James Taylor with SWEET BABY JAMES, Crosby, Stills, Nash & Young with DÉJÀ VU, Bob Dylan with SELF PORTRAIT, Joni Mitchell with LADIES OF THE CANYON and Creedence Clearwater Revival with COSMO'S FACTORY, while Miles Davis was perfecting his form of jazz-rock fusion with BITCHES BREW. In the meantime, Great Britain seemed to be experiencing a totally new swell of creativity. While The Beatles released their epitaph LET IT BE, Deep Purple consolidated their legendary status with IN ROCK, alongside other hard rockers such as Uriah Heep with ...VERY 'EAVY ...VERY 'UMBLE and Black Sabbath with PARANOID. And while King Crimson, Jethro Tull, Yes and Van Der Graaf Generator continued moving forward (respectively with IN THE WAKE OF POSEIDON, BENEFIT, TIME AND A WORD and THE LEAST WE CAN DO IS WAVE TO EACH OTHER), Supertramp brought out their debut album and Traffic released their masterpiece, JOHN BARLEYCORN MUST DIE.

Whilst this was an extraordinary period for the release of groundbreaking records (also worthy of mention are MONA BONE JAKON by Cat Stevens, with a very young Peter Gabriel on flute, ABRAXAS by Santana and Caravan's IF I COULD DO IT ALL OVER AGAIN, I'D DO IT OVER YOU) Genesis seemed unperturbed, as they forged ahead on their very own path. In October 1970, TRESPASS came out alongside releases by rock legends Led Zeppelin (III), Pink Floyd (ATOM HEART MOTHER), Frank Zappa (CHUNGA'S REVENGE) and Elton John (TUMBLEWEED CONNECTION). Despite such fierce competition, TRESPASS was declared 'Album of the Month' in December's edition of Melody Maker.

*Melody Maker,*
January 23, 1971.

## THE SONGS

### LOOKING FOR SOMEONE

The start of Genesis' second album is strikingly different to their debut record: an organ chord leaves the field open to the splendid voice of Peter Gabriel showing off his soul influences.

Gabriel: "That was a song which I'd brought to the band and the band then extended. It was a sort of blues, soul-influenced piece which went into this folkier journey. I can't remember if that mixture was more thanks to Ant or Ant and Tony. But it was fun to sing. I've always liked to try and have, in the different voices I work within, a bluesy one and one that was more soul-influenced. I was finding my voice and exploring things. I think the sort of folkier voice was probably more original, but I could sometimes get more emotion into the bluesier one." (2)

Phillips: "I always thought that Peter sounded like Stevie Winwood on this track: his voice had already got deeper and more powerful. The beginning is all Peter, with a good piano sound, but there are bits of King Crimson as well. Procol Harum influenced us, particularly Tony and Peter. I was influenced by Family, for the acoustic guitar parts, those played by John Whitney." (3)

After the last vocal sections, the almost military pace, driven by the guitars over the eerie arpeggio on the organ, leads to an instrumental ending lasting over two minutes.

Phillips: "I can't really remember who started these parts. A lot of the instrumental stuff on this song and on *The Knife* was done at my parents' place. We spent two weeks there with my father sitting next door trying to watch the TV." (3)

Under the arpeggio of the organ you can also hear a classical guitar played by Mike.

Phillips: "He had to wait seven minutes because John Anthony wouldn't let anyone drop in. Mike was sitting there getting more and more nervous with his hand shaking. In this piece, there's an acoustic guitar and an electric, but live there wouldn't have been the acoustic. Live would have been all electric because Mike was playing bass as well." (3)

In the scales preceding the final guitar solo, Phillips explains "there's extra piano here which Tony wouldn't have been able to do live. The organ is more powerful and reverts to piano again, with a nice tune. I didn't actually remember the last part at all. It's clever. There's some out-of-tune guitar there. I should be shot for that." (3)

The very limited songwriting contributions from the drummer are to be found in a handful of the lines in the lyrics to this song. Mayhew: "It was Peter who wrote the lyrics, it was his special conserve, his special thing. So I didn't contribute very much to the lyrics, although when I was twelve years old I had some poetry published in a London literary magazine. I have always been good with words, writing stories and poetry but don't think I wrote Genesis songs, I didn't. I only made some suggestions." (4)

### WHITE MOUNTAIN

Phillips: "I found the demo where Mike and I just start writing this, playing the tune together. You can hear Josie, Mike's then-girlfriend, saying "Ooh that's nice!" and I'm going "I'm sure that sounds like something else". I realise now why it

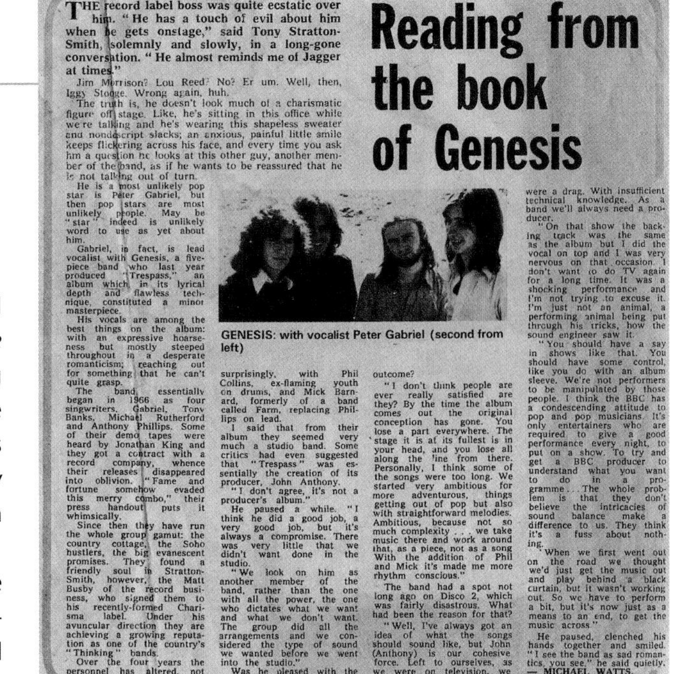

# Reading from the book of Genesis

THE record label boss was quite ecstatic over him. "He has a touch of evil about him when he gets onstage," said Tony Stratton-Smith, solemnly and slowly, in a long-gone conversation. "He almost reminds me of Jagger at times."

Jim Morrison? Lou Reed? No? Er um. Well, then, Iggy Stooge. Wrong again, huh.

The truth is, he doesn't look much of a charismatic figure off stage. Like, he's sitting in this office while we're talking and he's wearing this shapeless sweater and nondescript slacks; an anxious, painful little smile keeps flickering across his face, and every time you ask him a question he looks at this other guy, another member of the band, as if he wants to be reassured that he is not talking out of turn.

He is a most unlikely pop star is Peter Gabriel, but then pop stars are most unlikely people. May be "star" indeed is unlikely word to use as yet about him.

Gabriel, in fact, is lead vocalist with Genesis, a five-piece band who last year produced "Trespass," an album which, in its lyrical depth and flawless technique, constituted a minor masterpiece.

His vocals are among the best things on the album: with an expressive hoarseness but mostly steeped throughout in a desperate romanticism; reaching out for something that he can't quite grasp.

The band essentially began in 1966 as four singwriters, Gabriel, Tony Banks, Michael Rutherford and Anthony Phillips. Some of their demo tapes were heard by Jonathan King and they got a contract with a record company, whence their releases disappeared into oblivion. "Fame and fortune somehow evaded this merry combo," their press handout puts it whimsically.

Since then they have run the whole group gamut: the country cottage, the Soho hustlers, the big evanescent promises. They found a friendly soul in Stratton-Smith, however, the Matt Busby of the record business, who signed them to his recently-formed Charisma label. Under his avuncular direction they are achieving a growing reputation as one of the country's "Thinking" bands.

Over the four years the personnel has altered, not surprisingly, with Phil Collins, ex-flaming youth on drums, and Mick Barnard, formerly of a band called Farm, replacing Phillips on lead.

I said that from their album they seemed very much a studio band. Some critics had even suggested that "Trespass" was essentially the creation of its producer, John Anthony.

"I don't agree, it's not a producer's album."

He paused a while. "I think he did a good job, a very good job, but it's always a compromise. There was very little that we didn't want done in the studio.

"We look on him as another member of the band, rather than the one with all the power, the one who dictates what we want and what we don't want. The group did all the arrangements and we considered the type of sound we wanted before we went into the studio."

Was he pleased with the outcome?

"I don't think people are ever really satisfied are they? By the time the album comes out the original conception has gone. You lose a part everywhere. The stage it is at its fullest is in your head, and you lose all along the line from there. Personally, I think some of the songs were too long. We started very ambitious for more adventurous, things getting out of pop but also with straightforward melodies. Ambitious, because not so much complexity . . . we take music there and work around that, as a piece, not as a song. With the addition of Phil and Mick it's made me more rhythm conscious."

The band had a spot not long ago on Disco 2, which was fairly disastrous. What had been the reason for that?

"Well, I've always got an idea of what the songs should sound like, but John (Anthony) is our cohesive force. Left to ourselves, as we were on television, we were a drag. With insufficient technical knowledge. As a band we'll always need a producer.

"On that show the backing track was the same as the album but I did the vocal on top and I was very nervous on that occasion. I don't want to do TV again for a long time. It was a shocking performance and I'm not trying to excuse it. I'm just not an animal, a performing animal being put through his tricks, how the sound engineer saw it.

"You should have a say in shows like that. You should have some control, like you do with an album sleeve. We're not performers to be manipulated by those people. I think the BBC has a condescending attitude to pop and pop musicians. It's only entertainers who are required to give a good performance every night, to put on a show. To try and get a BBC producer to understand what you want to do in a programme . . . The whole problem is that they don't believe the intricacies of sound balance make a difference to us. They think it's a fuss about nothing.

"When we first went out on the road we thought we'd just get the music out and play behind a black curtain, but it wasn't working out. So we have to perform a bit, but it's now just as a means to an end, to get the music across."

He paused, clenched his hands together and smiled. "I see the band as sad romantics, you see," he said quietly.

— MICHAEL WATTS.

GENESIS: with vocalist Peter Gabriel (second from left)

was reminding me of something. I know what it is now: *Those Were The Days* by Mary Hopkin, a song from 1968 – the same summer we did FROM GENESIS TO REVELATION. This was around the same time *Hey Jude* was released and the tune is a little bit similar to that." [3]

On a base of light organ, the song is all 12-string tinkling arpeggios. Phillips: "People have copied this kind of music so much, but when we were doing this I don't think we were really like anybody. It was quite different, based on the two 12-string guitars. What was original, I now realise, was the combination of the two 12-strings with the organ. King Crimson were different; they didn't have much acoustic guitar and they had a Mellotron, not an organ. So that's where we got our original angle." [3]

Rutherford: "It's a favourite of mine. The lyrics tell a story, which we always seemed to do. I think Tony wrote the lyrics." [2]

In fact, Tony tells the story of Fang, a wolf condemned to death for having dared to see the crown of the king. Both Fang and another character in the lyrics, One Eye (already mentioned in *One-Eyed Hound*) come from the famous children's book *White Fang* by Jack London.

## VISIONS OF ANGELS

Recorded in 1968 at Regent Sound Studios for the first album, the song was discarded at the last minute. Phillips: "We did a crap version of it then. I don't know why; it was as good a song as a lot of the others. Tony was playing an upper piano part and John Silver's drums sounded a bit like *A Day In The Life* by The Beatles, loads of towels on the tom toms. We got caught somewhere between a pop song and *A Day In The Life*. If it had made it to the album, I'm sure we would have ditched it and we would never have developed the middle section with Tony's keyboard; the chords and all that glory made such a difference. Obviously, it was actually a song that was quite well suited to being dramatised a bit, both vocally and with the organ. It was definitely my flagship song for the first album. At the time I was rather heartbroken when it got chucked out. I didn't argue about it, but I didn't know if it was ever going to see the light of day. I kept wondering what I had done wrong, where did we not get it right. So it's a really nice bonus that this was the only song from that previous era that survived." [2]

Apart from "the middle section which we all did together, Tony and myself mainly", explains Phillips [3], the song was composed entirely by Ant on the piano.

● GENESIS: Charisma took them under their wing.

## Charisma's new baby

**BY DEFINITION, Genesis is the production of something new. And the group of the same name certainly justify their name, so much so that of all Charisma's array of talent, they are regarded as "the baby".**

The band was formed at Charterhouse school, and despite making an album for Decca they were wandering in the wilderness when Charisma took them under their wing, gave them a sympathetic and indulgent producer in John Anthony, and an extremely fat cheque to cover the cost of two months in Trident Studios.

This is exactly what Genesis required to compile the beautiful "Trespass" — the time and patience to achieve perfection. In recent months several eminent figures in the music business have acclaimed the group's talents and now, without doubt, they have come of age. At the famous Mothers Club, they are regarded as the best small band to have appeared there.

□ □ □

Their lead singer is Peter Gabriel, frantic and aggressive on stage, yet strangely correct and diffident off stage.

He explained: "Since the album was made, we've lost percussionist John Mayhew, and lead guitarist Anthony Phillips, who was one of the original four. We've had one or two drummers in the past, and we've now got Phil Collins, who actually played the part of the Artful Dodger in the West End production of Oliver Twist; Anthony was very good indeed but he was getting very depressed going on the road, so Mick Barnard has replaced him on lead guitar. We're just about settling down and finding our feet again now."

□ □ □

Genesis went into the studios in June and Charisma thought that they'd taken up permanent residence in Trident. "There was quite a lot of tracking and we spent quite a lot of time arranging songs; not only that but there are certain effects you can't try until you get into the studios," Peter explained.

Prior to this the group had rehearsed extensively at the Gin Mill Club, deep in Surrey where they live. "And before that we spent a time in a cottage in Dorking, but built up debts all the time," he added.

Peter recalled the formation of Genesis. "The four of us originally began as four separate songwriters in different groups at school. Then we thought we'd combine our talents so we made a tape that was pushed around to several people and pushed back again. We eventually got Jonathan King mildly interested; we'd written 300 songs between us and no-one was interested in any of them until Jonathan let us do a demo session and we got four songs into reasonable shape. This eventually led to the album and in order to make that, we began playing together; then in order to make something out of the album we decided to start working."

This album, incidentally, was called "From Genesis To Revelation", and like so many debut albums it was constructed at drastic speed, not really giving the group an opportunity to display their talents.

□ □ □

Then followed a worrying period for Genesis who were left wandering around aimlessly with little predictable future. "I was doing the hustling," Peter recalled, "driving round in an old taxi.

John Anthony saw the group playing at Ronnie Scott's, and was so enthusiastic that he brought down Charisma boss Tony Stratton-Smith for the remaining ten minutes of their act; and this was sufficient to convince Tony of Genesis' musical timbre.

"We didn't really have an album to record then, although 'Visions Of Angels' was already in our stage act," added Peter.

This is one of the six tracks on an extremely picturesque album where the lyrics are highlighted in the foreground of some fat, melodic chords. Liberal use of keyboards and twelve string guitars captures the mood of the stories admirably. Every structure and every scene has been meticulously threaded together, and to have rushed such a delicate operation would have been akin to imposing a time limit on a famous landscape painter.

□ □ □

"We've got very little ambition in terms of instrumental techniques — we are more interested in having available textures of sound. I think we are getting the more satisfaction out of writing and recording, and we will do that as often as possible. That doesn't go as far as saying we don't enjoy live gigs but we play very tightly and we can't always recapture the goodness of a song when it is first organised. It's very difficult to get the circumstances and the set-up to recreate the sound; for instance when you create a sound in a rehearsal room you get a really exciting moment when things haven't got a shape. But we can't always decorate this in a way which completely satisfies us, and on a lot of gigs it'll come out as just the skeleton.

"But we can grow up a hell of a lot." — JERRY GILBERT.

Phillips: "I couldn't play the piano at all in a conventional way. I used to play with three fingers in right-hand octaves and then I would cross over and play the tune which was very bizarre. I think Tony thought I was an idiot which would be understandable. But, like a lot of idiots, sometimes you can come up with something that's a little bit different. I was helped by the fact that I was very limited. Just occasionally I could come up with a nugget of a tune and there was a sort of plodding piano style that was very fashionable at the time; The Beach Boys had done it a lot, The Beatles were doing it in things like *With A Little Help From My Friends*." (2)

After a piano intro, the bass comes in alongside the 12-string arpeggio and light drumming. Phillips: "John did a bloody good job on this, you know. I'm sure Phil would have been a bit better, but John did pretty damn well. God bless his soul. The only thing with John is that sometimes he wasn't incredibly steady." (3)

The romantic verse gives us Gabriel's voice filtered and compressed over arpeggiated guitars.

Phillips: "This is all 12-string but not with a microphone, so you haven't got all that ssss. Listening to it now, maybe it's too mellow but it works well with the organ. At one point Peter was phasing his voice, which overall is quite dry, there's not much reverb on it. But it's so much more powerful than the version we did for the previous album." (3)

Oddly enough, the lyrics to the track are a love song which Ant wrote for Jill Moore, who would later become Peter Gabriel's first wife.

Phillips: "Peter realised that this song was written about Jill before we went on the road. I can't remember if the lyrics were changed for the new studio version." (3)

### STAGNATION

Partially composed by Ant and Mike at Ant's house, this song was first recorded as a demo in Ant's home studio at Send Barns, in August 1969.

Phillips: "Most of this was based on a lot of two 12-string sections Mike and I had written in the spring of '69. We used to sit in my parents' kitchen (I don't know why but it always sounded better in

*Sounds*, 9 January 1971..

the kitchen) and we wrote a lot of stuff during the summer when we were going around and trying things and auditioning drummers. We had a thing called *The Movement* which was a sort of an experiment with a longer piece. We tried it different ways but it didn't really go anywhere, but some of the original ideas went into *Stagnation*: we took out a two 12-string guitars section and Tony started working on it very early on, adding more than just solos." (2)

Banks: "It developed out of a piece that we had rather pretentiously called *The Movement* which we'd been rehearsing for a long time before we played it on stage and it developed. At one point this thing was about 30 minutes long. It sort of got a bit condensed; bits came and bits left, but the first bit stayed and so it was always a key song for us." (2)

Gabriel: "I think it started with an Ant and Mike thing and then bits were added, a 'journey song' as I'd call it. It didn't follow the normal verse/chorus, verse/chorus sort of structure but went through a series of landscapes and that was something that interested me and continues to interest me in the things I do, especially with my film soundtrack work. Some of my favourite pieces of music are when, as a listener, you get taken into different worlds made out of sounds or blends that you've not encountered before: I think that's what we were aspiring to and this is one of the most band-composed tracks on the record." (2)

The track opens with incredible cross harmonies played by Ant and Mike on 12-string guitars with open tunings. Banks: "The Fairport Convention folk influence and the general acoustic guitar style was quite a big thing. Ant and Mike used to play these two guitars together and do a lot of interweaving parts in the harmony, which was very much part of early Genesis and certainly led to the start of what was probably the best song on the album, *Stagnation*, which was then developed by the whole group. I think that was quite unique, no-one else was doing that sort of thing. But it did come from Fairport roots." (2)

After the vocals come in and a few muffled beats on the tom, the first real solo in Tony Banks' career takes off with a rather strange tone created on his organ using a trick for the descending note you can hear at 2'09" on the remastered version.

Phillips: "He got that swoop by turning the organ off and back on again. There was no pitch wheel you see. It was funny, this was the most experimental section. This is where we discovered a lot of things between 12-string and organ." (3)

Phillips again: "There's no bass. Mike may have played bass pedals, although it doesn't sound like a bass pedal. There are some strange sounds in the background – I don't know what they are. I know Pete used to play the accordion on it. This track must have been quite weird for people actually because it was very decorative, not really like a song. I mean, this is exciting now, but then they must have been thinking: "What are they doing?" There wasn't much for Pete to do actually. It was mainly us three with John." (3)

After a brief flute section, when the singing starts again (4'12"), Tony brings in the Mellotron. Phillips: "We had to really work hard to try and get Tony to play the Mellotron. He didn't want to to start with. And straight after [5'05"] I don't know where this section came from. It's guitar-based,

Single version of *The Knife*, German pressing.

but whether it was adapted from a tune of someone's, I don't know. I think it's Mike's riff. In this sequence you can see where *I Know What I Like* came from years later because its chords are quite similar." [3]

In fact, after 1977, Genesis would often feature Gabriel's flute melody in the extended ending of the live version of *I Know What I Like*.

Banks: "Peter used to play a lot of flute really and it was nice for us to have an extra instrument. You have to understand that, in those days, keyboards meant just organ and piano really, that's all there was. I used to put the piano through a fuzz box which got some good sounds on it, but the flute which Peter played was very strong. I mean he wasn't a great flute player, but it was a lovely touch and the big melody at the end of *Stagnation* shows that. Obviously later, once Mellotrons and synthesizers and everything came in, the flute kind of fell by the wayside, but it gave Pete something else to do when we were writing songs. I mean banging tambourines and the rest of it can obviously get a bit frustrating. He was a person who would have liked to have had his hands on the keys quite a lot of the time but I wouldn't let him." [2]

Gabriel's lyrics were inspired by the possible consequences of a nuclear war.

Phillips: "I always liked the words "bitter minnows amongst the weeds and slimy water". Good lyric. Peter sang it putting his voice through a narrow tube so it sounds as if he's underwater." [3]

Banks: "In those days, we used to have a thing about keeping the voice really low on the first verse, but we overdid it on the original version, you can hardly hear the voice on the first verse. The remixes have made a big difference – suddenly the voice is there. Particularly with the 5.1 mixes, you can spread the guitars out a bit, although, having said that, on this particular album we had to do a lot of sub-mixing because it was done on an 8-track. The bottom end was very weak on the original version and you couldn't really do a lot with that." [2]

## DUSK

Written by Ant and Mike at Send Barns, a first version of this song was recorded on 20 August 1969 (released 30 years later as part of GENESIS ARCHIVE 1967–75). The version on TRESPASS, however, is shorter, more compact, and is again dominated by Ant's 12-string and Mike's classical guitar. Phillips: "Nice sound. Mike's playing classical guitar there. This is quite mellow." [3]

Gabriel's voice, which is strong in the verses, disappears completely in the choruses where the main voice is Ant's. Phillips: "I think Peter was singing at the bottom. It's such an ensemble piece. This is probably the first song we did of the new era, after FROM GENESIS TO REVELATION." [3]

After the second chorus, Peter plays a flute solo which closes with a guitar arpeggio.

Phillips: "I always liked this bit [2'28"]. It's a very haunting chord that actually sounds slightly like Family. On MUSIC IN A DOLL'S HOUSE, there's a track called *The Breeze* which is quite similar. This is a really good track. It's better than I thought." [3]

Anthony was also the main author of the lyrics. Phillips: "On this one, we imagine someone who is what we call morbid, someone whose life is slipping away and is looking back on life. The funny

thing is, we were only seventeen, eighteen or nineteen. Why were we imagining somebody dying looking back on their life?" (3)

## THE KNIFE

Gabriel: "It used to be known as *The Nice*, because we were big fans of The Nice. Not many people know much of their work nowadays, but it was what actually drew us into Tony Stratton-Smith, and although Keith Emerson is associated with some of the more extreme departures of prog rock on the keyboard, back then The Nice was a hip, underground band that Hendrix wanted to join. Now, people forget that, but they were amazing, their music was powerful, inventive, driving. Maybe Soundgarden might be a modern-day reference. And obviously Emerson was a great performer, he used to sort of rock backwards and forwards with The Nice. And there we would be, you know, sitting on stools twiddling away at 12-strings and we'd be thinking: "Where's the balls in this? Let's get something with a bit of energy and something a little dangerous." We didn't have anything like that in our repertoire, so I started to try and write something that would have that energy. Then Tony added a section to it, and obviously the keyboard part at the end. It was the first peak of a darker energy that we'd discovered." (2)

Phillips: "This song was obviously very much Peter and Tony, while the instrumental part was all of us. It was inspired by The Nice. Just as Mike and I were greatly influenced by blues guitarists, Tony was the same with Keith Emerson, but this was slightly before Wakeman and people like that. This would have been around '66, '68." (2)

A track which was unusually heavy, with the organ playing the lead and Mayhew's tarantella rhythm under Ant's solo guitar and Mike's bass which often went along in sync, even though every now and again the guitarist goes off into some solo sections to support Gabriel's aggressive voice. Once the main structure comes to an end, before proceeding with the long instrumental part, there is an interlocutory phase full of fine details and effects.

Phillips: "Mike's bass is great here, while my guitar is a bit out of tune. Funny, I don't remember playing with the volume pedal [3'18"]; I remember when it starts to get going with the flute. Even the flute's a bit out of tune." (3)

There follows a chaotic phase with people chatting, apparently talking nonsense. The voice of John Anthony stands out [5'08"] and there are female shouts, "I don't know who did it" (Phillips). (3)

The song closes with a long guitar solo almost always echoed by the bass.

Banks: "The end sections developed out of improvisations. We actually performed *The Knife* on stage one time, it was like 20 minutes long. We just pruned it right back and took what we felt was the best part of it. This song and *Looking For Someone* started out as concise songs which when we started to play them and rehearse them started developing ideas. That developed into what became the Genesis trademark of extended solos." [2]

The lyrics (a parody of a protest song which, at first sight, may seem like an invitation to violence) were written by Gabriel with a little help from Phillips, who remembers:

"This is the song where I sat with him to try and come up with extra lyrics. He had the first verse but he was singing the same thing all the time, so we had to come up with some extra words. We sat in the kitchen and I came up with "carry their heads to the palace of old"." [3]

## THE ALBUM ARTWORK

Rutherford: "For the first two or three albums we had Paul Whitehead, who was a good artist involved in doing album covers at that time. Gatefold record sleeves were fantastic, you could let the artist go away and do something that excited them. The cover for Trespass looked great with the big knife slash across it." [2]

Paul Whitehead is an English artist whom Genesis contacted because they were convinced their music deserved the right packaging. This is why the artist spent time with the band in the rehearsal room where he was particularly influenced by the lyrics to *White Mountain* and *Visions Of Angels*. But the stroke of genius lies in the knife slash on the back cover.

Gabriel: "Paul heard some of the folky stuff and mythical bits. I felt it was getting a bit too twee, so I suggested that we get a big knife and slash it. There was a lot of discussion about this in the band, but in the end they went for it. I was going to go for quite a crude knife, but Paul chose this sort of more elegant dagger, which wasn't quite what I'd had in mind, but it did a job and for fans it had its own personality, which is what we wanted." [2]

Banks: "I think it was quite a nice idea, because a lot of the music we'd done was very pretty and romantic music but we had this one song, *The Knife*, which was completely different, a sort of violent song. So pictorially we did that, we asked this guy to draw a fairy drawing and a knife slash through the middle of it with the knife sticking out. Genesis is deceptive sometimes. We've always had those two sides to us: there's the romantic side and the more aggressive side. So I thought that particular cover was really good. I think it was the best of the first three covers." [2]

Phillips: "I think the album was a pretty good compromise between the kind of folky tendency towards medieval echoes and then there's the harder-edged stuff, and we wanted to draw people's attention to that as well. So, the cover, with that knife slash, was a great way of combining the two things, and you could see commercially why that was a good move." [2]

## EPILOGUE

Compared to the blatant naivety of the debut album, TRESPASS reveals a band which had matured in all aspects: technique, composition quality and personality. The disparity is so great that the two records seem to be the work of two completely different bands.

Rutherford: "On FROM GENESIS TO REVELATION we were really a bunch of kids on holiday time, but between that album and TRESPASS we'd become a band. We'd done live concerts, we'd done the cottage era, where we wrote stuff for six months and the band started to take shape... and it's a strange album because it's the only one we ever did where we actually played it live before we recorded it. Which I wouldn't do again, funnily enough. To be honest, I could barely play bass on the first album. I'd been playing more guitar with Ant and, of course, he's the lead player so I had to play bass as well as acoustic guitar." (2)

Phillips: "I don't like much of the guitar playing, I'm afraid, but apart from that, the sound could have been better, the sound wasn't powerful enough, but it had its moments. Quite creative for the time. Not as good as King Crimson but not bad at all." (3)

Rutherford: "*Stagnation* and *The Knife* are a great example of what we do. The contrasts are always how we think to create our music in a sense, and that album contained both those things. *The Knife* was our heaviest song and a popular live song too and with a good performance from Pete. On that album we were still working in pairs. Myself and Ant wrote the acoustic sound with guitars picking out harmony parts. *Stagnation*, *Dusk* and *White Mountain* were very atmospheric and that was a part of what we were doing on stage and on the record." (2)

Banks: "I think it was a pretty good second album. *Stagnation* is great, as is *Looking For Someone*. The other songs on the album don't do much for me anymore. I always felt *Dusk* was a bit of a B track whereas *White Mountain*, well we used to do that live and it was quite atmospheric, but I don't think it's as strong as what was to come." (2)

Rutherford: "What the album did suffer from was the fact that we'd played the songs for so long live, so when we met in the studio we were fairly inflexible. We'd found a sound and that's the way it stayed, and it was in a way a little frustrating. The way we worked after that, we went in with songs we'd never played live, so actually you could mess around with the sound. You didn't quite know where you were going sonically. But with TRESPASS, we'd defined how the parts went, so in a way that was kind of a unique experience." (2)

Phillips: "I think of TRESPASS as a very good early Genesis album. Obviously, there were many better later ones, but I think there's a sort of prototype there, in a lot of the tracks, for things that came later. I mean the 12-string stuff we did on this album is developed more later. And obviously, the longer format songs like *The Knife* and *Looking For Someone* were the precursor of things like *The Musical Box*. It was a very important, early stage in the band's later development." (2)

Rutherford: "We were considered part of that era with bands like Yes, Emerson, Lake & Palmer and stuff, but actually they were very different. I

Anthony Phillips in London, 27 February 2007.

mean you only have to listen to songs like *Stagnation*; it's an acoustic album. We were always about songs. The playing came secondary to the songs." (2)

Gabriel: "TRESPASS was a good start. It definitely had a personality that was different to other prog bands. We had some minor success in Belgium, which felt like conquering the world at the time." (2)

Unfortunately, by the time TRESPASS had reached the record shops in October 1970, the band was already desperately seeking a solution to what would be the most dramatic defection in its still very short history: the departure of Anthony Phillips.

Rutherford: "In a sense, people never realised that in a way, apart from Peter, who was always very get up and go with agents and managers and the business side of thing, in many ways during that first era, Ant was the strongest driving force. He was an extrovert on stage, musically he was very strong, so the concept that he might leave was probably nowhere near our thoughts at all." (2)

Phillips: "My leaving was nothing to do with the music, it was just due to stage fright and my health, really. I found it really tough. There was no kind of 'left for musical differences' or huge personality clashes. I just found the touring had taken a huge toll. You know people glamorised this life, they imagine it's all high-living and groupies and stuff but we were living a fairly monastic life. I mean, we were living on top of each other in a cottage. We never went anywhere else, nobody saw anybody else. At one stage we got so irritated with each other that we wouldn't talk. I mean it's understandable if you're living in the same place for six months. I didn't have a girlfriend at the time but two of them never saw their girlfriends. So, looking back on it, the idea of getting together in a country cottage and never get away from it, living 24-hours-a-day music was pretty silly. Pete has pointed out that I was probably the most driven member of the band. I loved the illusion, I believed in it..." [2]

Banks: "There was parental pressure on Ant and that was probably one of the factors that made him leave. It was certainly the reason our previous drummer, John Silver, left. You should remember that, back in those days, pop music was not a respectable profession, but those of us who just love music, just wanted to be in it and didn't really care one way or the other how it was, we stuck at it. For me, Anthony was the group leader, he was the one who wanted to go live, he was the one who wanted to go professional, he kind of motivated the rest of us really. Peter and I were not sure at all it was what we really wanted to do. Initially, I think we said we'd stay just for the first summer, with the intention that we probably wouldn't stay, that they'd find somebody else. And then, of course, we got more into everything after that, so we were very surprised when Anthony was the one who suffered from stage fright." [2]

In January 1970, Phillips, who was still battling with the after-effects of glandular fever, began to suffer from accute stage fright. Then in April, he contracted bronchial pneumonia. Phillips: "I stopped touring when I got bronchial pneumonia. I had to stop for two weeks, which felt really bad, but I realised the problem wasn't going to go away. I was advised by the doctor to leave, but there was a part of me that didn't want to let go of the dream and I also didn't want to let the others down. But I was pretty clear that I was dispensable. So, whilst there was a feeling of not wanting to let the others down, things had moved on. Tony was very confident now with the organ and Mike had grown hugely into an all-round musician and writer. Their success was all very gradual, the right way really, which makes you appreciate it and not take things for granted. I used to go and watch them to start with [after leaving]. I used to enjoy it. You used to know all the people in the audience, but then obviously things got bigger and more impersonal. It would be unnatural if I had walked away and then never thought "wouldn't it be great to be part of that", but there are lots of things in life you just aren't cut out for. If I said, I've got no regrets about it, no-one would believe me anyway, but if I look at the situation at the time it was just untenable. The combination of unresolved stage fright (which I never spoke or sought advice about) and physical frailty made the decision to leave unavoidable. And, to be honest, you can't have four composers all in the same sort of space. I think they ended up with a very workable unit because everyone (Phil, Mike and Tony) made their own separate power blocks. You hear stories of groups where there's no co-composing, where they all fall out and hate each other and throw guitars at each other. But you try co-composing where you get someone saying "if you take my chorus, I'll take your verse", it comes down to who's got the strongest will, and if the person is just not prepared to back off, it gets quite wearing. I think they got it to a stage where it really worked, there was just mutual respect with no treading on anybody else's toes. That doesn't mean to say you loved everything." [2]

Gabriel: "Ant's departure was a great loss. In many ways, he was the most musically gifted of all of us. He was also the most obsessive and transmitted that culture to the band: it was a bit like joining the Army, there was this really powerful group mentality that it had to be one hundred percent total commitment. But this also has its costs. I think Ant was very uncomfortable playing live. It was also extremely stressful, which in part was self-imposed and partly group-imposed. He was definitely the most closely focused on becoming a professional musician, whereas the rest of us were just aspiring musicians and songwriters." (2)

Rutherford: "After hearing Ant's side of things in the band's biography [*Genesis: Chapter and Verse*, 2007], I was kind of saddened that I hadn't quite clocked what was going on at the time. Ant and I were very close, but at this stage I had a girlfriend and we saw each other less, I kind of drifted away a bit. I wasn't really aware of just how bad his stage fright was, along with his other health issues. I'd have thought, knowing him so well, that I would have been able to pick up on what was going on but… I often miss things. So in a sense, it was a shock when he told us he was leaving." (2)

Anthony Phillips' departure put Genesis in the very difficult position of having to decide whether to quit or carry on. They opted for the latter, albeit with heavy hearts, mainly thanks to the sheer determination of Richard Macphail.

Macphail: "When Ant announced he was leaving, I found myself in the van at the back of the Marquee Club in the summer of 1970 with Peter, Tony and Mike who were seriously thinking of calling it a day. I convinced them to carry on, and it has since been said that if I hadn't insisted so much, there's a chance they would have quit. Tony agreed to carry on but said we needed to find a better drummer. And it was obviously one of the best things that ever happened because the difference that Phil made…we just couldn't believe it…it was unbelievable." (1)

Banks: "When Anthony left I thought we would probably split up. He was certainly the most influential person in the group. Mike and Pete were very keen to carry on and Richard Macphail, who was our roadie and good friend, wasn't for letting us quit. We decided that we had to do better on the drums. We liked John and everything, he was good, it's just we felt we needed someone more creative in the drum seat." (2)

Phillips: "He was a good drummer but we were very, very demanding and I think he always felt he came up short. He didn't really, he did a fine job. The trouble is that history hasn't treated John well because his successor just so happens to be one of those very, very special drummers, not only a drummer but a singer and a brilliant musician. I think, had they found a more prosaic drummer afterwards, then history would speak more kindly about John, but he's cast in a rather dim light, which I always think is rather unfair. We were very demanding and we spoke the same musical language, we'd grown up in the same environment for a long time and there was no way John could really understand what we were on about most of the time. He lacked that sort of sunny character and confidence which I think it's best for a drummer to exude. I think a drummer is the foundation of the group, like the goalkeeper in a football team: if you have a dodgy goalkeeper, there's a

Genesis

chance the defence will feel more insecure." (2)

John Mayhew quite literally left the scene, emigrating to New Zealand and then moving to Australia. He disappeared without a trace for 30 years. He eventually came back to the UK at the end of 2002, without anyone knowing about it, until he was recognised by a colleague in the company he was working for as a carpenter. In 2006, Mayhew agreed to take part in some Genesis fan conventions held in England, Italy and Germany and as a result came into contact with the band's management. Shortly afterwards he was given all the royalties which had accumulated from the sales of TRESPASS in his absence, a considerable sum of money with which he intended to go back to Australia. Fate, however, decided differently and on 26 March 2009, the day before his 62nd birthday, Mayhew died from complications associated with a heart condition shortly after being admitted to a hospital in Glasgow.

Once the decision to carry on without Ant had been taken, the Gabriel-Banks-Rutherford trio officially set out to recruit two new band members. The first step was taken by Tony Stratton-Smith who placed an ad in Melody Maker looking for "...a drummer sensitive to acoustic music, and a 12-string acoustic guitarist".

Gabriel: "As a sort of drum fanatic, I took a big role in the auditions. We auditioned a lot of people, including some really quite useful drummers, at my parents' house where Tony and I used to do all the writing and some rehearsing. I suggested, I think, that we devise a series of tests because we didn't have long in an audition – I hate auditions anyway – but one of the problems with John was that he was quite...uh...you know, once he'd got something he could do it and deliver it well, but he was very slow learning. So when we wanted to try different arrangements, different grooves, different feels, it was a painful and really time-consuming process, so we thought, okay we will throw some different tests at these drummers and see how quickly people pick up these ideas." (2)

Phil Collins: "I didn't know their music at all because I was always playing with my band [Flaming Youth] even if we weren't actually gigging, but I used to see their name constantly in the back pages of Melody Maker where they advertised all the gigs for the Greater London area. It seemed that Genesis were always working, and I remember complaining to our manager because they were always playing and we weren't. One day when I was scouring the back pages looking for jobs I spotted an advert with a box round it. I knew Tony Stratton-Smith very well, I'd known him for years, so I knew where to find him. I went

John Mayhew in Orvieto,
23 September 2006.

to the Marquee Club bar and asked him about it. He said it was for Genesis. And I thought, at last I get to find out what their music's like." (2)

The audition was held at Peter Gabriel's parents' house in Chobham, where a handful of aspiring drummers and guitarists were met by the three remaining members of Genesis.

Collins: "I was given Peter's phone number as he was arranging the auditions. I went down there with Ronnie Caryl, who was in the same band as me back then (and still plays with me now). That was the first time I'd ever met them, seen them or heard anything by them. My only recollection of Trespass was that it had an arty cover. Anyway, they gathered the three or four drummers that were there that day in the living room to listen to a couple of tracks off the album. I specifically remember *Looking For Someone* and *Stagnation*. Maybe *The Knife* as well. The music had a soft edge to it. I came from a blues band and Genesis didn't have that kind of sound. It was a summer's day and I came away with feelings of Crosby, Stills & Nash, their harmonies, the 12-string guitars, it was warm, fuzzy music. I didn't think the band sounded that great. The drums sounded a little woolly, but I think that was due to bad production rather than anything else." (2)

Gabriel: "Phil arrived early, he was always the most punctual member of the band, with his mate, Ronnie Caryl, and he was there listening to the other two drummers. So by the time he sat down, he knew everything. As an ex-drummer, I knew just from the way he sat down in the saddle that he knew exactly what he was doing, It was clear that he could lift the music. They always say that a band is only as good as its drummer and Phil is a great drummer. I connected with Phil immediately, he had this cheerful chap personality and a really good sense of humour, and he'd had real experience of real bands on the road whereas we were still getting our feet wet. He impressed me because he said he'd played on a George Harrison session (even though I think he'd only actually done third tambourine...)." (2)

Straightforward and easy going, Phil found himself thrown into a well-off, vaguely aristocratic and slightly eccentric environment.

Rutherford: "Whatever he says, I was not wearing a smoking jacket when I came down the stairs to greet him! I was probably wearing a dressing gown and it probably had the same effect actually. But the story's kind of grown over time. It's a good story but he tells it much better than I do." (2)

Collins: "I left with Ronnie Caryl. We packed our stuff up and got back in his car, and he said "I think you blew that". When I asked why, he said "I dunno, but I think I did pretty good"". (2) However, Caryl was wrong: Collins was the only one to pass any of the auditions (for drummer and guitarist) held on that day.

Collins: "Turned out of course that a couple of weeks later, Peter Gabriel called me back, said they liked me very much and asked if I would join the band. I was very, very happy. I think I must have gone up to London to meet them." (2)

It was 4 August 1970 when Genesis told Phil Collins that he was their new drummer. They then took a couple of weeks' break, cancelling what few dates had been scheduled before Phillips left (including one in Plumpton on 9 August and one at the Marquee Club on 30th, where Genesis should have been opening for Amazing Blondel).

Collins: "And then they all went on holiday for two weeks, to sort of gather their strength. I guess they felt they had a huge barrier to cross without Anthony being there, because he was obviously a big writer (and I wasn't) and he was no longer in the band. In that time I got my first, my one and only ever job outside music, decorating people's houses. That was a terrible experience." (2)

On 24 August, Peter, Tony, Mike and Phil went to stay at The Maltings (a range of buildings in the heart of Farnham, Surrey, which is now a creative arts centre) to start rehearsing. While they were waiting for the right guitarist to come along, the band decided to keep busy and perfect new material, testing out their new compositions, albeit temporarily, as a four-piece. It must be said that Genesis music didn't require many guitar solos, but what was worrying was the absence of Ant as a songwriter and, in the live context, as the main performer of complicated 12-string guitar parts. Consequently, during rehearsals Tony and Mike took on additional tasks: Mike took charge of guitar parts, forcing him to start using bass pedals, while Tony began running his electric piano through a distortion box to fill in for the missing lead guitar, basically taking on all of the solos. This technique proved to be a really important step forward in the further growth of Genesis' technical abilities, and as a four-piece they perfected the execution of a number of songs previously rehearsed with Phillips, such as *Going Out To Get You* and *The Musical Box*.

Banks: "*Going Out To Get You* and *The Knife* were competing to be the big number. *Going Out To Get You* went through many, many transformations, at one point it was about 20 minutes long; it had lots of bits in it that came and went. The version we ended up with, the one in the box set [ARCHIVE 1967–75], was a simpler version, with a good basic riff, a Rolling Stones kind of thing, which was written by Ant. Paradoxically, when we were down to being a four-piece, we carried on doing it because we were a bit short of material which we could actually play. Some things, without Ant, were rather difficult, but this was a song we could do." (5)

Rutherford: "We were trying to function in a four-piece scenario, with Tony playing the lead parts. Funnily enough, the first time I felt that the band worked in this set-up was with *The Musical*

Charisma advertising poster

*Box*, with me playing bass pedals and Tony playing keyboards. The song worked well on stage as a four-piece and shows what direction the band might have taken if we had continued along this route. I'm glad we didn't because all the other tracks were missing the guitar." (2)

But while the lack of a guitarist may well have represented a handicap, the fact that they now had a great drummer in Phil Collins was immediately evident.

Gabriel: "The grooves felt better. People nowadays think of Phil through his own songs and his solo work; they often forget that he's someone who can pick up almost any instrument without knowing how to play it and make some sort of sound that feels good. He has a lot of natural talent and people sometimes fail to see him as a musician." (2)

Collins: "I never met John Mayhew, but I kind of feel that he wasn't able to climb the wall to get inside. I mean the drummer's role has always been to deflate the tension really, you know, the guy who sits there, drinks too much, cracks the odd joke." (2)

Rutherford: "We were all a bit serious and Phil, as drummers should be, was the joker. He brought this lightness to the band… I know he got a shock when we first started rehearsing at The Maltings because suddenly we'd have these huge rows and Tony would stomp out or I'd stomp out for 10 minutes, and he didn't know what was going on. For the first 10 days or so of rehearsing, around the time we were writing *The Musical Box*, I remember he stayed at my house, met my mum and dad, and then he went and stayed with Pete. I think he always thought that I didn't like him or that I'd kicked him out and sent him off, but it wasn't that way at all, it was just so we could all get to know him." (2)

After spending the whole of September rehearsing, Genesis were ready to go back on stage. The first show with Phil Collins on drums was in Chatham on 2 October. Two days later the band played at the Marquee.

Alternating between days rehearsing in Farnham, Genesis went on to play a series of concerts for which it is almost impossible to establish the setlists. What is known, however, is that these concerts revolved mainly around Trespass which was finally about to be released. Conceptually the four musicians perfected their already tried-and-tested approach to live shows based on a continuous crescendo, starting out with acoustic songs and building up to a more aggressive finale.

Banks: "We used to start acoustic. I managed to play a lot of guitar for the first 2 or 3 songs. And then *Stagnation* would be the first song that had anything else in it. The song itself starts off with just the guitars and then the keyboards come in and then there's an organ solo and then the whole thing becomes drums and everything comes in. *The Knife* was the final song in the set and the audience, even those who weren't quite sure what we were on about, always loved it, their heads were all going, you know, so for that first year or two of touring it was very much the key song, the trademark Genesis song." (2)

Gabriel: "I'd always felt that it was a good thing to try and build up from small to large, from light to dark and so on. We'd come on as a sort of folk act and then we'd end up electric and smashing things. We wanted to shock people. I think Ant

STRATTON SMITH MUSIC LIMITED ARTISTE GENESIS DATE W/E 13.11.70.

| DATE | VENUE | ARRIVAL TIMES | PAYMENT | HOTEL | OTHER INFORMATION |
|---|---|---|---|---|---|
| Friday 13th November | Rutherford College The University Canterbury, Kent. | Equipment: 6.30pm Artistes: 7.00pm On stage: Bet. 8.00-11.00 1 x 60 mins spot | £40 cheque | Tel No. | |
| Saturday 14th November | EVENING Main Hall, Watford Tech. College Hempstead Road, Watford, Herts. | Equipment: 6.30pm Artistes: 6.30pm On Stage: Bet. 8.00-12.00 2 x 45 mins spot | £60 c.o.n. | Tel No. | AFTERNOON Disco 2. Arrive 1.00pm T.V. Centre, Wood Lane, Shepherds Bush Steve Turner. |
| Sunday 15th Nov. | Free | Equipment: Artistes: On stage: mins spot | | Tel No. | |
| Monday 16th Nov. | Free | Equipment: Artistes: On stage: mins spot | | Tel No. | |
| Tuesday 17th Nov. | Free | Equipment: Artistes: On stage: mins spot | | Tel No. | |
| Wednesday 18th Nov. | Free | Equipment Artistes: On stage mins spots | | Tel No. | |
| Thursday 18th Nov. | Scotland To be advised. | Equipment: Artistes: On stage mins spot | | Tel No. | |
| Friday 19th Nov. | Scotland t.b.a. | Equipment: Artistes: On Stage mins spot | | | |

had some of these instincts about how to interact with an audience, more than the rest of the band. They learned over the years, but it was sometimes like trying to talk to a brick wall. As the frontman, I felt I was the vehicle through which the audience connected to the music and I was painfully aware when things weren't working. Ant had this great body of other melodic and classical things within him, he was from The Stones mould of rock guitar. Another loss, for me, when he went was that I didn't feel anyone else quite understood what actually happens between band and audience." [2]

While some songs from the repertoire already tried out with Phillips survived, such as *Peace*, *Twilight Alehouse* and *Going Out To Get You*, other songs like *The Musical Box* took on a more definitive form when Genesis were playing as a four-piece. More importantly, during the rehearsals at The Maltings, existing pieces of music were developed and completely new songs written, for example, the instrumental track *Moss*, previously called *The Epilogue*, (which recycled a few sections from *The Movement*), and *Wooden Horse* (which later became known as *Wooden Mask*). Songs from the four-piece period also include *The Light* (from one of Phil's ideas) and a primitive version of *The Return Of The Giant Hogweed*.

Banks: "When we recorded Trespass, we only recorded about 50% of the music we were playing live. By the time we got to recording Nursery Cryme, we'd written new material and didn't really want to do the old stuff again. We had about half a dozen songs which we did in those early shows that just never got recorded. *The Light*, for example, had some good bits on it which saw the light of day on The Lamb..., and there were two or three other songs like that." [5]

Having no intention of carrying on as a four-piece, Genesis continued auditioning guitarists.

Despite not being fully accepted into the band, Ronnie Caryl (former guitarist in Flaming Youth and friend of Phil Collins) did maintain contact for some time. Caryl: "After the first audition, where Phil was playing by the house and I was playing on a chair with Mike Rutherford, I went back and did three days of rehearsals. But Genesis wanted somebody to play more or less rhythm and I wasn't that kind of guitarist; I was into blues. I basically saw a guitar solo as something I made up and not something somebody else told me to play. Mike was very technically gifted as a 12-string guitar player. I think I lacked certain skills." [6]

Caryl did play live with the band on occasions, for example at the Kempston gig on 23 October 1970 (on electric guitar only).

In the meantime, David Stopps, promoter of the Friars Club and big Genesis fan, suggested guitarist Mick Barnard who played in a local band, The Farm. After having gone to a few of their gigs (including the one with Caryl on guitar), Barnard auditioned for Genesis in mid-October, first at The Maltings and then again in West Hampstead (which is why the band skipped the performance at the Grand Benefit Festival held at Sussex University in Falmer on 31 October and 1 November) before finally appearing on stage in Salisbury on 3 November.

For a time it seemed that Genesis had found the answer to their problems because Barnard had a certain amount of experience, even though he didn't play 12-string - only a Gibson 335 electric guitar. With Barnard in the band, Genesis further perfected songs like *The Musical Box*, for which he outlined the essential parts of the guitar solo.

At this point in time Genesis still weren't that well-known (so much so that occasionally their name got misspelt on posters and flyers, appearing, for example, as Genisis) but they were starting to get noticed, even if most of the time they were still supporting other bands (on 7 November they opened for Argent and on 10 November for Jackson Heights). They were also supposed to open for Fleetwood Mac in Brighton on 13 November, but the schedule got changed and they ended up supporting Fairport Convention in Canterbury.

On 14 November Genesis made their first ever TV appearance, live in the BBC Shepherd's Bush studio on the 'Disco 2' music show. The band, including Barnard, all mimed *The Knife* except Gabriel who actually sang live. After their TV performance, unfortunately deleted from the BBC archives, Genesis rushed up to Watford where they had a gig that same evening.

Between 15 and 22 November the band toured Scotland and on the 28th they had an important and unexpected gig at Imperial College London. The evening's main attraction was Van Der Graaf Generator, the most popular band in the Charisma catalogue, and Genesis were called in at the last minute to replace the original support band, Cochise.

As Genesis weren't 100% convinced about keeping Mick Barnard, they continued to keep an eye out for another guitarist. On 12 December Peter spotted an ad in Melody Maker saying: "Imaginative guitarist/writer seeks involvement with receptive musicians, determined to strive beyond existing stagnant music forms".

Steve Hackett: "I stuck loads of ads in Melody Maker. It was the most powerful music paper at the time. Loads of bands were formed off the back pages of Melody Maker. I think the odd Rolling Stone or the odd member of Led Zeppelin, possibly the whole band, found work like that. Five years of ads and eventually this crazy guy called Peter Gabriel phoned me up. I figured he was at least as mad as I was, so I thought OK, why not join the band. I didn't have anything better to do at that time." (2)

Instead of inviting Steve to an audition, Peter and Tony went round to his flat.

Hackett: "To be honest, I didn't realise that I was auditioning. I mean I hadn't queued up with 40 other guitarists. Had I known, I think I probably would have been more nervous. Pete and Tony came to the flat that I shared with my brother and family, it was all very low key. They turned up with overcoats, looking like they might have been

Mick Barnard, 1970.

were attracted to. I had a Gibson Melody Maker that I was playing through a little radio. And I probably had a Macari's fuzz-wah pedal, a very small, red pedal but it had both sounds. I'd also used it to record the Quiet World album [THE ROAD released in 1970]." (7)

Steve was invited to hear the band play live at the Lyceum in London on 28 December where they were doing a charity gig. Despite the rather odd time (it was a lunchtime show), there was a good turnout and the audience enjoyed their performance.

Unbeknown to him at the time, Mick Barnard played his last ever concert with Genesis on 5 January 1971, at High Wycombe. Ironically, the support band that evening was his old band, The Farm.

Mick Barnard: "The Farm had a new singer and a new guitarist. We played the gig and it went down quite well. At the end, Peter called me to have a talk in the back of the van. It was just Peter Gabriel and me. I think the rest of them were having a drink. And that's where he explained to me that they'd got another guitarist." (8)

The news didn't come as a complete surprise to Mick who had never really felt he was part of the band.

Barnard: "I pretty much tried and tried to get them to say if I was in or out because I had really dropped my career to be with them. I didn't think I was going to be in the band that long, obviously not knowing what success was to come. I don't feel cheated by anything. It was just not a very nice experience at that time. I do feel that they could have been a little bit more honest with the situation instead of just keep saying "we'll let you

understudies for *Doctor Who*, with long woolly scarves, long coats, borrowed trousers and shoes. That was the look, it was very anti-image in those days, so I sort of fitted in because I was all sort of beard and glasses and dodgy safari jacket. It was hardly glamorous." (2)

Rutherford: "The problem was that I was trying to find Ant II, but there was no such thing. Then I had a terrible sort of ulcer and had to stay in bed for a week, during which time Tony and Pete found Steve. I think my not being around enabled them to find someone. And it worked great. I think the reason we hadn't been able to find anyone was probably my fault. I was the stumbling block trying to replace Ant with a similar sort of person. But you couldn't do that." (2)

Hackett: "I remember that my brother and I played three different kinds of music for them. One was pastoral with the flute, one was atonal and dissonant and aggressive, and the other was blues with harmonica. It was the first one they

*The Knife*, UK single release

know". They were all excellent musicians. They were brilliant, all of them. Peter, I found quite easy to talk to. He was a very straight person. He had quite a stutter but he didn't seem to have that on stage. Phil was much more of the type of person I was – the same upbringing. The others had a very privileged upbringing. Mike Rutherford was very friendly and very good. He would help me out with some guitar parts. We used to go down and play parts together. I wouldn't say I really ever had a fall-out with Tony Banks, but I always got the impression he felt somewhat superior. Maybe that was just his general attitude. I just felt that he kept me at a distance. With the others we had a great time on tours, especially with Peter because he had a brand new Hillman Imp at the time and we used to go off and tour the Lake District, while the roadies took the equipment to Scotland in the van." (8)

Hackett: "Seeing the band live somewhere like the Lyceum, my perception was that they weren't very loud. But in a small rehearsal room, they were deafening! And I thought: "My god, how is it possible to play through thunder?" I used to play in the bedroom with this big amp that I thought was deafening, but when I tried to use it in the rehearsal room it just wasn't loud enough to cut through the drums acoustically, so it got replaced with something louder." (7)

After the last set of gigs as a four-piece, mainly opening for other bands (such as Hawkwind in Slough and Kevin Ayers in Ewell), Steve Hackett made his debut with Genesis on 14 January at University College London. Even though it might not have been one of their finest performances (Phil wasn't at his best having had slightly too much to drink, while Steve was beset with a series of technical problems), it was still plain to see that with the arrival of Hackett, Genesis were finally complete.

Gabriel: "We were all worried because Ant had been a sort of driving force in the band, so we were going to have to find a different sort of energy to feed off. Steve had a more contained, hiding-behind-his-glasses personality, I think, and at that time he was more used to building these worlds of sound that were beautifully crafted but quite internal and it took him a while before he got comfortable. In fact, he only got comfortable being a guitar hero way after I left. But he was a fine player and it was his interest in sound that attracted me particularly to Steve." (2)

Rutherford: "I missed Ant as a person. But Steve had his great sounds, little weird fuzz boxes and these little dark atmospheres he created. It was great." (2)

Banks: "It was fairly easy to select Phil out of the drummers we auditioned because he was definitely the best and he was a very likeable person which was important – someone we thought could fit in. When it came to the guitarist, Mike was doing most of the auditioning and he hadn't found anybody. Steve sounded interesting and we went there and he seemed good; it was just luck we happened to end up with someone who worked. Phil had gone to a stage school and he acted differently to us. Having both Steve and Phil sort of changed the way the band was seen a little bit, although you could never stop the press from calling us 'ex-public schoolboys', they still say it, I think. There are so many of them around now that it doesn't seem to make much sense, but back then we lived a very sheltered life and we were still only 21 or something at this point and quite recently out of school. But that upbringing really marks you for quite a long time." (2)

The positive experience of the concert at Imperial College at the end of November led Tony Stratton-Smith to embark upon an even more ambitious project: the Charisma Package Tour, with bands from his label sharing the stage at events with affordable tickets. This operation, which became known as the 'Six Bob Tour' because tickets cost just six shillings, included performances by Van Der Graaf Generator, Lindisfarne and Genesis. Being the least famous of the three, Genesis were often expected to open but there were times when it was their music that totally enthralled the audience. The tour started on 24 January at the Lyceum in London and went on until 13 February (in Bournemouth), although not all three bands played every single date (for example, Genesis didn't play the Bristol gig on 26 January because on that particular day they were supporting Johnny Winter in Watford).

Banks: "We did this tour with two other Charisma groups, Van Der Graaf Generator and Lindisfarne, called the 'Six Bob Tour' because you could see all three groups for six bob. For the time it was quite cheap and a lot of people came to see it. We went on first, which of course was a gift really because it meant you couldn't really lose. If you didn't go down too well, it was because you were the first on; if you went down great, then it was troublesome for the other two. It was never trouble for Lindisfarne, mind you, because they always went down well, but it was trouble for Van Der Graaf, sometimes it was very difficult for them closing the show. We were getting more together in every sense, we learnt how to construct a set and how to play our instruments a lot better." (2)

On 7 March 1971, Genesis played their first overseas gig in the Woluwe-Saint-Lambert district of Brussels, Belgium. The concert, captured on tape by a member of the audience, was distributed to collectors in 1994, making it the oldest Genesis bootleg in existence. The setlist was: *Happy The Man / Stagnation / The Light / Twilight Alehouse / The Musical Box / The Knife / Going Out To Get You.*

The song which most enthusiasts rave about is *The Light*, no other recording of which exists (some fragments of the song would eventually end up being recycled in *Colony Of Slippermen* and to an even greater extent in *Lilywhite Lilith*, over three years later). But there are other aspects of the bootleg which make it extremely interesting. *Happy The Man* was a brand new acoustic composition played on three 12-string guitars (by Mike, Tony and Steve) and sung by Peter and Phil almost in unison. This song would only be recorded a year later in a distinctly faster version. *The Musical Box* is also quite different to the version which was officially released a few months later, with Steve Hackett's solo still not completely defined and with an extended central section.

Before returning to England, Genesis spent another two days in Brussels to take part in a television show between 8 and 9 March, all trace of which has, alas, been lost.

Banks: "In England we were just one of hundreds of bands going up and down the country playing wherever we could. Trespass seemed to go down quite well in Belgium... We were lucky because there was this guy, quite an influential journalist out there, Piero [Kenroll] who liked us. We received quite a good offer to go there, and it was quite an adventure for us really. We went over on the ferry and we played a couple of shows that weren't that fantastic, but there was this sort of enthusiasm there that was quite fun. It was the first time we felt we were wanted." (5)

Stratton-Smith, meanwhile, was continuing to focus on promoting the top Charisma bands and after the 'Lyceum Easter Festival' on 9 April (with Genesis, Van Der Graaf Generator, Audience and other bands) he came up with the 'Charisma tour' with 8 concerts between 11 and 26 April. With Van Der Graaf Generator firmly billed as headliners, Genesis performed at all the shows while the third group varied between Lindisfarne and Graham Bell & Arc.

After a relatively quiet May, the highlight of which was the session for the famous BBC DJ Bob Harris on the 10th (Genesis played *The Musical Box* and *Stagnation* live), June proved to be quite an important month: the band performed at the London Lyceum again, only this time as headliners (the opening acts were Lancaster and Bell & Arc), while on the 19th they were back at Friars, the Aylesbury venue (which in the meantime had moved to larger premises) that had hosted them so often and with such enthusiasm in the previous months. Here, in a sudden burst of overconfidence, during the encore of *The Knife*, Gabriel took a running jump into the audience which, instead of catching him, moved out of the way leaving the lead singer to crash to the floor and break his ankle.

As a result of the accident, Peter was forced to go on stage in a wheelchair and use crutches in the following shows, including their performance at the prestigious Reading Festival, held over three days from 25 to 27 June. Genesis played on Saturday 26 June, even though their name was one of the smaller ones on the event posters, which included East of Eden, Lindisfarne and Wishbone Ash to name but a few.

Before taking a break to write and record the

songs for their third album, Genesis managed to play the Marquee again in the summer of '71 (9 July) and participate in the 'Rock Against Racism' event on 20 July (Redditch, with support band, Sonny's Disco).

The last show was again in Belgium; this time at the 'Fétes de la Djote', a pop festival held in Jemelle over four days (5–8 August). Genesis played on the Sunday, the last evening, as the event's main attraction, even more important than Dutch band Golden Earring, a small indication as to how the band was becoming more popular abroad than in the UK.

Gabriel: "Two clubs were key to us around then, Friars and The Angel in Godalming and we did well in Newcastle and Glasgow. It was quite strange because we seemed to get through in tougher working-class cities and Southern Europe; it was harder for us in the cliquey cultured world of London and some of the big cities. We wanted to develop our music, we wanted to get more energy into it, more of a darker feel too and to expand, if you like, the horizons of the musical world that we were living in. And things were beginning to work live." (2)

The growth of Genesis from both a technical and theatrical point of view was undeniable.

Gabriel: "My flute playing, which was never great, was something that gave our music a bit of character. I was an aspiring drummer, that's where I started off. I loved grooves, always have done, and, to me, an absolutely critical part of getting any piece of music to work is to make it feel right. In the beginning, with our first drummers, Chris Stewart and John Silver, they were at my level in the rhythm department, but when Phil arrived it was quite clear he was in a superior league. So my kit sort of gradually shrank until I was left hanging on to my bass drum because I hated the idea of being just the singer. As soon as the lyrics (which never even got heard much in those days because of bad PA systems) ended, you were left with nothing to do musically, so you either had to prance around or get off stage or stand still, whereas I wanted to play, I was full of music." (2)

As well as the poor quality of the equipment, the lead singer had to invent something for other reasons.

Gabriel: "I started telling stories based on some of the ideas that were in the songs because back then we had three 12-string guitars on stage and it used to take ages to tune them. We'd build up some energy with the audience from a song and then we'd be tuning for what seemed like a lifetime, and everyone would be looking at me and I'd be thinking "Oh shit, I've gotta do something". The ideas would evolve as the tour went along and then I would try and act out some of what I was improvising about in the stories." (2)

Banks: "It was a difficult period with some great moments and some awful moments. But then, once we started playing on the road, once you started getting this audience response, it all started to make sense. Peter had to develop a way of coping with being on stage. In the early days he wasn't natural on stage at all, so like a lot of people he found a kind of persona to hide behind. It wasn't initially theatrical really, he just started off by telling these stories because we had such long gaps between songs to tune up and everything, and he slowly developed his way of communicating. We weren't a group who came fully formed in any sense, it took us 10 years, I think, to get anywhere near it. You couldn't just go up there and play the songs, that wasn't enough; if you wanted to attract the audience's attention, someone had to actually talk to them and communicate with them. We used to argue a lot because we were passionate about our music. We were young, sexually frustrated... looking back on some of the arguments we had, they were just about pretty trivial things, but that's how it is when you're living on top of each other, little things can trigger an argument. Like in the cottage period when we were all living together and we weren't even taking weekends off or anything." (2)

**NOTES**

(1) Mario Giammetti's telephone interview with Richard Macphail, 12 May 2005, partially published in the article "Il Sesto Genesis" in Dusk, Issue no. 50, August 2005

(2) Mike Kaufman's Genesis interviews, Chicago / London, October 2007, partially used in the bonus disc accompanying the 2008 remasters

(3) Mario Giammetti listening to Trespass with Anthony Phillips, London, 7 May 2011

(4) Mario Giammetti's interview with John Mayhew, London, 28 May 2006, partially published in the article "Working Class Hero" in Dusk, Issue no. 53, July 2006

(5) Mario Giammetti's telephone interview with Tony Banks, 16 February 2012, partially published in the article "Six not simply shrouded pieces" in Dusk, Issue no. 70, April 2012

(6) Mario Giammetti's telephone interview with Ronnie Caryl, 27 February 2002, partially published in the article "Come Talk To Me – Ronnie Caryl" in Dusk, Issue no. 39, June 2002

(7) Mario Giammetti listens to Nursery Cryme with Steve Hackett, Twickenham, 1 December 2011

(8) Mario Giammetti's telephone interview with Mick Barnard, 3 December 2001, partially published in the article "Looking For Someone" in Dusk, Issue no. 38, February 2002

# Trespass Tour

## 1970

### OCTOBER

2 **Chatham** (ENGLAND), Medway Technical College • *First concert with Phil Collins. 4-piece line-up*
3 **Farnborough** (ENGLAND), Technical College
4 **London** (ENGLAND), Marquee Club
6 **Princes Risborough** (ENGLAND), British Legion Hall • *At the last minute Genesis replaced Writing On The Wall, who were supposed to be the main attraction.*
7 **Harlow** (ENGLAND), The Birdcage
9 **Wallasey** (ENGLAND), Tomorrow Club
10 **Colchester** (ENGLAND), Corn Exchange
13 **Wood Green** (ENGLAND), Fishmongers Arms
16 **Cambridge** (ENGLAND), Rex Cinema
23 **Kempston** (ENGLAND), Addison Centre
*Genesis (with Ronnie Caryl on guitar) opened for Medicine Head.*

### NOVEMBER

3 **Barnet** (ENGLAND), Resurrection Club
*First gig with Mick Barnard on guitar*
6 **Salford** (ENGLAND), Main Hall - Salford College of Technology
7 **Uxbridge** (ENGLAND), Student's Hall - Brunel University
8 **Chelmsford** (ENGLAND), Victoria Hall
10 **London** (ENGLAND), Marquee Club
13 **Canterbury** (ENGLAND), Rutherford College - University of Kent • *This concert was originally planned at Brighton's Big Apple Club, where Genesis were engaged as Fleetwood Mac's support act.*
14 **London** (ENGLAND), Shepherd Bush BBC TV Studios • *In the afternoon, the band appeared at the TV programme 'Disco Two'.*
14 **Watford** (ENGLAND), Watford Technical College
*Evening show*
20 **Edinburgh** (SCOTLAND), Heriot-Watt University
21 **Edinburgh** (SCOTLAND), Garry's Club
22 **Dunfermline** (SCOTLAND), Kinema Ballroom
25 **Hitchin** (ENGLAND), Hermitage Ballroom
26 **Blackpool** (ENGLAND), Dead End
27 **Durham** (ENGLAND), Neville's Cross College
28 **London** (ENGLAND), Imperial College
29 **Southall** (ENGLAND), Farx - The Northcote Arms
30 **Letchworth** (ENGLAND), The Leys

### DECEMBER

4 **Worcester** (ENGLAND), College of Education
6 **Birmingham** (ENGLAND), Mother's Club
9 **London** (ENGLAND), Marquee Club
*'Charisma Christmas Party' closed to the public*
11 **London** (ENGLAND), Café Royal
16 **Aylesbury** (ENGLAND), Aylesbury Grammar School
17 **Ipswich** (ENGLAND), Civic College
18 **Hatton** (ENGLAND), The Hatton Centre
19 **Cleethorpes** (ENGLAND), Clee Humberstone School
20 **Godalming** (ENGLAND), Angel Hotel
28 **London** (ENGLAND), Lyceum Theatre
*Free concert*

## 1971

### JANUARY

3 **Manchester** (ENGLAND), Arts Lab
5 **High Wycombe** (ENGLAND), Technical College Hall • *Last gig with Mick Barnard*
7 **London** (ENGLAND), College Hall - City University
*Various artists concert. The headliner was the Henry Lowther Band.*
8 **Slough** (ENGLAND), Slough College
9 **Ewell** (ENGLAND), Technical College
10 **Southall** (ENGLAND), Farx - The Northcote Arms
14 **London** (ENGLAND), University College
*First concert with Steve Hackett*
15 **High Wycombe** (ENGLAND), Technical College
17 **Blackpool** (ENGLAND), Tower Ballroom
18 **Bangor** (WALES), Student Union Hall - University of Wales
22 **London** (ENGLAND), College Hall - City University
24 **London** (ENGLAND), Lyceum Theatre
*First date of the 'Charisma Show - Six Shilling tour'. Genesis supported Lindisfarne and Van Der Graaf Generator.*
25 **Birmingham** (ENGLAND), Town Hall
26 **Watford** (ENGLAND), Town Hall • *Originally, on this day, Genesis were supposed to perform at the 'Charisma Show' at Bristol's Colston Hall.*
27 **Sheffield** (ENGLAND), Oval Hall - Sheffield City Hall

28 **Bradford** (ENGLAND), St. George's Hall
29 **Hatton** (ENGLAND), Civic Centre
30 **Manchester** (ENGLAND), Free Trade Hall
31 **Newcastle** (ENGLAND), City Hall

## FEBRUARY

5 **Leeds** (ENGLAND), Polytechnic
6 **Leicester** (ENGLAND), Student Union Hall
11 **Brighton** (ENGLAND), The Dome
13 **Bournemouth** (ENGLAND), Winter Gardens
14 **Peterborough** (ENGLAND), Cloud Nine
19 **Hull** (ENGLAND), Hull City Hall
20 **Southampton** (ENGLAND), University Of Southampton – Students' Union
22 **Bristol** (ENGLAND), The Granary
23 **London** (ENGLAND), Blaise's
25 **Liverpool** (ENGLAND), Mountford Hall - University of Liverpool
26 **Haverford West** (ENGLAND), Technical College
28 **Stowe** (ENGLAND), Roxburgh Hall - Stowe School

## MARCH

4 **Blackpool** (ENGLAND), Tower Ballroom
5 **York** (ENGLAND), Great Hall - York University
6 **Birmingham** (ENGLAND), Lyceum Theatre
7 **Brussels - Woluwe St. Lambert** (BELGIUM), Ferme V • *First concert abroad ever*
8 **Brussels - Cité Reyers** (BELGIUM), RTB TV Studios • *Uncertain session*
9 **Brussels - Cité Reyers** (BELGIUM), RTB TV Studios • *Recordings for the TV show 'Pop Shop', never broadcast*
10 **Leicester** (ENGLAND), De Montfort Hall
13 **Colchester** (ENGLAND), Great Hall - University of Essex
21 **Cardiff** (WALES), Sophia Gardens
24 **Greenford** (ENGLAND), Big Brother Club

## APRIL

2 **Hemel Hempstead** (ENGLAND), Dacorum College
3 **Farnborough** (ENGLAND), Technical College Hall
5 **Godalming** (ENGLAND), Angel Hotel
9 **London** (ENGLAND), Lyceum Theatre *'Lyceum Easter Festival'*
11 **Croydon** (ENGLAND), Fairfield Hall *First show of the second 'Charisma Tour', with Van Der Graaf Generator and Lindisfarne, the latter sometimes replaced by Graham Bell & Arc.*
13 **Portsmouth** (ENGLAND), The Guildhall
15 **Guildford** (ENGLAND), Civic Hall
17 **Durham** (ENGLAND), Dunelm House - Durham Technical College
22 **Southport** (ENGLAND), Floral Hall
23 **Glasgow** (SCOTLAND), Green's Playhouse
24 **Dundee** (SCOTLAND), Caird Hall
25 **Edinburgh** (SCOTLAND), The Caley Picture House
26 **Manchester** (ENGLAND), Free Trade Hall
30 **Kingston-upon-Thames** (ENGLAND), Arts College

## MAY

1 **Hitchin** (ENGLAND), Hermitage Ballroom
4 **Portsmouth** (ENGLAND), The Guildhall
6 **London** (ENGLAND), Marquee Club
7 **Norwich** (ENGLAND), Assembly Hall - University of East Anglia
8 **Halifax** (ENGLAND), Clarence's
10 **London** (ENGLAND), BBC T1 Studios *'Sounds of the 70's' radio broadcast*
14 **Whitley Bay** (ENGLAND), Rex Hotel
21 **Bletchley** (ENGLAND), Bletchey Youth Centre
22 **Watford** (ENGLAND), Kingham Hall

## JUNE

6 **London** (ENGLAND), Lyceum Theatre
12 **Edinburgh** (SCOTLAND), Queen Margaret College
18 **Cheltenham** (ENGLAND), Cheltenham Town Hall
19 **Aylesbury** (ENGLAND), Borough Assembly Hall *During the performance of The Knife, Peter Gabriel broke an ankle jumping from the stage.*
26 **Reading** (ENGLAND), Thames-side Arena *'Reading Festival'*
28 **Southall** (ENGLAND), Farx - The Northcote Arms

## JULY

2 **Kempston** (ENGLAND), Addison Centre
3 **Potters Bar** (ENGLAND), Farx - Elm Court Youth Centre
9 **London** (ENGLAND), Marquee Club
18 **Wolverhampton** (ENGLAND), Civic Hall
20 **Redditch** (ENGLAND), Windsor Club *'Rock Against Racism'*
22 **Scarborough** (ENGLAND), Penthouse Club

## AUGUST

8 **Jemelle** (BELGIUM), 'Fètes de la Djote'

# Nursery Cryme

(Charisma 1971)

***The Musical Box / For Absent Friends / The Return Of The Giant Hogweed /// Seven Stones / Harold The Barrel / Harlequin / The Fountain Of Salmacis***

- **Release date: 12 November 1971**
- **Recorded at Trident Studios, London, August 1971**
  **Engineer: David Hentschel**
- **Producer: John Anthony**
- **Artwork: Paul Whitehead - inspired by *The Musical Box***

- **Tony Banks: organ, Mellotron, piano, electric piano, 12-string guitar, voices**
- **Michael Rutherford: bass, bass pedals, 12-string guitar, voices**
- **Peter Gabriel: lead voice, flute, bass drum, tambourine**
- **Steve Hackett: electric guitar, 12-string guitar**
- **Phil Collins: drums, voices, percussion (lead vocals on *For Absent Friends*)**

## THE MAKING OF

After Trespass, chaos reigned for Genesis. Getting over the departure of Anthony Phillips would prove to be the most arduous test in the history of the band which, as already mentioned, had also decided to change its drummer. In order to focus on fresh material and tackle the new challenges posed by live performances, as soon as Philip David Charles Collins (born in Chiswick, 30 January 1951) had been welcomed into the fold, Genesis threw themselves into a long period of rehearsals, working as a four-piece at The Maltings, Farnham.

Collins: "We were like two worlds colliding. It's extraordinary that we got on so great because at the beginning we were from totally different backgrounds. I was a grammar school boy, actually I had just finished two or three years in drama school where anything went. I went out with all the girls, whereas they'd come from public school where there were no girls. I was very light-hearted and jokey and fully comfortable on stage, even though I was behind the drums, whereas they all seemed quite uptight. Part of that was because Anthony had just left and they didn't really know what was going to happen; he was a quarter of their songwriting team. Sometimes we'd be playing and suddenly something would happen and there'd only be three of us left because either Mike or Tony had stormed off. Something had been said by somebody and I hadn't even noticed. A couple of hours later they'd come back... There was a lot of tension. It took a long time to get used to and a long time for it to disappear slightly." (1)

During this time, songs like *Wooden Mask* and *Moss* were written, while other material dating back to when Phillips was still in the band was perfected (*The Musical Box, Harlequin* and part of *The*

*Fountain Of Salmacis*). Rehearsals at The Maltings went on for three weeks in September 1970. Then, after a handful of shows, the band were back in the rehearsal rooms in mid-October, this time with new guitarist, Mick Barnard (born in Aylesbury, 5 March 1948) who, despite writing most of the guitar solo for the *The Musical Box*, never really managed to get into the spirit of Genesis.

Banks: "We found the drummer quite quickly and quite easily, I mean Phil was a fantastic find. But the guitarist was more of a problem; in fact, we went out as a 4-piece for about 2 or 3 months. This taught me a lot because I ended up playing all Ant's guitar parts on the piano through a fuzz box, all the ones I could anyhow, while at the same time playing the organ part. So suddenly I was doing this two-handed stuff which I'd never really done before. We started writing this piece which became *The Musical Box* as a 4-piece. We had a guitarist very briefly, for a month or two, called Mick Barnard. He was actually good, he probably just wasn't assertive enough." (1)

They finally found the man who would become the band's full-time guitarist towards the end of the year. A member of Quiet World and with an album already under his belt (The Road), Stephen Richard Hackett (born in London, 12 February 1950) joined Genesis (after Barnard was fired on 5 January 1971) and made his first stage appearance with the band on the 14th of that month.

Banks: "Mike was always looking for someone to replace Ant, which he was never going to be able to do because he was a good friend and everything. So Peter and I went and auditioned Steve and we were really impressed with him. We really liked the way he approached things. His brother [John] was on flute and he was playing these things on guitar which were slightly more

classical than we were used to but we thought he had a lot of imaginative ideas. He didn't want to be a mad guitarist: most guitarists either wanted to be on lead guitar playing solos or else they were just purely acoustic guitarists and we wanted someone who could cover both roles, so Steve was a very important addition." (1)

Hackett: "Phil had been to stage school and I'd been a grammar school boy. There was a mixture from my background, some people were posh, some people weren't. I think my school was maybe more of a level playing field." (1)

The new arrivals without a doubt took the already high technical standard of the band up a notch. Collins was already a superb drummer and probably the most instinctive musician of the five. As well as being gifted with a great voice, Collins also turned out to be a talented arranger as well as the band member with the most outgoing character, in sharp contrast to the rather more reserved nature of the ex-Charterhouse boys. Hackett, on the other hand, despite being less able than Phillips on the 12-string, possessed superior technical skills on electric guitar and as a soloist. Furthermore, he also had a predisposition towards experimentation, something which would improve the overall quality of Genesis' music.

Rutherford: "Whereas it took Steve a little while to become what he is, on drums Phil was immediately a huge lift. We had never had that kind of energy from the engine room before; it was just a whole different level." (1)

Gabriel: "Phil can get on with anyone, although on occasions I think it was an alien world to him, whereas Steve is more of a loner, I think, in terms of personality. I think I get on with most people fairly easily but Tony doesn't. Nowadays he's a whole lot different, much more mellow and open, but it took him a long time to open up to Steve. The same goes for Mike, to some extent, but less so because Mike had moved into guitar territory and so they were two guitarists working together. The Lamb Lies Down On Broadway period was a more difficult and darker time; the arguments were more about life issues whereas on Nursery Cryme we only had musical differences." (1)

Hackett: "It was a little bit hard to understand them when I first joined. They'd been at school together for all those years, all talking the same sort of language. It was almost as if the band had their own way of communicating, the equivalent of cockney rhyming slang. They used expressions I'd never heard before and there were some fairly deep-seated issues that went back to their schooldays, which obviously Phil and I weren't privy to. I think it was tougher for them because there was a lot of affection for the guys who'd been through the ranks previously, people like Anthony Phillips, whom I got to meet subsequently. I realise that had we all been in the band together at the same time, we probably would've enjoyed working

Peter Gabriel and his wife Jill in Genoa on 22 August 1972.

together." [1]

Collins: "We rehearsed at The Maltings in Farnham, where Mike and his parents lived. And I stayed with them while we wrote what would become NURSERY CRYME. We wrote *The Musical Box* there. When they wanted The Maltings back, we moved to Tony Stratton-Smith's country residence (Luxford House) in Crowborough in Sussex. That was fantastic, it was lovely and we rehearsed in the garage or the barn. We wrote *The Return Of The Giant Hogweed* there and me and Steve wrote *For Absent Friends*." [1]

Luxford House is a somewhat eerie looking 16th-century Tudor house. It was here that Genesis were aiming to give their new album a more definite form, something which turned out to be easier said than done.

Hackett: "We wrote it over the course of one summer in 1971. I think it took about three months but it was recorded rather more quickly, in about a month. We stopped doing gigs because the new band, that is with Phil and myself, did try and write on the road, but I think everyone was just too stressed travelling around everywhere that we couldn't really write as a team. We needed time off to really get to know each other, work together and relax." [2]

Rutherford: "I remember the sessions being quite hard. Steve and Phil had just joined the band so we had these two new members on board. I mean it had all changed, sonically, and as players we were improving a lot, but writing some of the songs wasn't easy, although some of them are really strong." [1]

Hackett: "I was the only person in the band who didn't have a girlfriend. They probably thought I was gay, but the truth is I had given up on romance to really concentrate on music and all my time was spent on that. So it was quite an emotional time for me as I couldn't really put my arms around anyone at the end of the day. It was hard but it was wonderful as well. We stayed in this place which was called a cottage but was, in fact, a large house; for me, it was like a manor house compared to anything I had known. I had my own room and the English summer and all that beautiful music. We used to sit out on the grass, because it was such a glorious summer, playing 12-strings together, writing and performing. I remember sitting out there playing *For Absent Friends* and *Harlequin* for John Anthony. We were like country boys. This was all new to me because I was from the city, I was from Pimlico, near Battersea power station, the one on the Pink Floyd album cover [ANIMALS]. It was the fulfilment of a dream working with a Mellotron and a band that was capable of sounding like an orchestra, a choir, a rock band and a pantomime troupe because of the humour. It was many things and it filled a very big void in my life at the time." [2]

Collins: "I have very fond memories of the period. We were a real great five-piece working unit. I mean, we all got together for the meetings about the cover and we were all pretty much involved in the writing, apart from the lyrics which were written in pairs." [1]

Of course, there were still some heated arguments between the three founding members of the band.

Hackett: "We just let them get on with it, knowing that soon all would be forgiven. I think we were just dead serious about getting things right.

*Zig Zag* n. 29, March 1973.

It was extraordinary how it could go from a blazing row one minute to someone sitting down playing the most exquisite, gentle music the next. I think they wanted people who were ambitious about their music rather than, you know, the idea of having hit singles. In those days, the band really didn't get any radio support; there was only the BBC and we weren't really a singles band, we were firmly set on albums. And that was great for me because I liked the idea of long songs that developed." (1)

The album was mainly recorded in August at Trident Studios in London. Although they hadn't done much in terms of writing, Steve and Phil's presence in the band proved decisive in other ways.

Banks: "Phil and Steve's contribution, particularly at this stage, was to bring a bit of musicianship into the group. As musicians, Mike and I were still learning. Phil came and he was a really high-quality drummer right from the word go, with a great sense of rhythm, and Steve was obviously technically a better player than we were at that time. That gave us the ability to have a bit of technique in there as well as everything else, which gave us a better chance to do things. The contribution from Phil on drums is what transformed it really. The rhythm section was a bit stiff on Trespass, whereas those complicated songs like *The Return Of The Giant Hogweed* have a much better flow about them. And Phil's other contribution, which we were aware of right from the start, was the fact that he could sing. The rest of us sort of made vague attempts at doing backing harmonies which were OK, but, with Phil, we actually had someone who had a really strong voice. He and Pete used to do a lot of singing in unison and Phil was also very good at just picking out little harmonies, a bit like Crosby Stills & Nash." (1)

Hackett: "If I were to talk about the differences between myself and Phil, I'd say his was more of a jazz lover's approach, whereas I love classical music and blues. There was a kind of natural fusion of lots of elements that the band had. Tony liked classical music too, he liked hymns and I liked those chord shapes, those harmonic inversions. Then Phil had me listening to Buddy Rich and Mel Tormé, which sounded strange to me at first, but I realised that that was where he got the basis for all those accents he was putting in. We sort of learnt off each other and then during the course of Nursery Cryme, I'd come up with this idea of a guitar technique called tapping which meant you could play the fretboard like a keyboard and then Tony and I would do harmony duets." (1)

Gabriel: "Each person in the band had his own little corner of songwriting that they'd sometimes do on their own and there'd be this bigger area which was the band and because we were the old timers, Tony, Mike and I, we got more air time in those days. In the band there was this sort of dark, contained personality that was struggling to get out and I think that's partly why we connected with people; there was this compressed energy that needed to explode. We didn't always manage to get it out but people could feel and touch the vibrations humming beneath the surface. Steve definitely had a good dollop of unfulfilled frustrations that gave the band a good personality." (1)

The production was once again in the hands of John Anthony and his young assistant engineer, Dave Hentschel.

Genesis • Eagles • Everly Bros • Captain Beefheart
Byrds • Johnny Speight • grist'n'goodies galore
zigzag 29
15 pence
Vol 111: Nº 5

Hackett: "I liked John very much, but it was Dave Hentschel who was the engineer. We tried to do the songs all in one go, and the same with the mixing. No-one was editing, no-one was experienced enough to do that. Sometimes we worked very late at night and people would get very tired. If there was a mistake you had to go right back to the beginning. Editing was a razor blade slicing the tape, so it was laboriously slow to mix. Had we been more experienced who knows how it would have sounded. But there was a lot of passion and instinct going on, intelligence would only be employed later."[2]

Collins: "I found I couldn't really listen to the old albums. I just didn't like the sound; it didn't sound as good as it had in the rehearsal room. I used to put everything on a cassette (later on DAT) and I'd play them in the car on the way home wondering what happened, why things hadn't come out as good on the record. But, of course, it's just that bit of roughness. The compression of the cassette player and nerves in the studio. Without a doubt we were working against the clock and, of course, we weren't the ones putting the fingers on the buttons, that was John Anthony and the sound engineer. My real frustration was that we all used to go into the studio and play the song that we had rehearsed or taken out on the road. The drummer's first takes are usually the best, first, second, third possibly, after that he's playing safe because he doesn't want to fuck it up. I think we once got to take 31 or something and I said "enough". And then we had this wonderful moment when Tony said "Right, well I'll go and replace my keyboards" and Mike said he wanted to replace his guitar and a bass as well. I was the only one that was stuck with my part which probably was actually better three hours before. There was a lot of that in those early albums. Nowadays, of course, it's all different. On the last album we did together [We Can't Dance, 1991], we just put a skeleton track down and then went in to replace everything. But back in the old days we tried to play it as a band."[1]

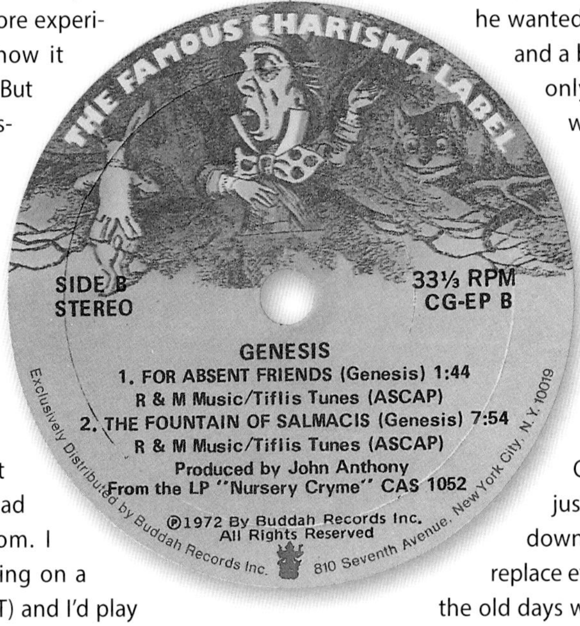

Hackett: "I was very intense about the band. I probably didn't have much of a sense of humour at the time. I just kept asking the sound engineer, Dave Hentschel, or John Anthony how we could make it better all the time. We worked long hours but it was probably recorded in about a month at Trident Studios in Soho. I was thrilled with it, you know. I refused to hear the rough edges at the

Promotional Extended Play of Nursery Cryme, American press.

time, I just wanted to bask in the glory of the fact that I'd done an album with what was destined to become a great band. Occasionally the sound was wonderful and that was great for me. I think the new mixes have improved things sonically also because everyone's had decades to reflect on how things could be improved. They could have gone further with the new mixes, of course, in terms of the timing and tuning, as it is, it's still preserved pretty much as it was; it's almost as if it's just had a bit of a dusting rather than a total facelift." [1]

## THE ALBUM

Nursery Cryme was perhaps the most difficult album for the band to write. Having started out with the intention of becoming a team of writers, Genesis suddenly found themselves without Anthony Phillips, the leading light of the songwriting process. Despite the obvious progress over the pop songs put together for From Genesis To Revelation, on Trespass the Banks-Gabriel writing input was clearly weaker than that of Phillips. Moreover, Rutherford had not yet shown any great talent as a songwriter, acting mainly in a supporting role to Phillips.

Consequently, carrying on without Phillips must have seemed an impossible task. However, Nursery Cryme was the result of numerous songwriting sessions and still included some of Phillips' compositional work. *The Musical Box* and *Harlequin* were written mainly by Mike and Ant and were then developed and elaborated on by the whole band, transforming the first into an extraordinary track. Tony and Peter, on the other hand, were the main authors of *Seven Stones*, *Harold The Barrel* and *The Fountain Of Salmacis* (the intro to which, however, dates back to a year earlier, when Ant was still a part of Genesis), while the very first versions of *The Return Of The Giant Hogweed* came about while the band were working as a four-piece. Finally, the two newcomers, Phil and Steve, wrote *For Absent Friends* together. Allowing this song to be included in the tracklist may, at first glance, seem like an act of generosity granted by the three 'old boys', but the fact of the matter is that during this period of confusion, Genesis were in need of new talent also on the writing front.

With knowledge of the different writing sessions, one could consider Nursery Cryme a transitional album but, if truth be told, it was more a case of Genesis triumphing, not for the last time, in the face of adversity. The apparent fragmentation and undeniable personality clashes between the three founding members of the group would always fall into second place when it came to working hard, revealing an unexpected level of cohesion within the group which would transform songs that had previously only been rough outlines into masterpieces (*The Musical Box*). Collins on drums lifts the entire rhythm section, together with Rutherford, who had evolved further still following the already remarkable improvements witnessed on Trespass. Despite still maintaining a strongly acoustic sound (without doubt inherited from Anthony Phillips), the new Genesis appeared more interested in the rhythmic aspects, and whilst on Trespass this manifested itself gradually (for example on *Stagnation*), it was not a primary focus until the album's closing song, *The Knife*. On Nursery Cryme, however, the contrast between acoustic and electric instrumentation is marked, strident even. The two songs which are without a doubt the mainstays of the album (*The Musical Box* and *The Fountain Of Salmacis*) live and breathe their own rhythm changes, alternating between calmer, more romantic moments and crazy, electrifying excursions. Hackett and Banks both play decisive roles in achieving this. The new guitarist certainly displays greater fluidity as a soloist over Phillips. In fact, his solos, despite not being outstanding from a technical point of view, are formidable in terms of experimental inventiveness (we should perhaps once again mention his first, pioneering attempts at tapping, a revolutionary technique which years later would be perfected and made famous by Eddie Van Halen) and their highly original sound. Banks, on the other hand, after being forced to play a solo on *Stagnation* and having practised during their time as a four-piece, had acquired a new level of confidence and was about to become the leading soloist in the entire history of Genesis, supported by a rich assortment of keyboards (by now the band had its very own Mellotron). The result is the transformation of a primarily acoustic and pastoral band into an ensemble with increasingly broad horizons, a real rock band when it wanted to be, as in on *The Return Of The Giant Hogweed*, while continuing to prioritise their attention towards acoustic music, which still dominates in *Harlequin* and *For Absent Friends*.

Throughout all of these changes, Peter Gabriel's personality was continuing to grow. His voice manages to be unusually aggressive (in the final section of *The Musical Box* and on *The Return Of The Giant Hogweed*), mellow and expressive (*Seven Stones, The Fountain Of Salmacis*) and even similar to pantomime in *Harold The Barrel*, this also thanks to the second voice provided by Phil, who was also given the honour of singing a song on his own (*For Absent Friends*). While Tony's and Mike's voices continue to be used here and there (especially on *Harlequin*), it is evident that with Phil Collins now in the band, Genesis had acquired a second top-class vocalist. In this regard, Gabriel proved he was prepared to share some of the limelight with the drummer, thus allowing the band to evolve in another direction.

Peter was also continuing to perfect his ability to write beautiful lyrics, where poetry blends with cultural references. The words to *The Musical Box* are a miracle of lyricism and literature, somewhere between Oscar Wilde and childhood memories, while in *The Return Of The Giant Hogweed* the young songwriter imagined a gigantic toxic plant rebelling against the human race. Standing as a case apart we have *Harold The Barrel*, a grotesque yet thrilling story with a slightly Dickensian feel.

Gabriel wrote around half of the lyrics on the album, with the other band members writing the rest. These other lyrics, although less sophisticated, are still of a very high level: Tony once more takes his inspiration from mythology for *The Fountain Of Salmacis* (in collaboration with Peter) and *Seven Stones*, putting pastel-coloured poetic phrases together for *Harlequin*, while Steve (with a little help from his friend Phil) paints a beautiful and typically English image in the track *For Absent Friends*.

NURSERY CRYME, therefore, presents itself as a totally unique album in the abundantly fertile music scene of the early '70s. After TRESPASS went on sale, the end of 1970 saw the release of THE MAN WHO SOLD THE WORLD by David Bowie, ALL THINGS

Must Pass by George Harrison, Layla And Other Assorted Love Songs by Eric Clapton's Derek & The Dominos and the first self-titled album by Gentle Giant. In addition, although still very much part of a niche market, we should mention the seminal recordings released by those two melancholy songwriters: Nick Drake (Bryter Layter) and Tim Buckley (Starsailor).

The first months of 1971 saw the release in America of the groundbreaking albums (If I Could Only Remember My Name by David Crosby, Tapestry by Carole King and What's Going On by Marvin Gaye), all of which had very little impact on the young Genesis. On the other side of the Atlantic, alongside the evergreen Rolling Stones with Sticky Fingers, the world was witnessing the growth of other names linked to the new genre of progressive rock: Steve Howe joined Yes who then released The Yes Album and Jethro Tull, Emerson, Lake & Palmer and Caravan released their own respective masterpieces (Aqualung, Tarkus and In The Land Of Grey And Pink) with Gentle Giant releasing the magnificent Acquiring The Taste. However, the idea of trying to pigeonhole Genesis into some kind of movement or musical category remains a purely academic exercise. The acoustic sections alternating with explosive rock and the refined and yet humorous lyrics are unique in style at this point in rock history and the technical level shown by the new members (with Hackett more ideologically inclined to follow the experimentations of Robert Fripp rather than the virtuosity of the classic guitar hero icon) further lifts the group which was already promising to achieve some of the best progressive rock ever.

## THE SONGS

### THE MUSICAL BOX

Collins: "Because we were starting from scratch, obviously some of the good bits that hadn't been used before were bought back into the fold, as is normally the case. They had this bit called *F Sharp* left over from when Ant was still in the band" [1]

Banks: "It developed when we were playing as a 4-piece, but it originally went back to the early days with Ant and Mike playing on 12-string guitars. I played guitar on it as well in the beginning part." [1]

A good two thirds of this track was written in September 1969 by Rutherford and Phillips and the original title of the song was due to the unusual way the 12-string guitars were tuned.

Rutherford: "I had this Rickenbacker guitar and I started doing weird tunings. The tuning in this song is very bizarre with all the top three [pairs of] strings tuned to F sharp, which is just mad. But it made that jangly sound and it meant that the big chord which comes after had this lovely open stringed feeling." [1]

Mike's Rickenbacker 12-string originally belonged to Charterhouse school friend John Alexander (the same friend who had given the demo tape to Jonathan King back in 1967). Alexander: "Whilst still at school my 12-string Rickenbacker went to Mike and it indeed became a Genesis icon over the years. I believe it was one of the originals as owned by the Beach Boys, Townshend and Harrison, but unfortunately it was stolen many years later at Madison Square Garden; so when I got its replacement back probably 30 years later, it was a later version." [3]

Hackett: "Mike used to use an electric 12-string with the top 6 strings tuned to F sharp, because that was a keyboard player's key, and I played an electric 6-string. Mike and I played electric guitar and Tony played an acoustic 12-string which he used to put through a Leslie cabinet. We had two of them for the organ and he sometimes used one for his guitar." (2) The original demo of *F Sharp* (recorded by Mike and Ant) was eventually released in 1998 on Anthony Phillip's album The Archive Collection Volume One.

The song starts with a solitary guitar phrase played by Rutherford. Hackett: "Mike's guitar was recorded at half speed so when its played back it sounds higher than it did originally. It was a technique Genesis sometimes used called Varispeed, The Beatles used it a lot." (2)

Hackett's contribution is only very minor as the song was all but complete when he joined. Hackett: "The structure of the song was done, but I joined the band on the basis that, if I added anything to the details of the song, then I would be considered one of the writers. So I tried to create a musical moment that sounded like a musical box [1'14"]. When I listen to this now, however, there are so many things I would do differently to the mix. For example, why did we have the hi-hat at the beginning, it doesn't really need to be there." (2)

At 3'39" a heavy riff from Mike kicks off the first instrumental bridge.

The Genesis 1971/1975 formation.
From the left Tony Banks, Phil Collins, Steve Hackett, Peter Gabriel and Mike Rutherford.

Gabriel: "Mike and I were big fans of The Who and I really wanted to try and persuade Mike to play something like Pete Townshend, you know, an arm waving, ballsy attacking section. We were in the rehearsal rooms in West Hampstead, on the 28 bus route, and it was exciting when it first came to gel as a piece." (1)

Hackett: "It's just Mike first of all, then I join him and then the organ answers. Tony put his Hohner Pianet through a fuzzbox because he was trying to sound like a guitarist and in the last phrase (4'20") you can hear me using the tapping technique. It's the earliest recorded example of that technique because I was trying to sound like a keyboard player. So Genesis had a keyboard player trying to sound like a guitarist and vice-versa. I had tried it [tapping] at home for this song and I tried it out live and it worked OK. I just used a fuzz box, probably a Marshall Supa Fuzz." (2)

As the first guitar solo takes off, the drums explode onto the scene.

Collins: "There was a song by Family called *The Weaver's Answer*, with a kind of rolling rhythm. I had a pretty good foot and they liked that. So I put that with their rhythm and suddenly we were off." (1)

Rutherford: "We'd had endless drummers up until then, but none of them were the same calibre as Phil; he brought a real lift in energy to the band. For example, if you take the second half of *The Musical Box*, we couldn't have done that with the other drummers ". (1)

The metamorphosis in the sound is stunning and *The Musical Box*, from an acoustic and bucolic opening section, transforms into something rhythmically overwhelming.

Rutherford: "This is my favourite track on Nursery Cryme, it's a prime example of how we were going more electric. It starts soft and then it builds and builds and by the end everything's going. And I think this must be the first time with the bass pedals, which we didn't need on Trespass, when there were five of us. It's funny how things happen; you get stretched and you're forced into doing something. I'm sure, if we hadn't been a 4 piece, I'd never have bothered to pick up the bloody bass pedals." (1)

Once the first electric phase ends, the song curls in on itself with a 12-string guitar arpeggio played by Mike and later joined by the organ [8'34"].

Collins: "Tony had this wonderful chord sequence at the end of the song. I don't think he had envisaged vocals on it and Peter came in with "You stand there with your fixed expression", sort of trampling all over this nice chord sequence. But, of course, it worked fantastically well." (1)

Banks: "I think the real strength of the song comes towards the end, when the organ comes in playing this little sort of fugue-type thing, which I originally saw as an instrumental part. And then suddenly Pete started singing over it. I must admit, initially I wasn't too sure about it, and, in fact, when we did the mix of the album, we mixed the voice too low. But when we started playing this on stage, I realised just how strong it was; the vocal just gave it a real capping quality and it was a real stand-up moment on stage. The version on the album is OK (it sounds a lot better now it's been remixed), but it probably developed even more live. It was a very good track that created a sort of fantasy with the lyrics relating to this old Victorian quality and the album cover which related to it as well. It was a very atmospheric piece and it was musically interesting as it went through all these changes: it was a sort of precursor of what was to come later, with a lack of repetition, starting off with a really strong section, the opening part, that never comes back again. We used to quite like the idea of having a very quiet bit going into a very loud bit and then a sort of serene bit. It's a song about a lot of contrasts, which for some people is very appealing, while other people just find it irritating, because it never settles into a groove but keeps changing time and chords. So it's a very typical Genesis song, a follow-on from *Stagnation*, I suppose, but perhaps a little bit more dramatic." (1)

The grand finale of this mini rock opera reaches an exceptional and emphatic climax.

Hackett: "When we did it live all the audiences liked it very much. I think they liked the wide dynamics of one moment quiet, the next minute very loud. So in a way it's typical of the band at that time. Right at the end of the song I track my guitars in a three-part harmony, but for some reason you can only hear two. Brian May said to me that this track was an influence on him and listening to the way it sounds at the end you can see why that might have been the case." (2)

So, even if Hackett's songwriting role was purely marginal, it can be said that his stylistic influence was felt from the word go.

Hackett: "In terms of playing, yes. There were some things that became influential for other people, and you have to remember that this album was not a huge success in its time; it found its audience over a long period of time." (2)

This extraordinarily evocative music is accompanied by some equally amazing lyrics. Peter took his inspiration from his grandfather's house located in Coxhill, with its garden, croquet lawn, conservatory, vines and fig trees. The friendship between two children becomes a morbid allegory steeped in sexuality.

Gabriel: "I think my head at the time was in this Victoriana world which I pictured around the house my Dad had grown up in, this sort of controlled English mental landscape under which festered violence and sex. This was the sort of flavour I was trying to bring into the lyrics and vocals. This was one of the regular battlegrounds with Tony; blissfully unaware of the audience, he would want to stretch things out for 10 or 20 minutes for a big keyboard and instrumental part, whereas I was trying to tell a story too. There were a lot of arguments about those types of issues, probably more so in the latter days, like over *Apocalypse In 9/8* in *Supper's Ready* and some of THE LAMB, because I just felt some of the keyboard solos were too long and we risked losing people. And it was important, because you didn't want all the up moments to be instrumental only and all the down moments to be the vocal bits. I certainly didn't!" (1)

## FOR ABSENT FRIENDS

Oddly enough, Tony, Mike and Pete gave newcomers, Steve and Phil, their own spotlight on the new album.

Collins: "Steve and I wrote the song because we were the two new boys and we wanted to see what we could do. The fact that it was on the album, I guess is because it was very different from anything else, and I think we were quite

FRIARS
HOME COUNTIES
**GENESIS FREAKS**
UNITE
YOUR TIME HAS COME TO SHINE
WEDNESDAY, JUNE 28th
**WATFORD TOWN HALL**
Visions of Angels all around dance in the sky. Leaving me here forever. Goodbye.

happy to have that variety of tastes and musical output. Some people see this as very positive, while others see it as a lack of direction because there wasn't any one in particular." (1)

The song is based mainly on a simple chord sequence led by Mike and Steve on 12-string guitars.

Hackett: "Mike and I played 12-string on it and Tony played a little bit of Hohner Pianet. And that was the whole orchestration of the track. The tuning on this one is regular but the guitar is being used almost like a harpsichord. The thing about Genesis is this combination of 12-string guitars; when they all work together the distinction between guitars and keyboards is no longer there. Whenever a song was guitar-based it usually meant 12-string and using chords that might not necessarily be obvious, but you can tell the classical and folk roots were there." (2)

This song was shaped in the rehearsal room. Hackett: "I think most of it was written during the sessions at Tony Stratton-Smith's country house. Phil and I would go off into a corner in the garden." (2)

One of the most surprising aspects is that the lead vocals were given to Collins. Hackett: "It was the first thing I ever wrote for Genesis in my own right, and I was too shy to present it to the lead singer because Pete was very much the star. The thing is, a lot of people didn't realise it was Phil singing. I remember seeing them live, before I joined the band, and I thought there was some sort of automatic double tracking effect going on with Pete's voice, and then I looked a little closer and I could see that Pete and Phil were in perfect sync with similar vocal tones. This made it much easier later on when Pete left." (1)

The fact that Phil sang lead vocals on the track wasn't a problem for the band.

Rutherford: "I think Pete enjoyed having Phil sing it. As a band, if anyone could do something and bring something new to the table, we would always encourage it." (1)

Hackett: "The band's reaction to it was very good and Pete was fine with it as well; I don't think anyone perceived it as a threat. Phil was probably thinking "I'll sing it and if Pete likes it he'll sing it". They also used to sing things together; they had similar voices so sometimes it would sound like one singer. It was very fortunate for Genesis to have two singers with such strong voices." (2)

Banks: "It's not my favourite moment on the album but Phil's voice sounds very nice, very pure; it had a sort of James Taylor quality about it, before he got the rasp that was to come later. It showed that he had a nice voice, so we thought it would be great to feature it as a solo thing and Pete was quite happy with that." (1)

The lyrics, so beautifully English, are set in a churchyard and feature a pair of widows.

Hackett: "The song is mine musically; lyrically it's

50/50. I think it was one of the first things Phil wrote as well. I was never sure that people would be able to understand the story just by listening to the lyrics because it's not obvious... the references on this album are quite wide. The first track, *The Musical Box*, is best described as Victoriana, the world of mechanicals and musical boxes, and I think it explodes into life very well, it is a clever song, but this one is a lot simpler. It's a simple, direct little Cinderella song; it's very shy but it has charm, like a miniature in a gallery of portraits. I was trying to think of something that wasn't a love song. I was thinking of two old women at the end of their lives, and I was trying to describe a typically English scene. I think the love of places, trying to describe them in a song and your relationship to the place is just as important as describing the individuals you might be with. Sometimes those landscapes are a little bit like paintings; I think I confuse writing songs with doing paintings or writing books." (2)

## THE RETURN OF THE GIANT HOGWEED

It would appear that the seeds for this song were sown when the band was working as a four-piece, just after Collins had joined.

Hackett: "At the time, whenever we played live, we used to play *The Knife* as the last number of the set, and we wanted to have something to replace that, so we could have a big finish. So this was really designed with that in mind." (2)

*The Return Of The Giant Hogweed* is a gutsy song with a strong rock impact and features phenomenal drumming from Collins.

Hackett: "It was written as a kind of joke, a long elaborate joke, but the rhythm is interesting, Tony always used to call it 5 against 2, like a shuffle ['5 against 2' is a polyrhythm, i.e. the simultaneous use of two or more conflicting rhythms, that are not readily perceived as deriving from one another.]." (2)

In fact, the song took on its definitive form when Steve arrived and played the introduction using his tapping technique in sync with Tony on the electric piano.

Praise from Keith Emerson in a Charisma advert published in Melody Maker.

Hackett: "I was tapping on the guitar, on the bass string, while Tony was playing his Pianet in harmony to it. The introduction is my major contribution to the song." (2)

At 4'15" a truly original instrumental section takes off with electric guitar and flute playing together.

Hackett: "It's not really a classic guitar solo, it's more of an arranged thing with my melody on the top doubled with the flute. And the piano arpeggio later [4'53"] is not really a rock keyboard thing, is it?" (2)

At 5'21" another, very subtle guitar solo melody comes in. Hackett: "I was trying to sound like a synth here, pizzicato. I was still using a plectrum at that time, but the tapping was with the nails rather than the pads of the fingers. At 6'31" you hear the Mellotron brass come in (it's mixed brass because you had different types). He [Banks] sometimes used to put the Mellotron through the Leslie cabinet, so ironically it came out sounding more like an organ at times, but we tried to do sounds that were very complementary to each other." (2)

In the lyrics, Gabriel tells the story of the plant world turning against humanity in the form of the Giant Hogweed (*Heracleum mantegazzianum*).

Hackett: "Again, the meaning of the lyrics has a Victorian feel, Kew Gardens comes into it." (2)

## SEVEN STONES

The opening is a magnificent chord sequence played on the organ using a little trickery. Hackett: "This song uses organ and English accordion but quite distorted on the Mellotron." (2)

After two verses, at 1'17", the singing by Gabriel and Collins almost acts as a lament.

Hackett: "This bit was mine. These days I would probably make that into a whole chorus. You can hear the distortion on the tapes of the Mellotron, [the crescendo at 1'34"] I think it's Mike's Vox bass pedals. The effect is quite hymn-like, almost similar to what Procol Harum were doing, the stuff they did with Matthew Fisher with an admiration of and respect for church music. I think Tony's classical influence is Shostakovich, whereas in my case it was Bach and Vaughan Williams." (2)

After repeating the entire structure reached to this point and a short and emotional distorted guitar phase from Steve, we get to the magnificent orchestral section.

Hackett: "At the end you get Mellotron strings [3'56"] trying to play very high, like a harp, while the guitar sounds like brass... In spirit, it's quite close to Sibelius and at the end [from 4'36" to the last notes on the Mellotron] it gets quite strange." (2)

A song written mainly by Tony (Hackett: "going off the chord changes, I'd say so" (2)), who was also the author of the lyrics in which an old man tells his tales. Even though, according to Hackett, "Pete was interested in the ideas he had read in the *I Ching*, so the lyrics were influenced by *The Book of Changes*". (2)

## HAROLD THE BARREL

This is followed by a sort of progressive mini-operetta. In fact, the next track presents itself in a very different way, with a thumping piano and excited feel.

Hackett: "I always felt that there was something

Mike Rutherford and Steve Hackett during performance of *The Musical Box* in Viareggio on August 20th, 1972.

of *Summer In The City* [by Lovin' Spoonful] about the chord sequence. It's a clever idea, but, if I'm honest, I think it's a bit of a filler on the album. It's like one of those deadpan English humour jokes put to music, perhaps it could've been funnier; some of the subsequent things we did became very funny." (1)

Collins: "It was a good-fun song which showed the kind of humour that there has always been in Genesis; people might take us very seriously but we don't." (1)

Gabriel: "It was part of a little subsection of Genesis, these odd quite English bits of songwriting which continued with *Willow Farm* and I can see the connection in *Father, Son* [from Ovo, 2000] and in what I've been doing in recent years. You could call it 'English Gabriel writing'." (1)

Thanks to the switches between the different characters in the song (man in the street, man on the council, British public, Mrs. Barrel…), this song steeped in British humour has, in the words of Hackett, "an aspect of Gilbert and Sullivan about it" (2), and almost all of it is sung with two voices, those of Peter and Phil.

Banks: "They sing it together; in fact, they're actually mixed together on the tape so you can't separate them, which maybe wasn't a great idea, because sometimes it sounds a little Phil biased. But it's a clever song that works really well." (1)

Gabriel: "My voice has got quite a lot of bass content whereas Phil's has a much higher element, so he's sort of the centre of gravity, harmonically speaking. So if you put the two at exactly the same level, you'll hear more of his voice than mine. Even though *Harold The Barrel* was all my song, you hear just as much of Phil, if not more, in some places. When I left and that voice continued as lead singer, it was easier for people to get used to. Phil is a very natural singer so I think it should have occurred to the others to try Phil earlier than they did." (1)

Collins: "On this song, vocally speaking, me and Peter bonded quite well. Neither Mike nor Tony, nor Steve for that matter, were singers. So, if there was any other singing to be done, it was always going to be me. They did have a couple of little bits of harmonies, but they always asked me to do it because they said I was quicker and better at it than they were. So I remember sitting around a piano with Peter while he came up with *Harold The Barrel* and we both wrote the lyrics for it." (1)

At one point there is a repeated line ("We can help you. We can help you" at 1'36" and 2'26") where the timbres of the two vocalists are unrecognisable. Hackett: "The idea was to do a parody of a British policeman. It was Phil or Pete: even then Pete didn't like anyone to be around when he was doing his vocals. I quite understand it, you don't want to be performing to the gallery when you are trying new things. At the end of the track there was a voice loop that kept going, although it seems to have faded out here, so perhaps it's not the same as the original. It might have been slowed down." (2)

## HARLEQUIN

Rutherford: "*Harlequin* was an acoustic song that I think I did. I'm not convinced it's much good, but at the time it was an area I worked quite well in. We were playing more and more gigs and starting to drop some of the softer side

because half an hour of acoustic stuff on stage, well it didn't work that great; people were at the bar and not listening. So we found a compromise between where we'd come from and where we were going." (1)

Written by Mike with the help of Anthony Phillips, this piece has a relatively simple acoustic structure. Hackett: "This is mainly two 12-strings with a little bit of Mellotron, a little bit of organ and just a tiny bit of electric guitar playing one phrase, while at 0'34" you have Mellotron vibraphone which sounds nothing like a vibraphone. But then the Mellotron flutes on *Strawberry Fields Forever* [The Beatles] sounded nothing like flutes." (2)

Banks: "Starting from Nursery Cryme we had 16 tracks, so particularly with this album and Foxtrot we were just suddenly able to find space that wasn't there before. I was there all the time, with every track on this album, helping or hindering (as the case may be) Nick Davis while he was doing the 5.1 mixes, trying to give the group's point of view, because sometimes some songs end up further away than they should and others end up sounding great straight away. So revisiting these songs was great for me because I hadn't heard a lot of them for a long time and I had pre-conceived ideas about them. For example, I used to think *Harlequin* was a very weak song, but on hearing it again I realise it was pretty good. It was a strange process though, spending two years being able to reassess what you feel, exploring and reliving the past." (1)

Hackett: "Right at the end I play a thing called a sleigh tambourine very high. I was trying to make it sound very sweet, so it sounds quite Christmassy in a way. Sometimes, when I was playing 12-string with Genesis, I would play it almost outside the range of the guitar to make it sound very sweet. So in a way, I thought it was a very feminine, chocolate box type of a song." (2)

The vocals are the main feature of the track.

Hackett: "I think the vocals could have been recorded more strongly, because when we rehearsed it everyone sounded much fuller, it sounded a lot more like Crosby, Stills & Nash." (2)

Tony and Mike also sang on the track alongside Peter and Phil. Hackett: "I was too shy to sing in those days, I thought I would sing out of tune. I became a singer much later on." (2)

Banks: "We all sang it, there was a castrati chorus. We did it as a vocal harmony which was something we used to do in the garden at Tony Stratton-Smith's country house when we were writing Nursery Cryme. It was beautiful weather so we used to just go outside with our guitars and just strum along. We were trying to have our Crosby, Stills & Nash moment, and it almost worked. We all had reasonable voices. Mike and I aren't character voices, but we can sing in tune and up to that

Mike, John Alexander and Richard Macphail at Peter Gabriel's wedding. The foot being pushed in from the right is John Anthony's

point we always used to do it, starting with From Genesis To Revelation and Trespass, but once Phil came into the band, his voice was so much better. It was much better for him and Pete to double track if more than two harmonies were needed."[4]

## THE FOUNTAIN OF SALMACIS

Banks: "When we got together at Tony Stratton-Smith's house and started putting all these ideas together, the writing was easier than it was on Trespass, but it still wasn't that easy, I suppose we drew from a few old songs that we had around. I had this piece that I'd written when I was at university. It was just a simple organ part really which I then started developing once we decided to buy a Mellotron. We bought it because we loved the sound, we had used it a little bit on Trespass. We loved the first King Crimson album, where obviously it was used more extensively. So we went and bought one, off King Crimson actually. We tried this little riff I'd started on the Mellotron and with the organ it really developed these great big swells and it sounded fantastic, and that's how the opening part of *The Fountain Of Salmacis* came about."[1]

In fact, the intro of the song makes an appearance, with few variations, in *Provocation*, one of the tracks commissioned by the BBC for the planned 1970 documentary on the painter Michael Jackson.

Hackett: "One day I heard Tony playing this introduction by himself, mixing organ and Mellotron, and I told him it sounded really good. He said it was part of another song called *Ketch*, that had never been recorded. I suggested we use it, encouraging him and trying to bring out what was natural to Tony."[2]

At a stage when his songwriting input was still rather limited, the guitarist proved useful in other ways. Hackett: "I felt that my role was complementary and often it was quite difficult to work out what a lead guitarist was going to do, because they were already fairly self-sufficient even as a 3-piece, as they later became. So I would be forced to think a little bit like an orchestral arranger as opposed to someone required to do heroic guitar solos. That's why we were all credited with writing all the songs, because we considered the arrangements to be as important as writing the actual material. All of the detail was equally important but I think most bands don't function like that. Genesis may be a one-off in that department."[1]

*The Fountain Of Salmacis* is an intricate song which alternates calm sections with more uptempo passages, where Rutherford demonstrates significant progress as a bass player.

Hackett: "Mike played bass and I played both electric and 12-string guitar on this and occasionally electric guitars in harmony, right at the end, and 12-string in the chorus. Well, what we would call a chorus isn't, in fact, a chorus. Our songs are distinct from most other people's in that they don't have choruses. In those days we didn't know how to write choruses, I didn't really understand what a chorus was, and the band often disagreed about what was a verse and what was a chorus. I think the nearest thing to a chorus is the bit at 3'06". But it has no repeated phrase, there is always a vocal variation and then it goes into a shuffle. At 3'25" there is a keyboard and guitar duet, an aspect reminiscent of Sibelius, along with other things peculiar to Tony."[2]

While the opening section was composed solely by Banks, the keyboard player remembers that "we all developed the rest with a lot of jamming which produced a strongly romantic track".[1]

It is extraordinary to hear the complexity of the songs played by these five young lads who were only in their early twenties.

Hackett: "At the time it was my favourite song on the album because it had got as close to fully symphonic as we could manage. I believe its true home is on the stage where you can be enveloped by those crescendos. It deserves to be played live again and I know that some tribute bands do it. There is something unique about it, like the change at 6'27", and the bass pedal under the Mellotron gives it is a very beautiful melody. In the rehearsal room I remember there was a lot of reverb on Peter's voice which gave it a more operatic feel. It's got an Italian spirit and it's probably closer to opera than it is to rock. I love the end part [7'31"]: I wanted more reverb on the guitar but I couldn't voice that at the time. We had something in the rehearsal room that was special, but we weren't skilled enough producers to realise that we could have changed the perspectives. I agonise about all of that now and I think it's such a shame that people didn't get to hear what it sounded like when it was originally written. I wish it could have sounded as good as it did in the rehearsal room. I remember when we worked on what became the end of the track, we'd all had dinner one night, but we went back in to the rehearsal area, which we'd named Toad Hall from the story *The Wind In The Willows* [by Kenneth Grahame], for reasons best known to ourselves, and we were all very relaxed. I played a guitar solo over the top of it and we had a few coloured lights around and it felt absolutely magical, it was a new kind of music... No-one was using the term symphonic rock back then, but I think that's probably what that was; you had the strings, you had the choir, the guitar solo... For me, it was a very big emotional moment. I was really moved by it: I had refined the guitar part, I'd written it, rather than just improvising, so you had this crying guitar over a beautiful sea of sound. As a piece of music it was very crescendo-based, like classical music."[2]

In terms of the lyrics, according to Hackett, "Tony and Peter wrote the words based on Greek mythology".[2]

Banks: "The lyrics are based on the myth of Salmacis and Hermaphroditus, something very different from anything on the previous album. It took us in another direction; it's an area that some people really like about us while others really don't. It's a defining kind of song: overblown and quite romantic and goes through lots of musical changes. It was an exciting moment I think."[1]

## THE ALBUM ARTWORK

Gabriel: "Paul Whitehead captured a mood, although in an external scene because of the croquet game; a sort of suppressed violence which I think was accurate for the vibe we were trying to portray at the time."[1]

Rutherford: "The image of the little girl, the croquet lawn and the heads helped to create a slightly quirky atmosphere about the band, together with the songs and Pete's performance. I felt we were starting to become something a little unique in the music business in England and I think that was a good thing. The picture represents images from *The Musical Box* and other parts of the album. It's an area where Paul Whitehead worked very well. I think later on we kind of lost the plot a bit there but initially it was good."(1)

Collins: "Paul Whitehead came up with the idea for the album cover having discussed a couple of ideas over the phone with Pete. It was in the days before e-mail, so if you wanted to see something you actually had to all get together in a room and look at it. The croquet with heads idea was all very off-the-wall. Fortunately, it wasn't as romantic and wistful as the Trespass cover (even though there was a knife on it). Which was good because it showed that there was a little bit of an unusual side to the band."(1)

Banks: "We got on well with Paul and so we stuck with him for the first three albums. I've always felt that the album covers got slightly less good as they went along: the first was a great idea and well executed, the second worked quite well for the album, the third one I think was less good. After that, we parted company. If you're in a group you can't really change the members (even though it happens) but you can change other things like producers or engineers or covers just to give a different feel to the different albums. Whom you have as a cover artist is an arbitrary choice and there was no reason to stick with the same one forever. In a funny way, I almost prefer this cover now than I did at the time, it's so much part of my past and youth. I signed so many copies of it that it's rather difficult to have an objective viewpoint, but I think it's a strong image and it fits well with the idea of the title of the album and the association with *The Musical Box*."(1)

## EPILOGUE

Nursery Cryme was released in November 1971. Despite public praise from Keith Emerson in Melody Maker, on the whole the press didn't warm to the album, and it sold fewer copies than Trespass in the UK. However, following their success in Belgium, Italy too began to show significant interest in the band.

Rutherford: "I think it's a good example of how we were moving on. Some of it's good and some of it is just OK."(1)

Hackett: "We were doing loads of gigs at the time, and we'd spend the odd day in a windy church hall trying to write songs together, but it wasn't working. So we pulled out of gigs for the entire summer of 1971. We'd just bought a new Mellotron and I had a new Les Paul and amplifier. I still get people writing to me asking what fuzz box I was using back then! I think people like the fact that it was very mechanical, that things were held together by sticky tape and chewing gum. It made it all a lot more individual. Happy accidents abound all over it, none of it was that focused. I remember this crazy thing about mixing *The Musical Box*, we kept working all night long because everyone refused to do edits, one mistake and you went back to the beginning of the song. It beggars belief now but that's how we worked back then."(1)

Banks: "For me there was definitely an improvement in the writing compared to Trespass, so we

genesis

Promotion by Charisma Records, 1972.

were certainly pleased with the artistic progress. But even though we were making progress in the live sense, commercially we weren't going anywhere. NURSERY CRYME did no better than TRESPASS. So it was slightly disappointing for us because we thought that songs like *The Musical Box*, *The Fountain Of Salmacis* and *The Return Of The Giant Hogweed*, in particular, were really strong pieces and on stage were going down really well. But, for some reason, we only sold about five or six thousand copies." (1)

Hackett: "It was a very creative period and I was very happy to be working on the first really professional record with a dedicated team. It seemed to be a great opportunity for all of us. I think my perception of it may have been slightly different to that of the other guys who were more experienced. For me, it was divine, heavenly to be in that position of making a real record and I wanted to make it very strong. I didn't always know how to fulfil those ambitions, because I was quite inexperienced. I felt I wasn't an experienced songwriter but I could recognise good things in others and could try to bring that out. I wanted to encourage other people to be at their best." (2)

Collins: "Generally speaking it was a very strong album, I think. At the time I was much more of a player, I wasn't really writing apart from the few lines in *Harold The Barrel* with Pete and *For Absent Friends*. We were jamming a lot together to write songs but I wasn't actually a bona fide writer. The two voices style happened like this: I did the harmonies so when we were writing something I would always sing. Rather than singing the melody I'd sort of sing something else which then became part of the song." (1)

Hackett: " When I listen to it now I am more critical than I was then, and I think you'll find all the band members are probably like that. If I were doing it now, I'd make sure it was all in time and in tune with all the right compressors and with all the technology of now, but we didn't have any of that. But we had such a huge well of talent all working towards the same goal. I also think Richard Macphail was very important to the band at the time. He was part roadie, part manager, part enthusiast, coach, critic, overseer, friend... I loved his input; he had a very quiet way about him, but at live gigs he was a roadie and mixing sound and he knew how to get a job done. He could be quite tough despite his public school background. He was quite fierce and loyal. If I said, "I don't know if I'm good enough for this", he would say, "Of course you are and you must continue in the same way". When, years later, Chester Thompson joined for live work, I tried to do the same thing with him as the first concert did not go well. I said, "Don't worry you'll be great, it will be fine, it's just one gig". Let's just say that to hold things together is very important. Of course, you have to be critical because music can't afford to be sacred until it's finally on record. So I could sometimes be critical, but also I like to think I could be very liberal with praise; it was a bit like trying to be the glue, I wanted this band to work. The album has a lot of good things on it, and I think the people who like it hear it with the same ears as when they were teenagers, so they forgive it lots of things, just like me when I listen to the early Beatles and early Stones." (2)

# THE CONCERTS

Hackett: "It was strange working with Genesis, it was different. We ended up playing gigs at places like Stowe and Eton and these all-male audiences were tremendously enthusiastic." [1]

After just a month's break from touring, used to record NURSERY CRYME, Genesis were back on the road with a handful of live shows in September, before undertaking a more packed schedule in October which included a dozen or so dates in the UK. The one at The Lyceum on 14 October with Van Der Graaf Generator marked the start of a joint tour known as the 'One Price' Concerts. During this period of their history, Genesis often shared the stage (usually as openers) with other Charisma bands (particularly Van Der Graaf Generator, but later also with Audience and Lindisfarne).

The tour continued through to November; in the meantime, the first record with the new line-up had finally hit the high streets and on more than one occasion Genesis turned out to be the headliner (for example on 20th in Letchworth, Circe opened for them).

For the month of December, the Gibus Club in Paris had organised a series of concerts featuring some foreign bands such as Amon Düül II from Germany and Mungo Jerry from England. Genesis were also contacted and their name was added to the billboard for Friday 17 December. However, the idea of a sortie to continental Europe in the middle of a series of UK dates proved to be unworkable and so the band's debut performance in France had to be postponed.

1972 immediately promised to be an important year. Following a couple of days rehearsing in West Hampstead, and after a gig at The Friars in Aylesbury scheduled for 8 January was cancelled, on the 9th Genesis had a session in the BBC's Studio T1 in Shepherd's Bush (which would later be aired as part of the well-known radio programme 'Sounds Of The Seventies' with John Peel). This was the second time the band had entered the famous London studios with its new line-up, only this time the programme envisaged a longer performance with the band playing four songs from NURSERY CRYME: *Harold The Barrel / Harlequin / The Fountain Of Salmacis / The Return Of The Giant Hogweed.*

Between 22 and 24 January, Genesis returned to Belgium where they also took part in a festival in Charleroi (with Supersister and Wil and Paolo supporting). A bootleg recording of this show (probably only partial) survives to this day revealing the following setlist: *Happy The Man / Stagnation / The Fountain Of Salmacis / Twilight Alehouse / The Musical Box / The Return Of The Giant Hogweed.*

After a pretty hectic February, during which the band continued to play up and down the UK, including venues such as the Queen Elizabeth Hall, London (on the 4th) and the Oval Hall at Sheffield City Hall (on the 17th), Genesis received their third invitation to the BBC for 2 March, this time in the Paris Studios. Here they played *The Fountain Of Salmacis, The Musical Box* and *The Return Of The Giant Hogweed* (this performance was aired in its entirety as part of the 'In Concert' programme).

Two days later, in Watford, the setlist included *Harlequin / Stagnation / The Fountain Of Salmacis / Twilight Alehouse / The Musical Box / The Return Of The Giant Hogweed / The Knife.* By this time the band's live shows were pretty much defined, with the tried and tested formula of a soft acoustic start with three 12-string acoustic guitars, including Tony Banks, starting with *Happy The Man* or *Harle-*

genesis
CHARISMA

**SONO IN ARRIVO**

**GENESIS**

| | | | | |
|---|---|---|---|---|
| 14 8 | RIMINI | LA LOCANDA DEL LUPO | ore | 17-22 |
| 16 8 | FANO (Pesaro) | CORTE MALATESTIANA | » | 21,30 |
| 18 8 | MONSELICE | Dancing LAGO DELLE ROSE | » | 21,30 |
| 19 8 | RAVENNA | JOLLY CLUB | » | 17-22 |
| 20 8 | VIAREGGIO | PIPER 2000 | » | 18-22 |
| 21 8 | ALBENGA | PALASPORT | » | 21,30 |
| 22 8 | GENOVA | TEATRO ALCYONE | » | 21,30 |

*quin*, both sung by Peter and Phil with the drummer, in the latter case, standing alongside the lead singer in the centre of the stage while also playing maracas. The first part of the concert was rather sedate from a visual point of view, with all the band seated except for Peter. It wasn't until about halfway through *Stagnation* that Tony put down his guitar and began playing the organ, while all the other electrical instruments only made their appearance during the third song: Hackett on his Gibson and Rutherford on bass and later on his electric 12-string Rickenbacker while at the same time using bass pedals.

Collins: "I think people tend to like things when it's all the same. I mean, if you go and see a Metallica concert, you know what you're going to get and you don't really want to see three acoustic guitars halfway through. Variety was something we played on back then, which is why the band used to open shows with acoustic guitars, like *Happy The Man*. But it didn't go down very well. Then gradually, throughout the first two, three or four songs, we got more electric and then, of course, we ended up with *The Knife*, which was the other end of the scale. That appealed to us, you know, and it appealed to a lot of our fans; I mean, there weren't many of them but those that did follow us around were very supportive." [1]

With Hackett and Collins in the band, the electric percentage shot up. *Stagnation*, despite incorporating some uptempo sections, still preserves a mainly acoustic matrix, *The Fountain Of Salmacis* is a symphonic piece, beautifully constructed by Tony Banks' keyboards, whereas an atypical but fundamental song in this phase is *Twilight Alehouse*, with its unusual structure, its psychedelic sounds and its blues and jazz overtones. Surprisingly for Genesis, the only real solo in the song is by Peter on flute, while Hackett tirelessly embellishes the rhythm of Rutherford's 12-string.

The final triptych, starting from the second half of *The Musical Box* when Mike remains on his own with his arpeggio, is absolutely magnificent. Hackett: "When we played this live, Tony would put the guitar down and get ready to play the keyboards for the big organ moment." [2]

Another core song was *The Return Of The Giant Hogweed*. Hackett: "It's very symphonic and live it was deafeningly loud. In the rehearsal room I used to put my foot full down on the pedal; you didn't want to be standing in the way of the amp. In those days I was either inaudible, in other words too quiet, or I was far too loud, there was nothing in between. Pete sometimes used to run around on stage and crash into my amplifier and send it flying. I remember it happening during this song in Hemel Hempstead. He crashed into my amp and suddenly – no sound." [2]

With *The Knife* the transformation can be considered complete, throwing one mighty punch at the enthralled audience by the sheer, almost violent, transformation of what initially started out as a group of sweet and sensitive musicians, yet also characterised by a touch of typical English eccentricity, enlarged by the surreal stage presence of Gabriel: a profoundly timid person in real life, the singer was unwillingly forced to come up with something to keep the audience entertained during the all too frequent technical problems and pauses needed to retune the guitars.

Hackett: "I was less keen to use different tunings because I knew what a nightmare it would be

The second Italian tour announced on *Ciao 2001*.

using all these different 12-strings with different tunings live. It could take two hours before the gig to tune them up and sometimes we would have to start all over again. Sometimes Mike would say, after we had been tuning for what seemed like hours, "I'm going to change the strings"! We didn't have anyone to tune them up for us and we didn't have tuners, we had a note from the organ and had to hope that the organ stayed and that the 12-strings stayed and sometimes they didn't. The Mellotron was a joy as well; when we did *The Fountain Of Salmacis* we were lucky if it ended up in the same key as the rest of the band. We needed a voltage stabiliser (which we got eventually), but we didn't know that at the time. A promise of greatness that brought great frustration when it sounded all off-key. It was a cross between the fulfilment of a great dream and a nightmare." [2]

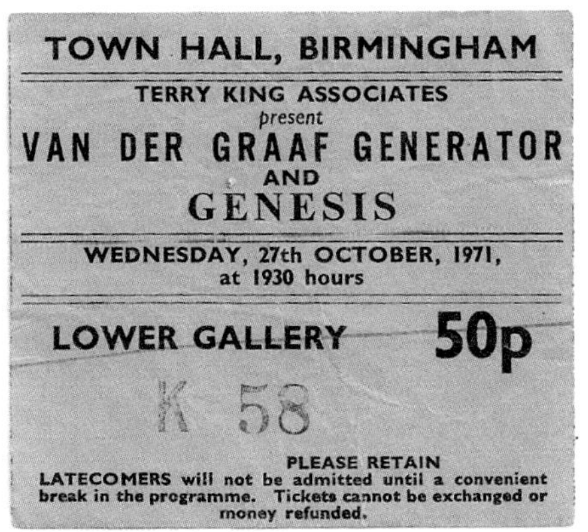


March, despite the odd concert here and there (including one on the 11th at Friars), was dedicated mainly to intensifying rehearsals: 7–9 in West Hampstead, 13–15 at Woolwich and 29–31 in Blackheath.

Mid-month the band was included in the line-up for the Fête Saint Gratien in France, a two-day festival (18th and 19th) hosting an array of bands (Van Der Graaf Generator, Wishbone Ash, Ten Years After, Nico and Gong). In order to play their slot on Saturday 18th, Genesis were forced to cancel their gig at the Boat Club in Nottingham.

Immediately afterwards the band were invited to a Belgian TV studio to record four songs live (*The Fountain Of Salmacis, Twilight Alehouse, The Musical Box, The Return Of The Giant Hogweed*) which were aired on 22 April as part of the programme Pop-Shop '72 (also broadcast in some locations as Rock of the 70's). It is an eye-opening clip with the musicians lined-up in the studio, concentrating on their instruments. From the left: Mike Rutherford, with 12-string guitars (acoustic and electric), bass and bass pedals; Steve Hackett, seated with his black Gibson Les Paul on his lap; Phil Collins on drums; Tony Banks on keyboards and 12-string. At the front is Peter Gabriel, thin with long straight hair, dressed in black with a heavy gold-coloured pendant round his neck. The vocalist is still in his pre-make-up days but nevertheless captures the spectator's attention with his charisma, even though he sometimes appears to be sheltering behind his bass drum, tambourine and flute.

At this point, Genesis were ready for a new challenge: an Italian tour with half a dozen dates running from 6 to 19 April. The man behind the tour was Maurizio Salvadori, a young Milanese promoter who was learning the ropes with Franco Mamone. Maurizio deserves all our praise for going beyond the call of duty, also with the press, to make sure Genesis and Van Der Graaf Generator

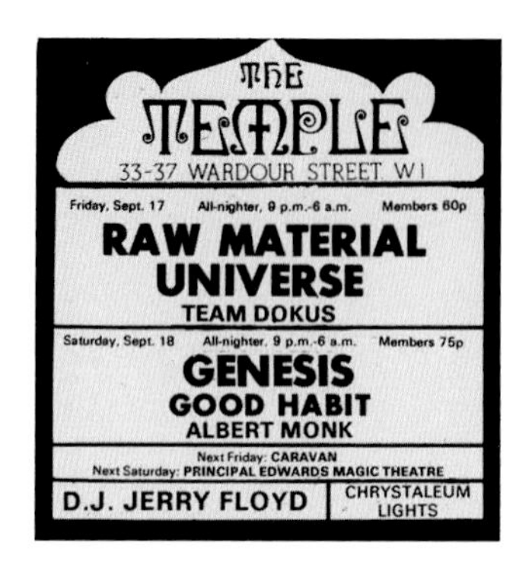


found an Italian distributor and managed to play live in Italy.

Alas, his commendable enthusiasm was not matched by impeccable organisational skills. The first concert, on 6 April, should have been in Belluno, but for reasons unknown ended up being rescheduled at the last minute and moved to Adria, about 100 miles away. After a concert in Godega di Sant'Urbano (Province of Treviso), serious issues arose with the third date, scheduled for Trieste on 8 April: while the band were driving the 87 miles between one gig and the next, the police closed the venue where they were supposed to be playing, Dancing Paradiso, for security reasons. This episode would be mentioned the following day, Saturday 9th, by Gabriel during their performance in San Martino Buon Albergo, near Verona, a partial recording of which exists featuring *Happy The Man / The Fountain Of Salmacis / Drum Solo / Twilight Alehouse / Rock Me Baby / The Musical Box*. The drum solo, which Gabriel emphatically presents as being performed with only one hand, is obviously a way of covering up the usual technical issues. *Rock Me Baby*, on the other hand, was the title given on this occasion to an as-yet-unreleased track which made its live debut on Italian soil: a primitive version of what would later become known as *Can-Utility And The Coastliners*.

Hackett: "It was a difficult song to get across and some of the parts weren't that refined at the time we were doing them. We found that it didn't really work live. Perhaps, if we'd persisted with it, it would have worked out, but if an audience won't be quiet it's impossible to get across a song that's based on acoustic guitar. Something like that would never have worked in the USA, Americans just want to boogie, they want to rock and Genesis did anything but." [2]

The band played two concerts in Verona: one in the afternoon and one in the evening, a pleasant occurrence which was due to the high demand for tickets and something which would be repeated in other locations across the country.

Banks: "There was a very variable response from audiences. Sometimes we didn't get that many people, but there were some shows where you seemed to get a lot of people who were quite enthusiastic. The point was you were trying to put together a tour so you had filler shows between one major concert and the next." [5]

Two palasport shows followed: one in Pesaro (with none other than Italian progressive rock band Premiata Forneria Marconi opening) and one in Reggio Emilia. During soundchecks, Tony used to play a chord sequence to check out the sound of the Mellotron (the instrument which was giving the band the most hassle due to its poor tuning stability). The power and impact these chords had in the Italian palasports (indoor sports arenas) led to the band developing them further, which is how they became the intro to a new song.

Unfortunately, the concert on 13 April in a dance hall in Cuorgnè (Province of Turin) was adversely affected by Tony Banks falling ill. Banks, who spent much of the next 24 hours getting closely acquainted with some of the primitive Italian toilets of the time, says: "We'd gone to see this place where they made drums and on the way there I'd had some Parma ham or something. Anyhow, I got there and I just felt like death really, I mean I had the whole thing of squatting over holes in the ground, all that. They took me to a hospital where

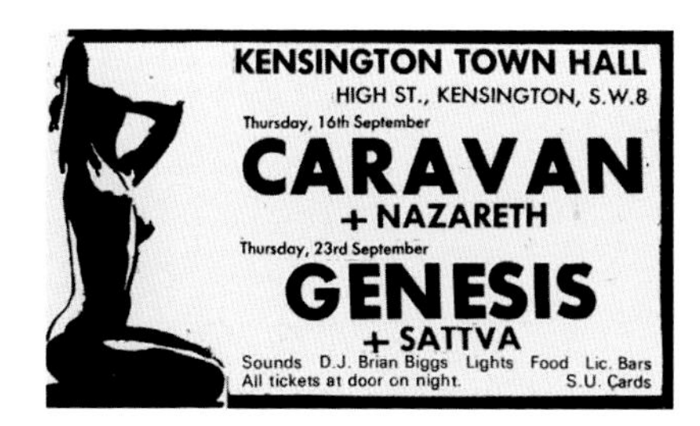

they gave me what I assume was an anti-nausea injection and it made me feel like my hands were on fire! It was awful. I went on stage anyway but I couldn't really do anything at all. The other guys decided to try and do the songs which didn't feature too much keyboard and *The Knife*, which was about all I could do. We did what we could, but rather than doing an hour and a half we ended up only doing about 40 minutes. And then the promoter wouldn't pay us because we hadn't done the full show, even though there weren't too many people in the audience, so I don't think they cared that much. It was a bad experience. It really took me about two or three weeks to get over it. It wasn't until we ended up in Marseilles where this doctor gave me lots of injections and things, that I managed to get better. I found it very depressing because every time we went out for a meal in Italy, I'd go there with great intent but as soon as I looked at food I felt sick again." [5]

Beppe Crovella, who would later become the keyboard player in the jazz-rock band from Turin, Arti e Mestieri, has recently restored the priceless tape which he himself recorded of the concert giving us a precise setlist of this one-off and rather brief show: *Happy The Man, Stagnation, The Musical Box* and *Twilight Alehouse*, with the first and last songs played by only four members of the band, without Banks, and only the two central songs being played by the whole band.

On the 14th, at Palazzo delle Esposizioni in Pavia, Genesis performed two concerts, one of which was recorded and included *Happy The Man / The Fountain Of Salmacis / Twilight Alehouse / Bye-Bye Johnny* (the new title given by Gabriel to the provisional version of *Can-Utility And The Coastliners*) / *The Musical Box / The Return Of The Giant Hogweed / The Knife*. The Pavia date is remembered most of all for the stone throwing incident which involved the audience complaining about the price of the ticket (1,500 Lire) and resulted in a police officer receiving a head injury.

Banks: "In Pavia, they sort of broke the glass doors down and stuff. When we planned to go back to do another tour they said we couldn't because it was too dangerous. It always seemed to me that people wanted to come on stage, you'd get the odd person leaping up and grabbing the microphone and you got people making political speeches and they'd always be either to the far left or the far right. They seemed to me very polarised, but I think the Italians are more excitable people than the English so you kind of accepted that. And there was this thing about free music, which is the other thing everyone wanted." [5]

On 5 April, Genesis arrived in Lugo in the Emilia-Romagna region where they played in a club called Hit Parade. Thanks to a recording made at this event, a rare version of *Going Out To Get You* can be listened to. A staple of their shows back to when Anthony Phillips (the song's author) was still in the band, *Going Out To Get You* was a cornerstone of the set when Genesis were playing live as a four-piece (before the arrival of Steve Hackett). The band would continue to play it occasionally as a four-piece, with Banks dominating the performance with a clearly '60s-inspired organ part, reminiscent of Keith Emerson, and Rutherford's distorted bass following Phil's surging drums. It was a song which usually got brought out for particularly enthusiastic audiences as a second encore after *The Knife* to which

Viareggio, 21 August 1972.
Beside, Peter Gabriel with his wife Jill;
on the next page, Gabriel and Jill
with Tony Banks and his wife Margaret.

it is similar in some ways; in fact, it came close to taking its place on TRESPASS when the time came to record the album.

Banks: "I had forgotten we played that on the Italian tour as well. It had some good bits, if I remember rightly." (5)

After a concert in a club in Travagliato, near Brescia, Genesis played the Palasport in Siena. Banks: "In England we played wherever we could and we got a variable reaction, sometimes good, sometimes bad. NURSERY CRYME aroused a bit of interest in Italy, so we had a bit more of an audience when we toured over there. We seemed to be able to play reasonably sized places in a way we couldn't begin to do in England. So it was quite exciting for us. The tours are all very muddled up in my mind, but I remember doing the show in Siena which was in a very bizarre palasport, very tall with all this echo due to the structure of the building. The Mellotron never sounded better thanks to all that fantastic resonance." (5)

The tour ended in style in the two biggest cities of central and southern Italy, Rome and Naples. In Rome (with Tony Stratton-Smith flying in especially from the UK) at Alberigo Crocetta's legendary Piper Club, where, despite the usual technical issues (Collins was forced to perform his customary drum solo, while the sound from Hackett's guitar literally disappeared in the middle of his solo in *The Musical Box*), the crowd were bewitched by a powerful performance which to their delight included two encores. The setlist was: *Happy The Man / Stagnation / The Fountain Of Salmacis / Twilight Alehouse / Drum Solo / The Musical Box / The Return Of The Giant Hogweed / The Knife / Going Out To Get You.*

The Rome concert was also blessed with a visit from a television crew: the RAI (Italy's public broadcasting company) interviewed the band in the dressing rooms and filmed some extracts of the first two songs on the setlist. This brief TV coverage, which was never completed (some of the footage has no audio) and never aired, would eventually be released as part of the bonus material in the 2008 remastered issue of FOXTROT, revealing the earnest expressions on the faces of the audience as captured by the TV cameras. Banks: "Genesis audiences tended to be quite quiet and attentive like us. In the early days we attracted a sort of intense person to our shows. I would say that Italy took to us a bit before England did; you got people who would be listening very intensely, and by that stage we had a little bit more of an audience over there. But we were starting to get the same kind of response in England. It wasn't until we started doing the big venues later on that the audience got noisy, before that there wouldn't be a lot of noise in the audience throughout the whole show. When we did these very quiet pieces, with just acoustic

guitar, there was total attention, which was great, I mean it was a really nice experience." (5)

The grand finale was in Naples. In the afternoon, Mike and Tony wrote the lyrics to the new song dominated by Banks' Mellotron, *Watcher Of The Skies*, inspired by the view from the roof of their hotel (The Domitiana) overlooking the Mostra d'Oltremare, (Naples' trade exhibition site) where the Mediterraneo Theatre is located. Here the band played its tried and tested setlist, without any major incidents except for one covered by the usual drum solo before the concluding song, *The Knife*.

An enormously successful tour, despite the incredible variety in venues (theatres, palasports, small clubs). Banks: "In those days it didn't make too much difference to us because we didn't really have the equipment to sort of make much difference. I think we were probably happiest in the middle-sized venues really, but playing the palasports in Italy was great fun. I mean we were playing palasports in Italy and then going back to playing really tiny clubs in England. It was a real contrast of places. When you're playing in the smaller places, you're much more conscious the audience can hear you much more clearly, so it's more nerve-racking because every note can be heard and people are hanging over you and can actually see you. Once you get to the bigger places you're on a big stage and a bit removed from everything and those big places are a bit echoey and the sound is less precise." (5)

With their first Italian tour under their belt, Genesis went on to do some more dates in other European countries, playing yet again in Belgium (Arlon) on 22 April and their first ever gig in Germany (Frankfurt) on the 23rd.

May was dedicated to touring the UK with a dozen or so gigs culminating on the 29th at the Great Western Express Festival near Lincoln. Despite the problems caused by the adverse weather conditions, the line-up of artists from diverse genres (Joe Cocker, Humble Pie, Sha Na Na...) and the rather poor slot (in the afternoon), Genesis had the chance to play in front of a reportedly 50,000-strong crowd, with Gabriel wearing

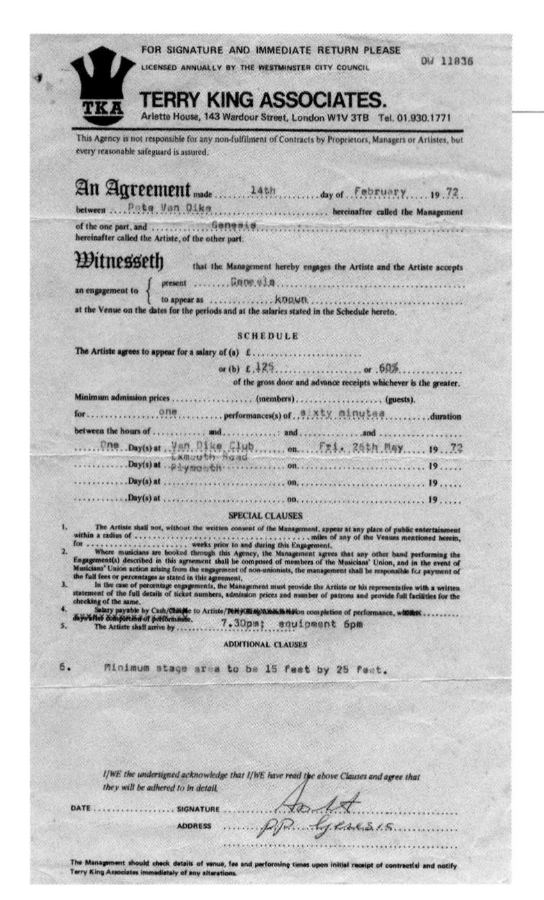

FOR SIGNATURE AND IMMEDIATE RETURN PLEASE

LICENSED ANNUALLY BY THE WESTMINSTER CITY COUNCIL

DW 11836

TKA

**TERRY KING ASSOCIATES.**

Arlette House, 143 Wardour Street, London W1V 3TB Tel. 01.930.1771

This Agency is not responsible for any non-fulfilment of Contracts by Proprietors, Managers or Artistes, but every reasonable safeguard is assured.

**An Agreement** made 14th day of February 19 72 between Pete Van Dike hereinafter called the Management of the one part, and Genesis hereinafter called the Artiste, of the other part.

**Witnesseth** that the Management hereby engages the Artiste and the Artiste accepts an engagement to present Genesis / to appear as known at the Venue on the dates for the periods and at the salaries stated in the Schedule hereto.

SCHEDULE

The Artiste agrees to appear for a salary of (a) £ ........ or (b) £ 125 ........ or 60% ........ of the gross door and advance receipts whichever is the greater.

Minimum admission prices ........ (members) ........ (guests).

for one performances(s) of sixty minutes duration

between the hours of ........ and ........ and ........ and ........

One Day(s) at Van Dike Club, Exmouth Road, Plymouth on Fri. 26th May 19 72

........ Day(s) at ........ on ........ 19 ....

........ Day(s) at ........ on ........ 19 ....

........ Day(s) at ........ on ........ 19 ....

SPECIAL CLAUSES

1. The Artiste shall not, without the written consent of the Management, appear at any place of public entertainment within a radius of ........ miles of any of the Venues mentioned herein, for ........ weeks prior to and during this Engagement.
2. Where musicians are booked through this Agency, the Management agrees that any other band performing the Engagement(s) described in this agreement shall be composed of members of the Musicians' Union, and in the event of Musicians' Union action arising from the engagement of non-unionists, the management shall be responsible for payment of the full fees or percentages as stated in this agreement.
3. In the case of percentage engagements, the Management must provide the Artiste or his representative with a written statement of the full details of ticket numbers, admission prices and number of patrons and provide full facilities for the checking of the same.
4. Salary payable by Cash/Cheque to Artiste/Terry King Associates on completion of performance, within ........ days after completion of performance.
5. The Artiste shall arrive by 7.30pm; equipment 6pm

ADDITIONAL CLAUSES

6. Minimum stage area to be 15 feet by 25 feet.

*I/WE the undersigned acknowledge that I/WE have read the above Clauses and agree that they will be adhered to in detail.*

DATE ........ SIGNATURE ........

ADDRESS p.p. Genesis

The Management should check details of venue, fee and performing times upon initial receipt of contract(s) and notify Terry King Associates immediately of any alterations.

noticeable make-up, a large necklace and two bracelets over his black sweater. From a musical point of view, this performance included the debut of the previously unheard and still to be released *Watcher Of The Skies*.

June began with a gig in Hastings (on the 2nd, where for the first time ever the band had its own lights) and ended with further important steps forward for the band: in fact, on the 26th they performed on stage at the prestigious Olympia Theatre in Paris along with Van Der Graaf Generator and Lindisfarne. The setlist was: *Watcher Of The Skies / Twilight Alehouse / The Fountain Of Salmacis / The Musical Box / The Knife*.

Then on the 28th, their old friend David Stopps decided to stage a special concert in Watford, a kind of Genesis Convention for their most dedicated fans, accompanied by an advertising campaign in the press. There is a bootleg recording of this event revealing the usual technical problems and the following setlist: *Watcher Of The Skies / Stagnation / One-Handed Drum Solo / The Fountain Of Salmacis / Happy The Man / Twilight Alehouse / The Musical Box / The Return Of The Giant Hogweed / Instrumental Jam / The Knife*.

After three days rehearsing in Blackheath (3–5 July), Genesis made their debut in Holland, playing at the Paradiso in Amsterdam on the 7th and in Meerlo the following day at a festival with various artists including Focus and Ekseption.

They then had a few shows back home in the UK, the most important of which was the 'Midnight Court' at The Lyceum on the 24th, which began at midnight with performances from Capability Brown and Audience and closing with Genesis.

Throughout this period and for the first half of August, the primary objective was to get the new album recorded. Nevertheless, the band still managed to put another feather in its cap by taking part in the famous Reading Festival on 11 August, albeit supporting better-known bands (Nazareth, Curved Air, Mungo Jerry ...) and with only a forty-minute slot. The setlist was: *The Knife / Twilight Alehouse / Watcher Of The Skies / The Musical Box / The Return Of The Giant Hogweed*. What is immediately striking is the decision to open with *The Knife*, obviously in an attempt to capture the attention of the crowd, who presumably knew very little about Genesis, with their heaviest track.

After just a couple of days' break, it was time for their second tour in Italy, right in the middle of recording Foxtrot. The first date of the tour was supposed to be on 14 August, in Rimini, but the

The contract between Terry King Associates and Genesis for the performance in Plymouth on May 6th, 1972; the band was hired for £125.

second Italian tour, just like the one four months earlier, got off to a bad start.

Banks: "We were travelling with Maurizio [Salvadori] and these two drivers, Sandro and Gianni, and a guy called Walter, they were basically friends of Maurizio who kind of liked us, while Richard Macphail had a van with all the gear in it. By the time we did those tours we had a slightly bigger van which only took the gear. The very first tour might have been with the Transit van, but after that we had a bigger one, a three-tonner. When we played Rimini, Richard didn't turn up at all because he got stuck at the border." (5)

The gig had to be postponed and some of the band members took consolation by joining the nocturnal jamming session which used to be held at the Altro Mondo discotheque. Here Italian and foreign artists in the area would meet up after finishing their concerts. It was a period of great experimentation and Lello Brandi, bass player with Italian band Osanna (who together with Jumbo were openers for Genesis on some of their tour dates), distinctly remembers jamming with Collins on this occasion.

Forced by circumstances to be tourists for a couple of days (it is said that they had a gig in Fano on 16 August, but there is a measure of doubt surrounding this), Genesis subsequently had a gig booked in Monselice (15 miles from Padua) for the 18th, but for some reason or another the venue (Dancing Lago Delle Rose) was not available and the gig had to be moved at the last minute to Feltre in the Belluno Dolomites. Flyers were used to inform fans of the change in plans and they had to hastily make a journey of nearly 70 miles to reach the new venue. The concert took place, oddly enough, at a local sports ground, where Gabriel was clearly annoyed at the distance between himself and the audience, who were on the other side of a wire fence.

Things didn't always go that badly, however, as most of the summer tour dates were indoors and usually in dance halls, such as the Dancing Jolie Club at Marina di Ravenna, normally used for ballroom dancing, where the band played on 19 August. The following day the tour took them to the Versilia Riviera: Genesis arrived in Viareggio and played in the Piper Club 2000, which that summer had already hosted Rory Gallagher, Brian Auger, Atomic Rooster and Van Der Graaf Generator, as well as a number of Italy's best progressive rock bands. Genesis were closing the summer gig season and delighted the audience with a double concert, one in the afternoon and one in the evening. In the first they played *Watcher Of The Skies / Can-Utility And The Coastliners / The Fountain Of Salmacis / Twilight Alehouse / Get 'Em Out By Friday / The Musical Box / The Return Of The Giant Hogweed / The Knife*. The bootleg recording of the evening show reveals the same setlist minus *The Musical Box,* but with a special treat for their Italian fans: a performance of *Harold The Barrel* as a second encore, practically the only time in the Nursery Cryme tour it was ever played.

Hackett: "We did it a few times live, but we didn't think it really worked. It's a short song, another one of those miniatures in the middle of the epics. I was having this conversation with Roine Stolt, the guitarist with The Flower Kings and Transatlantic. He was saying it is much harder to write a short song than an epic. We'd written both, but it was much harder to write a short song that worked. At

the time we probably thought there was strength in length, but I'm speaking for myself, that's just my take on it."[2]

The setlist also included songs from FOXTROT (still to be released) and was already becoming quite impressive with *Watcher Of The Skies, Get 'Em Out By Friday* and *Can-Utility And The Coastliners* (at long last presented with its definitive title). In the meantime songs such as *Happy The Man* and *Going Out To Get You* had been permanently dropped from the live shows.

The band then moved on to the Liguria region where they first played a gig in Albenga on 21st, in what was pompously called a 'palasport' but which, in fact, turned out to be a boules club, and then on the 22nd they played in the far more suitable Alcione Theatre in Genoa. The setlist of the bootleg circulated amongst fans is: *Watcher Of The Skies / Can-Utility And The Coastliners / The Fountain Of Salmacis / Twilight Alehouse / Seven Stones / The Musical Box / The Return Of The Giant Hogweed.* Yet another gift for the Italian audience: a unique (at least amongst the recordings which have survived) rendition of *Seven Stones.* "I remember it sounding very good when we rehearsed it," says Hackett, "there was a lot of reverb on the voice and on the piano accordion...".[2]

The tour was supposed to wind up in Genoa, but they had to make up for the concert they'd had to cancel in Rimini on the 14th. So on 23 August, Genesis played two concerts in the Adriatic tourist resort, both at the Locanda del Lupo. To celebrate the end of the tour there was another jam session with Osanna, but this time way bigger than the previous one. Basically, the two bands merged, with Hackett and Danilo Rustici on guitars, Collins and Massimo Guarino on percussion, Elio D'Anna on sax, Lino Vairetti on bass and Gabriel on keyboards. It should also be pointed out that, at this time, Osanna, who were already famous in Italy thanks to albums like L'UOMO and the soundtrack to the film MILANO CALIBRO 9, used to appear on stage wearing habits and heavily painted faces. Something which evidently did not go unnoticed by Gabriel.

## NOTES

(1) Mike Kaufman's Genesis interviews, Chicago / London, October 2007, partially used in the bonus disc accompanying the 2008 remasters

(2) Mario Giammetti listens to NURSERY CRYME with Steve Hackett, Twickenham, 1 December 2011

(3) Mario Giammetti's e-mail interview with John Alexander, 13 May 2015, partially published in the article "John Alexander: Mr. Bad Example" in Dusk, Issue no. 80, July 2015

(4) Mario Giammetti listens to THE LAMB LIES DOWN ON BROADWAY with Tony Banks, Chiddingfold, 10 May 2011

(5) Mario Giammetti's telephone interview with Tony Banks, 16 February 2012, partially published in the article "Six not simply shrouded pieces" in Dusk, Issue no. 70, April 2012

# NURSERY CRYME TOUR

## 1971

### SEPTEMBER

5 **Hemel Hempstead (ENGLAND)**, Pavilion
16 **Gravesend (ENGLAND)**, Civic Centre
18 **London (ENGLAND)**, The Temple
22 **Kennington (ENGLAND)**, Surrey Rooms - The Oval
23 **Kensington (ENGLAND)**, Kensington Town Hall
25 **Letchworth (ENGLAND)**, The Leys

### OCTOBER

9 **Watford (ENGLAND)**, Kingham Hall
12 **Windsor (ENGLAND)**, 1832
14 **London (ENGLAND)**, Lyceum Theatre
*'One Price Concerts'. Genesis supported Van Der Graaf Generator for this series of concerts.*
16 **Preston (ENGLAND)**, Public Hall
19 **Dorking (ENGLAND)**, Dorking Halls
21 **Oxford (ENGLAND)**, Town Hall
22 **Exeter (ENGLAND)**, Great Hall - Exeter University
23 **Colchester (ENGLAND)**, Dance Hall - University of Essex
26 **Southampton (ENGLAND)**, Southampton Guildhall
27 **Birmingham (ENGLAND)**, Town Hall
28 **Newcastle (ENGLAND)**, City Hall
29 **Birmingham (ENGLAND)**, Lake Hall
31 **Plymouth (ENGLAND)**, Plymouth Guildhall

### NOVEMBER

1 **Brighton (ENGLAND)**, The Dome
2 **Crawley (ENGLAND)**, Starlight Club
3 **Derby (ENGLAND)**, King's Hall
4 **Blackpool (ENGLAND)**, New Sands Casino
*Uncertain concert*
6 **Slough (ENGLAND)**, Slough College
7 **Salisbury (ENGLAND)**, City Hall
20 **Letchworth (ENGLAND)**, The Leys
22 **Kennington (ENGLAND)**, Surrey Rooms - The Oval
24 **London (ENGLAND)**, Lyceum Theatre
25 **Cambridge (ENGLAND)**, Corn Exchange
26 **Windsor (ENGLAND)**, Eton College
30 **Sheffield (ENGLAND)**, Oval Hall - Sheffield City Hall

### DECEMBER

1 **Atherstone (ENGLAND)**, Memorial Hall
3 **Leytonstone (ENGLAND)**, The Red Lion
4 **Cottingham (ENGLAND)**, Lawns Centre
7 **Wimbledon (ENGLAND)**, Hobbits Garden
8 **King's Lynn (ENGLAND)**, Technical College
9 **Middlesbrough (ENGLAND)**, Teeside Polytechnic
10 **Abingdon (ENGLAND)**, Culham College
11 **High Wycombe (ENGLAND)**, Cranbrook School
12 **High Wycombe (ENGLAND)**, Windrush Twylight Club
15 **Greenford (ENGLAND)**, Big Brother Club
16 **Weymouth (ENGLAND)**, Grammar School
21 **Portsmouth (ENGLAND)**, South Parade Pier
23 **Watford (ENGLAND)**, Kingham Hall

## 1972

### JANUARY

1 **Dagenham (ENGLAND)**, The Roundhouse
7 **Bradford (ENGLAND)**, Technical College
8 **Epsom (ENGLAND)**, Baths Hall
9 **London (ENGLAND)**, BBC Studio T1 Shepherds Bush • *'Sounds of the 70's' radio show, DJ John Peel*
15 **Cambridge (ENGLAND)**, New Canteen - Cambridgeshire College of Arts and Technology
19 **Coventry (ENGLAND)**, College of Education

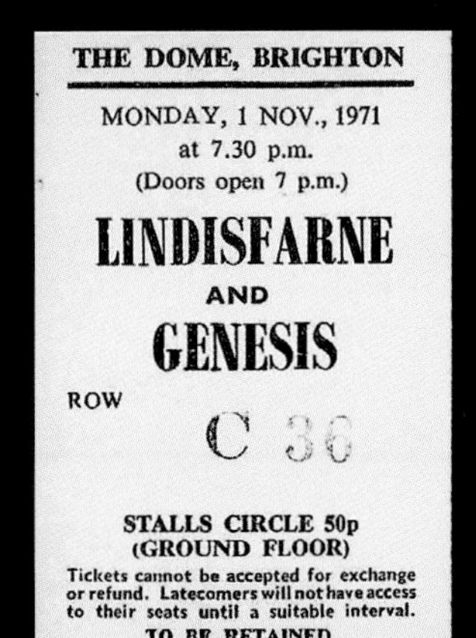

20 **Manchester** (ENGLAND), St. John's College
22 **Woluwe St. Pierre** (BELGIUM), Athénée Royal
23 **Charleroi** (BELGIUM), Palais des Beaux Arts
24 **Liège** (BELGIUM), Trocadero
27 **Tolworth** (ENGLAND), The Toby Jug
28 **High Wycombe** (ENGLAND), Town Hall
29 **Guildford** (ENGLAND), University of Surrey
30 **Bexley** (ENGLAND), Black Prince

## FEBRUARY

4 **London** (ENGLAND), Queen Elizabeth Hall
*Two shows*
5 **Luton** (ENGLAND), Luton College of Technology
6 **Lancing** (ENGLAND), Great School - Lancing College
11 **Penzance** (ENGLAND), Winter Gardens
12 **Plymouth** (ENGLAND), Van Dike Club
14 **Aberystwyth** (WALES), University College of Wales
17 **Sheffield** (ENGLAND), Oval Hall - Sheffield City Hall
19 **Salisbury** (ENGLAND), Alex Disco
20 **Croydon** (ENGLAND), The Greyhound
24 **High Wycombe** (ENGLAND), Town Hall
25 **Sunderland** (ENGLAND), Locarno Ballroom
26 **Bracknell** (ENGLAND), Bracknell Sports Centre

## MARCH

1 **Chelmsford** (ENGLAND), Chelmsford Civic Theatre • *Originally scheduled for 28 February*
2 **London** (ENGLAND), BBC Paris Studios
*'In Concert' radio show*
4 **Watford** (ENGLAND), Watford Technical College
10 **Portsmouth** (ENGLAND), South Parade Pier
11 **Aylesbury** (ENGLAND), Borough Assembly Hall
16 **Hull** (ENGLAND), Princess Theatre
*Uncertain concert*
17 **Birmingham** (ENGLAND), Aston University
18 **Troyes, Aube** (FRANCE), Halls de la Foire de Champagne • *'Féte Saint Gratien'. To be able to perform their first concert ever in France, Genesis cancelled the show originally scheduled at Nottingham's Boat Club.*
20 **Brussels** (BELGIUM), TV Studios
*Recording of the TV show 'Pop Shop'*
21 **Brussels** (BELGIUM), TV Studios
*Recording of the TV show 'Pop Shop'*
24 **Chelmsford** (ENGLAND), Essex University
25 **Carshalton** (ENGLAND), College of Education

## APRIL

6 **Adria, RO** (ITALY), Teatro Comunale del Popolo
*First concert ever in Italy. Originally scheduled at Belluno's Palasport.*
7 **Godega di Sant'Urbano, TV** (ITALY), Apollo 2000
9 **San Martino Buon Albergo, VR** (ITALY), Dancing Lem • *Two shows*
11 **Pesaro** (ITALY), Palazzo dello sport
12 **Reggio Emilia** (ITALY), Palasport
13 **Cuorgnè, TO** (ITALY), Dancing 2 Rotonde
14 **Pavia** (ITALY), Palazzo delle Esposizioni
*Two shows*
15 **Lugo di Romagna, RA** (ITALY), Hit Parade
16 **Travagliato, BS** (ITALY), Supertivoli
*Two Shows*
17 **Siena** (ITALY), Palasport

Luton College S.U. Nº 0520
Saturday February 5th. 1972 at 7.30 p.m.
RORY GALLAGHER
GENESIS
S. U.: 75p Others: 85p
tickets from S. U. Office Only

2 ROTONDE DANCING CUORGNÈ
13 APRILE 1972 ore 22
"GENESIS"

18 **Roma** (ITALY), Piper Club
*Two shows*
19 **Napoli** (ITALY), Teatro Mediterraneo
*Two shows*
22 **Arlon** (BELGIUM), Salle de la Jeunesse
23 **Frankfurt** (WEST GERMANY), Zoom Club
*First concert ever in Germany*
28 **Kingston-upon-Thames** (ENGLAND), Kingston Polytechnic
29 **Isleworth** (ENGLAND), Isleworth Polytechnic
30 **Guildford** (ENGLAND), Civic Hall

## MAY

5 **Leytonstone** (ENGLAND), Red Lion
6 **Bangor** (WALES), Auditorium
*Uncertain concert*
8 **High Wycombe** (ENGLAND), University of Essex
9 **Oxford** (ENGLAND), Town Hall
11 **Derby** (ENGLAND), Cleopatra's Club
19 **Newcastle** (ENGLAND), Mecca Ballrooms
20 **St. Albans** (ENGLAND), City Hall
21 **Bletchley** (ENGLAND), Bletchley Youth Centre
25 **Penzance** (ENGLAND), Winter Gardens
26 **Plymouth** (ENGLAND), Van Dike Club
27 **Farnborough** (ENGLAND), Farnborough Technical College
29 **Bardney** (ENGLAND),
*'Great Western Express Festival'*

## JUNE

2 **Hastings** (ENGLAND), Pier Pavilion
3 **Luton** (ENGLAND), Luton College of Technology
4 **London** (ENGLAND), Lyceum Theatre
6 **Colchester** (ENGLAND), College of Technology
*Uncertain concert*
9 **Leeds** (ENGLAND), Leeds Polytechnic
10 **Cambridge** (ENGLAND), Corn Exchange
16 **Bedford** (ENGLAND), Corn Exchange
17 **Wellingborough** (ENGLAND), The Rock Club
19 **Swansea** (WALES), Top Rank Suite
23 **Durham** (ENGLAND), Durham Castle
24 **Felixstowe** (ENGLAND), Pier Pavilion
26 **Paris** (FRANCE), L'Olympia
28 **Watford** (ENGLAND), Watford Town Hall

**PIPER 2000**
Viareggio
domenica 20 agosto - ore 18-22
**GENESIS**
sconto del 15% presentando questo tagliando.

29 **London** (ENGLAND), Shoreditch Town Hall
30 **Slough** (ENGLAND), Community Centre

## JULY

1 **Folkestone** (ENGLAND), Leas Cliff Hall
2 **Croydon** (ENGLAND), The Greyhound
7 **Amsterdam** (THE NETHERLANDS), Paradiso
8 **Meerlo** (THE NETHERLANDS), 'Midsummer-Pop Festival '72'
13 **Rutland** (ENGLAND), Uppingham School
14 **London** (ENGLAND), Lyceum Theatre
16 **Redcar** (ENGLAND), Coatham Hotel
21 **Leytonstone** (ENGLAND), Red Lion
22 **Salisbury** (ENGLAND), Alex Disco
23 **Epping** (ENGLAND), The Wake Arms
25 **Solihull** (ENGLAND), Solihull Civic Hall
27 **Cleethorpes** (ENGLAND), Winter Gardens
28 **Billericay** (ENGLAND), Archer Hall

## AUGUST

2 **Worthing** (ENGLAND), Assembly Halls
*Uncertain concert*
11 **Reading** (ENGLAND), Thames-side Arena
*'Reading Festival'*
18 **Feltre, BL** (ITALY), Campo Sportivo Zugni Tauro
*Originally scheduled at Monselice (PD), Dancing Lago della Rose*
19 **Marina di Ravenna** (ITALY), Dancing Jolie Club
*Two shows*
20 **Viareggio, LU** (ITALY), Piper 2000 Club
*Two shows*
21 **Albenga, SV** (ITALY), Palasport
22 **Genova** (ITALY), Teatro Alcione
23 **Rimini, FO** (ITALY), La Locanda del Lupo
*Two shows. Originally scheduled for 14 August*
24 **Travagliato, BS** (ITALY), Supertivoli

# Foxtrot

(Charisma 1972)

***Watcher Of The Skies / Time Table / Get 'Em Out By Friday / Can-Utility And The Coastliners /// Horizons / Supper's Ready: a) Lovers' Leap; b) The Guaranteed Eternal Sanctuary Man; c) Ikhnaton And Itsacon And Their Band Of Merry Men; d) How Dare I Be So Beautiful?; e) Willow Farm; f) Apocalypse in 9/8 (Co-Starring The Delicious Talents Of Gabble Ratchet); g) As Sure As Eggs Is Eggs (Aching Mens' Feet)***

- **Release date: 6 October 1972**
- **Recorded at Island Studios, London, July and August 1972**
- **Engineer: John Burns**
- **Producers: David Hitchcock and Genesis**
- **Artwork: Paul Whitehead**

- **Tony Banks: organ, Mellotron, piano, electric piano, 12-string, voices**
- **Steve Hackett: electric guitar, 12-string and 6-string solo**
- **Phil Collins: drums, voices, assorted percussion**
- **Peter Gabriel: lead voice, flute, bass drum, tambourine, oboe**
- **Michael Rutherford: bass, bass pedals, 12-string guitar, voices, cello**
- **Richard Macphail: Equipment & stage sound (sound friend)**

## THE MAKING OF

In March 1972, Genesis went into the recording studio with the specific intention of making a single. "I seem to remember," says Hackett, "that Richard Branson gave us a free day at The Manor [Studio]."[1] The chosen track was *Happy The Man*, an acoustic folk ballad written by Mike Rutherford which had already been part of their live set for at least a year. The idea was to try out the market with something short (just three minutes long) and catchy.

Banks: "We always used to like the fact that, in the early days of The Beatles, their singles weren't on their albums, *She Loves You* wasn't on With The Beatles or whatever. We always thought of *Happy The Man* as a single, so we were keen to do it in that format, hoping it would be a hit." [2]

In the same period another song was also recorded, *Wooden Mask*, for the purpose of making a possible follow-up single; alas, these tapes have been irretrievably lost.

In the meantime, the new album was being written in fits and starts due to the fact that the band was nearly always touring. During the first Italian tour, the one in April 1972, a song introduced as *Bye-Bye Johnny* featured at some of the gigs. *Bye-Bye Johnny* would eventually evolve into *Can-Utility And The Coastliners*, while another track set to become of great importance to the band, *Watcher Of The Skies*, also started to take shape in terms of music and lyrics during this tour. Notwithstanding their hectic schedule, during quieter periods the group would try and find the necessary concentration to write new material, every now and again renting a rehearsal room.

Collins: "We never managed to rehearse for more than one week in the same place. I remember one week in Woolwich and another at 'Una Billings' [a dance school in London]. Some of the album was written in Chessington because a friend of a friend had a house there." (3)

Hackett: "We rehearsed in different places. There was a place in Chessington and a rehearsal room in West Hampstead, near the station. I can't remember if it belonged to John Mayall or his son. 'Una Billings' is where we wrote *Supper's Ready*." (1)

After their initial period of euphoria, the two new members (perhaps still not completely integrated into the band) went through a rather unsettled period.

Hackett: "Every now and again Phil and I would threaten to leave. Luckily, on the first day of recording FOXTROT, Mike and Tony told me they didn't want me to leave and that they really liked my guitar playing. It may seem strange, but I hadn't understood it at that point, mainly because within the band we didn't compliment each other very much. I felt very insecure and I thought maybe it was better to leave before I got sacked. When I realised they liked what I did and wanted me to stay, it was an epiphanal moment for me. I was allowed to play this solo piece, *Horizons*, which meant I had one minute and 30 seconds all to myself on the album. I know Phil considered leaving from time to time (but I don't know if he admits it these days). I think Lindisfarne wanted him to join at one point and he was thinking about it. I think it's because we were so very, very tired." (3)

Fortunately there was no lack of new material; in fact, not only was it flowing freely, it was also exceptionally good.

Hackett: "As a band we were trying to find our feet, hoping that the record company would

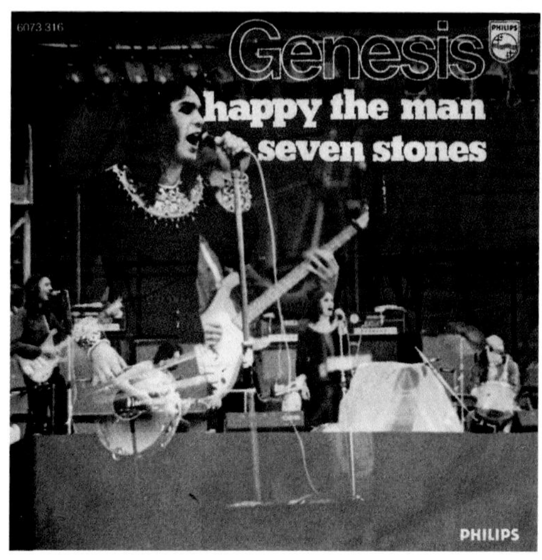


renew the contract and we were being given the thumbs up to develop very, very slowly thanks to Tony Stratton-Smith, a wonderful man who signed acts he felt passionately about. He would give them, and us, many, many albums to make it. There was nothing meteoric about the rise of Genesis, it took a long time to make it happen and you really needed to be putting bums on seats in those days. You played to people and when you went back to the same town you hoped there would be a bigger audience and luckily for us that's how it went." (3)

Most of the recording was done at the beginning of August at Island Records Studios in Basing Street, London, but just a few days in and the sessions had to be stopped so that they could accept a request to go back to Italy and tour for another week. The sessions turned out to be anything but plain sailing, mainly due to the fact that the producer's seat remained empty following the split with John Anthony in May, in part possibly due to the lack of success achieved by the single *Happy The Man / Seven Stones*.

Hackett: "I don't know if it was because of that. I think Tony Stratton-Smith felt that the power of the live band wasn't being captured on record, so he felt that we needed a new producer and suggested Bob Potter." (1)

Potter was a young sound engineer who had worked with Bob Johnston, a producer with an impressive track record (Bob Dylan, Simon & Garfunkel, Leonard Cohen) and who had just produced Lindisfarne's highly successful album Fog On The Tyne. Stratton-Smith evidently thought Johnston's assistant, Bob Potter, who in the meantime was learning the ropes on other English folk and rock albums such as Please To See The King by Steeleye Span and Bell + Arc by Bell & Arc, would more than suffice for Genesis. Unfortunately, however, he soon started to clash with the band over their musical tastes and their attitude in the studio.

Hackett: "It used to take us a long time to set up and get the sound right. He thought we should be able to rock out a lot quicker than that, but we weren't that kind of band; at times work was produced at an almost leisurely pace. I remember once, Mike was doing some 12-string stuff and he didn't think the strings sounded bright enough and he wanted to re-string, something which could take two hours. Bob Potter couldn't handle it. I think the only thing that worked [with Potter] was the night I recorded *Horizons*. It took four takes to get it right. I played it all the way through, so the version on the record has no edits. He said that was the only thing he enjoyed doing. I was

The *Happy The Man* single came out with two different covers for the English (left) and Italian (right) markets.

aware that the chemistry wasn't working and I wanted to try and make it work with him." (1)

Banks: "Charisma were very keen for us to work with Bob Potter, who had worked with Lindisfarne, mainly because they wanted the lead vocals to sound louder and because they thought a real producer might be useful to us. So we went into the studio and started to record. But the minute I started playing the opening to *Watcher Of The Skies*, Potter said he didn't like it and that he didn't think we should use it. After we'd tried a couple of other things we realised that he might have been a good engineer but he didn't actually like what we were doing. That meant we simply couldn't work with him, so we got rid of him." (3)

From this distance in time, it is not entirely clear whether Potter was fired or decided to leave of his own accord.

Hackett: "He was quite young and inexperienced and he seemed to be on a collision course with the guys in the band. He ended up abandoning the project and it was a very worrying time for us. It's very depressing when your producer quits. Personally I don't think he should have got involved with Genesis, because I don't think he liked our music, he liked more obvious rock'n'roll. I think the subtleties of Genesis were lost on him, although he did like *Horizons*. I gather that was the only part he liked, probably because he wasn't dealing with the whole band, just one member of it." (1)

Potter's replacement as producer was David Hitchcock, who was again brought in by Stratton-Smith. Hitchcock: "Strat asked me if I was interested in producing Genesis. He knew I had just produced In The Land Of Grey And Pink by Caravan, which contained the suite *Nine Feet Underground*, which took up one side of the album, so I knew how to do that kind of recording. Genesis had written *Supper's Ready* which was similar in length and structure, consisting of several pieces of music that were very different but were conceived as one suite. I was also starting to get a reputation for producing prog rock having done successful albums by Caravan and East of Eden and various other similar bands. So I met them [Genesis] and we went into the studio which I knew, with an engineer I didn't know [Tony Platt] that I wasn't too happy with, so I changed to another engineer that I did know and who I knew I could work with called John Burns, who worked very well with the band and went on to produce the next two albums." (4)

Banks: "[When Potter left] we ended up working with just the engineer [Platt], but we weren't too sure about him either, so we changed engineer halfway through the recording of *Supper's Ready*. We recorded the first half of the song with the first engineer, then we got this other guy, John Burns, and we finished off the song with him." (3)

Hackett: "When John Burns heard the 12-string stuff we'd already recorded for *Supper's Ready*, he really liked it and said we should continue with it. And that was very important for the band; this new team was much more encouraging. I liked David Hitchcock very much as a person, but the dialogue was between us and John Burns because he was an engineer and consequently much more hands on. Ironically it was John Burns who was to stay the course in the long term because he was very enthusiastic and a great

Steve Hackett's first marriage, celebrated in September 1972. From the left, we can recognise Banks, Rutherford, Hackett (with his wife, Ellen), Collins, Steve Hackett's mother, June, and, at the extreme right, Gabriel.

engineer who seemed to know how to deal with everybody, he had a nice way about him. He worked with us on Foxtrot, Selling England By The Pound and The Lamb and he was also a guitarist, so he was good at getting guitar sounds." (1)

During these studio sessions, *Twilight Alehouse*, which dates back to the Anthony Phillips' days, was finally recorded, even if it never made it to the final tracklist.

Banks: "This song was already around when we did Trespass but for some reason or other we didn't record it. We kept back one or two songs from the time of Trespass that we could have done. There was another song called *Let Us Now Make Love*, one of Ant's songs, which we kept back as a possible single. We knew *Twilight Alehouse* was a good stage song and we finally got round to recording it during the Foxtrot sessions, but we had other material by then and it became an extra, so we decided to leave it off and it eventually ended up as the B-side of *I Know What I Like* [released as a single the following year]. Now I think it was actually really good, definitely better than half the ones that ended up on the record. Tastes change. We just had a different attitude at the time." (2)

## THE ALBUM

After that 'difficult' third album Nursery Cryme, (difficult because of the changed band line-up and especially because of the loss of Anthony Phillips who had been the leading songwriter), Genesis made a giant leap forward in their creative growth and musicianship with Foxtrot.

Foxtrot is above all associated with *Supper's Ready* the band's first and only recorded suite (other suites were planned for the Duke and Abacab albums but were abandoned during album recording sessions). *Supper's Ready* is 23 minutes' long, takes up almost the whole of Side Two on the album and represents a broader, more variegated and artistically relevant songwriting effort than comparable works by other artists of the same period. It is made up of seven movements, beautifully fitted together, with an ending which restates themes from earlier parts of the song, with a profusion of styles and atmospheres in the middle, ranging from pastoral to symphonic, from grotesque to dramatic. *Supper's Ready* is considered by many to be the crowning glory of Genesis' entire career, an extraordinary epic which never becomes tiresome nor repetitive throughout its long evolution.

That said, anyone trying to heap all of their praise for the album on the suite alone would be misguided, as this record is the logical evolution of the previous one. Side One, in fact, contains three songs which are milestones in the history of early Genesis: the monumental introduction of the syncopated *Watcher Of The Skies*, the theatrical and composite *Get 'Em Out By Friday* (and its

satirical lyrics laced with social comment) and the intricate top-level progressive rock displayed in *Can-Utility And The Coastliners*. And while *Time Table*, in its absolute agreeableness, has to make do with a minor status, *Horizons*, a delicate sketch for 6-string acoustic guitar which opens Side Two ahead of *Supper's Ready*, became a musical symbol for the band, especially for its author and performer, Steve Hackett.

Hackett, now at his second album with Genesis, is the musician showing the most encouraging progress in his songwriting ability, composing not only *Horizons* but also much of *Can-Utility And The Coastliners*. He also managed to get his proverbial finger into different parts of the pie that is *Supper's Ready* while still continuing to develop his technique and creativity for the band. A guitarist with little inclination for pyrotechnics, Hackett knew exactly what was needed for the sound of Genesis and limited himself to providing just that: very subtle solos, often highly original in their melodic structure, and background work on the electric guitar (and on the 12-string at the beginning of *Supper's Ready*), maybe a little inconspicuous but absolutely delightful and ultimately essential for achieving the end result.

The other new element, Collins, still wasn't a fully-fledged songwriter at this stage. However, with his amazing drumming technique and touch he managed to bring extraordinary gear changes into certain sections of songs (*Watcher Of The Skies, Get 'Em Out By Friday* and some parts of *Supper's Ready*) which without his prowess would never have reached such formidable heights. Furthermore, his voice supports Gabriel's vocals in many places, becoming a sort of echo and counterbalance.

Mike Rutherford, on the other hand, was continuing to grow as a bass player (his parts on *Watcher Of The Skies* and *Get 'Em Out By Friday* are outstanding) and he also confirmed himself as the binding force for the whole band with his 12-string guitar and his supporting role in the more adventurous parts like in *Apocalypse In 9/8*. That said, his songwriting contribution still hadn't reached maximum level as Mike was more inclined to write brief sections as opposed to whole songs.

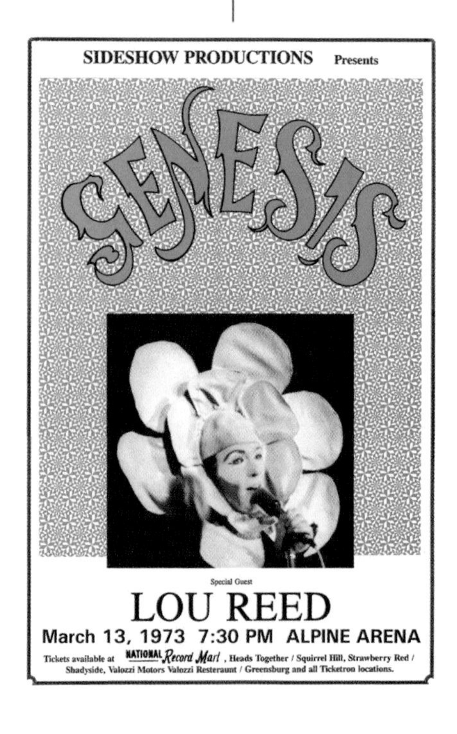


On this album Tony Banks' songwriting capabilities finally came to the fore: *Time Table*, the intro to *Watcher Of The Skies*, the structure of *Get 'Em Out By Friday* and almost half of the music which went into creating *Supper's Ready* (including much of the improvisation with Mike and Phil of the *Apocalypse In 9/8* section) were written by Banks. So, at their fourth album, the keyboard player won himself the role of Genesis' chief songwriter (despite being in a band full of writers), a position he would never relinquish.

And Gabriel? His vocals had acquired even more shades, interpreting different characters within the same song and expertly exploiting the tricks of the trade in the recording studio. Although musically he limited himself to composing *Willow Farm*, Gabriel concentrated on writing complicated lyrics for *Supper's Ready* and proved to be a sophisticated fantasy storyteller full of irony on *Get 'Em Out By Friday*. Gabriel, therefore, remained the main author of the lyrics, but the others also made their contribution: Steve wrote the words to *Can-Utility And The Coastliners*, Tony the lyrics for *Time Table* and *Watcher Of The Skies*, in the latter case with the help of Mike.

1972 was an extraordinary year for music. Starting on the other side of the Atlantic, Creedence Clearwater Revival released their seventh (and last) album Mardi Gras, Neil Young and Lou Reed released two radically different masterpieces: the pastoral Harvest for the Canadian and the louche Transformer for the ex-Velvet Underground singer. Meanwhile, thanks to Weather Report's I Sing The Body Electric, jazz was becoming appetizing even to the rock lover's palate.

The British rock scene was also vibrant with Pink Moon, Nick Drake's third and final album, Deep Purple's Machine Head, David Bowie's The Rise and Fall of Ziggy Stardust and the Spiders from Mars and

Pittsburgh concert poster from 13th March 1973, when Genesis shared the stage with Lou Reed.

not forgetting Exile On Main Street by the already legendary Rolling Stones. The progressive rock scenario was also stronger than ever. However, whilst Gentle Giant (with Three Friends) and Emerson, Lake & Palmer (with Trilogy) released strong records, Genesis boasted a creative supremacy which at this stage (and arguably for the last time) only Yes with Close To The Edge seemed able to counteract. Of particular note is that Jon Anderson's band, among other things, created a convincing suite for its album which took up a whole side, while Jethro Tull took it one step further by writing a single song for the entire record (Thick As A Brick, divided into two parts, of course).

Foxtrot, however, took the top spot as best prog album of the year, an accolade gained in a highly creative musical context.

## THE SONGS

### WATCHER OF THE SKIES

Gabriel: "It was a very important track for us; on the live side it was a key number. Although Tony was the lead writer of the song (in particular the Mellotron chords in the intro are his) I did some work on the verses and chorus." (3)

Producer David Hitchcock: "We wanted to get a big sound from the Mellotron. We were working in the Studio 2 at Basing Street in London which was a small studio [Island Studios, now called SARM Studios, but also known as Basing Street Studios, established by Chris Blackwell and located in Notting Hill, London] and I think it was John Burns who suggested we use Studio 1 upstairs, the big studio, and put up some big speaker stacks and use distance mikes and record all the room, as well as recording directly from the Mellotron. That is how we got that sound which some producers have asked me (about) afterwards." (4)

Rutherford: "I remember hearing Tony playing those opening chords in one of those big palasports on an Italian tour; the echoes were booming round and it sounded fantastic. The band was gaining some darkness, in terms of the music. I think it's got a fantastic intro and the rhythm's great. Looking back on it, however, I think it's a little too busy." (3)

Collins: "Every Wednesday I used to go and see Yes at the Marquee. I wanted to bring a little bit of that musicianship into the band, the tricky arrangements they used to have. I used to say, "it's a shame we can't do stuff like that". Certainly the intro is all Tony, of course, but the next part came from my drumming." (3)

Hackett: "It was actually a combo of everybody. The intro is Tony's, the rhythm is Phil's, while the crescendo and the dynamics of the 6/4 riff being done very softly and then very loud were my ideas. Tony was using the Mellotron [MKII], a mixture of brass and strings, while the bass part on the intro is done with Mellotron piano accordion. He also used to like putting the Mellotron through Leslie cabinets which made it sound more like an organ. The recorded version is much faster than the live version used to be. I think it would be impossible to play it live at that speed." (1)

In the melodic part of the track, Hackett is doubling Mike's bass line.

Hackett: "The staccato rhythm idea was Phil's,

*Qui Giovani* n. 46,
16 November 1972.

he thought it should sound like Morse code. The rhythm changes towards the end of the song, going from 6/4 to 4/4. It's very difficult to do a melody line over a rhythm like that so the melody line floats over the top. For some people there might be too much punctuation and not enough statement, so arguably the best part of the song lies in the instrumental at the beginning and right at the end. I love the song very much; it was unlike anything anyone else was doing up to that point, half classical and half rock. A song that used to divide people. In America they found it too classical, too removed from the roots of rock'n'roll." (1)

Banks: "I don't think this song stands the test of time as well as some of the others. I find some of the vocal parts are a bit embarrassing." (3)

The lyrics were written by Tony and Mike one afternoon while the band was touring in Italy in April 1972. Inspiration was provided by the desolate landscape which they could see from the roof of the Hotel Domitiana in Naples looking over Viale Kennedy and the Mostra d'Oltremare trade exhibition site.

Rutherford: "I remember writing the lyrics with Tony, sitting on a roof outside the bedroom window of a hotel in Italy. Looking around you could see all these other tar roofs and there was no-one around, a sort of lunar landscape. This song is definitely a period piece. With the passing of the years I've learnt that you can't just use the words you want to say, they've got to sing well. "Watcher of the skies, watcher of all" is a bit of a stiff lyric." (3)

The lyrics combine elements from literature and comic books.

Banks: "I had just read *Childhood's End* by Arthur C. Clarke, where the population moves on to the next level and disappears, which was fun, and we combined that with The Watcher, a Marvel Comics character who just observes and can't take any active part or anything. So we combined these ideas and wrote the lyrics inspired by this very hot day and this 'where's everybody gone?' sensation." (5)

## TIME TABLE

Banks: "In the early days I was perhaps more free. With this song, for example, I came in with a complete piece saying, "right, this is this" and we did it." (3)

Tony is therefore the sole writer of this song, conducted by a piano sound of times gone by, classical with a Renaissance touch. Hackett: "It's quite simple for a Genesis song: a piano intro and I'm doubling part of the piano work while Mike plays bass and there's a single vocal. It was a lovely song in the rehearsal room, but the recorded version sounded a bit dry. The remix of this song is brighter and you can hear the sound of the guitar which was put through a Leslie cabinet which was a Beatles' trick." (1)

Even in a simple song like this, there is always room for a touch of genius.

Hackett: "At 1'37" we used tubular bells, while the solo melody which comes in at 1'43" was played with the piano but by picking the strings inside the lid with a plectrum so it doesn't sound like a guitar or piano. The sound that plays out from inside the body of the piano is beautiful, it reminded me of Henry Mancini when he played on *Charade*. He wrote *Moon River* and other hits

QUI
giovani
NUOVE
MOTO
1973
in abbonam. postale - Gruppo II/70
La "volpe" dei Genesis
nel grande
concerto di Londra

and there's an element of that, so this track is a very accessible aspect of Genesis. This is not the sort of thing you hear from most rock bands as it modulates from key to key." (1)

Tony also wrote the lyrics, something which seems to cause him some slight embarrassment: "It was pretty early days when I wrote it. We used to distribute the lyrics between us, but then as time went by Peter wanted to write more and more, which was fine by me, after all he was the singer and I didn't really care; I'm not in the business to write lyrics, I'm in it to write music. The same thing happened with Phil really, by the end he was writing more of the lyrics than anybody else. I think he's a very good lyric writer so that was OK." (5)

## GET 'EM OUT BY FRIDAY

Starting with some fragments of the 1969 track *The Movement*, this song took shape thanks to a collective effort.

Banks: "I had this riff which we developed as a group. Both ways of writing worked, but I think when the group all felt involved in the composition it tended to produce a better result. *Get 'Em Out By Friday* is definitely the second best song on the album [after *Supper's Ready*], I think it's much better than *Watcher Of The Skies*." (3)

Hackett: "It's a kind of 6/8 rhythm and at the beginning you can hear Pete who was learning to play the oboe. So we had guitar and oboe playing together, which again is not a regular rock combination and the divisions at 0'26" are typical of Phil. Then [1'58"] there is a guitar bit which I suggested to them." (1)

Rutherford's bass in this track is particularly effective. Hackett: "Mike played bass but he had the sensibility of a guitarist, so he played melodic lines. I think the best bass players think of it as counterpoint, they are coming up with another melody entirely to the vocal one. Mike was very good at that and he was also very good at using bass pedals, so he was free to play the 12-string." (1)

Steve's guitar solo is truly original. Hackett: "I used a fuzz box and a small Fender Champ amp. I

Advertising poster for the 8th April 1973 Sherbrooke University concert in Canada.

was playing double notes and everyone says I had a great sustain but I wanted the guitar to have better sustain than that... I was using jazz tone in those days which made little impression on the overall sound." (1)

The song is characterised by different sections with strong rhythm parts and parts which are unusually soft. Rutherford: "This is an example of where we had too much stuff on a song. I mean, the track was great without any vocals, it sounded good, but when the vocals came on, despite the very clever lyrics and great performance from Peter, there was almost too much in there. Later on, we started to realise that there's a danger in not getting the voice laid down early on when you're actually playing tracks. In those days we'd often do the track instrumentally, then someone would go away and come back with a lyric and vocal ideas which hadn't been sung much beforehand. In later songs we realised that you can just play the chord of A for eight bars, which instrumentally sounds a bit boring, but when there's a great vocal on top it really works because it gives you more space. This song suffered a bit from having just too many good ideas in it." (3)

Collins: "Because there was nothing to sing to start with, Peter would be playing his bass drum, his tambourine or the flute and shouting some things. We couldn't really hear him because it was a rehearsal room and the PA wasn't very good, so we'd write these great things that actually sounded like instrumental tracks. Then Pete would go away and come back with a lyric but then the song would become too crowded. Adding a voice at that stage meant things would come back a little dense, but by that time it was too late because we'd already recorded the backing tracks." (3)

Banks: "There's a clever idea in the middle of the song where Peter plays real flute and I'm playing Mellotron flutes [4'56"] in harmony. It's a lovely, sad piece." (3)

Hackett: "In the middle of this rocking tune we decided to strip it right back to the silence and minimalism of real flute and Mellotron flute together. Phil's drums, with a fast tom break [5'27"], is a funny characteristic of Genesis, combining energy and restraint. This song has a level of stasis in it that most rock bands wouldn't have touched. There's no feeling of the need to entertain here and I always thought this was a very nice part. There's a sense of old English music in it." (1)

At 6'05" Gabriel starts singing again with a range of bizarre vocal effects. Hackett: "Pete used to like doing this thing; if you put headphones on you can hear a repeat echo of the voice, but not the original singer. In the middle of this song he acted out different parts, it's almost Gilbert and Sullivan with a Dickensian character." (1)

Gabriel: "I tried to put some sort of Dickensian feel into this song. In a way, musically that was something I don't think we managed to deliver. On the recording side, some of the things were too stretched and on other things we were still trying to find our way with sound and arrangement." (3)

The lead singer doesn't deny there were problems with the metric. Gabriel: "I think it did end up too wordy. The song was essentially about people being kicked out of rented accommodation. It was based on some of the Rachman stories, about bad landlords [Perec Rachman was a landlord

Press announcement for FOXTROT UK tour dates.

who operated in Notting Hill and became notorious for his exploitation of tenants] and I put in a little extra thought about evolving the species. The idea of making people shorter so that you can get more apartments in the same building was meant to be a comment on the attitudes of landlords towards tenants along with the idea that genetic engineering may at some point in the future be used to control our evolution, maybe not in my lifetime but in my children's lifetime. There may be a decision to go smaller as a way of using less of nature's resources. So in part social comment and in part prophetic." (3)

Hackett: "It's about people, the corruption of Government. It's an interesting track, it's multifaceted but mainly it has a claustrophobic feel about it. Funnily enough, when we were working on it, Donovan walked into the studio. I went out to speak to him and he said that the part where the flute and Mellotron flutes play together sounded like rows and rows of houses." (1)

Banks: "I think it's one of Pete's best lyrics." (3)

## CAN-UTILITY AND THE COASTLINERS

Banks: "Every piece on this worked pretty well and the end section is really good. I know a lot of people consider it one of their favourite tracks and it is a really good song, but it does suffer from being a bit fragmented." (3)

Divided into three main sections (the first is acoustic, the second is characterised by a long, flowing Mellotron part while the third is more rhythmic) this song sprang mainly from an idea provided by Steve.

Hackett: "I wrote everything up to 1'50" but the guitar break is Mike's, played with two 12-strings in harmony. I think the part from 2'11" is one of the best bits of Genesis' music as you've got the bass pedal, very simple, but Tony is doing this whole impression of a string orchestra with the Mellotron strings and he's being quite free with the use of chords, he's basically ignoring the chords and doing what he wants. It really shouldn't work because the chords are being drowned out by the weight of the strings but it works in a way that music shouldn't, while the 12 strings are not moving at all, just repeating the same thing, very clever. This idea of the organ and Mellotron [from 3'23"] playing together was influenced by Procol Harum's *Wreck Of The Hesperus*. I remember Phil wanted Mike to play bass [at 3'44"] but he refused. So the bass kicks in later and you have the influence of Chris Squire, the fast bass playing." (1)

Again, also in this case the guitar solo is extremely original. Hackett: "Yeah, strange isn't it, all faded in. Hearing this now, I think it is a solo I would have played again, it was difficult to play anything over that chord sequence. The guitar sounds like a synthesiser on this, as it fades in it goes to distortion. At 5'17" you can hear Phil's influence. And I wrote the vocal melody at the end of this section." (1)

CARLOS SANTANA COLOUR POSTER

MUSIC IS THE MESSAGE

sounds

JANUARY 13, 1973 7p

Brinsley Schwarz Talk-In

SEE PAGE EIGHTEEN

**BRITISH TOUR FOR GENESIS**

**Fifteen dates for February**

Steve was also the author of the lyrics. Hackett: "The lyrics tell the story of an English King called Cnut. He was concerned about his people flattering him and telling him he could do anything. So he had his throne put on the seashore and he commanded the waves to go out and they didn't. He was just trying to prove the point that he was only human and not immortal. He was trying to demythologise royalty. He's an interesting character to me as most leaders are self-aggrandising and he seemed to be the opposite. So he had a certain amount of modesty." (1)

## HORIZONS

Irritated by the exasperatingly long time it was taking Rutherford to change his guitar strings, the soon-to-be-replaced producer, Bob Potter, asked Steve if he had anything ready. When Hackett played him his short acoustic piece, Potter was so pleased with it that in the end, *Horizons* ended up being the only track he produced in full.

Hackett: "I had been trying to get an acoustic guitar sound like that for ages. At that time I was hearing people playing 6-string acoustic and thinking what beautiful sounds they were getting. It is beautiful, if you've got the right melody it can sound wonderful. I used an acoustic guitar, a Japanese Yairi, fed through two Leslie cabinets to give it that phasey sound which was typical of Genesis. A lot of the arpeggiated guitar work was put through them, it was a favourite of ours before the days of using chorus or pitch shift." (1)

Gabriel: "It's a lovely piece, almost like a classical guitar piece. But being played before *Supper's Ready* meant it sort of became absorbed by this bigger entity." (3)

Even though, at the end of the day, its inclusion in Foxtrot was down to chance, the track had in any case been proposed to the band by Steve.

Hackett: "I played it to the rest of the band on electric guitar because it was easier in the rehearsal room, saying "I don't know if this is right for the band as it is just a solo piece, about a minute and a half long". Phil said it sounded like there ought to be applause at the end of it. I'd been influenced by the length of a piece called *The Earl of Salisbury* by William Byrd, and what I liked about it was the brevity of it. It took me a whole year to write this short piece of music which is based on a Bach piece for cello. When it was done, I was very proud of it and thrilled that the band thought it was good enough to use. In the early days I really had an inferiority complex, you know, and before we were due to start recording FOXTROT I offered to leave the band because I didn't feel I'd contributed enough. I was frustrated that I had all these ideas but I couldn't really get them out. But they said, "No, we really like your guitar playing and want you to stay", and that made a real difference to me. I remember Ringo Starr telling a similar story about The Beatles: he offered to leave but they said no, they liked what he was playing. I think I underestimated my effect on the band. I was a bit too modest and what I hadn't realised was that the band was quite competitive, and so just because you didn't get an idea through it didn't mean it wasn't up to scratch. That was the case when Mike wrote the end of *Shadow Of The Hierophant* [a track which Hackett later elaborated and used on his first solo album VOYAGE OF THE ACOLYTE]. It was an amazing sound, it was like a whole world within itself, it had this circular effect of energy; the band sounded like an orchestra and yet it had the power of rock as well. It was rehearsed with the band and it could have (and I think should have) been on FOXTROT, I couldn't believe we could pass it by." (1)

Charisma Records celebrate the fifth anniversary of Charisma Records with an advert in *Ciao 2001*

## SUPPER'S READY

Gabriel: "We were gaining confidence. Live, we were going very well at that point, even though, you know, financially things weren't good. There was a great rapport with the audience building and it was beginning to move around other countries. That gave us the mental platform on which to build something like *Supper's Ready*, which is still one of the things I like best." [3]

*Supper's Ready* is a suite divided into seven movements lasting just over 23 minutes; a web of melodies, great progressive rock, typically English pantomime and an alternating of soft and loud sections which is pure genius.

Collins: "We didn't know what it was going to sound like till we spliced the tape together. *The Guaranteed Eternal Sanctuary Man* I think was Peter's, and *Willow Farm* was another one of his *Harold The Barrel* type things. The big instrumental parts took shape when we were rehearsing at 'Una Billings School of Dance' in Shepherd's Bush." [3]

Banks: "I think we were writing better together as a group, although a lot of the individual stuff was still there. On this album we'd come in with ideas, a riff, or something. The beginning of *Supper's Ready*, and what became the end section, was something I'd written on guitar at university. But the strongest stuff was written as a group, like *Apocalypse In 9/8*, which was something that Mike, Phil and I just wrote, improvising, working out a big keyboard solo together and a way of playing it." [3]

Rutherford: "*Supper's Ready* is the track that really made the album very special. And to think we never knew what we were doing. We had a whole lot of bits and then we started to string them together. The second half showed a bit more freedom. It was really just myself, Phil, Tony and Steve sort of jamming. We were just playing down at the bottom all the time, but with no movement, so Tony could move around the chords a lot, building up to that '666' bit, which was one of those few moments in our career where we actually got a great sounding thing and then Pete came in with a vocal line we hadn't sung together, he just laid it on top. We hadn't been rehearsing it like that, he just came in and it sounded fantastic. I would liken it to *Mama*, where the middle section came about in a similar way; we just went in and then Phil laid this vocal down which was just fantastic, you know, so strong. It shows a bit more freedom, because we [now] tend to write songs which are much more compact, here we would stay on a section for a bit longer and let things happen. What I've always loved about this business, as a writer, is that you learn it as you go along and there's luck. Things that seem quite effortless, as this was, are always good. The end section is very powerful but one of my favourite pieces is *Willow Farm*, which I think is like *Harold The Barrel* because it has a bit of that humour in it which was always important for us... had it been just a long song without this piece, *Supper's Ready* would have been a little straight." [3]

Hackett: "*Supper's Ready* works because it's so unusual; there are lots of bits in it. If you don't like one bit, that's over fairly quickly and you're onto another bit. If you didn't like the little acoustic folky bit, then you've got another bit full of time

*Ciao 2001* n. 44, 3 November 1972.

signatures and you've got a bit of 9/8... then eventually it all meets up because all roads lead to Rome in the end, and you've got Pete's apocalyptic take on it, lyrically speaking." (3)

Banks: "We decided we were really going to go for the long one this time. We'd done *The Musical Box* and *Stagnation* and we thought "well, let's just go for one whole side of an album, you know, 23 minutes of music and see what we can do". The song started off just like *Stagnation*: the first two or three minutes were based on this guitar piece I'd written which I thought was a really strong opening part with a lovely melody which we carried on developing. We added little tinkly bits and a few vocal bits, and I suddenly thought, if we weren't careful, it could end up sounding exactly like *The Musical Box*. So I said we should just stop the song, after a really romantic bit, and go straight into this other piece we had which was *Willow Farm*. We thought having this really *pretty* bit with this really *ugly*, cool sequence suddenly coming in after that would sound great. And so that's what we did. That suddenly took the whole song to another dimension, with the drums coming in and everything else. The second half of *Supper's Ready* becomes very electric and I think that produced our best piece of composition during the period with Peter, particularly from *Apocalypse In 9/8* onwards. It was just a coincidence to some extent, what happened there. It was another of those places where I had this keyboard solo that ended on these big chords and I had this idea of there just being some sort of vocal harmonies going on. Then Peter started singing on top of it you know, and I thought, "oh shit, here he goes again!" But when I heard it back I thought it sounded fantastic and it was the real peak of the song. You have the long build-up of this keyboard solo, which starts off very sweet and then gets slightly more sinister and then suddenly it's this big chord and then '666' comes in. It's an incredibly strong moment and I think for the early fans, it was the big moment on stage; it was tremendous. But I think *Supper's Ready* needed all the extra stuff at the beginning; it's like foreplay, you had to have all that to get to that one big moment. When we first heard it played back, I was very proud of it." (3)

David Hitchcock: "The end of *Supper's Ready* with the *Apocalypse In 9/8* section with the "666 is no longer alone" part. It is just so powerful. That part was spine tingling!" (4)

Hackett: "This was a time when rock music was getting more articulate, the chords were getting more complex. It was still very English sounding but there was a lot of humorous stuff as well, like the wonderful moment called *Willow Farm*, a very funny and very witty piece. I remember Pete and I telling the others that we couldn't present this great long piece of music live if we didn't have everything going for it, and so it had to have the lights, it had to have the sound effects. There was a certain resistance within the band that maybe it wasn't musical, maybe it was a bit gauche. I realised that they were going to crucify us if we didn't sling everything at it, and so we did and we got away with it. When you read interviews at the time, everyone felt very exposed, they felt they'd gone out on a limb. I think with *Supper's Ready*, this great long piece of meandering music going all over the place, we wondered if it wasn't indulgent and stretch-

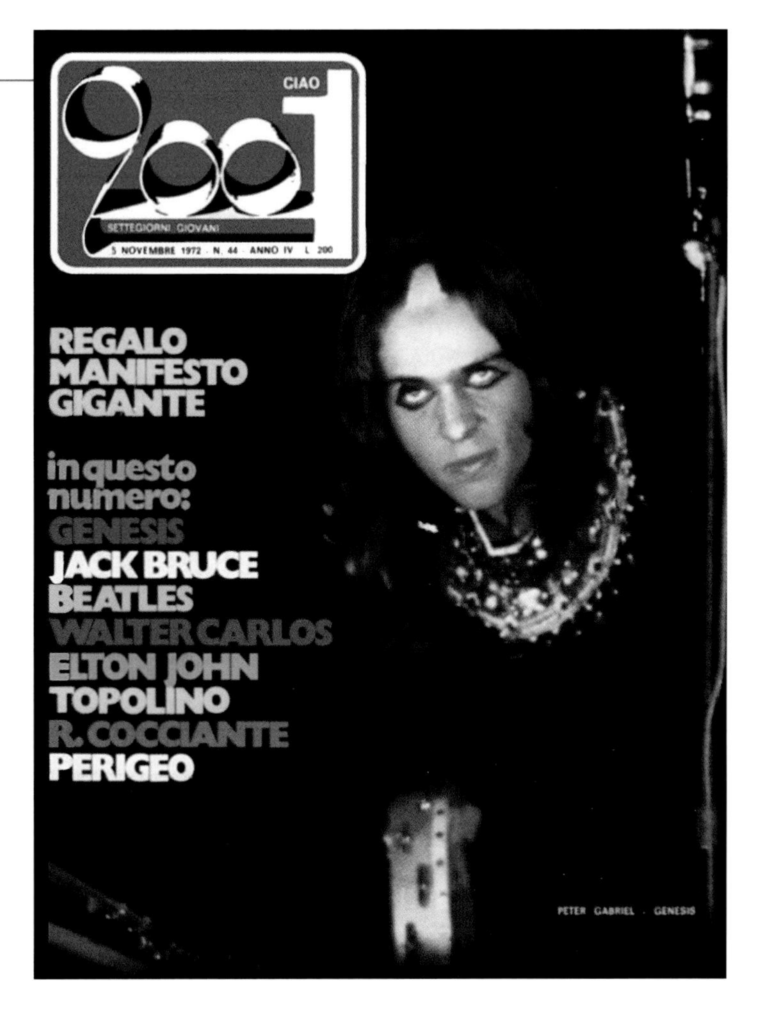


ing the attention span of a fickle audience. Luckily people came out in favour of it, saying it was really wonderful. We weren't preaching to the converted at that stage, we were in search of an audience so it was the antithesis of what was to follow (short songs, snappy videos and rhythm). In those days the audience was your judge and jury: there was no media back-up at that time, no radio support. If you did songs that were long, you weren't on the radio. That was that. Even if you did a short one, you had to queue up with all the rest. If the BBC didn't like you, you could wait in the wings forever. Luckily, we played to lots of great audiences and I think the theatrics helped tremendously. Everything got better, it got more professional." [(3)]

Banks: "Back in the 1970s they used to have these sort of polls, and I remember on Nicky Horne's show on Capital Radio, the number one rock track of all time was *Stairway to Heaven*, inevitably, but number two was *Supper's Ready*. That wouldn't happen now. One of the reasons for that is because it subsequently never gets played because it's too long. No radio station is going to play a song that's 23 minutes long, is it? That applies even in England, so it's not really known apart from by people who know and like the group and bought the album or saw the live shows. We were always tempted to try and do it on stage, but it is 23 minutes of a show and that's an awful lot of time to give over to one piece from that period. If we had done it on the tour [in 2007] we wouldn't have been able to do the *In The Cage* medley which has the advantage of being able to go into lots of different areas. Nor could we condense *Supper's Ready* into a 15-minute version because the fans would want to hear the whole thing." [(3)]

Mike Rutherford and Phil Collins in concert in St. Gallen, Switzerland, December 18, 1972.

Due to the length of the track, it was recorded at different times and even in different studios.

Banks: "Mike and I went into another studio to actually stick the two parts together because we'd run out of studio time. Incidentally, they were actually slightly out of tune, so we had to slow down the track in order to make it work; something we were able to rectify in the remixes." (3)

Hackett: "The new mixes have fixed certain things, for example, there was a moment of confusion when we had machines running at different tape speeds. I expect there are all these bands out there trying to copy that, wondering how we managed to get that quarter tone moment. It's lovely to hear our music sounding really good, but at the same time there's always this problem, when you do remixes, with the purists thinking that you're messing with their childhoods, "how dare you remix that?". But you've just got to accept that these are different mixes. If you liked it the old way, the older grainier stuff, that's still there, you can compare it." (3)

The first section of the song, *Lovers' Leap*, is a delightful acoustic sketch based (albeit not exclusively) on a piece of music written by Tony.

Hackett: "The opening sequence is Tony Banks', it's the same chord sequence Procol Harum used on *A Salty Dog*. There are three 12-strings at the beginning playing the same part: me, Mike and Tony, with Tony's guitar going through two Leslie cabinets. Mike also played cello and I think bass pedals as well. He used Vox bass pedals in those days. Now Pete, when he sang this originally, he sang up an octave, you can hear the strained voice at the top. It didn't sound right to my mind, so I suggested he sang an octave down and we had the two at the same time." (1)

Before the second subsection of the song, there is a long acoustic interlude [from 1'58"] upon which Peter and Phil's vocal harmonies and subsequently the electric piano are layered.

Hackett: "This was my bit, with two 12-strings playing in harmony. The idea of the vocals fading in and out [2'11"] was mine as well and then Tony plays the melody on the Hohner Pianet. All of this part with the acoustic guitars was recorded with Bob Potter but I think that's as far as we got with him. This was a substantial way into the song and we were worried that it didn't sound right because the producer didn't like it. It turns out there was nothing wrong with it, just the wrong combination of characters. There's this thing about the Genesis 12-string; it sounds like a harpsichord, like a keyboard. So even when we used

guitars they sounded like keyboards and sometimes the keyboards sounded like guitars." (1)

*The Guaranteed Eternal Sanctuary Man* is again mainly Tony's work and dates back to a much earlier period. Hackett: "This was from another song that we already had, a very '60s early chord sequence, very deliberately naive. I did this, very economical guitar work." (1)

It is a section in which the song builds up rhythmically with the drums coming in and the heart-wrenching riffs of the solo guitar while Gabriel strains his voice almost to breaking point. Hackett: "I think it was a difficult area for Pete. It's very high for him as you can hear." (1)

This takes us to the part where children's voices sing a slightly menacing chant [5'30"].

Hackett: "I don't think I was in the studio when that was recorded. It's a parody of *The Rocking Carol*, actually. Peter just went out in the street and got a whole bunch of kids in and said, "Do you want to come and record something?" and so they did." (1)

*Ikhnaton And Itsacon And Their Band Of Merry Men* is a much more dynamic and lively section.

Hackett: "This is really based on Mike's strumming on the 12-string but my guitar is very loud in the mix, so you can hear I'm playing a note but I'm also flicking the toggle switch to give it different tones. The idea behind the line "And they're giving me a wonderful potion 'Cos I cannot contain my emotion", I may be wrong, but I think we were talking about Vietnam, about guys who were out of their brains in battle. Of course, it's not a new idea is it? People often went into battle drunk, the English Navy with their tots of rum.... At 7'39" I play harmonics, but unfortunately my guitar playing is very out of time, I should have relaxed more. Then [8'03"] there's some tapping, with Tony

*Watcher Of The Skies* in the short version for Italian jukeboxes.

doing it in harmony as well on the Hohner Pianet, through a fuzz box, and echoing my phrase on the organ. This section was a kind of collaboration of everyone, really. The sustained guitar note [at 9'00"] sounds almost like a flute. I also used a small amp, a Fender Champ Jazz Tone." (1)

The scene slows down into the gentle *How Dare I Be So Beautiful?*, where Peter's singing lies on top of a bizarre keyboard crescendo and diminuendo.

Hackett: "From here the album gets very interesting sonically. It's piano [9'39"] but each time a chord is played, a fader on the desk comes in after the note has been struck. It's the sort of thing that guitarists do, play a note and fade in the volume pedal later. I think this depicts the disorientation of battle very well [referring to the lyrics] and I think the sharp contrast between this section and the incoming section is very good. This part is more Genesis-like and the next one more Beatlesque: a Burlesque pantomime, but very good with the whole band playing as one." (1)

The guitarist here is, of course, referring to *Willow Farm*, fomented by a sudden change in pace it evolves into a section divided into two parts. This very English and bizarre part of the song was written entirely by Gabriel, who sings it with different voices.

Hackett: "The voice was modified with pitch shift over a base of Mellotron brass, organ and distorted guitar. Peter wanted to separate the two parts with "All Change!" So I said why not make it like a train station, why not have the sound of slamming doors and trains? So Peter found a tape and we used that on the recording and when we did it live as well. King Crimson had done LIZARD around this time, which has a similar sound sonically (Mellotron brass, organ and distorted guitar or distorted bass)." (1)

Strange and difficult-to-recognise voices sing "the soil, the soil" [13'20"]. Hackett: "I think it's Pete and Phil. Pete always wanted to be on his own when he recorded vocals, he didn't want anyone else around, so maybe just him and Phil. He wanted to be left alone. He didn't want the comments of everybody else, which I understand totally. In the end, his voice is very subconscious sounding, almost like *Coronation Street* [a well-known British television series]." (1)

After the final riff of *Willow Farm*, there is an almost sinister interlude. Hackett: "[14'14"] Here I'm playing very high notes on the Les Paul which sounds more like a celesta. The guitar and the flute playing together owe something to the *Dance Of The Sugar Plum Fairy* [by Tchaikovsky] because it has a sort of calm after the storm effect. But just when you think it's going to wind down and go out, the song really starts to brew up with the next section in 9/8; an unlikely 9/8 repeated riff with a keyboard solo over the top of it." (1)

*Apocalypse In 9/8* is without doubt the real gem in the whole of *Supper's Ready*, a long section with an irregular rhythm which starts and finishes with Gabriel singing, but which in the middle exploits a long instrumental improvisation with Mike and Steve on rhythm guitars, Phil's momentous drumming and a splendid organ solo from Banks.

Collins: "I remember I had something to do in the afternoon. When I came back, Mike and Tony had basically written *Apocalypse In 9/8*. Tony had written this riff without thinking about the time signature. I maybe played it once or twice, but never really thought about it too much and we went in to record it still not really knowing what it was. It was one of those moments where the tape was playing and recording and it just captured what was probably one of our best spontaneous moments. That's probably my favourite song on the album. I still listen to it and can't quite work out how it just all happened at the right time." (3)

Hackett: "I was trying to make the sound of a muted trumpet and I used to have to try and think metronomically about this riff and not allow myself to get distracted by anything that was going on around me. I'm playing in octaves and Mike's playing bass pedals. Live we would sometimes switch roles and I'd be playing the bass pedals; a very difficult thing to do whilst sitting down, you get repetitive strain injury playing bass pedals that way. Phil is really the only one who is improvising here, his part is spontaneous, with no overdubs. Something may have been overdubbed, but not the drums, we didn't overdub drums in those days; more's the pity for Phil, he was stuck with whatever he did first of all. At the end of this section you have Mellotron and organ again with Mike and I playing the riff and Pete doubling it on oboe as well [18'56"]." (1)

The music slows down after Peter's voice comes back in and the suite turns around on itself; *As Sure As Eggs Is Eggs* picks up the initial melody of *Lovers' Leap* [20'10"].

Hackett: "I suggested that the return of the vocal melody should be done, like a sort of salute, so I suggested the bells and the snare drum roll so it would be almost anthemic and sound almost patriotic... And then you have the same melody as "I know a fireman" [20'49"], from earlier. This was always an interesting sound, a combo of guitar and Tony's keyboards; there's something about that combination." (1)

After a last phase sung by Gabriel, the guitarist launches himself into some solo parts.

Hackett: "We were trying to finish the LP while we were touring in Italy. As soon as the second tour finished [August 1972] I flew back as I still had to do my guitar work on the end of *Supper's Ready*. I was the only one lucky enough to have a plane ticket, the rest were driving back overnight in a van that was moving very slowly. I wasn't trying to be a star about it, it's just that my parts needed to be done to complete the album. So I did these phrases on the end and luckily Phil liked them very much; they were his favourite..." (1)

In the 2008 remastered edition, a few extra seconds have been left in where you can hear additional, previously unknown, guitar parts. Hackett:

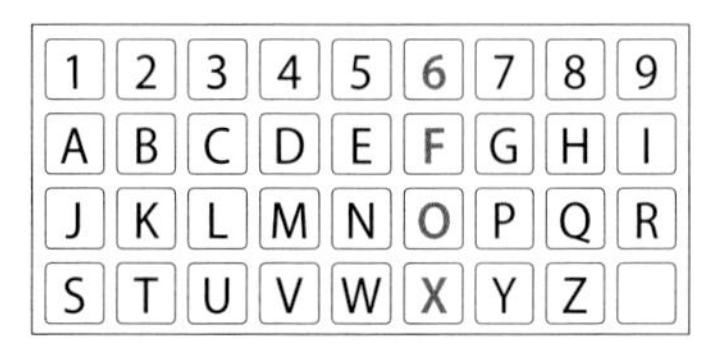


"I recorded a lot. There's tapping on some of the last phrases, a lot of reverb and repeat echo on the guitar which comes through it almost like a fanfare." [1]

The composite and multifaceted music is accompanied by transcendental lyrics, written entirely by Gabriel, full of references which cannot possibly be summarised in just a few sentences; in extreme synthesis, it can be said that it celebrates good triumphing over evil.

Hackett: "I know Pete felt particularly close to this piece, he really meant it. I gather that some of it relates to a personal experience that he had. It's very personal to Pete. I can tell you to what it alludes. There is a Turner painting called '*The Angel Standing in the Sun*', I think it relates to that, but there is also some stuff from The Book of Revelation, like '666' [the Number of the Beast in The New Testament]. Pete was also into this idea that Pythagoras used to write backwards in a mirror, codes and stuff for secrecy." [1]

Gabriel: "*Supper's Ready* was again one of those journey songs, where we really tried to take people along this dream/journey. When it worked and we got to the 'New Jerusalem' part at the end, you could really feel you were touching people. There was a guy who'd been Édith Piaf's promoter in Paris, I remember when he heard it for the first time, he invited us to perform it in his church in Normandy, and this was a guy who didn't normally relate to rock music. There were different ways you could capture people's imagination. We were beginning to know who we were as writers and also know how to deliver it as performers. It's a coming of age piece, I think, in lots of ways." [3]

## THE ALBUM ARTWORK

Arguably one of the most loved by Genesis fans, this album cover is, oddly enough, the one least liked by the band members.

Rutherford: "I think the album cover was a little weak. I was never convinced about this one and this was the last time we used Paul Whitehead. I think the lovely atmosphere on Trespass and Nursery Cryme lies in the fact that they felt like paintings and they had a nice texture. This felt a little bit… it was OK, but he just put together a bunch of images that were in the lyrics." [3]

Gabriel: "I was less happy with this sleeve than I was with the first two. We'd already worked with Paul and got identified with him, but I think the style was losing some of its appeal to me, even though I think the fox character, related to hunting and the hunted, worked. I was looking at all sorts of esoteric stuff and numerology at that time. In numerology each letter carries a certain value and so I wrote out abcdef... The next time you come round you get to O and then you get to X all of which are under the number 6 (see diagram above), so there was this Revelation reference, 666 and all that crap, you know, a sort of hidden element to it which we were just playing around with. It wasn't the backwards-playing-devil-worshipping version but this mixture of Christian and Pagan symbolism." [3]

Collins: "For me, the artwork was getting a little bit busy and I guess that was one of the reasons this was the last one Paul Whitehead did for us. I mean, Trespass did have, you know, an elegance about it, Nursery Cryme was more butch but this was just a bit busy... the lady figure with the fox's

The single *Watcher Of The Skies* for the German market.

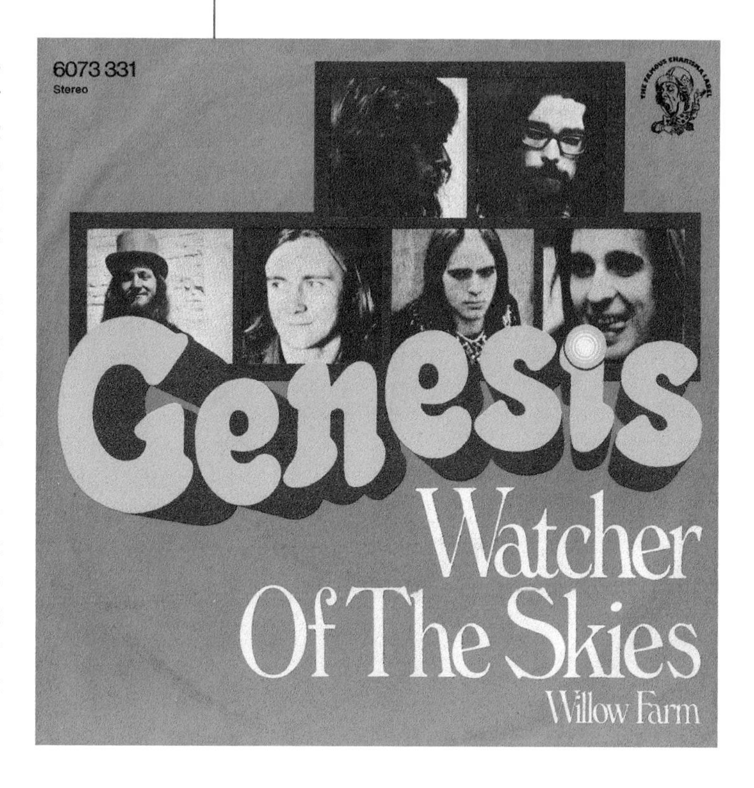


head, the bit of ice, the water. It didn't look professional for some reason. It's all a bit dated now. It does sum up the album, the period and I thought it was OK but not particularly special." (3)

Hackett: "When I first saw it I wasn't sure about it, to be honest. It looked rather like a collage of unlikely things, a number of cut-outs. Since then I've come to understand the concept of collage a little more and I think it works. It had this sort of flat, one-dimensional look because it was collage, but I don't know what was painted and what was pasted on." (3)

Banks: "I thought this was the weakest of the album covers Paul Whitehead did for us, certainly at that time, and it's rather difficult to view it objectively now. The mockery of the hunt was his idea and it doesn't really relate to anything on the album. We sort of managed to give it a sense with the album title, FOXTROT, you know to help rationalise it a little bit. Anyway, the album cover depicted Peter's costume after he started wearing it on stage and not the other way round." (3) [Banks is actually mistaken: Gabriel started wearing the red dress with the fox's head only at the end of September 1972, when the album was already finished and pressed ready for release the next month.]

## EPILOGUE

Released throughout the world on 6 October 1972, FOXTROT represents Genesis' first real commercial success. For the first time ever they made it into the UK charts (number 12) while in Italy, according to some music magazines from the time, it may even have reached the top of the charts.

Rutherford: "FOXTROT always appears to me as an album where things took us by surprise, particularly the end section of *Supper's Ready*. Later on in our career that happened a lot more often, but in those days there were five of us, full of ideas,

Peter Gabriel in the dressing room, freshly made up, before the concert on December 18, 1972 in St. Gallen, Switzerland.

almost too many ideas going around, so bits like this where things could just happen a bit more freely were great." (3)

Collins: "I have very fond memories of recording this album. We did most of it at Island Studios in Basing Street and John Burns was the engineer who helped us. Hearing those things and *Supper's Ready* put together, it was very strong. We felt we were actually getting somewhere, we had a great album and it came out and did better than the one before. There are a couple of songs that I don't remember at all, for example *Time Table*; I have no idea what that song sounds like or anything. Of course *Horizons* was the guitar thing that started *Supper's Ready*, but the ones that stand out are undoubtedly *Supper's Ready* and *Watcher Of The Skies*. There are some things in *Can-Utility And The Coastliners* that I liked and I think I wrote a little bit of that, but I can't remember what it was now." (3)

Banks: "On the whole, this is probably my favourite of the band's early albums. It felt like we really came of age with FOXTROT. It got to number 12 in the charts which was a staggering thing for us. It was the first album where we sounded convincing to the outside world; we only convinced ourselves and maybe our fans with the first two albums, but, with FOXTROT, people could hear this album who had never heard of Genesis before and be interested in it. It wasn't a big hit but it certainly sold a lot more copies than its predecessors." (3)

Hackett: "It's a multifaceted album. It's heavily influenced by classical music but there is English humour in there as well, and I think having that parody, that send-up, was a very British trait. I remember Tony Stratton-Smith saying that he thought FOXTROT showed the breadth of the band's writing. I think we were a lot less certain when we played *Supper's Ready* to him. We thought he was going to say, "Sorry boys, we're going to have to tear up your contract", because it was so extreme and long and convoluted. It touched on so many areas. I must say I was surprised when he received it so enthusiastically. He was more enthusiastic about that than he was about SELLING ENGLAND. Going back to the time when it was conceived, we had our critics and supporters and we didn't know who was going to win. It parallels on a much smaller scale with what the Beatles had with SGT. PEPPER'S; they never knew if people would like it or not, it was so drastically different, it's as far removed from pop as a band can go without moving into free jazz. I'm sure I have a different take on it all now than I did at the time: when I hear SGT. PEPPER'S I don't mind if it's not in time or in tune (because lots of it isn't), but when I hear Genesis I want to hear it played perfectly. But it wasn't to be, it was recorded quickly and between tours." (1)

Gabriel: "I never really listen to the old albums, unless I'm, you know, in an interview situation. [But when I do] it's amazing how quickly you fall back into those old roles and still want different things done in different tracks! I think you would probably get five different versions of all the songs if you allowed the different members of the band to do their own mix. And it's not just a question of the *'more me'* syndrome, it's just that sometimes there are different approaches and tastes. I didn't really get involved that much with the remixing. I made some comments on some of the stuff I was involved in and I encouraged adopting a certain approach with the 5.1, where you have three speakers at the front and the two at the back

Tony Banks in concert
in Reggio Emilia on 20 January 1973.

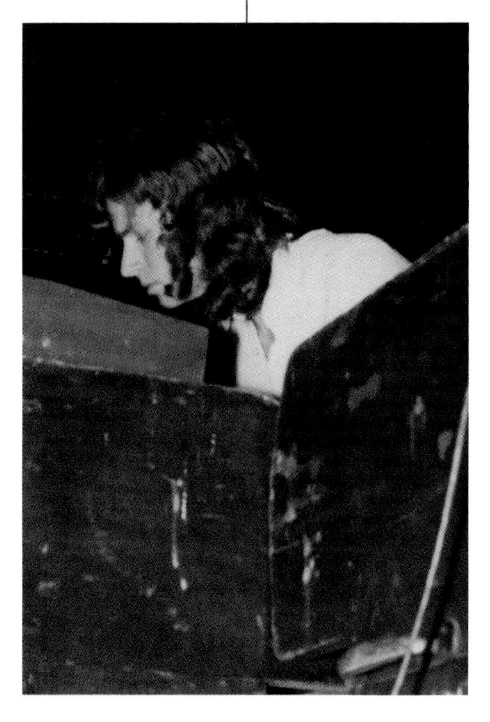

because a lot of people have two back speakers which are throwaway, you know, which cost half as much as the ones at the front. So you are either afraid of that and therefore mix very conservatively, like enhanced stereo, or you say "Fuck it! Let's just do it for people who have got the good systems and really make use and take advantage of being in this sort of three-dimensional environment". That's the way I prefer." (3)

Foxtrot proves just how much Genesis were a band open to external stimuli.

Hackett: "I think a lot of Genesis tracks are only nominally rock pieces; we were influenced by Joni Mitchell and Judy Collins, and Buffy Sainte-Marie, in my case, as much as we listened to Led Zeppelin. I loved Bach and blues, Mike liked folk as well as heavy stuff, and Tony loved classical music but he also liked a lot of pop, he was a big fan of The Beatles. I remember us being interviewed by Melody Maker, we were all asked the same question, which we answered separately, no conferring: what our favourite single was. And 4 out of 5 of us said *MacArthur Park* written by Jimmy Webb and sung by Richard Harris. When you listen to it you realise you've got this parallel with a lot of Genesis tracks where you've got this verse and chorus thing followed by a weird middle bit and then a long instrumental before you recapitulate towards the end. It's a little bit more like a sort of concerto form. We'd all listened to Jimmy Webb and thought he was brilliant and still do. How many bands would combine a love of big band stuff with Buddy Rich, Shostakovich, Prokofiev, Bach and, in my case, Howlin' Wolf and Paul Butterfield and masses of blues players?" (3)

But Foxtrot is also an album where the qualities of all the band members forcefully emerge, in a formidable collective which is the union of five great individuals.

Hackett: "The strange thing, when you're in a band, is that you don't really realise how great everyone is, you just see the others as the guys who play their own respective instruments. You haven't got time when you're a cog in the wheel of this thing that has to keep motoring. It's only when you've had years to reflect and listen to everyone's work both collectively and individually that you realise just how great everyone was individually and how they've all become gurus in their own right. A bit like Monty Python whom we shared the label with [Monty Python was also signed to Charisma]; everybody's work stood

Steve Hackett in concert in Reggio Emilia on January 20, 1973.

out, you realise it was more than the sum of the parts. It's funny because I think each of the guys has written a song at some point that could move me to tears, and you can't say that about most bands. Bands don't come like that. There's usually one guy who's the lynchpin and everyone sort of follows the indications of the one who is the musical director. Genesis wasn't like that, we were like a sort of musical co-op that had its strengths and weaknesses. Sometimes very good ideas could get shafted at the committee stage. Sometimes the best ideas just had to be fought through like a cavalry charge and that can be very difficult to do in a band that is a democracy. So, I mean luckily we gave each other enough leeway to make a lot of great things happen. I think it's true that the founding members did tend to hold sway, but nonetheless, we were all listened to and that's important. I quickly realised that the best way of working was to bring out the best in all the others, so if anyone did anything that I thought was remotely good, I would always say it sounded really good and we should use it in something. I felt I was being the glue, but maybe everyone else will have a different take on it and say I was always arguing against them, that I was always competing. Even these days, whenever I work with people, it's always the same thing, if someone does something absolutely fantastic, I tell him he can do it again. You've always got to have the tapes rolling from the word go." [3]

Charisma postcard from 1973 (the picture was taken in Central Park, New York, in December of the previous year.)

# THE CONCERTS

With the Italian tour over and the recording of FOXTROT completed, it looked like Genesis were back to the same old routine. In September they began touring the usual clubs in the UK, including Friars in Aylesbury, where they had built up quite a fan base, and the Marquee in London. They also managed to squeeze in an appearance at the Franche-Comté Pop Festival in Montbéliard, France, on the 9th, alongside Van Der Graaf Generator, Caravan and Matching Mole to name but a few.

The setlist during this phase was pretty well-defined and generally included *Watcher Of The Skies / Can-Utility And The Coastliners / Get 'Em Out By Friday / The Musical Box / The Return Of The Giant Hogweed / The Knife*, with the occasional appearance of *Twilight Alehouse* and *The Fountain Of Salmacis*.

The end of the month brought with it two very important events: on the 25th the band were back in the BBC's Studio T1 for another radio session, this time for the John Peel show 'Top Gear' (playing magnificent live versions of *Watcher Of The Skies, Twilight Alehouse* and *Get 'Em Out By Friday*) and on the 28th they had their very first gig in Ireland. And it was here, in Dublin, that the unimaginable happened thanks to Gabriel's fantastic imagination. While the band were playing the long instrumental part of *The Musical Box*, the lead singer sneaked off into the wings only to reappear wearing the most extraordinary costume: a long red dress (belonging to his wife, Jill) and a fox's head. The costume had absolutely nothing to do with the story of Henry, now transformed into the lecherous old man desperate to seduce his childhood playmate Cynthia, but brought to life the main character depicted on the FOXTROT album cover, even though the album still wasn't available in most record shops. Gabriel's initiative also took his unsuspecting bandmates completely by surprise. One of them actually found it rather annoying.

Banks: "Well, wouldn't it surprise you if your lead singer suddenly walked out on stage in a red dress and a fox's head? He did it in this boxing ring in Dublin, at the end of *The Musical Box*. When we first saw it, we didn't know what was happening, we thought the stage was being invaded. Then suddenly we realised it was Peter in a dress." [3]

Gabriel: "Paul Conroy (who was working as our agent), Glen Colson (Charisma press director) and I

Poster for the Oxford concert on 19th February, 1973. The support band on the British tour was String Driven Thing. Tickets cost just 70 pence.

were talking about ways of trying to market this record. Paul got the music but it wasn't really Glen's cup of tea at all. When they saw the cover with this fox character, they thought maybe we should pay someone a few quid to wear a fox's head. I thought, "if we were going to do that then I should try doing it". So I took a red dress from my wife's wardrobe. She's told me since that it was an Ossie Clark dress, probably worth quite a lot now, and I could just about get into it. The first gig where I put the fox's head on was actually in this old boxing ring in Dublin. Nowadays it is a very progressive, tolerant and open City, but at that point there was a shocked silence when I walked out on stage: seeing a man in a dress and a sort of animal head created this visceral sense of shock that you could feel, and I thought, "oh, that's interesting, we should do this a bit more"." (3)

Rutherford: "Pete probably realised that if he tried to run it by the band and get a committee vote on it, we'd all have said, "you've got to be kidding". So he cleverly appeared on stage with a red dress and a fox's head and we all kind of just went, wow! I think it was in a boxing ring in Belfast or Dublin, but, of course, it's funny how these things turn out, the next week we were on the front page of Melody Maker. It wasn't done intentionally for that reason but it makes you realise that, as is always the problem with the press, they like to write about stuff that's nothing to do with the music." (3)

Banks: "We were never going to compromise the music but something like that can get you a lot of publicity and obviously it developed from that into all the other stuff." (3)

Peter's gimmick gained a lot of visibility for Gen-

Steve Hackett in concert in St. Gallen, Switzerland, December 18, 1972.

esis, raising interest and curiosity in their music. A classic example, in other words, of the end justifying the means.

Two days later Melody Maker put on the so-called '1972 Poll Awards Concert' at the Oval in Kennington, London, featuring some of the best musicians of the year. Headlining were Emerson, Lake & Palmer, with Wishbone Ash, Argent and the Dutch band, Focus, also performing.

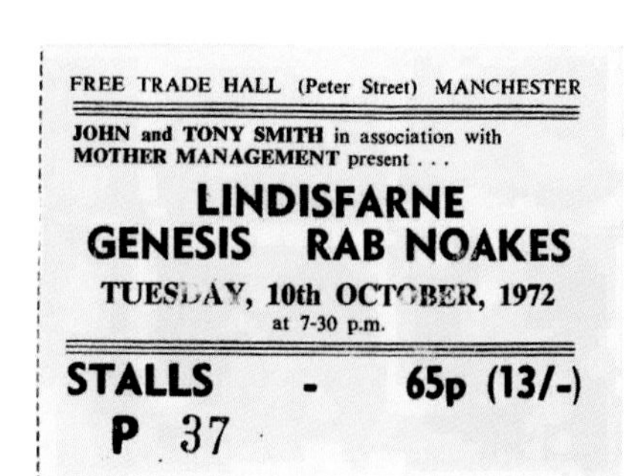


Genesis prepared a setlist with a completely different running order for the occasion, opening (as they had done at the Reading Festival on 11 August) with *The Knife* followed by *The Fountain Of Salmacis, Get 'Em Out By Friday, Watcher Of The Skies, The Musical Box* and *The Return Of The Giant Hogweed.*

For most of October, Genesis were busy with a series of gigs in the UK alongside Lindisfarne (usually the headliners) and Rab Noakes, although there were occasions when Genesis were the main attraction with Noakes sometimes opening for them. On 2 November at the Hard Rock Concert Theatre, Manchester, Capability Brown (another Charisma band) opened for Genesis. Genesis were becoming increasingly better-known and even though they were still occasionally opening for bigger bands, their growth in popularity was evident. During this period the band's stage set-up was changed around, with Hackett and Rutherford swapping places: the bespectacled guitarist was now on the far left of the stage with Mike placed slightly further back between Steve and Peter.

Apart from the odd familar episode dictated by the usual technical issues (to fill in the gap caused by the Mellotron breaking down in Aberdeen on 4 October, preventing the immediate start of *Watcher Of The Skies*, Phil came in with his usual drum solo), the UK tour saw yet another evolution in the setlist. Most notably starting on 10 November when Genesis presented the complete version of *Supper's Ready* for the first time ever at Uxbridge.

Rutherford: "The fact that we could go out and play one side of an album to people who had never heard it, and they actually loved it, was a compliment to the music. *Supper's Ready* still works today; we played it for quite a long time when Phil was the singer. I didn't realise till Phil sent me a YouTube link, how much he actually sang in the early days. I couldn't believe it: Phil doubled the whole of the first part of *Supper's Ready*! When Peter left and Phil started singing, people forget that Phil's voice had always been there." [3]

Including such a long song in the setlist obviously led to further changes: *The Fountain Of Salmacis* and *Twilight Alehouse* disappeared (although they were occasionally reinstated) along with *Can-Utility And The Coastliners* (gone for good). Banks: "I think you just move on to the next album and you have to ditch some songs. *Can-Utility And The Coastliners* was more difficult and we didn't feel it sounded quite so good live, the first part in

particular. It was a song we played live sometimes, but it's just we had too much material and it was one that the band wasn't too keen on playing." [2]

About a week later, on the 18th, Genesis were booked to play at Imperial College, London. The setlist they performed (*Watcher Of The Skies / The Musical Box / Get 'Em Out By Friday / Supper's Ready / The Return Of The Giant Hogweed / The Knife*) was now the standard and was continuously being tried and tested in preparation for a particularly important event: their first appearance in The States.

The band's US debut was anything but simple, mainly because Genesis wasn't particularly well-known and due to the fact that America is an immense country divided into different and culturally distinct states. In order to test the terrain, the group debuted with what can be described as a trial concert to which journalist and sector workers were invited at Brandeis University, Waltham, Massachusetts. This was a prelude to their first real concert on US soil, which took place on 13 December at the prestigious Philharmonic Hall in New York. The show was presented as a 'Christmas concert' by Charisma in collaboration with WNEW-FM radio, and had another British band, String Driven Thing, as openers. Things got off to a difficult start with Genesis being given only a very short time to soundcheck as the venue was occupied for hours by Leonard Bernstein, the famous conductor, who was rehearsing with his orchestra. Despite the various technical issues, mainly due to the different power supply voltage, Genesis' performance went down exceptionally well with the audience making the band's first brief appearance on US soil a positive experience.

The following day, the band and Stratton-Smith returned to London and on the 16th they went to Hamburg and then on to St. Gallen in Switzerland. Here, at the Hotel Ekkehard, the band played to an audience of about 500 and Gabriel, despite running a fever, managed to complete the show, thus saving the newly-established 'Swiss Rock Circus' company, which had organised the show as their business debut.

After a Christmas break (a very difficult time for Phil whose father died unexpectedly) on 10 January 1973, Genesis returned to Paris for a concert at the well-known Bataclan. This time, however, there was a television crew waiting for them. The resulting film footage, lasting 38 minutes (which would appear in fans' collections in increasingly better quality VHS versions and was finally officially released on the DVD accompanying the remastered SELLING ENGLAND BY THE POUND in 2008), includes a few short interviews and large sections of the four songs: *The Musical Box, Supper's Ready, The Return Of The Giant Hogweed* and *The Knife.* The first two are particularly interesting in that after the instrumental interlude of *The Musical Box,* Gabriel comes on stage wearing the red, low-neck dress and the fox's head, making it the only existing video of this particular costume, which was soon to be retired. *Supper's Ready,* on the other hand, was marked by a very poor performance by Gabriel, who was evidently not in good vocal shape and closed on a note in crescendo and not in fade-out as would be the case later on.

The international growth of Genesis was slow but unstoppable. Following their appearance at the Bataclan, other concerts had been booked for France, in Mulhouse and Strasbourg (already postponed to 12 and 13 January over the original dates of 19 and 20 December 1972) which, however, ended up being cancelled definitively, along with the date in Geneva, Switzerland on 14 January, so that Genesis could perform in Germany.

Genesis played four gigs in Germany together with headliners Lindisfarne and Capability Brown, the first of which, in Frankfurt on 14 January, was also recorded by a local radio station (although only two songs were actually aired: *Watcher Of The Skies* and *The Musical Box*). In Heidelberg, the following day (the 15th) *Twilight Alehouse* made a comeback to the setlist, ending on yet another Collins drum solo, which was added to cover up the usual technical issues before *Get 'Em Out By Friday.*

It was then time to return to Italy after the two tours of the previous year. This time, however, things were very different. After the initial success enjoyed with NURSERY CRYME, in Italy FOXTROT was a big hit and the results were immediately evident, even though the limited organisational capacity of the country once more came to light. In fact, what became known as the 'Charisma Pop Festival' due to the participation of Peter Hammill with David Jackson, Capability Brown and Lindisfarne (now all reduced to being support acts with Genesis headlining) was initially planned for 18 January in Rome and on the 20th in Milan. The show in Rome was

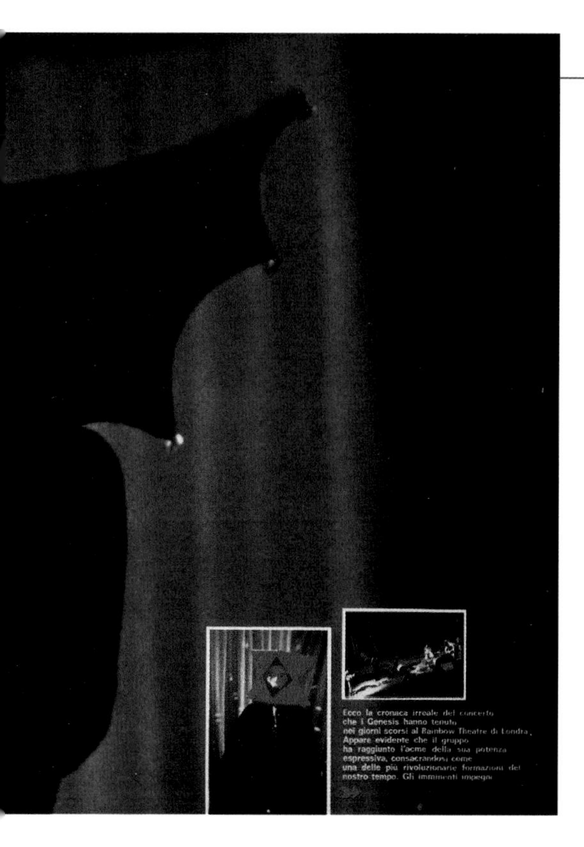


*Ciao 2001* n.15, April 15th 1973.

moved first to the 19th and then to the 22nd, so the first date in Italy became the one on the 20th which instead of being in Milan was moved to Reggio Emilia. The turnout, however, was spectacular: 8,000 tickets were sold for the Reggio Emilia date and 18,000 for Rome, an incredible number for a band which in its homeland, except for the occasional event, only managed to draw in audiences of a few hundred, sometimes less according to Richard Macphail: "I distinctly remember one week where we played in Rome to thousands of people in a huge stadium and then came back to England and we were playing the next gig in a basement club in Peterborough to twenty-five not very interested people. And the contrast was just really extraordinary." (6)

Once again, the concerts in Italy, as well as being a triumph in terms of audience, were also an amazing success from an artistic point of view. The biggest surprise in a setlist, which included *Watcher Of The Skies / The Musical Box / The Fountain Of Salmacis / Get 'Em Out By Friday / Supper's Ready / The Return Of The Giant Hogweed / The Knife*, was the return of *The Fountain of Salmacis*.

Hackett: "It's a complex song and it was difficult to play. You had to concentrate very hard and it went down very badly with audiences; every time we played it they were really stony at the end of it and we didn't understand why. So we stopped doing it. We believed in it so much, but audiences were left cold by it, except in Italy where it was more appreciated. It was so far removed from rock and roll, and we hadn't really found an audience for it at this stage, I don't believe they started playing it again live until after I left, when they did it with Daryl [Stuermer] when the band was more established internationally. It was a song out of time really, but it was the thing we were proudest of. We continued to do *The Musical Box* because it seemed that it was easier for audiences to get that, whereas the overtly symphonic nature of *Fountain Of Salmacis* was a bit much for them. Perhaps we did a better version of *The Musical Box* live as we had been playing it for a while already; there was a version of it before we recorded it and it had been honed in front of audiences and it already had its approval." (1)

For February another long UK tour was planned with tickets being sold for just 70p which was set to be a turning point in the band's popularity on home turf. All sorts happened, in particular on 9 February when Genesis played at the prestigious Rainbow Theatre, with String Driven Thing opening for them; regardless of the concerns within the band, Gabriel brought with him a whole trunk of costume changes to be adapted to the various songs, starting with the opening of *Watcher Of The Skies*.

Banks: "We used to bring in the whole show with this and it may sound like a cliché, but we had the dry ice and Peter had the make-up on and his bat wings and stuff. It was just a stunning intro; something you could only see at a Genesis concert, nothing else was like it. We put the Mellotron through the PA, with an echo so it had a big stereo effect which was very unusual in those days." (3)

Gabriel: "*Watcher Of The Skies* was sci-fi meets prog. I used to wear UV make-up. The show would start in darkness and then the UV lights would slowly come on and these big droning chords would appear out of nowhere. Then you'd see these two little points of light which were my eyes lit up and we had a white backcloth at that time." (3)

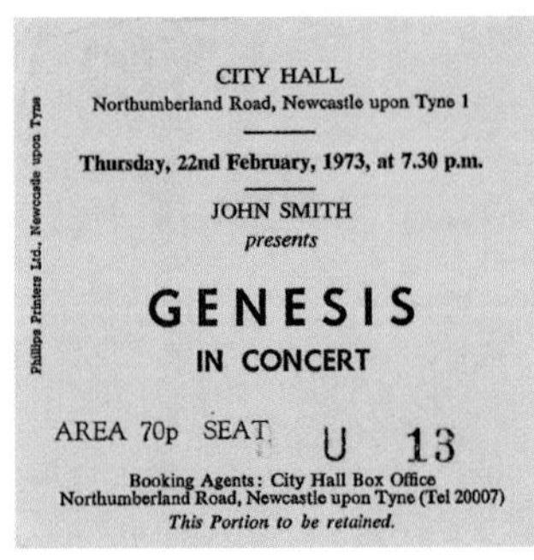


While in *Get 'Em Out By Friday* he would change various hats to interpret the different characters, Gabriel reached his biggest transformation yet in *Supper's Ready*, alternating a crown of thorns headpiece (*The Guaranteed Eternal Sanctuary Man*), his famous flower mask (*Willow Farm*) and the geometrical orange headdress for *Apocalypse In 9/8*.

Collins: "His wardrobe was well stocked with things by this point. And, of course, we never saw anything until it happened. The classic example is when he walked on stage halfway through *The Musical Box* wearing the fox's head and the red dress. We all kind of looked around wondering what the hell it was all about. I don't remember what the reaction was apart from surprise. I've read that Pete said he was tired of conferences about it, but I don't remember there being any conferences. I don't remember being asked or there being any trouble. Not till years later, when I said in the press that I was a bit frustrated about the fact that the five of us would be playing and responsible for the music but Pete would be getting all the praise. The record company executives were just sort of you know, "Excuse me, excuse me" [pushing past the other band members to get to Gabriel] and, of course, reviewers tended to talk about what he wore rather than the music. At that point we'd still have a laugh about it. It wasn't until we got to a couple of albums later, when he couldn't really get a microphone close enough to his mouth for him to be able to sing into it (or by the time he did he was too tired from having to) that we started to think it had gone a little bit too far." (3)

Gabriel: "Phil, I think understands and knows how to work with an audience now, but at that

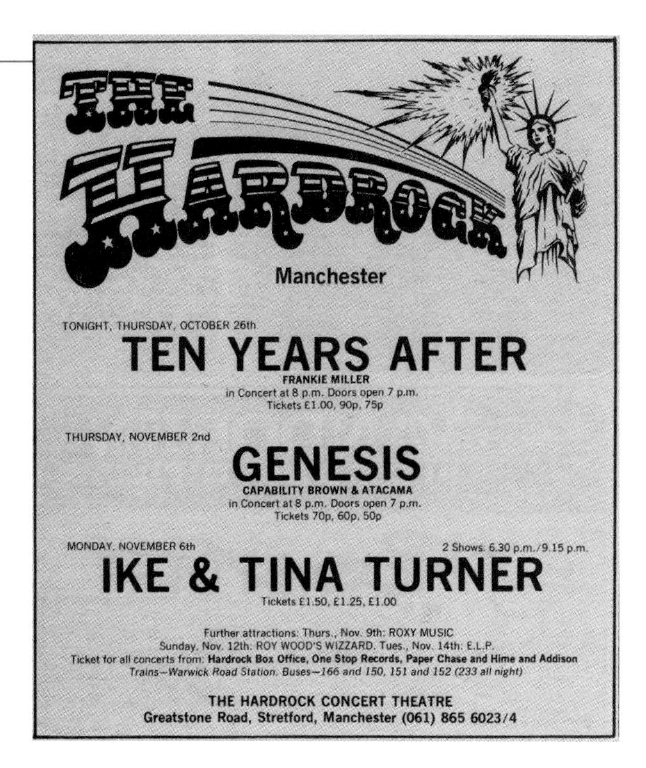


Event programme for The Hardrock Theatre, Manchester, November 1972.

point he was 'Mr. Pure-Jazzo-Muso', you know: "don't bother me with any of that rubbish and let's just get on with the music". So there was some sort of tension that arrived with the costumes, like at the Rainbow Theatre. There was a ton of arguments about it, you know, and I thought "fuck it, I'm just gonna do it". The band wasn't a real democracy because some people were more powerful than others and the more bloody-minded of us tended to get their way more often, as in every band the world over. At that point, they thought maybe I had something and perhaps they shouldn't fight me because it got us on the front page." (3)

Rutherford: "Pete started creating characters and becoming personalities on stage. Our audiences weren't big but we'd started to have a following. We'd play in France and Aylesbury [in England] and there'd be a great vibe there and in certain parts of the country we were sort of popular. We were still playing clubs but for once they weren't all empty all the time." (3)

Alongside the improvements in the visuals provided by the costumes, Gabriel's storytelling between songs evolved and, although still mainly improvised, by this time they had a more solid foundation. So, while *The Musical Box* was preceded by the story of Henry and Cynthia as described on the cover of Nursery Cryme, before *Supper's Ready* Peter would tell the bizarre exploits of 'Old Michael', singing the school hymn *Jerusalem* (renamed *Jerusalem Boogie* by Gabriel).

And this was all accompanied by a stage set-up which was finally up to calibre. Genesis' stage manager and lighting engineer, Adrian Selby, set up a curtain illuminated by UV lights which would hide a lot of the bulky equipment from the audience's view. The crowd was then emotionally (and sometimes almost literally) blown away by an explosion of magnesium powder at the end of *Supper's Ready*, which dissolved to reveal Gabriel dressed all in white holding a luminous tube in his hand.

Banks: "We were developing the light show as much we could in those days, trying to create a sort of fantasy on stage. We had this nice couple of guys who used to project these oil slides. We only had a few red and blue lights and stuff, but it was amazing what you could do if it was coordinated. Sounds a bit obvious now, doesn't it? But in those days it was kind of revolutionary. There was a particular Rainbow Theatre performance which I felt was a very, very strong moment in the group's history." (3)

Rutherford: "We always tried to present songs on stage so as to create an atmosphere. We bought this big gauze curtain and we hung it behind the stage at the Rainbow, I remember, and hid the amplifiers. And we bought some UV lights just to light it up and it looked sort of Gothic, all sort of pillars and temples, it had a real atmosphere. It cost fuck all really which was great, the best-value-for-money special effect we ever had, so Adrian Selby, wherever you are, well done (it was his idea). It was always a good sort of coupling of looks and music. It also worked thanks to the flower, the cloak at the end and the red mask. In other words, Pete's performance and what he did visually with costumes, trying to paint pictures, in a sense worked." [3]

Hackett: "Being as FOXTROT was complicated with difficult time signatures and the songs were invariably stories, I knew that it couldn't stand on its own without a carefully thought out production and presentation. We needed everything, lights, sound effects, everything to help it along, so it was the nearest thing an English band was doing to an Alice Cooper style show. He was about theatrics not just about the music, and in a way we were a more subtle version of that. We weren't biting heads off chickens or stabbing dolls or using guillotines... the energy of Genesis was much more subtle. If you read the classics there was a chance you'd enjoy what Genesis did. The criticism was that it sounded like it had been looked up in books rather than it being personal experience." [1]

When the technical difficulties exceeded the usual amount of time to resolve, there was always a life-saving drum solo from Collins to fill in the gap, such as in Glasgow on 16 February, while on the 17th, *The Musical Box* was interrupted about 3 minutes in by a power cut, so they went back to the beginning and started again.

The UK tour with support band, String Driven Thing, included around 15 live shows (it is impossible to give a precise number), two of which (Manchester 24 and Leicester 25 February) were recorded and became the source for a first live album, GENESIS LIVE.

After getting their first taste of America in the previous December, Genesis returned to the States in the spring for a longer stay. In fact, this time round the tour lasted around one month for around a dozen concerts which took the band not only to New York but also to other states on the East Coast and in the Midwest (Pennsylvania, Ohio, Illinois, Massachusetts), with a couple of stops in Canada. On some of these dates Genesis had to settle for being the support act again, albeit for some top flight acts, such as Lou Reed and Richie Havens, but special mention must go to the fantastic performance at the Philharmonic Hall in New York in early April with Sandy Denny opening. Another note on the set list, which was basically the same but with an important new twist: *Supper's Ready* was moved to the end, after *The Return Of The Giant Hogweed* and *The Knife*.

After a break, Genesis went back to work writing new music, so there were very few concerts scheduled for the months between May and August 1973, and even some of those were cancelled.

The band did, however, return to the Olympia in Paris on 7 May, moving onto Brussels in Belgium the following day, whereas an important event was scheduled for the 26th at the Empire Pool Arena in London, a much bigger venue than usual, but this, alas, was also cancelled due (according to

Advertisement for the Reading Festival, New Musical Express, 25th August 1973.

a newspaper article from that time) to tickets not being printed in time. Not the most credible of excuses and together with the statement in the same article ("Genesis will not be performing live for the next four months while they rehearse a completely new show. No new date for the Wembley concert has been set") leads us to believe that subsequent dates, for which newspaper ads exist (such as Slough on 30 June), might also have been axed.

The only certainty in this period is that the band took part in the Reading Festival on 26 August, where they played *Watcher Of The Skies / The Musical Box / Supper's Ready / The Return Of The Giant Hogweed / The Knife*. This time, Genesis were headliners ahead of other acts such as Jon Hiseman's Tempest, John Martyn, the American Roy Buchanan and Italy's PFM. A massive change in circumstances compared to their first appearance on the same stage just one year earlier!

## NOTES

(1) Mario Giammetti listens to Foxtrot with Steve Hackett, Benevento, 13 March 2011

(2) Mario Giammetti's telephone interview with Tony Banks, 16 February 2012, partially published in the article "Six not simply shrouded pieces" in Dusk, Issue no. 70, April 2012

(3) Mike Kaufman's Genesis interviews, Chicago / London, October 2007, partially used in the bonus disc accompanying the 2008 remasters

(4) Mario Giammetti's interview with David Hitchcock: Fasano, 1 June 2015, partially published in the article "In the land of grey and foxes – Intervista esclusiva a David Hitchcock" in Dusk, Issue no. 80, July 2015

(5) Mario Giammetti's telephone interview with Tony Banks, 1 October 2009, partially published in the article "Nei meandri della memoria" in Dusk, Issue no. 63, November 2009

(6) Mario Giammetti's telephone interview with Richard Macphail, 12 May 2005, partially published in the article "Il Sesto Genesis" in Dusk, Issue no. 50, August 2005

# Foxtrot Tour

## 1972

### SEPTEMBER

1 **Merton** (ENGLAND), Civic Hall
2 **Aylesbury** (ENGLAND), Borough Assembly Hall
3 **Bournemouth** (ENGLAND), Chelsea Village
9 **Montbéliard** (FRANCE), Halle Polyvalente
*P.E.M. Paris-Est-Music. 'V Franche Comte Pop Festival'.*
12 **Hastings** (ENGLAND), Pier Pavilion
13 **Greenford** (ENGLAND), Big Brother Club
14 **Worthing** (ENGLAND), Assembly Hall
16 **Bracknell** (ENGLAND), Sports Centre
17 **Croydon** (ENGLAND), The Greyhound
19 **London** (ENGLAND), Marquee Club
23 **Kelso** (SCOTLAND), Tait Hall
24 **York** (ENGLAND), Theatre Royal
25 **London** (ENGLAND), BBC T1 Studios
*'John Peel's Top Gear' radio broadcast*
28 **Dublin** (IRELAND), National Stadium
30 **Kennington** (ENGLAND), The Oval
*'Melody Maker Poll Concert'*

### OCTOBER

1 **Newcastle** (ENGLAND), City Hall
*First of a series of gigs with Lindisfarne as the headliners, and Genesis and Rab Noakes as support acts.*
3 **Sheffield** (ENGLAND), Oval Hall - Sheffield City Hall
4 **Aberdeen** (SCOTLAND), Music Hall
6 **Glasgow** (SCOTLAND), Green's Playhouse
7 **Edinburgh** (SCOTLAND), Empire Theatre
10 **Manchester** (ENGLAND), Free Trade Hall
11 **Bradford** (ENGLAND), St. George's Hall
12 **Leicester** (ENGLAND), De Montfort Hall
13 **Bournemouth** (ENGLAND), Winter Gardens
14 **Kingston-upon-Thames** (ENGLAND), Main Hall - Kingston Polytechnic
15 **London** (ENGLAND), London Coliseum
16 **Liverpool** (ENGLAND), Top Rank Suite
17 **Hull** (ENGLAND), The City Hall
*Uncertain concert*
18 **Watford** (ENGLAND), Top Rank - Watford Suite
19 **Stoke-on-Trent** (ENGLAND), Trentham Gardens
20 **Bristol** (ENGLAND), Top Rank Suite
21 **Oxford** (ENGLAND), New Theatre
22 **Preston** (ENGLAND), Public Hall
24 **Portsmouth** (ENGLAND), The Guildhall
25 **Birmingham** (ENGLAND), Odeon Theatre
26 **Cardiff** (WALES), Top Rank Suite
27 **Brighton** (ENGLAND), Top Rank Suite
29 **Lewisham** (ENGLAND), Odeon Theatre

### NOVEMBER

2 **Manchester** (ENGLAND), The Hardrock Concert Theatre
3 **Ipswich** (ENGLAND), Civic College
4 **Leeds** (ENGLAND), Auditorium - University of Leeds
5 **Epping** (ENGLAND), The Wake Arms
6 **Cleethorpes** (ENGLAND), Winter Gardens
10 **Uxbridge** (ENGLAND), Brunel University
11 **London** (ENGLAND), Marquee Club
12 **Croydon** (ENGLAND), Fairfield Hall
13 **Westcliff-on-Sea** (ENGLAND), Queens Hotel
17 **Colchester** (ENGLAND), University of Essex
18 **London** (ENGLAND), Great Hall - Imperial College
19 **Cheltenham** (ENGLAND), Town Hall
24 **King's Lynn** (ENGLAND), Corn Exchange Hall
25 **Sutton-Coldfield** (ENGLAND), Belfry Hotel
26 **Gravesend** (ENGLAND), Lord's Club Civic Hall

### DECEMBER

1 **Leicester** (ENGLAND), University of Leicester
2 **Slough** (ENGLAND), Slough College
*Uncertain concert*
6 **Mile End** (ENGLAND), Sundown
8 **Plymouth** (ENGLAND), Guildhall
*Uncertain concert. However, it was originally planned for 11 December.*
11 **Waltham, MA** (USA), Brandeis University
13 **New York, NY** (USA), Philharmonic Hall - Lincoln Center for the Performing Arts
18 **St. Gallen** (SWITZERLAND), Hotel Ekkehard
*First concert ever in Switzerland*

# 1973

## JANUARY

6 **Dagenham** (**ENGLAND**), The Roundhouse
7 **Croydon** (**ENGLAND**), The Greyhound
9 **Marseilles** (**FRANCE**), Salle Vallier
*Uncertain concert*
10 **Paris** (**FRANCE**), Bataclan
13 **Hamburg** (**WEST GERMANY**), Congress Centrum Hamburg
14 **Frankfurt** (**WEST GERMANY**), Jahrhunderthalle
15 **Heidelberg** (**WEST GERMANY**), Stadthalle
16 **Offenbach** (**WEST GERMANY**), Stadthalle Offenbach
17 **Düsseldorf** (**WEST GERMANY**), Rheinhalle
20 **Reggio Emilia** (**ITALY**), Palazzo dello Sport
*Originally scheduled at Milan's Palalido*
22 **Roma** (**ITALY**), Palazzo dello Sport
*Originally scheduled for 18 January, then moved to 19 January and eventually actually played on 22nd.*
30 **Peterborough** (**ENGLAND**), ABC Theatre
*Uncertain date*

## FEBRUARY

2 **Coventry** (**ENGLAND**), Main Hall - Lanchester Polytechnic • *'Lanchester Arts Festival'*
4 **Bristol** (**ENGLAND**), Hippodrome
9 **London** (**ENGLAND**), Rainbow Theatre
10 **Brighton** (**ENGLAND**), The Dome
12 **Plymouth** (**ENGLAND**), Guildhall
14 **Exeter** (**ENGLAND**), Exeter University Guild of Students
16 **Glasgow** (**SCOTLAND**), Green's Playhouse
17 **Sheffield** (**ENGLAND**), Oval Hall - Sheffield City Hall
18 **Birmingham** (**ENGLAND**), Town Hall
19 **Oxford** (**ENGLAND**), New Theatre
21 **York** (**ENGLAND**), Central Hall - University of York
22 **Newcastle** (**ENGLAND**), City Hall
23 **Lancaster** (**ENGLAND**), University of Lancaster
24 **Manchester** (**ENGLAND**), Free Trade Hall
25 **Leicester** (**ENGLAND**), De Montfort Hall
26 **Dunstable** (**ENGLAND**), Queensway Hall

## MARCH

28 **Princeton, NJ** (**USA**), Alexander Hall - Princeton University
31 **South Orange, NJ** (**USA**), Student Center - Seton Hall University

## APRIL

2 **New York, NY** (**USA**), Philharmonic Hall - Lincoln Center for the Performing Arts
6 **Québec, QC** (**CANADA**), Salle Louis-Fréchette
*Grand Théâtre de Québec*
8 **Sherbrooke, QC** (**CANADA**), Salle Maurice O'Bready - Centre Culturel - Université de Sherbrooke
9 **Toronto, ON** (**CANADA**), Massey Hall
11 **Rochester, NY** (**USA**), Clark Memorial Gym – Rochester Institute Of Technology
13 **Pittsburgh, PA** (**USA**), Alpine Arena
14 **Cleveland, OH** (**USA**), Adelbert Gym - Case Western Reserve University
17 **Cincinnati, OH** (**USA**), Reflections
20 **Chicago, IL** (**USA**), Aragon Ballroom
23 **Waltham, MA** (**USA**), Brandeis University

## MAY

7 **Paris** (**FRANCE**), L'Olympia
8 **Brussels** (**BELGIUM**), Cirque Royal

## AUGUST

26 **Reading** (**ENGLAND**), Thames-side Arena
*'Reading Festival'*

# Selling England By The Pound

(Charisma 1973)

*Dancing With The Moonlit Knight / I Know What I Like (In Your Wardrobe) / Firth Of Fifth / More Fool Me /// The Battle Of Epping Forest / After The Ordeal / The Cinema Show / Aisle Of Plenty*

- **Release date: 12 October 1973**
- **Recorded at Island Studios, London, August 1973**
- **Producers: John Burns / Genesis**
- **Assistant Engineer: Rhett Davies**
- **Artwork: Betty Swanwick, A.R.A.**

- **Phil Collins: drums, percussion, voices, lead voice on** *More Fool Me*
- **Michael Rutherford: 12-string, bass, electric sitar**
- **Stephen Hackett: electric guitar, nylon guitar**
- **Tony Banks: keyboards, 12-string**
- **Peter Gabriel: lead voice, flute, oboe, percussion**

## THE MAKING OF

In late spring 1973, with the second American tour behind them, Genesis stopped performing live to concentrate on writing their fifth studio album. They rehearsed in the same two places they had used for FOXTROT: 'Una Billing's School Of Dance' in Shepherd's Bush and a doctor's house in Chessington.

Rutherford: "Most of it was written near Chessington. Phil had a friend with an apartment in a big, old country house there and they had an area which bands could rent out." [1]

Hackett: "I remember us rehearsing this album in a house that a family lived in, near Chessington Zoo. Of course, it was a totally inappropriate place because it had no soundproofing, and quite naturally the neighbours started to complain. I remember one woman coming in and saying, "you're just making banging noises, it's not music at all!". Because it was a house that belonged to a family, it gave the music a sense of happy amateurishness. It made it fun because you felt you shouldn't really be there doing that kind of thing. It was designed as a canteen or a cafeteria, there was even a machine that used to dispense bubble gum for kids! The atmosphere was very different than a normal rehearsal space, and I think that helped put a smile into the music, it did for me anyway. And then there was 'Una Billing's', which is where we wrote FOXTROT and *Supper's Ready*, another very eccentric place. The sound of these girls dancing upstairs was like elephants dancing, believe me. Imagine what it's like when you've got twenty of them all making this noise together. It was so funny, we used to look at each other... Whatever we were doing at that moment, no matter how serious it sounded, was crazy." [2]

While writing the album, the band had some difficulties coming up with ideas for songs.

Banks: "We used to have writing sessions; we didn't necessarily write the album all in one go but I remember that on this particular record we were a bit stuck for ideas. There were two or three things we already had, for example there was this riff Steve had been playing on stage and all over the place. We developed that into the song *I Know What I Like*; it was quite a simple thing for us really but it had a very strong atmosphere. I had three bits I'd written which I originally assumed would go into different songs. As it is, they all ended up in the song which became *Firth Of Fifth*. Basically, we just strung the three bits together in a way that made sense of them. Then there was the riff that became the first part of *The Battle Of Epping Forest*, other than that we didn't have much. We were struggling a bit to find things, so we ended up playing these three things every day for a long time and kind of overworked them, particularly *Epping Forest*; we got way too many ideas into that." (1)

Collins, speaking in 2007: "Some people see this as a difficult album to make. I don't particularly remember it being that way. I do remember the Chessington sessions when we came up with *Cinema Show* and *Dancing With The Moonlit Knight*. Some of the instrumental stuff is me and Steve: I was starting to listen to the Mahavishnu Orchestra, so I was trying to put my weird time signatures into anything that would move. *I Know What I Like*, which we wrote at 'Una Billing's', was us doing our Beatles thing, really. We didn't see any harm in that because we had yet to have a hit single. I know Tony has said he could have done without *Aisle Of Plenty*. *Firth Of Fifth* was a big tour de force, while *Cinema Show* was a huge tour de

band rehearsals. So it was a sort of dual approach." (1)

Banks: "We always felt that our strongest moments seemed to come out of us all improvising and jamming with things just coalescing. We always liked that very much, it's what gives you the thrill." (1)

Hackett: "I think we were given six weeks to write an album and six weeks to record it at this point; we used to think anything else was excessive. With this album we were all working together as a group trying to write as much as possible face to face in the studio. Obviously Tony brought in *Firth Of Fifth* as a finished song himself. The first part of *Dancing With The Moonlit Knight* was Pete's and then it became everybody's. *I Know What I Like* started as a guitar riff of mine. The rest we all did together." (2)

force, it's got a lot of things in it that we still play. It became a huge stage classic and I particularly like it, I think the first half is great. We were definitely starting to sound a little bit better in the studio." (1)

Rutherford: "It wasn't until Hugh Padgham came along [i.e. not until 1981] that the band on record really started to sound like it did in the rehearsal room. At the time we used to have a good sound both live and in the rehearsal room, but in the studio we were always trying to get it back up to how it should be. The drums always sounded small on the record, but not live." (1)

Gabriel: "Very often people would come in with ideas that were starting points and then they would sort of get to be the captain of that song. Some things, on the other hand, emerged during

For the guitarist, these writing sessions became a place of refuge.

Hackett: "At the time my first marriage was in bad shape. When I was at home I was finding it very hard to write because the atmosphere was tense. I just turned up for the rehearsals of this album with lots of guitar riffs, so it turned into a very guitary album. I was talking to Anthony Phillips about this recently, he liked the album a lot. He was very generous about it considering he was my predecessor. He said to me, "you did exactly the right thing bringing in all these riffs, because if

Charisma promotion, 1973

you tried to bring complete songs into Genesis it didn't always work". Unless you were Tony Banks, that is! Tony basically got his way more than anybody else. It's a fact. That said, he came up with wonderful things, and it was both wonderful and terrible working with him." (2)

For this album the band had a much larger array of instruments and effects at their disposal.

Hackett: "I already had my volume pedal and my fuzz box and I had this thing called an Echoplex which could do tape echo with a moveable head. We used it on the vocals to *I Know What I Like* to make the voices go all wobbly, and it meant that, live, the guitar could sound like a studio recording. I didn't know any other bands that were using that, so we were state-of-the-art at that point. We also had everything that a Mellotron could do. Tony had got hold of a monophonic synth, that was something I pushed for because I was always very keen on enlarging what the keyboards could do, having a wider palette to draw from; the more tone colours, the better." (1)

Banks: "I would put the Hammond organ through fuzz boxes and things, I'd try using one drawbar or just the percussion sound. I'd be trying to get every little thing you could possibly get out of it, I'd be using 100% of the instrument, whereas now, with the modern synthesizer, you probably use only one half of one percent. A lot of people just switch it on and use presets and that's all they ever do. Mellotrons were great in the sense that they gave you these lovely string and voice sounds and everything, but you couldn't play fast on them. When synthesizers came in, they just opened up the keyboard world so much. I had this ARP Pro Soloist, a very simple monophonic synthesizer, which had a nice little range of tones on it. You didn't have to do any programming, it was just preset sounds. *Cinema Show* was very much based on that instrument, but I used it on little bits and pieces throughout the album. It was a really interesting addition to the armoury I already had (organ, piano, Mellotron). Having something alternative to play lead keyboards on suddenly opened up possibilities for me." (1)

When the time came to decide which tracks were to go on the album a series of arguments within the band occurred. Tony detested *After The Ordeal*; Steve and Peter thought the keyboard solo in *Cinema Show* was too long. In the end, to avoid upsetting anyone, they came to a compromise and decided to keep everything, which might explain why this is a particularly long album.

Hackett: "*The Battle Of Epping Forest* is very long and took that side of the album up to around 29 minutes; people didn't do that in those days because it meant you could get less bass response. We had arguments about what should and what shouldn't be included, but I'm very glad we left everything in." (2)

## THE ALBUM

In August 1973, Genesis went into the studio to record the album with the help of John Burns, the sound engineer who had worked with them on Foxtrot and was now promoted to co-producer.

As for past albums, Genesis made use of some pre-existing ideas which developed into more definitive versions in the rehearsal room. The continuous creative growth of the whole band (including the two latest additions who were by this time fully integrated members) was accompanied by their ability to improvise freely and intuitively.

From a writing point of view, with the exception of *Firth Of Fifth* (Banks) and *More Fool Me* (Rutherford), all the other songs came about as a result of collective interaction between the whole band or units made up of at least two or three members. Set against the early parts of *Dancing With The Moonlit Knight*, written entirely by Gabriel (and reprised in the last track *Aisle Of Plenty*), is the collective instrumental section written mainly by Steve, Phil and Tony. Steve wrote the underlying riff for *I Know What I Like*, but this was only shaped into a song thanks to Peter's verse and Tony's chorus. *The Battle Of Epping Forest* is a juxtaposition between Tony's music (written with the help of Mike in the intermediate sections) and Peter's expressive singing. *After The Ordeal* is an instrumental track written by Steve incorporating a section written by Mike, while *Cinema Show* is divided into two sections: the first acoustic part was written by Mike, while the second electric part came about from a jamming session between Mike, Phil and Tony.

In terms of lyrics, however, Gabriel definitely had the upper hand. Besides the mellifluous love song *More Fool Me*, Tony and Mike worked together (without much success) on the lyrics for *Firth Of Fifth* and *Cinema Show*, leaving their lead singer to pen the words to *Dancing With The Moonlit Knight, I Know What I Like, The Battle Of Epping Forest* and *Aisle Of Plenty*, authentic works of genius and verbal agility. Gabriel's lyrical prowess was head and shoulders above many of his contemporaries (and not just from within the band). Drawing his inspiration from things such as newspaper articles (as he had done previously with *The Return Of The Giant Hogweed*), his writing comes across as both refined and sophisticated. In this album, the usual references to mythology and literature are relegated to a marginal role (albeit still present) in favour of historical references and social comment. In an intertwining and exquisitely English play on words, the lyrics form the framework of the most 'British' album Genesis ever wrote thanks to the fantastic descriptive identity of the characters who would later come to life on stage.

Paradoxically, when more or less individual compositions were being written (although the songs were, as always, credited to the whole group), Selling England By The Pound turns out to be the first Genesis record which could realistically be credited 20% to each member. While the first two albums were created by the work of two songwriting pairs (Banks-Gabriel on the one side and Phillips-Rutherford on the other) and Nursery Cryme and Foxtrot essentially represented the primary compositional fusion between Banks and Rutherford with the support of Gabriel and contributions from the newcomers (just a little from Hackett and even less from Collins), Selling England By The Pound is the album where Genesis achieved a perfect creative balance for the first time ever.

What's more, during the recording sessions a special kind of synergy developed between Tony and the rhythm section (Phil and Mike), the trio which would later go on to constitute the second and more commercially successful phase in the band's history. In a group where, apart from for the more instinctive Steve and Phil, the idea of

improvising had been a totally foreign concept, the three developed an enviable level of understanding with Tony acting as the driving force and inventor of original melodies driven by fantastic and creative rhythms. The most striking case, a precursor of which was seen in *Apocalypse In 9/8*, is the long instrumental section in *Cinema Show*.

Maybe due to this sense of unity (despite the initial difficulties) Selling England By The Pound, although preceded by three extraordinary albums, is often considered Genesis' real coming-of-age. The band's evolution continued to follow a logical and seemingly unstoppable thread. From Genesis To Revelation contained the first frail attempts at songwriting, while Trespass revealed the band's progressive side, despite it still being closely linked to folk influences thanks to Anthony's and Mike's 12-string guitar parts. Where Nursery Cryme suffers from a lack of synergy within the new line-up, with the band having changed two of its five members, Foxtrot turned out to be a successful album by what had by then become a consolidated and technically skillful band.

The artistic standing of Selling England By The Pound, on the other hand, is all the more brilliant at a time when progressive rock seemed to have already reached its peak and was about to go into decline. In fact, the new records released in 1973 by Genesis' most reputable counterparts all showed a marked change in direction. Albums such as Pink Floyd's Dark Side Of The Moon or King Crimson's Larks Tongues In Aspic, while undoubtedly representing milestones in the history of rock, both unequivocally show that these bands were already moving beyond their purely progressive phase. Floyd, it has to be said, had barely touched upon it with Meddle, whereas the return of King Crimson, a couple of years after their first break-up, indicates a much harder direction with their romantic moments reduced to a mere flicker.

And then there were the other prog giants: Emerson, Lake & Palmer (with their passable Brain Salad Surgery) and Yes (with their heavy-going Tales From Topographic Oceans) along with the equally indigestible The Six Wives Of Henry VIII (Rick Wakeman's solo album) confirm that delusions of grandeur had hijacked the musical genre which seemed to be merely running its course and becoming increasingly unpalatable, while in the field of prog folk, Jethro Tull, with their pretentious A Passion Play, got slated by the critics.

The odd innovative spark did appear, albeit from unexpected sources. If Tubular Bells by the phenomenal Mike Oldfield remains an isolated case, the fusion found in Birds OF Fire by the Mahavishnu Orchestra represented, according to Collins and Hackett, a source of inspiration for Genesis in this era, while the electronic experimentation in No Pussyfooting by Fripp & Eno would leave its mark on Genesis just a year later. In the meantime, glam rock (to which Gabriel's theatricality has been unfairly likened) was still at its height with David Bowie's Aladdin Sane, Roxy Music's For Your Pleasure, Gary Glitter's Touch Me and Tanx by T. Rex.

In this artistic scenario, Selling England By The Pound became the perfect progressive rock album, the maximum level to which any band in this sector could aspire at that time.

It has to be said that the album is lacking an opus, such as *The Musical Box* or *Supper's Ready*. On the other hand, the musicality of the band is seen

Tony Banks in Reggio Emilia, 4 February 1974.

to be open to more diverse influences than ever before. At the end of the day, only *Firth Of Fifth* and the instrumental section in *Cinema Show* can be considered classic progressive rock. The rest of the album reveals alternating disparate influences whose roots are to be found not only in Europe (folk and baroque) but also on the other side of the Atlantic (jazz-rock, West Coast). In the midst of all this lie the seeds of pop, planted in a compositional soil which would soon prove to be very fertile.

At this point, however, one question remains: how would the band follow up this masterpiece?

## THE SONGS

### DANCING WITH THE MOONLIT KNIGHT

This song is essentially divided into three sections: an acoustic opening (with the acappella introduction by Gabriel, who wrote the whole melody), an audacious instrumental (created by band improvisation) and a final section with a delicate atmosphere.

Gabriel: "There was a growing sense of confidence in this track, which I started off writing. I was trying to get a folk reference, you know, to protect and preserve some of the Englishness. In the opening part, I was particularly trying to capture something that had more references to Henry VIII than to American song music." [1]

Hackett: "When it starts out you really don't know where the song is going to go. There was this melody [0'22"] which Pete wrote on piano and mainly becomes a guitar figure throughout the song. It was someone else's melody interpreted on guitar in two different ways." [1]

Banks: "I like the way it starts very much, but it's not my favorite song, although I know a lot of people really like it. It's a slightly weaker track for me." [1]

Hackett: "I love the fact that the album starts off with Pete singing on his own, something that was influenced by Scottish plainsong, in other words songs that were sung without any accompaniment, like a man standing in the wind just singing in the open with a few stragglers; just the elements to carry his word on the wind or in the rain. So it starts off with that bleakness, that starkness, almost like a song with no furniture, sparse, bereft of support. And then it becomes a romantic reflection on the state of England selling off its history which moves quite naturally into the fusion that we associate more with the American influence." [2]

Gabriel: "We were attempting to mix some traditional folk elements with more contemporary band arrangements. Even the colour of the voice I was using at the time was folk influenced. In the opening part it was fairly easy to get a mood going but once the band kicked off, that transition was quite awkward. I probably remember it more from playing it live than from the record; it was a very effective shift in gear." [1]

Rutherford: "I think the first part of the song was great whereas the 'moonlit knight' bit [2'24"] was OK but a bit busy." [1]

The central section is notable for its variety of instrumentation: Banks not only plays piano but also organ, Mellotron and some individual synth phrases; Rutherford plays 12-string and bass; while Hackett passes from the nylon guitar to

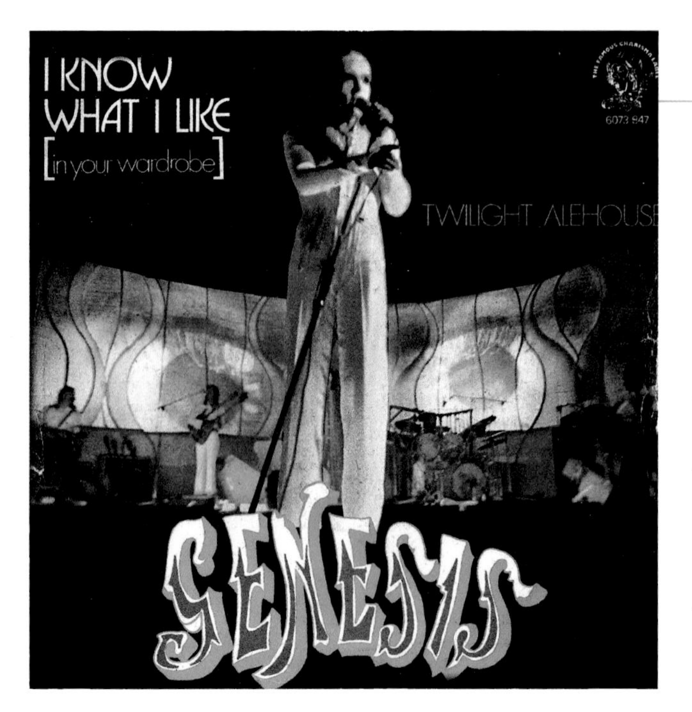


because we thought it sounded like a cartoon. Classical musicians would call it a tone poem really because it creates pictures. Often this is used on television even now in England, normally to do with nature programs. It somehow makes you think of the natural world; it's like a meditation on a lake. I find it very English sounding. We always used to improvise it, so every time we played it it came out different. I don't find it too long." (2)

electric where he gives us his famous tapping sequence (2'35").

Hackett: "It was the fastest a guitarist had ever played. You couldn't play that fast with regular picking but with this tapping technique, using the nail, you could play phenomenally fast. In the instrumental part we had Mellotron, and guitar which together sounded like a brass section; it's almost like classical fusion, and then you get guitar and piano ensemble playing." (2)

In the finale, the atmosphere suddenly rounds back on itself, becoming repetitive and yet evocative (6'17"). Collins: "I'd forgotten all about that bit until recently when someone played it to me. It was being used in a documentary and I asked where it came from. It goes a bit like clockwork. You know, like a wind-up clock. Sometimes you forget about these little bits that actually could have been the beginning of something else." (1)

Hackett: "The noises in the background are Peter playing the oboe reed to make it sound like ducks. Everybody was improvising except for one fixed part which was Mike Rutherford on the 12-string. We used to call this the Disney section

Gabriel's lyrics contrast the decadence of Old England and its progressive Americanisation, as highlighted by the reference to the Wimpy Bar burger chain. It is packed with historical and social references exploiting very clever wordplay, like the union of *uniform* and *faun* to create 'unifaun', the Queen of Maybe or the "citizens of hope and glory" to mimic the patriotic song, *Land Of Hope And Glory*.

Gabriel: "The lyrics were, in a sense, about the commercialisation of English culture. Even we were selling ourselves to foreign audiences, including the Americas. One of the aims of the record was to look at Englishness in a different way and therefore the title SELLING ENGLAND BY THE POUND seemed like a good title for the album. So that was my recommendation." (1)

Rutherford: "I think it's one of our best album titles actually. "Selling England By the Pound" is a great phrase. On stage, with that sort of headgear thing, Peter looked like [the depiction of] Britannia on the back of a coin; it was a great setting for the song." (1)

Single release for the Italian market, February 1974.

Promotional single for France, 1973.

## I KNOW WHAT I LIKE (In Your Wardrobe)

As a single, this was Genesis' first moderate success in the hit parade. It starts with a fixed synthesizer drone sound accompanied by an unusual rhythm from the bongos. Peter's spoken intro leads into the rather elementary structure of the song: a verse sung by two voices over an insistent riff played on electric guitar (Steve) and sitar (Mike) and a very catchy chorus characterised by a lovely bass guitar sequence. Hackett: "This is a very simple song of course. It's based on a guitar riff of mine. We were practising this riff round about the time of FOXTROT; Phil and I used to play it all the time, but the rest of the guys in the band said it sounded a bit too much like The Beatles, so we didn't use it. When it came to the following album, Phil and I were still playing it together only this time the rest of the band joined in and the song was written from a jam." (2)

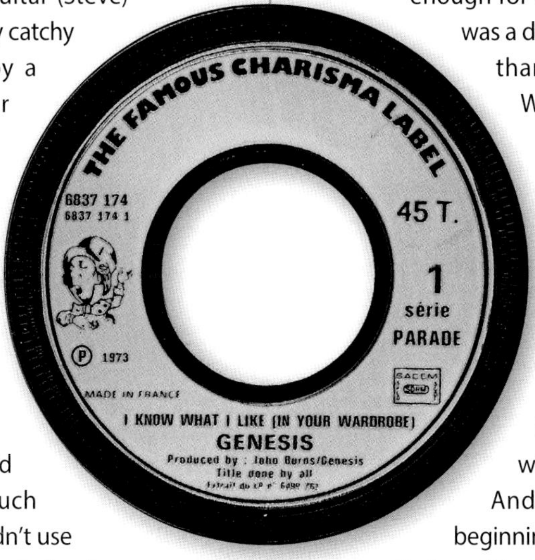

Rutherford: "We grew up with The Beatles. The best band in the world. This word 'pop' has come to mean something different now, but a great song is a great song. Although our writing wasn't bad at all, there were different pieces in our songs. I suppose *I Know What I Like* was one of the first songs where we actually managed to take a short, simple idea and develop it rather than having (as we often did) too many small bits in a song." (1)

Quite unusually, the song is sung entirely by Peter and Phil together.

Hackett: "When it came to the mix I remember Pete wanted to make it a single line and not have Phil's harmony on it. I insisted on it having the two voices because that's what makes it more immediate. It just seemed to me that it wasn't strong enough for a single line, but when it was a double, it became stronger than the sum of the parts. What really makes the song work is what we were all doing: the crazy percussion that's going on, filling up milk bottles and running drumsticks along them, all that tingly stuff that people became fond of, that's what really makes it work. And the *drone* right at the beginning... everybody is playing that and it's slowed down to half speed and I think some of it might be backwards as well, because in those days guitars didn't *sustain* long enough. I could get a great sound with an *octave divider* and a fuzz box but then the sound would run out; it would go for a while and then just stop. At half speed we were able to re-trigger things and make it work." (2)

Gabriel: "Although it may have looked as if there was more of a pop sensibility on this record, I think *I Know What I Like* was in part an accident. Often, when we tried to chase things, we'd fail miserably.

Rutherford, Gabriel and Collins
in Reggio Emilia, 4 February 1974.

I think we'd got to a point where we'd learnt that when we were ourselves and allowed things to happen, we seemed to have more success and resonance with audiences than if we tried to write something which none of us really felt was true to the core of the band." (1)

Hackett: "Sometimes you've just got to be tenacious, you've got to be stubborn and stick to your guns. I remember joking to journalists saying, "you should hear our latest hit single", as if it were a done deal but I was just joking! When it did become a hit, I was thrilled of course; it was years before the band had another one." (1)

Banks: "We always loved pop songs, you know, and even though we're always associated with being a heavy progressive group we came into the business writing pop songs. We were really pleased that we'd actually written one that we thought was pretty good and probably would have been quite a big hit if it hadn't had this wardrobe in the title, which no-one could understand. It was a really nice sort of effect, you know. We developed the chorus very well, it was very strong." (1)

Gabriel: "I never really loved the chorus; it was one of Tony's melodies and after a while I got very bored of it. But it was fun playing the sort of jerkier and jumpier melodies of the verse with Phil. The lyrics certainly weren't conventional pop lyrics. Again, I think I was trying to explore what lurked beneath the surface." (1)

As confirmed by the album liner notes included with the original release, the lyrics were inspired by a painting by Betty Swanwick called *The Dream*, which (with the later addition of a lawn mower) went on to become the album cover. The main character in the story is Jacob, apparently a good-for-nothing who gets comfort from mowing the lawn, but whose identity isn't very clear as in the concluding phrase, steeped in deliciously British surrealism, the words seem to be talking about a lawnmower rather than a human being who mowed lawns.

## FIRTH OF FIFTH

Banks: "I'd written a piece for FOXTROT which had this piano bit that ended up as the introduction to *Firth Of Fifth*. I was quite excited about it but the others less so. I carried on working on the idea and wrote a piece I thought sounded really good on its own and that, if I could swing it by the rest of them, I could do it as an introduction. We'd done *Horizons*, so I thought the idea of letting one person just do a bit was acceptable." (3)

Hackett: "There's something almost religious about Tony's famous introduction. It's a cross between gospel, blues and classical." (2)

There have been suggestions that the piano solo was influenced by mathematical theory and specifically Fibonacci's golden ratio, but this was not the case. Banks: "I wasn't thinking about mathematics for the introduction... I didn't worry about time signatures because with those runs of arpeggios and 4s and 3s, you can always follow it without it being a strict time signature, so I just let it take me where it wanted. It wasn't a particularly difficult thing to write, although I wasn't quite sure how to use it." (3)

The body of the song develops with verses and riffs repeated twice, with Hackett doubling the notes of the bass. Hackett: "The bass and the guitar playing together creates this idea, it's almost like brass and organ together. And just about every time we played it, it sounded good. The fact that you could see the bass line descending makes it similar to baroque music and Bach." (2)

Between the first and second verse there is a variation in melody followed by vocal harmonies. Hackett: "At 2'14" it's volume pedal for guitar with echo. Although I wasn't around for the actual recording of the voices, I think they were speeded up to sound higher than they actually were." (2)

The long instrumental section is preceded by swooping guitar (from 3'04") which Hackett achieved with a "slide volume pedal, some repeat echo and some reverb as well". (2) The main theme is played by Gabriel on the flute, then by Banks on synthesizer and finally Steve's guitar solo comes in.

Collins: "We were steamrollered into *Firth Of Fifth*, but it worked. Tony was good at that and still is. When someone comes in with something and

Mike Rutherford backstage in Reggio Emilia, 4 February 1974.

it's full of odd time signatures and odd bar lengths with a few speed-ups and a few slow-downs, it's a drummer's nightmare; you go: "Oh my god, how am I gonna play this and make it sound natural?" But that's what we did. He came in with this fully composed thing which we ended up doing as he wrote it. We didn't record a great version of it. I remember it was a bit wonky in the middle. I tried to correct it by putting a cabasa on it and it just made it worse." (1)

Rutherford, speaking in 2007: "We're still playing a big section of it today. We're taking the main theme from the song and just letting it run for about four minutes with a lovely guitar solo playing the melody and some lines in between. We were starting to give the sections more space and more time to sit in one mood rather than move on too fast." (1)

Hackett: "When what was the piano solo becomes the synth solo [4'32"], the rhythm section is doing all sorts of extraordinary things, with this furious punctuation behind it. I think a lot of bands, when they're trying to copy what they think is progressive music, they often spend too much time concentrating on the punctuation, without spending enough time on the statement. That's where I think Genesis scored because there was something to say with the song. The same applies to bands like Yes and ELP, you know bands where you had to spot the time signature, "how does that work?", "how does it link up?". It rotates but you can't count it, you can't tap your foot to it." (1)

Banks: "The way the guitar solo evolved is quite interesting really because the second bit I'd written was really just a flute and piano melody, I mean that's how I saw it, but we played it live a few times and it sounded really nice. Then one time Steve started playing it and I thought it was great. I liked putting these big Mellotron chords in, it was almost like a joke, and suddenly we were doing it à la King Crimson. So, for the reprise of that melody, when it came in the second half of the song, we decided to try and do it in this big way to see how it sounded. It worked really well, it gave a chance for Steve to actually do a proper guitar solo, basing it around the melodic line I'd written, but doing more with it." (1)

Hackett: "I think we recorded this song edited into different parts which is why the speed is different from one bit to another. When it came to doing the guitar solo, I tried to play Tony's melody and I thought if I bent the notes over it would sound more oriental, more exotic. I wasn't really trying to be a guitarist, I was pretending to play oboe or a reed instrument with the ability to be able to bend and sustain." (2)

Collins: "The theme was something that Tony had written. You know, the actual beginning and the end of it. But what goes on in the middle, obviously, is Steve stretching out. I always felt that Steve was a better sound man than player. Back then I didn't think he was a particularly fluent player, that's not to say he isn't now." (1)

Hackett: "Originally Tony wrote this as a piano part, but then you never heard it as a piano part; it

Playbill
of the Lausanne concert
of 29 September 1973.

was always piano with flute or piano with guitar or organ with guitar or Mellotron and guitar. Not only that, the piano melody was played on two synths. One is played at regular speed and the other one is played at half speed, so when it's brought back, you have two octaves. This sounds like typical progressive music to me, especially when you've got the drums doing this sort of punctuation along with the sound of Mike's bass, which was very Chris Squire-influenced". [2]

When the guitar solo comes to an end, passing onto a major chord (8'00"), the interaction with the music is so strong as to evoke the calm after the storm. Hackett: "I think it's very visual and descriptive, almost as if it comes after an area of trouble or something. Yes, very much the calm after the storm. I've always liked that in music, this contrast of moods, the intensity of the minor part which brings a bit of anguish perhaps, but there's something very majestic about the minor part as well. And the major part that follows is a little bit closer to Hendrix than it is to me." [2]

Banks: "Steve had obviously always contributed, you know. A lot of Genesis' music required acoustic guitar picking and stuff, which people notice less than a lead guitarist playing a solo. Steve was really starting to find his feet as a live player and everything, and I suppose on this it was more of a genuine guitar solo; some of the others he did were a bit more tricksy. You know, he was always thinking very hard about every note he played so nothing had soared in quite the way this does. I think he allowed himself to have a bit more freedom with it, particularly before the main melody starts where there are some really nice little phrases [5'45"] and it sounds more like a real guitarist." [1]

Hackett: "It's the longest and best-known electric guitar solo in Genesis' history. I think in the early days of the band it wasn't always easy to find the appropriate moment to do electric guitar work. It wasn't a band that was blues-based like Eric Clapton with the Blues Breakers or Cream that were dominated by lead guitar work. As a band, Genesis was dominated by chord work, but it just seemed as if this was a glorious melody to interpret in this way, and I just happened to be the right man for the job at that time. I'm very proud of the way that guitar solo sounds even though I know it's not as perfect as I can do it today. The tuning isn't as good as it could have been. In those days I was overdubbing in headphones and we didn't have strobe tuners. Now, of course, in the age of studios that we own ourselves and with experience and technology, there is no excuse for anything going out of tune ever again. But in those days it was a band in the studio for a short time just going for it and trying to make it sound as good as possible." [2]

Gabriel: "Steve had definitely gained in confidence. *Firth Of Fifth* is very much a Tony piece in terms of how it started and how it's built, but Steve did let loose and I think probably in the best way right up to that point at the end. It was his coming-of-age album in a lot of ways." [1]

The title, in true early Genesis style, is a play on

Peter Gabriel backstage in Reggio Emilia, 4 February 1974.

words; the Firth of Forth is an estuary (*firth*) on the east coast of Scotland into which the River Forth flows. The lyrics, written by Tony and Mike, are not of the highest quality and swing in a muddled manner between mythology and numerous water/ocean references (waterfall, sea, undinal songs, river of constant change), which caused a certain measure of embarrassment to Peter and Phil when performing the song in later years.

## MORE FOOL ME

Written by Mike and Phil while sitting on the steps outside Island Recording Studios, this track is the first in a series of simple (some might say cheesy) songs which would appear much more frequently in later stages of the band's history. Rutherford plays the 12-string with a lot of reverb while Collins sings, mainly in falsetto, the banal lyrics of this simple and short love song; a song recorded by just two of the band members, with the drummer on lead vocals.

Asked about the song featuring just two-fifths of the band, Hackett says: "It was fine because it gave a different atmosphere again. It was a nice dynamic compared to everything else; it was completely different. It was a love song and I think it was a refreshing change from everything else. The idea of just a guitar and a voice with the occasional harmony is good. It's a bit like on Foxtrot when I played *Horizons* on my own. It provides the same function: the picture empties out and becomes very peaceful, so silence comes into play. The idea of a song like this works as a miniature amongst most of the other songs which are epics. This and *I Know What I Like* are the two brief moments and they work as light relief, almost like something to clean the palate between courses, and it's in a style which would become very familiar with Phil." [2]

## THE BATTLE OF EPPING FOREST

A complex song (and the longest on the album at over twelve and a half minutes) driven by the incessant organ and Rickenbacker bass, while Tony uses the synthesizer in some passages and where the falsetto vocals in the choruses are provided by Phil. Various elements are reprised and intertwine to create a musical fabric with sometimes less than convincing results.

Hackett: "I don't think it's a totally successful song. I think maybe other people in the band might regard it as a total failure. I think Phil would because there are so many sections and it's so complicated. Yet it's a very simple idea. Perhaps it should have been done much more simply to reflect the lyrical content, but then again you've got a rhythm section trying to be very clever with rhythms, so it means you've got more punctuation than statement. It's a criticism that I would level at most progressive rock. In progressive rock, especially among the new purveyors of the genre, there is a tendency to think that it should sound like this; you shouldn't be able to tap your foot to it. This was a style that Phil was using at the time: rhythmically the drums are working in counterpoint to the main stream of the music. It parallels the approach that was being used by Bill Bruford. I sense a tremendous influence of Yes in the rhythm section with this song." [2]

The march at the beginning of the song is very

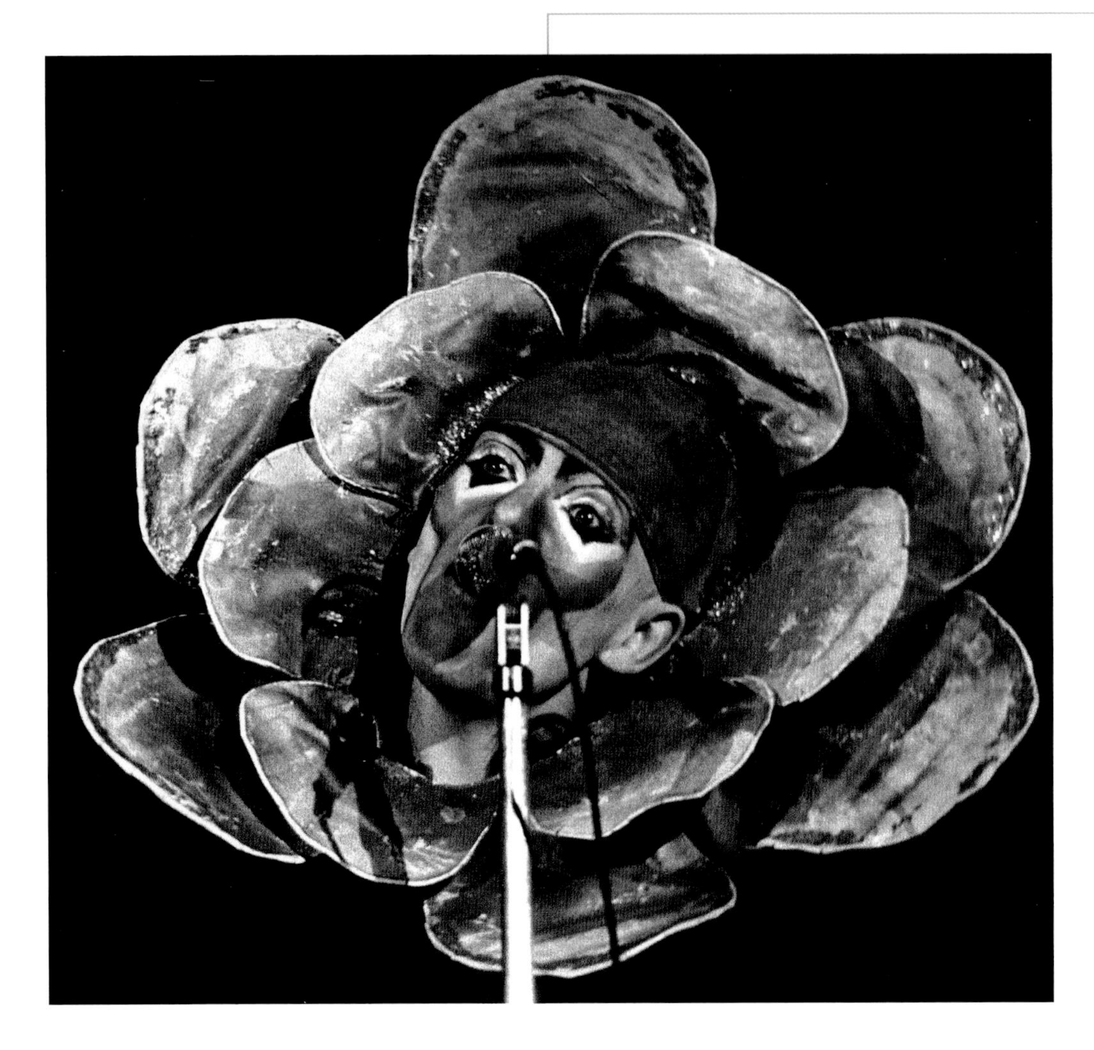

bizarre. Hackett: "The beginning is Mellotron flute and the marching feet of the soldiers is done with the guitar using a fuzz box, an *octave divider* and an echo so it's doubling on itself and sounds like multiple echoes. You had to play in time with the echo which never worked in America because the voltage was different so the echo speed would come back too fast." (2)

At the end of the first part (4'03") there is another guitar section played with repeat echo. Hackett: "As a guitar sound I'm very proud of it because it almost predates reggae playing. This is what reggae is all about, this idea of playing in time with echoes. Maybe no reggae band had ever heard it but it was the same use of technology. Just this little section predates reggae in the same way that THE LAMB LIES DOWN ON BROADWAY predates punk, in the same way that the use of tapping predates the whole orientation towards that by American guitarists." (2)

It is a particularly adventurous track with, according to Hackett "contrary rhythms the whole time, five against two [a drum polyrhythm] and lots of other things going on as well, like the hand claps which sound like Spanish flamenco" (2) whereas in the chorus it's "all straight four-four," Hackett explains, "but with the bass doing contrary time signatures. The drum work is all punctuation. Most modern drummers would just go bass drum and snare. Nobody does that anymore

Gabriel with the flower head used in *Willow Farm*. San Francisco, March 24th 1974.

unless you're a prog band of course. There's a very clever moment, but it's swing with accent, so it really comes from the Buddy Rich jazz school approach. Whether Phil was aware of them or not I don't know, but he reminds me of a drummer who worked with Miles Davis, Jack DeJohnette, when they were playing be-bop." (2)

The real problems arose when Gabriel recorded the vocals. Collins: "*The Battle Of Epping Forest* is a classic example of what had happened previously on *Can-Utility And The Coastliners* and *Get 'Em Out By Friday*. We were writing it and we had some really good counter-polyrhythmic bits happening, and then Peter took the song and wrote the lyrics. Then he came in to sing the lyrics and there were like 300 words a line. There was no space, it was like all the air had been sucked out of it. I'm not saying that he was in the wrong or we were in the wrong, it's just that if we'd known we could have thinned it out a bit. In those days we didn't go back and re-record things. It was a classic example of when stuff got a little bit out of hand." (1)

Banks: "It's a great backing track and it's a great vocal but the two together at times do conflict. Having said that, it's a fun track. I mean, it's a lovely idea of this gangland warfare; it gave a lot of scope for Pete to put on his voices and everything. And it worked quite well live." (1)

Gabriel took his inspiration for the extremely lengthy set of lyrics, which are very descriptive, full of double meanings, allegories and wordplay, from a newspaper article on the territorial battles of two rival gangs in London's East End. Hackett: "The words are very funny with very funny English puns and the nuances are very English, of course." (2)

Gabriel: "I'd spent a lot of time, you know, building up the story with all these characters and setting scenes, and I was quite reluctant to edit as severely as I should have done. So I think it did end up too wordy. The *groove* didn't really work on that particular take. If I were to do it now I'd maybe slow it down a little and speed it up at the end; try and get a punchier undercarriage." (1)

Musical conflicts aside, Gabriel's vocal interpretation is nothing short of outstanding, for example, in the part where he impersonates the vicar (5'28"). Hackett: "I think you have to be English to understand what Pete's doing here. He's doing an impression of an English churchman, a vicar, and the way vicars tend to pronounce their A's, typical of the way a certain class of churchmen would preach their sermons in this very superior sort of way. There is a chord sequence here that Tony came up with on guitars which for me didn't work. Then Pete came up with this thing which made it into a totally humorous statement, it was like a woman in clothes that are frumpy and very unsexy, a turn-off for men, that almost made her into a transvestite." (2)

## AFTER THE ORDEAL

Despite what the title may appear to imply, this instrumental has nothing to do with the battle described in the previous song. Hackett: "I can't remember if it was intentional to place it after *The Battle Of Epping Forest*. I just thought that was the kind of title that might dissipate all the tensions in the rest of the album. *After The Ordeal* was supposed to be the equivalent of today's *chill music*. After all that, you get something simple, again this

Charisma poster (circa 1973).

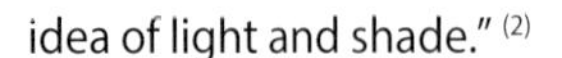

idea of light and shade." (2)

A track written by Steve where he is also the main player on his guitars: his nylon in the initial section and electric later on. Hackett: "It was really designed as an electric tune, but for some reason we couldn't make it work. It could have just been a section in another electric song but we didn't manage to do that, so we were not going to record it. Then in the studio, Tony came up with his part and on the spot we decided to switch it to an acoustic tune where I would play the electric line on the nylon guitar instead. This was the first time the nylon started to creep into Genesis music, both here and with the return of the theme on *Aisle Of Plenty*." (2)

The song caused a lot of arguments in the band. Banks: "I really don't like, I've never liked it, and I would have liked it not to have been on the album. In the end, we compromised by putting everything we had on the album." (1)

Hackett: "I know Tony hates it and thinks it's the worst thing that Genesis ever did. I could point out many other moments that I think are a lot weaker, but, as a diplomat, I won't. All I can say is that in *Cinema Show* I think the keyboard solo is far too long. There was a contest as to whether we were going to let the keyboard solo be on the album or not. Pete didn't want it on. Other people didn't want *After The Ordeal* on. We were all fighting each other, we were all emphatic that we wanted our ideas on. I think this was a new dynamic for the band, because I don't think they were used to me coming on as strong as them. I was thinking, "fuck it! this is a really strong guitar album and I don't want to have it diminished just because someone else thinks their part is more important"." (2)

The part where the electric guitar comes in (2'12") was written by Mike. Hackett: "I thought it was nice for the electric guitar to come to the fore. I felt that I had a real job to do in that band at the time and they were good memorable melodies. They could all of them be played better now, of course, in time and in tune. I can criticise this song and I can also praise it; I think Mike's is a lovely melody and I think this album would have been weaker had it been excluded." (2)

In the closing section, a twisting lead guitar (3'13") reaches an emotional peak before the song's conclusion where a magical touch of flute from Gabriel leads it up to fade. Hackett: "This is a lovely melody that I wrote and it's my melody at the end [3'19"]. The guitars are dubbed with harmony and then everyone did their improvisation around it." (2)

## THE CINEMA SHOW

This is a musical opera which is clearly divided into two parts: the first is an acoustic song written by Mike Rutherford, the second is a drawn-out instrumental part written and played by the trio

On page 188: Phil Collins in Naples, 6 February 1974.
On page 189: Steve Hackett in Lausanne,
29 September 1973.

Banks, Collins and Rutherford.

Rutherford, speaking in 2007: "Normally, you've got 12 strings and they're paired up and you tune each pair to the same note. I started tuning each pair to harmony notes, which is how the song starts with that sort of run down. Now, I haven't got a clue what the hell the tuning is. The other day, in New York, they were saying, "Oh let's do the first half of *Cinema Show*, maybe", and I said: "I've no idea how I played it. You have to work a compromised version out."" (1)

Hackett: "Now I've come to enjoy this song very much, but at the time I didn't feel it was strong. I realise it's very much a people's favourite, they like it very much and I've tried to understand why. I think it's probably because it's very romantic. It has a lot of sections in it and a lot of good bits, but I wouldn't necessarily say the actual song is the strongest bit of it. But it did work very well live." (2)

The initial structure includes two 12-strings (played by Mike and Tony) with Steve adding the finishing touches on his electric guitar. Hackett: "I was trying to make my guitar sound like Ian McDonald's flute, almost like a woodwind instrument, creating melodic phrases. In the introduction there were two guitars playing; one is at regular speed and one is at double speed. It was recorded at half speed and played back so that it comes back higher. So you hear a very high sounding 12-string and then a very sweet one above it." (2)

The first two verses are followed by a long acoustic interlude made up of various instrumentation [2'45"] and a two-voice vocal melody without words. Hackett: "Pete played oboe and flute, Phil played wood blocks, while Mike and Tony were playing 12-strings. Tony used to put his through the Leslie Cabinet to give it a very cloudy sort of sound. I used to do that with my electric guitar as well. The semi-improvised vocal part [4'05"] in counterpoint was very clever melodically. It's a lovely melody; something Crosby, Stills & Nash could have sung. Only, if they had sung it, I think it probably would have sounded better." (2)

When the arpeggio returns, with the drums coming in (4'35"), "if you listen carefully to the 12-string parts," says Hackett, "you'll notice there are lots of missed notes". (2) The first part closes on a short solo (5'21"). Hackett: "Guitar and synthesizer playing together. I was using a fuzz box and passing the guitar through the Leslie Cabinet again." (2)

Banks: "It sounds wonderful in 5.1, especially the first part: the way the guitars and voices sort of come in and out is really good. Sometimes with 5.1 the best thing is being able to position the guitars all over the place; often in our songs there were three of us playing guitar." (1)

The instrumental section of the song, played by the trio Tony, Mike and Phil is completely different. Collins: "It was obviously a song in two halves and it was even rehearsed separately. Probably, with the recording, Tony went in there and fooled around, but it was based on a 7/8 guitar riff and drum thing; something which we still do to this day." (1)

Rutherford: "We (myself, Phil and Tony) started the second part. I'm not excluding Steve, but it was more about us just jamming together, getting these instrumental moments like this one and the back end of 9/8 in *Supper's Ready*, which became a large part of our trademark. It was a great live

song and that instrumental part was a huge crowd-pleaser. In a sense, it was frustrating when Peter left because the audience didn't know that some of their favourite live sections, like *Cinema Show*, weren't actually written by Peter; they tended to think that the singer wrote everything. It was in the live set for a long while because we were sort of saying: "if only you knew that a lot of the stuff you liked before was actually written by the guys who are still here..." But, of course, we wrote in the credits "all the songs by Genesis", so you couldn't tell people that." (1)

Hackett: "It was tremendous playing by Phil but, as he said, in those days the drums were the only instrument that wasn't overdubbed, whereas there was a chance to overdub the keyboard parts and fix them. He had to accept a *take* that was done when he was really tired and he wouldn't be happy in the end because he'd end up playing safe. Even so, this is very good drumming. On the other hand, I think the synth solo goes on too long. It's a very lovely melody, especially when the Mellotron and voices kick in [7'29"]. Live it was great because it used to shake the foundations: bass pedal, choir, melody, as a trio they sounded huge. I think the 7/8 bit finds focus and becomes melodic and memorable. I far prefer it to all the *widdly widdly* up and down stuff that comes before it. But then again, I can't criticise my playing on this because I'm not playing on it!" (2)

Banks: "The instrumental at the end was probably the best one we did at this stage of our careers. Mike had this riff in 7/8 which just went *dang dang dang* and he'd just be playing along. So we put all this together and I just improvised for hours and got all the little bits and pieces going. We changed

the chords and we ended up with this piece and I think it has such a strong rhythm; a lot of things you play on it could be really good, but I got one or two quite good melodies on top of it and it built up to a very nice climax. It was probably better on stage than it is on the album in many ways, because on the album it fades out into the next bit which I'm not too sure is quite so good. It was an exciting thing to create at the time and we were very pleased with it. The funny thing about it was, when Tony Stratton-Smith heard the album, he didn't like that part. He thought we were trying to do something different and that we should stick with what we knew best. But we were very convinced that this should go on the album, so we stuck to our guns. You look at it now and realise that to have left that off the album would have been a bit of tragedy really." (1)

Towards the end of the long galloping synthesizers, the chords become major [9'42"]. Hackett: "I like this very much, I like it when the Mellotron strings kick in. It's a real up, the band starts to sound like an orchestra again, and I'm always relieved when it sounds like an orchestra or a choir. When it's ego-driven pyrotechnic playing, frankly I think it's a sport that I've heard others do better." (2)

The song slows down for a final synth riff [10'30"] which, surprisingly enough, was the drummer's idea. Hackett: "Phil had this riff on keyboards and we always tried to do it as another song. It was going to be another sort of Crosby, Stills & Nash influenced thing but we never did it, we just used a bit in *Cinema Show*." (2)

The lyrics were written by Tony and Mike; the first part clearly inspired by T.S. Eliot's *The Waste Land*. Gabriel: "I don't think I had much to do with

Charisma promotion from 1973

the lyrics; it was very much Mike and Tony's song, although it became sort of band thing as it took off. Although he had some good ideas, there were some things Tony would come up with that I would just refuse to sing, because the sound of the words and how you put them together is as important as the meaning. At times I felt lumbered and at [other] times really comfortable and liked the pictures being built. As time went on, I realised I did a better job when I'd written stuff or when I felt very comfortable with the lyrics. I could sing other people's lyrics if I thought they were really great and well-balanced. I got that sometimes with the others in the band but probably only 50 percent of the time. There were one or two things I wasn't 100 percent on. And then, of course, Phil had exactly the same experience when he had to sing my lyrics. There is such a thing as karma." (1)

In the live shows, when the instrumental part came along, Steve would leave the stage. Hackett: "I know that Daryl [Stuermer, Genesis' post-'77 session man] used to play along to this when they did it live, but I decided to distance myself from it rather than just play the same thing as Mike. He didn't really want me to play along with him during that part and I was OK with that. There was already this orientation towards the trio, so I just let them do that. There are plenty of other great guitar moments on the album. I didn't feel the need to keep playing one note. For me, it would have just been a repetitive strain injury." (2) In recent years, Hackett appears to have changed his mind as he does play on the instrumental part when the song is performed by his own live band.

Banks: "It was very popular live. It just sounded very good, particularly in later years when we had the double drummers, first of all, Bill Bruford and then with Chester Thompson. It was always a very, very strong moment, very driving, which is interesting really because it's in 7/8. But it sounds so natural that you're not really aware that it's in a funny time signature. As a keyboard player it's quite interesting because it gives you scope to try funny things; most of the time you play with it, without really thinking about it, but at other times you can actually construct things in 7/8, playing on top to see what happens. Some of that worked really well, so it was quite a fun thing to do." (1)

## AISLE OF PLENTY

The closing track acts as a coda to *Cinema Show* and reprises other parts of the album. It picks up from where the previous tracks slows down to its conclusion before flowing into Hackett's classical guitar riff taken from *Dancing With The Moonlit Knight*, from which it also inherits the melody sung by Gabriel.

*Aisle Of Plenty* is the perfect conclusion to the album, both musically and in terms of the very short lyrics, full of double meanings and wordplay, with an odd reference to *Supper's Ready*: "It's scrambled eggs" (which answers the question of what will be for supper).

Gabriel: "This song was the back bookend. Using the same melodies and harmonies that I'd written at the front on *Dancing With The Moonlit Knight*. At that point, it was full of these tarmac and supermarket images. It was what had happened to England." (1)

Hackett: "Pete's singing at the end, the impression of supermarkets I find very clever, especially

in terms of the lyrics because it's all a play on words. When it says "Tess co-operates" for example, Tess is a woman's name and at the same time it sounds like 'Tesco' which is a supermarket chain. So it's a combination. It could either be the woman or it could be the supermarket. The nuances of language are used very well on this. It's an album John Lennon said he liked. He used to listen to this in New York and, without doubt, all this play on words, when the various voices at the end are on top of each other, was influenced by Lennon and The Beatles." (2)

## THE ALBUM ARTWORK

After three albums characterised by the wonderful paintings of Paul Whitehead, the band decided on a change for this album. However, they were not drawn to the idea of featuring photographs of the band for the cover image. Gabriel: "We were quite obsessive about that. Me in particular, I think, about trying to have images do the talking rather than mugshots of the band." (1)

Instead, they were attracted to the work of an English artist, Betty Swanwick.

Rutherford: "I just like seeing stuff. You know, when you see an image and say, "That's the cover!" or "Let's develop that". I prefer seeing things and saying, "that's it!", rather than commissioning things because you spend a long time waiting for a drawing or painting and then maybe you get it and you don't like it. Betty Swanwick was a great artist. She was a great old lady and it was nice having someone who wasn't from the music world but from the art world. This was the first time without Paul Whitehead. I think that the Foxtrot album cover was a bit weak, so it was time to change and move on." (1)

Peter Gabriel in the dressing room,
Reggio Emilia, 4th February 1974

Collins: "For me, it was a great cover. It showed that there had been a change of sorts, you know, from that kind of almost schoolboy graphics we had on FOXTROT and NURSERY CRYME to something with Betty's characters which was kind of elegant." (1)

Banks: "Peter said, "why don't we get a real artist?". So we went to the Royal Academy and looked around and we saw this picture which we thought was great. So we went and had tea with this fantastic lady. We had tea in her garden but what was great was that she just put the table on the lawn, and when she put the tea on it, everything was sort of sliding down the thing. And the whole time we were there, there was this parrot sat on Peter's shoulder, sort of nibbling his collar. It was a somewhat surreal moment! Anyhow, she was a reasonably old lady and she said, she'd love to do it [the album cover] but that she couldn't do anything from scratch in just a month, which is what we needed. So we asked if she could modify the picture she already had. And that is what she did: she just took the picture she had and she added a lawn mower to it, so that it fitted with the lyrics of *I Know What I Like,* and some people in the background. It worked really well and in many ways it's the best piece of art we've ever had on a front cover. Whether it's the best cover or not, I don't know, but it's the best piece of art on a cover. I've got the original at home, I'm glad to say; it's a lovely piece." (1)

Gabriel: "I'd seen this artist, Betty Swanwick at a Royal Academy Show. She seemed to have a good combination of Englishness while exposing the underbelly. I went down to see her with Tony and Margaret [Tony Banks' wife}. She had a parrot and she kept on talking to the parrot in the middle of the conversation, so you weren't quite sure if you

Tony Banks in San Francisco, March 24th 1974.

The banknote printed by Charisma to promote the new album, with Gabriel instead of the Queen.

were being addressed or the parrot! And then she'd say, "right let's swap chairs", so you'd swap over. When she heard some of the things I was thinking about with the lyrics, she wanted to add a leather glove to the painting or sketch that she'd already done. I can't remember now if it was a drawing or a painting originally. She was a wonderful woman, a little bit like Miss Marple or an Agatha Christie character. Full of life, very smart and mischievous. She added the lawnmower because I had this line in a song: "me, I'm just a lawnmower, you can tell me by the way I walk". Again, I think it was the sense of the actor mowing the lawn, a way for people to clear some of the angst. I don't want to upset anyone, but this album cover was better than some that had gone before." [1]

Hackett: "Betty said she would work on this black and white thing we had seen over and over again and do it in colour. So we had this great artist doing this cover and I think it was perfect for the type of music: it was English, it was eccentric, it was gardens, it was dreamlike and it's a great work of art in its own right. She's sadly no longer with us. I believe she employed a dry brush technique but, then again, I'm no expert so it may have been pencil and crayon. It was just beautiful and I felt the whole package worked." [1]

## EPILOGUE

Selling England By The Pound was released in October 1973. In America, it never went higher than number 70 in the charts, but for the first time ever Genesis managed to make it into the UK Top 10 Albums Chart with an impressive number 3 spot, making this the band's first major commercial success. Alongside the album, the single, *I Know What I Like*, spent seven weeks in the charts, reaching number 21.

Collins: "It was another stage towards getting more confidence. There was a feeling that we'd finally gone somewhere, you know. We were still very much a road band, but we were learning the ropes in the studio." [1]

Gabriel: "I think people were growing into themselves and getting to know their quirks and eccentricities so the personalities were easier to feel. There was a sense of, you know, "look I can do this", and Steve definitely felt more of his own power in this record." [1]

Banks: "The line-up was stable and it felt stable too. Phil and Steve had both very much found their feet in the group, particularly as players, with Steve even starting to write a little bit, although it was still quite early days for him really. It was a more integrated sort of thing, even though, in all honesty, it was probably still a case of three senior and two junior members, but that was changing as time went by." [1]

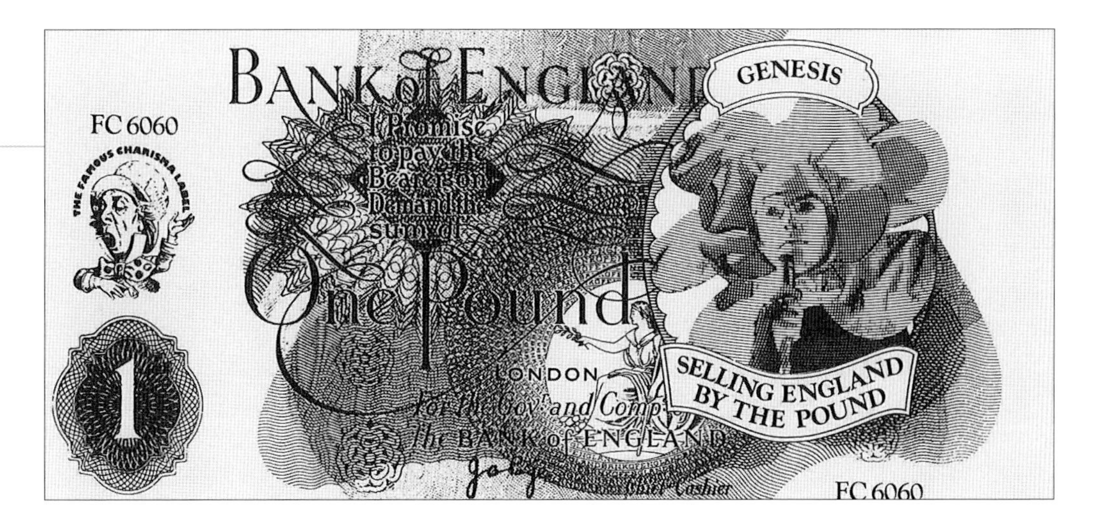


Hackett: "I think of this album as quintessentially English, it's like English fusion before the term was invented. Or even English collusion you could say, because it's too many different styles of music put side by side. I don't think Genesis or any modern band would be capable of making this now because they would be too frightened of failure. A modern band won't take a chance of making an album like SGT. PEPPER'S. Even The Beatles were terrified that SGT. PEPPER'S was going to be above people's heads. When we played this album to Tony Stratton-Smith, he said, "I don't like it, but we'll put it out anyway". He didn't think it was as strong as FOXTROT, but then again I thought it was an album with lots of great, wacky ideas and lots of guitar moments that work." [2]

Rutherford: "I've always likened SELLING ENGLAND BY THE POUND to NURSERY CRYME; they are sort of similar feeling albums in my mind. I think the good bits are good and the bad bits are a bit dodgy. But I think there are definitely some strong bits in there. And, of course, our first semi-hit single." [1]

Hackett: "I think albums like this provided a bridge over the chasm between what rock music was and what pop music was. The whole thing was a huge experiment. I think it's very English and not always an act of genius: it's very much a bunch of guys all forcing their ideas through and sticking to their guns and that's why there are times when it's an uncomfortable mix. Everyone was being strong on it and that's what I like about it. I think everyone plays, sings and writes with conviction, saying "no, my idea is as important as anyone else's". I still maintain that it's my favourite Genesis album because I felt most at home there. It was the life raft that I clung to at a time when I was operating in a stormy sea in my own private life. When I was working with them, I really felt that I was playing in the world's best band. When we were playing in America, particularly in Los Angeles at The Roxy (where we couldn't get a gig anywhere else) I felt that those shows in front of a small audience were some of the finest we ever did and I felt completely at home. When I was on stage playing this material, I felt as though I had the world of music in my hands. I felt that we were head and shoulders above everybody else at that time. There wasn't a band on the face of the earth that could do jazz moments like that and improvisation and cohesive arrangements and humour and little bits from classical music and hymns side by side with this kind of clever mathematical punctuated drumming." [2]

Banks: "On this album I think we came together much more as players, it was the first one where we sound really convincing; there's a bit more technique in there. However, I always like to think that technique is just another sort of paintbrush,

Peter Gabriel.
Reggio Emilia, 4 February 1974.

Phil Collins sings *More Fool Me*
in San Francisco, March 24, 1974.

something you can use and it can be very effective at times, but it should never take over. I think with some groups it sort of takes over; you get a guitarist who can play so fast that he can't stop doing it and everything, whereas we're very happy to sort of sit down... I'm just very happy to sit down and hold chords, which I do a lot of the time. Then other times you can go mad and the contrast works, it illustrates something; something you are trying to create with the piece of music you're writing." (1)

Collins: "Speaking frankly, my problem at that time was that we weren't a *groove*-oriented band. I was desperately trying to bring in my roots of Motown and Atlantic and sort of soul music into this thing that was very, very English. Sometimes it just didn't happen but at this point we were still struggling to sort of stay in time." (1)

Gabriel: "There were things I was less happy with than others and obviously I think everyone was trying to follow their own bits and pieces further through than anyone else's. Some things could have been a bit sharper, for example, the chorus of *I Know What I Like*, which for me didn't last as a pleasurable experience, even though it got us a hit. Most of our stuff took a few plays for a listener to open up to it, but once they got it, it would stick around for quite a long time. The old school allegiances had broken down quite a long time before really and I think Phil and Steve were on an equal footing in terms of power-broking." (1)

Banks: "This album was sort of commercially a success, I think that the odd light bit did help. Suddenly it started getting played on the radio a bit. I think what happened was that with the live shows we were picking up new fans all the time, so when the album came out, suddenly there were a lot of people going out and buying it all at the same time. That gave us a bit of chart presence. It came in at number three or something and stayed there for the second week and then suddenly it was down at 25, but it still made us feel that we had got somewhere." (1)

Gabriel: "I think I started to have some frustration about not being part of the keyboard side of things. I have very strong ideas on how things should sound and how you mix things together, so I think there may have been some frustrations in that department. There was a little riff on *I Know What I Like* which I played and there was a big battle to persuade Tony to let me play that bit [in the end, the keyboard part recorded by Gabriel was never used]. He was very possessive and I think a little afraid it would be the thin end of the wedge. But you know, I was never interested in trying to take over keyboards. It was just that I think sometimes when other people play things they bring different personalities into it. It was just a question of getting these new colours. When we were out gigging, quite often there'd be a piano in one of the dressing rooms and it was always Phil and I who would be there, busy playing keyboards and singing our stuff, but then there wouldn't be any of that within the Genesis performance. So there was this mild frustration. It wasn't burning at me or pissing me off also, because we were getting a lot of other stuff achieved and there was plenty to do." (1)

Hackett: "It's only over time that you have the ability to focus on this and analyse why it worked. It's an album that's full of nuances and digressions and side alleys, little side streets that sometimes

lead off and go nowhere; nonetheless, it doesn't sound like any other album anyone else has ever done. Not even Genesis did another album that sounded like this. If I were to speak for Mike, Tony and probably Pete, I don't think they would feel it's the strongest album because they would be thinking in terms of songs rather than atmospheres. I think this album is largely atmosphere-driven because they weren't the greatest songs around. Although it sounds nothing like them, this record is in some ways closer in spirit to a Pink Floyd album. There were fewer ideas but there are more moments of allowing the music to run. I think the idea of "why don't we just have a drone for a bit or just hit and knock bottles..." was influenced by Eno talking about music that was drone-driven. Drone music is ancient. It's Gregorian chant, it's hurdy-gurdy men doing their stuff, it's Greek Orthodox music and the music from the southern plains of Hungary; improvisations that have no fixed notes, no fixed point, it's very early use of two-note harmony. All I know is that the band went up a notch and fans liked it better each time, so it seems. This was not an album that disappointed fans who enjoyed Nursery Cryme or Foxtrot. And don't forget we were still working with the 12-string style at this time which was hugely influenced by the genius of the young Anthony Phillips. I don't think he's given enough credit for architecting the sound of Genesis and he was very important, almost like Matthew Fisher was for Procol Harum. I believe Anthony Phillips was for Genesis someone who cracked the whip, made them work harder and gave them a run for their money." (2)

# THE CONCERTS

The band's performance at Reading Festival on 26 August 1973 officially brought the FOXTROT tour to a close. By this time they had already recorded the new album, SELLING ENGLAND BY THE POUND, which they were set to take out on the road in less than a month's time to coincide with its release. After the first tours, decidedly basic in terms of presentation (depending almost entirely on Gabriel's charisma and imagination), this time round the music was going to be accompanied by a first-rate stage show. The stage set-up was dominated by the colour white: the four musicians were dressed in white, the drum kit and part of the keyboards were white and white light illuminated the whole scene. And that's not all: white, wavy curtains hung behind the musicians along with three screens on which slides were projected to create the right atmosphere for specific moments in the show.

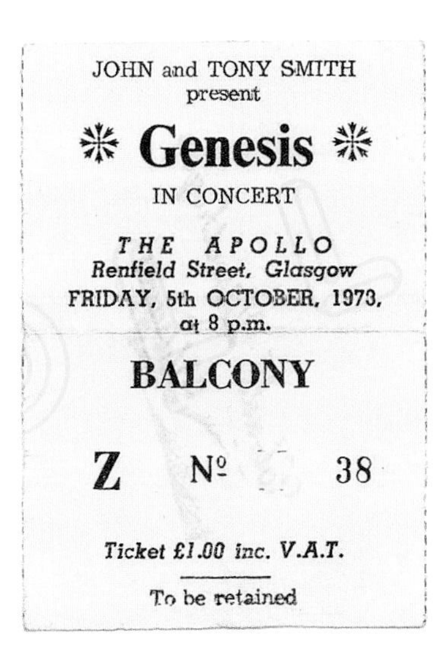
JOHN and TONY SMITH
present
Genesis
IN CONCERT
THE APOLLO
Renfield Street, Glasgow
FRIDAY, 5th OCTOBER, 1973,
at 8 p.m.
BALCONY
Z Nº 38
Ticket £1.00 inc. V.A.T.
To be retained

The setlist for the first few gigs was: *Watcher Of The Skies / I Know What I Like / The Cinema Show / The Battle Of Epping Forest / Dancing With The Moonlit Knight / Firth Of Fifth / The Musical Box / Supper's Ready* with *The Return Of The Giant Hogweed* as an encore. This last song was played to please audiences who had no intention of leaving at the end of *Supper's Ready*, which the band considered to be the logical conclusion to their show.

In fact, as early on as Lausanne, on 29 September, *The Return Of The Giant Hogweed* was taken out of the setlist to make room for *More Fool Me*, which usually came straight after *The Musical Box*. Shortly afterwards the band also changed the running order of the songs, moving *The Battle Of Epping Forest* further down the setlist and bringing *Dancing With The Moonlight Knight* forward to become their second number. At this point, the setlist became pretty much settled and normally included: *Watcher Of The Skies / Dancing With The Moonlit Knight / The Cinema Show / I Know What I Like / Firth Of Fifth / The Musical Box / More Fool Me / The Battle Of Epping Forest / Supper's Ready.*

This was a very different setlist to the previous tour due to the considerable presence of new songs (all the tracks off the new album were included except *After The Ordeal* and *Aisle Of Plenty*). To make way for the new material, classics such as *Get 'Em Out By Friday* and *The Knife* were dropped (although the latter did occasionally reappear as an encore). Even though the setlist was largely settled, occasionally there would be some variations. For example, *Harold The Barrel* from NURSERY CRYME would sometimes make an appearance (only once returning as an encore; more often than not it was added as a bonus in the second half of a concert).

Another significant variation concerns *Horizons*; Hackett's acoustic guitar solo (which funnily enough had never been played during the FOXTROT tour) quite often appeared instead of *More Fool*

Gabriel in concert. San Francisco, March 24th 1974.

*Me*, although sometimes both songs were played (the opposite also occurred, with neither of them being played, and occasionally *The Battle Of Epping Forest* was also left out).

This confirms an interesting trend which in all probability had something to do with Gabriel's by now overwhelming personality: with his increasingly predominant stage presence, the singer was (albeit involuntarily) beginning to overshadow his bandmates, something they didn't take too kindly to. Consequently, the band quite wisely decided to show their audiences that Gabriel was not the only shining star in the Genesis firmament and that it held four others of equal standing, even though they may have appeared to shine less brightly. So the group was frequently divided into different numerical entities: Hackett held the spotlight with his *Horizons*, while for *More Fool Me* drummer Phil took centre stage to sing accompanied by Mike on the 12-string. Tony was allowed an opportunity to play solo on piano with his intro to *Firth Of Fifth*, albeit for only a short while (starting from the English tour in January 1974) and the whole instrumental section of *Cinema Show* was played by Tony, Phil and Mike, the trio which would characterise the second stage in Genesis' career.

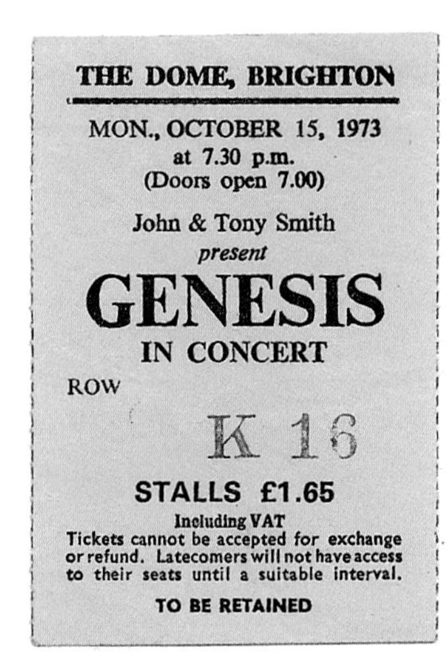


Musically speaking, the concerts were quite simply outstanding with a band on top form and, for the very first time, perfectly balanced. Rutherford once more proved to be the essential binding force with his great work on 12-string guitar and consistent use of the electric bass, often fed through a fuzz box, and making much use of his iconic Rickenbacker double-neck guitar (allowing him to move easily between bass and 12-string).

Collins, by this time consolidated in his position as second vocalist, gave extraordinary performances with increasingly more complex drum scores, appearing with vibraphone, glockenspiel, tubular bells and a vast array of other percussion instruments on stage.

Bolstered by his improved studio performance, Hackett went on tour with his confidence at an all-time high, playing electric and acoustic guitar and occasionally a Danelectro sitar while all the time making the most of his Echoplex (a device which helped to bring out experimental sounds). There were still occasional missteps, however. On some (possibly all) shows on the tour, Hackett would play a strangely-timed sequence of notes early in the solo on *Firth Of Fifth*, which seemed at odds with the rhythm section.

Genesis' most important player, though, was still Tony Banks, even more so now that he had better equipment. Although his primitive RMI electric piano left a lot to be desired (the short keyboard and lack of touch-sensitivity was so inadequate as to affect his playing, with him frequently getting the notes in the intro to *Firth Of*

Peter Gabriel performing *The Musical Box*, San Francisco, March 24th 1974.

*Fifth* wrong), having an ARP Pro-Soloist synthesizer definitely made his life much easier when playing his solos and especially in the long instrumental section of *Cinema Show*.

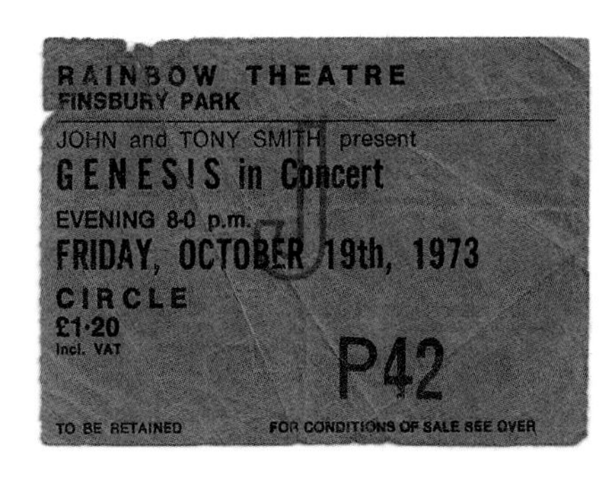


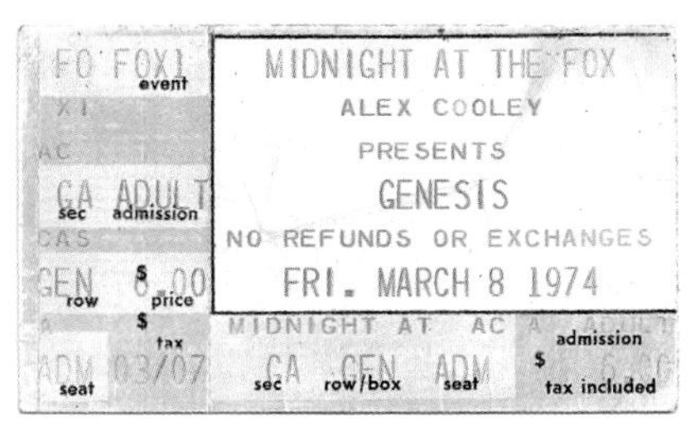


But, despite the undeniable high calibre of the four main instrumentalists, the absolute star of the show was still Gabriel: with a voice that had reached full maturity and playing some very pleasant flute, Peter continued to capture the audience's attention with his charisma and further developments in his stage costumes. While *Watcher Of The Skies* and *Supper's Ready* continued to be performed with the ingenious presentation ideas used in the previous tour, albeit with a few adjustments (the addition of gloves and cape for the former), Gabriel brought in some other theatrical elements to accompany songs from the new album, in particular for *Dancing With The Moonlit Knight*: "My name is Britannia", he would tell the audience, proudly wearing a helmet, cape and shield painted with the Union Jack. Slightly less picturesque but still evocative were his various interpretations for *The Battle Of Epping Forest* (including a vicar and a thug wearing a stocking mask over his head) and the lawnmower man complete with an ear of wheat in his mouth for *I Know What I Like*.

But possibly Gabriel's greatest theatrical moment came at the end of *The Musical Box*: after the long instrumental interlude, Peter would walk back onto the stage, hunched over and wearing a mask of an old man. After a series of unambiguous hip thrusting movements to act out the precociously-aged Henry's desire to possess his nursery playmate, Cynthia, he would fall to the ground as if exhausted.

Added to this, Gabriel continued to invent surreal stories which he would tell before songs, like his take on Romeo and Juliet before *Cinema Show*, the description of five rivers for *Firth Of Fifth*, the rather disturbing story of the girl on the tube (written on the back of the Genesis Live album sleeve) or the story of Old Michael before *Supper's Ready*, this sometimes with a little help from Phil on drums.

The Selling England By The Pound tour included around 120 shows, running from the second half of September to the beginning of the following May, with just a couple of short breaks (for Christmas and in the second half of February).

A handful of concerts in Europe (the first at the legendary Olympia in Paris followed by a few shows in Germany) gave the band a chance to musically shape the new songs before they started out on the first UK tour made up of 15 or so dates. The first (Glasgow, 5 October) was, unfor-

*Ciao 2001* n. 5,
3 February 1974.

made. Increasingly better quality copies of this roughly one-hour concert (with the following setlist: *Watcher Of The Skies / Dancing With The Moonlit Knight / I Know What I Like / The Musical Box / Supper's Ready*) would start to appear in fans' collections in the '80s and it was finally officially released as part of the bonus material in the 2008 remastered version of SELLING ENGLAND BY THE POUND.

At around the same time, the band renewed their request to Tony Smith (already famous for having worked alongside his father with bands such as The Beatles, The Who and Led Zeppelin) to become their manager. After declining the previous year, when he limited himself to organising the UK tour for February, Smith accepted, starting with the North American tour, which was much more comprehensive than the previous rather timid approach and ran throughout November and December. After a few days rehearsing at the beginning of November at the Cap-Rouge College in Québec City, the tour kicked off in Canada, not without the odd setback (the concert on 8 November in Toronto went ahead without a light show as the equipment had not arrived in time).

Tackling the East Coast with determination,

tunately hit by critical electrical issues and after the support act, Ron Geesin, finished his performance, Genesis were forced to postpone the show until the night of the 9 October.

Towards the end of the tour (30/31 October) Genesis spent two days at Shepperton Studios, Surrey, where, in front of a small audience of technicians, roadies and fans, the promo film *Tony Stratton-Smith Presents Genesis In Concert* was

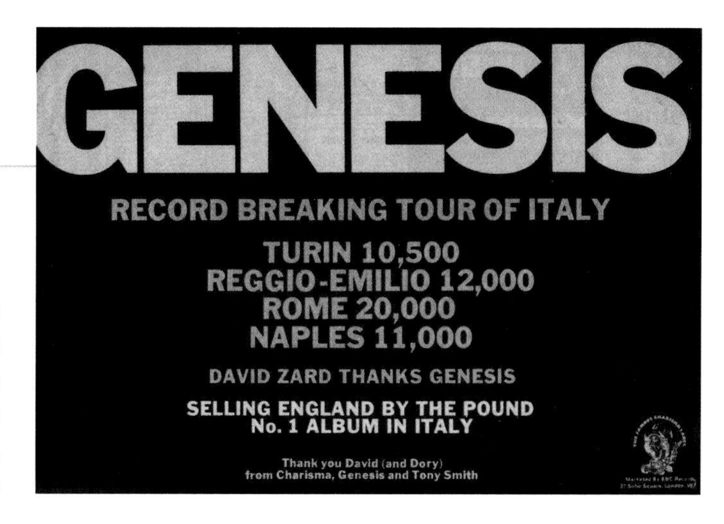


*Melody Maker* emphasising the enormous success of the Italian tour.

some of their concerts were in high-status venues, such as the Tower Theatre just outside the city limits of Philadelphia, the Felt Forum in New York, although most of them were still part of the college circuit. Genesis then ended the year by moving over to the West Coast for six concerts (two each day) in Los Angeles on 17, 18 and 19 December (for the last show Gabriel went on stage dressed up as Father Christmas and inhaling helium so he could talk with a funny voice). The Roxy wasn't a very large venue but Genesis managed to fill it with enthusiastic audiences for all six shows.

Before returning home the band managed to film a TV appearance for NBC which was aired on 25 January as part of the show *Midnight Special* (they played *Watcher Of The Skies* and a slightly abridged version of *The Musical Box* complete with a series of Gabriel costume changes).

But, although their fame was slowly starting to spread, Genesis didn't exactly make things easy. In fact, when they were invited to appear on *Top Of The Pops*, unhappy with the results, they rejected the film prepared for *I Know What I Like* forcing the BBC to air the song, which had entered the charts, accompanied by a Pan's People dance routine.

1974 began with another series of UK dates: after the concert in Birmingham, Genesis had three dates planned for the Theatre Royal Drury Lane in London, which would then become five to meet the enormous demand for tickets. These concerts in the British capital were the scene for Gabriel's umpteenth theatrical feat: at the end of *Supper's Ready* almost invisible steel wires hoisted him into the air as if he were flying.

After a few dates in Belgium, Germany and Switzerland, Genesis went back to Italy at the beginning of February for four concerts in Turin, Reggio Emilia, Rome and Naples. The band's success was huge and was reported back home in *Melody Maker* which published the amazing (and quite possibly slightly exaggerated) results of the tour organised by David Zard: 10,500 spectators in Turin, 12,000 in Reggio Emilia, 20,000 in Rome and 11,000 in Naples. A total of 53,000 tickets sold at a time when Genesis, despite their increasing popularity, were anything but stars on home turf. These concerts would long be remembered for the band's absolutely incredible performances, with their loyal Italian fans being rewarded with *The Knife* as an encore at all four venues and a

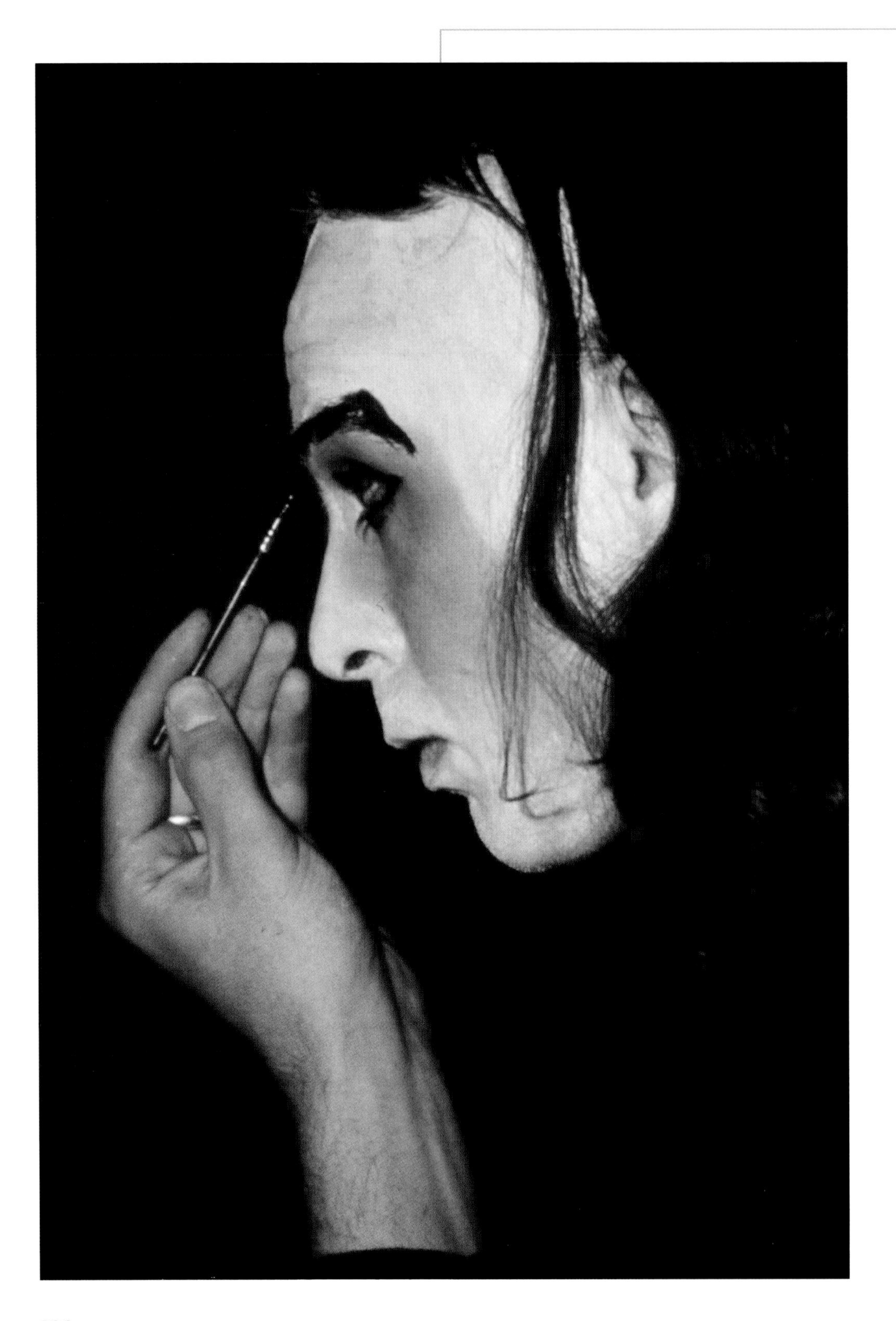

Gabriel, backstage at Reggio Emilia, 4th February 1974.

rare performance of *Harold The Barrel* in Reggio Emilia.

Before a brief break, Genesis played a couple of shows in France, stopping off in Paris on 12 February to record a live performance of *I Know What I Like* and *Supper's Ready* at the ORTF television studios. This appearance on the TV show *Melody* was recovered by enthusiasts many years later and was finally released as part of the bonus material of the 2008 remastered version of THE LAMB LIES DOWN ON BROADWAY.

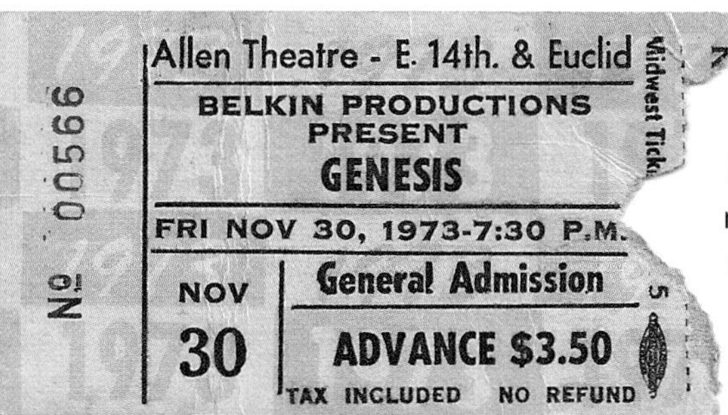


March and April were dedicated entirely to the United States. Genesis were set on extending their fan base on the other side of the Atlantic without giving second thoughts to the organisational effort required nor to the amount of travelling it would involve. As well as touring both the East and West Coasts, the group set about penetrating the interior states, those which were much more attached to tradition and therefore less open to the very European (nay, English) music offered by Genesis. So the band headed into Missouri and Iowa, into states along the Canadian border (Minnesota, Michigan) and into the Deep South (Texas, Georgia), even though the most acclaimed shows were obviously those in Philadelphia (where Gabriel once more flew during the performance of *Supper's Ready*, only this time almost strangling himself in the wires), New York, Chicago and Cleveland.

The US tour in spring 1974 brought with it, among other things, a visual innovation. The scene, which had previously been characterised by the colour white, this being the dominant colour of the instruments and the big backcloth (with two round screens on which slides were projected), had turned black.

The last concert was scheduled for 4 May at the Academy Of Music in New York. The massive enthusiasm shown by fans in the Big Apple meant another show was added for the following day. Unfortunately, however, during the night, six guitars were stolen. The band moved the repeat show to 6 May to give them time to recover some of their instruments (upon payment of a ransom) and hire others. And at the end of *Supper's Ready* Gabriel flew through the air on metal wires one last time.

## NOTES

(1) Mike Kaufman's Genesis interviews, Chicago / London, October 2007, partially used in the bonus disc accompanying the 2008 remasters

(2) Mario Giammetti listens to SELLING ENGLAND BY THE POUND with Steve Hackett, Twickenham, 27 January 2008

(3) Mario Giammetti listens to THE LAMB LIES DOWN ON BROADWAY with Tony Banks, Chiddingfold, 10 May 2011

# SELLING ENGLAND BY THE POUND TOUR

## 1973

### SEPTEMBER

19 **Paris (FRANCE)**, L'Olympia
23 **Osnabrück (WEST GERMANY)**, Städtische Bühnen
25 **Münster (WEST GERMANY)**, Halle Münsterland
26 **Hamm (WEST GERMANY)**, Kurhaus Bad Hamm
27 **Darmstadt (WEST GERMANY)**, Staatstheater Darmstadt
29 **Lausanne (SWITZERLAND)**, Théâtre de Beaulieu - Palais de Beaulieu

### OCTOBER

6 **Manchester (ENGLAND)**, Opera House
7 **Oxford (ENGLAND)**, New Theatre
9 **Glasgow (SCOTLAND)**, Apollo Theatre
*Originally planned for 5 October, the gig was then moved due to electrical problems.*
11 **Southampton (ENGLAND)**, Gaumont Theatre
12 **Bournemouth (ENGLAND)**, Winter Gardens
15 **Brighton (ENGLAND)**, The Dome
16 **Bristol (ENGLAND)**, Colston Hall
18 **Leicester (ENGLAND)**, De Montfort Hall
19 **London (ENGLAND)**, Rainbow Theatre
20 **London (ENGLAND)**, Rainbow Theatre
21 **London (ENGLAND)**, Rainbow Theatre
23 **Liverpool (ENGLAND)**, Empire Theatre
25 **Sheffield (ENGLAND)**, Oval Hall - Sheffield City Hall
26 **Newcastle (ENGLAND)**, City Hall
28 **Birmingham (ENGLAND)**, Hippodrome
30 **Borehamwood (ENGLAND)**, Shepperton Film Studios • *Video recordings for the film 'Tony Stratton-Smith Presents: Genesis In Concert'*
31 **Borehamwood (ENGLAND)**, Shepperton Film Studios • *Video recordings for the film 'Tony Stratton-Smith Presents: Genesis In Concert'*

### NOVEMBER

7 **Québec, QC (CANADA)**, Théâtre Capitol
*Two shows*
8 **Toronto, ON (CANADA)**, Massey Hall
9 **Kingston, ON (CANADA)**, Bartlett Gym - Queen's University

10 **Montréal, QC (CANADA)**, Centre Sportif - Université de Montréal
16 **Upper Darby, PA (USA)**, Tower Theater
17 **Medford, MA (USA)**, Cohen Auditorium - Tufts University
18 **Paramus, NJ (USA)**, Gymnasium - Bergen Community College
22 **New York, NY (USA)**, Felt Forum
24 **Princeton, NJ (USA)**, Alexander Hall - Princeto University • *Two shows*
27 **Rochester, NY (USA)**
*Venue unknown*
29 **Columbus, OH (USA)**, The Agora
30 **Cleveland, OH (USA)**, Allen Theatre

### DECEMBER

1 **Buffalo, NY (USA)**, New Gym - Buffalo State University
3 **Evanston, IL (USA)**, Cahn Auditorium - Northwestern University
7 **Fort Wayne, IN (USA)**, Ballroom - Walb Studen Union – Indiana University-Purdue University
8 **Ypsilanti, MI (USA)**, Frederic H. Pease Auditorium - Eastern Michigan University

9 **Toledo, OH** (USA), Hara Theatre
17 **Los Angeles, CA** (USA), The Roxy • *Two shows*
18 **Los Angeles, CA** (USA), The Roxy • *Two shows*
19 **Los Angeles, CA** (USA), The Roxy • *Two shows*
20 **Burbank, CA** (USA), NBC Studios
*Recording of the US TV show 'Midnight Special'*

# 1974

## JANUARY

13 **Bristol** (ENGLAND), Hippodrome
15 **London** (ENGLAND), Theatre Royal Drury Lane
16 **London** (ENGLAND), Theatre Royal Drury Lane
18 **London** (ENGLAND), Theatre Royal Drury Lane
19 **London** (ENGLAND), Theatre Royal Drury Lane
20 **London** (ENGLAND), Theatre Royal Drury Lane
26 **Brussels** (BELGIUM), Forest National
29 **Hamburg** (WEST GERMANY), Grosser Hall - Laeiszalle
30 **Düsseldorf** (WEST GERMANY), Rheinhalle
31 **Offenbach** (WEST GERMANY), Stadthalle Offenbach

## FEBRUARY

1 **Winterthur** (SWITZERLAND), Eulachhallen
3 **Torino** (ITALY), Palasport
4 **Reggio Emilia** (ITALY), Palasport
5 **Roma** (ITALY), Palasport
6 **Napoli** (ITALY), Palasport
9 **Marseilles** (FRANCE), Palais Des Sports
10 **Lyon** (FRANCE), Palais d'Hiver
12 **Paris** (FRANCE), ORTF TV Studios
*Recording of the French TV show 'Melody'*

## MARCH

1 **Passaic, NJ** (USA), Capitol Theatre
2 **Upper Darby, PA** (USA), Tower Theater
3 **Upper Darby, PA** (USA), Tower Theater
4 **Baltimore, MD** (USA), Eastwind Ballroom
5 **Washington D.C.** (USA), Warner Theatre
8 **Atlanta, GA** (USA), Fox Theatre
9 **Miami, FL** (USA), Gusman Philharmonic Hall
12 **Memphis, TN** (USA), North Hall - Ellis Auditorium
17 **Austin, TX** (USA), Armadillo World Headquarters
20 **Phoenix, AZ** (USA), Assembly Hall - Phoenix Civic Plaza
21 **Santa Monica, CA** (USA), Santa Monica Civic Auditorium
22 **Santa Monica, CA** (USA), Santa Monica Civic Auditorium
24 **San Francisco, CA** (USA), Winterland Arena
26 **Seattle, WA** (USA), Seattle Center Arena
27 **Vancouver, BC** (CANADA), Garden Auditorium

## APRIL

3 **Davenport, IA** (USA), RKO Orpheum Theatre
5 **Fort Wayne, IN** (USA), National Guard Armory
6 **Toledo, OH** (USA), Student Union Auditorium - University of Toledo
7 **Columbus, OH** (USA), The Agora
11 **Chicago, IL** (USA), Auditorium Theatre - Roosevelt University
12 **Indianapolis, IN** (USA), Indiana Convention Center
13 **St. Louis, MO** (USA), Kiel Auditorium
14 **Kansas City, MO** (USA), Memorial Hall
16 **Detroit, MI** (USA), Ford Auditorium
18 **Québec, QC** (CANADA), Centre des Congrès
19 **Ottawa, ON** (CANADA), Ottawa Civic Centre
20 **Montréal, QC** (CANADA), Centre Sportif - Université de Montréal
21 **Montréal, QC** (CANADA), Centre Sportif - Université de Montréal
22 **Rochester, NY** (USA), Auditorium Theatre
24 **Boston, MA** (USA), Music Hall
25 **Allentown, PA** (USA), Agricultural Hall - Allentown Fairgrounds
27 **Buffalo, NY** (USA), Century Theatre
28 **Cleveland, OH** (USA), Allen Theatre
29 **Cleveland, OH** (USA), Allen Theatre

## MAY

1 **Pittsburgh, PA** (USA), Syria Mosque
2 **Toronto, ON** (CANADA), Massey Hall • *Two shows*
4 **New York, NY** (USA), Academy of Music
6 **New York, NY** (USA), Academy of Music
*Extra concert added after the show of 4 May. It was originally planned for the 5th, but during the night some of the equipment of the band was stolen, so the second gig was postponed to 6 May.*

# The Lamb Lies Down On Broadway

(Charisma 1974)

***The Lamb Lies Down On Broadway / Fly On A Windshield / Broadway Melody Of 1974 / Cuckoo Cocoon / In The Cage / The Grand Parade Of Lifeless Packaging /// Back In N.Y.C. / Hairless Heart / Counting Out Time / Carpet Crawlers / The Chamber Of 32 Doors /// Lilywhite Lilith / The Waiting Room / Anyway / Here Comes The Supernatural Anaesthetist / The Lamia / Silent Sorrow In Empty Boats /// The Colony Of Slippermen: A) Arrival; B) A Visit To The Doktor; C) Raven / Ravine / The Light Dies Down On Broadway / Riding The Scree / In The Rapids / It***

- **Release date: 22 November 1974**
- **Recorded in Wales with the Island Mobile Studio, August–October 1974**
- **Mixed at Island Studios, London, August–October 1974**
- **Engineer: David Hutchins**
- **Producers: John Burns and Genesis**
- **Artwork and photography: Hipgnosis**

- **Michael Rutherford: bass, 12-string guitar**
- **Phil Collins: percussion, vibing and voicing**
- **Steve Hackett: guitars**
- **Tony Banks: keyboards**
- **Peter Gabriel: voices and flute**
- **Brian Eno: Enossification**

## THE MAKING OF

Having finally achieved some success in both the charts and on the road, packing venues wherever they went (and not just in Italy), Genesis were getting ready to enter a new and exciting phase in their artistic career. The band had spent the previous four years constantly touring, rehearsing and recording, and, now that they had finally managed to get above outsider status, they were also aware of the fact that their increasingly large audience had ever higher expectations of them.

However, the long and triumphant SELLING ENGLAND BY THE POUND tour caused devastating effects from a psychological point of view. With Gabriel now being idolised way beyond his expectations, the other four musicians were starting to feel the need to make music with different people, so while Mike continued to work with his old friend Ant Phillips (THE GEESE & THE GHOST, the album they made together which would be released three years later under the sole name of Anthony Phillips, is one of the most underrated prog treasures of all time), Phil Collins joined a pub band called Zox & The Radar Boys (with the intention of performing music in a looser, less-structured style than Genesis).

Alongside these extra-curricular activities and

now under the prestigious management of Tony Smith, Genesis began thinking about their artistic future: how to follow up a masterpiece like SELLING ENGLAND BY THE POUND?

Banks: "When we started writing, we thought it would be adventurous and quite nice to try and do a double album concept. We had no idea what the concept was going to be or anything but we felt that our audience would be able to take it. Peter seemed quite keen to do all the lyrics, which was something that had never been done before; prior to this they had been very much split throughout the group, so we weren't really in favour of this. We felt it would give the album a bit of a one-dimensional quality and, for me, lyrically speaking, that is what happened. What's more, the relationships in the group weren't quite as easy as they had once been, probably because Peter was being thrust out as the star, you know, the media would only concentrate on Peter really, which was kind of strange in a group that was as democratic as we were." (1)

The band seemed really enthusiastic about the idea of making a concept album, an ambitious experiment already undertaken by numerous other bands from diverse genres, such as The Who with TOMMY, Pretty Things with S.F. SORROW and The Kinks' ARTHUR (OR THE DECLINE AND FALL OF

The British Empire). Although Mike Rutherford's proposal to base it on the children's book *The Little Prince* by Antoine de Saint Exupéry was also taken into consideration during the very early stages of the project, in the end the band opted for what was then still a very vague storyline, put forward by the lead singer, about a half-Puerto Rican immigrant called Rael who was living on the margins of society in New York.

Gabriel: "When we were about a fifth of the way into the process, I started to write some of the lyrics and I thought, "yeah, there's a way of linking all this up and getting a sort of singular thread". A lot of people don't follow the thread very much but, in my head, it made a lot of sense. From the time of *Supper's Ready* I'd always wanted to try a bigger piece. We had a lot of discussions about the album and the writing of the story because I maintained then (and still do) that not many stories are written by committee. I was dreading fighting over things: the characters that I wanted to introduce, the words they would say or things someone else might want to include but that I didn't feel were appropriate." [1]

Collins: "I have no idea why Peter chose Broadway. I do remember us being part of Macy's parade on Broadway, it must have been in 1972/3, maybe it was during The Lamb period. We were all in white and we kind of jumped into the parade next to the white Michelin man or something, maybe that's why. Or maybe it was just because we'd been to America a couple of times and there was a fascination with the size of the place; the steam in the streets coming up through the grills fascinated everybody. It was like, "What goes on underneath there? What is it? The centre of the earth?"." [1]

Rutherford: "You need to ask Pete about the concept. It almost doesn't matter sometimes, because you just get on this journey and it takes you along. People hear songs, lyrically, the way they interpret them. I don't think they can actually hear the lyrics and I'm sure they don't understand them, apart from the choruses maybe. But they sound great anyway; lovely phrases." [1]

Hackett: "It's a weird album, isn't it? A modern

Hackett, the Slipperman (Gabriel) and Rutherford at Berkeley on 22 January 1975.

tale of redemption. It was Pete's concept as a lyrical venture but everyone's concept musically. There is often this misconception that Pete wrote the whole thing. I don't think it's the strongest thing that the band ever did." (1)

Gabriel: "The story is like *The Pilgrim's Progress* but on the streets of New York. So it's a spiritual journey into the soul but there's quite a tough world feeding the imagery. One of the influences was a film called *El Topo* by Alejandro Jodorowsky, whom I later invited to work with me on a screenplay for The Lamb Lies Down On Broadway [something which was never completed]. It was a rough, visceral cowboy spiritual film. It was unique at the time and had a really strong cult following. When I was working with Scorsese (on Passion, the original soundtrack for the film *The Last Temptation of Christ*) I talked about this film and he hated it, he thought it was really pretentious I loved it and I wasn't the only one, in fact now Jodorowsky is getting recognised, that film in particular. It had these extraordinary images and this character, played by Jodorowsky himself, who had to learn lessons from each sort of guru and then kill them on his way to finding his own self. So it was a real mix of esoteric images and spiritual journey, with urban street images and that was the blend I was trying to put together in a way that would allow more people to travel with me." (1)

As he only had the basis of an idea, Peter asked his bandmates to work separately for the first time ever: he would write the lyrics while the other four wrote the music (even if at times roles crossed). Rutherford: "I think Tony and I did one lyric, but it was very much Pete's project. He wrote some music too, but it became a little bit sectionalised." (1)

Gabriel: "There were parts of it where we'd be discussing lyrics and throwing some of the words around for different bits, for example in the title track, which was Tony's, musically speaking, and *Here Comes The Supernatural Anaesthetist*, which Steve had brought to the band. They would discuss some of the lyrical stuff with me because, well, they'd sort of got the writer's ticket. But I was pretty anal about hanging on to some lyrical flow and I really wanted a tougher edge to this record than we'd had previously. I didn't think anyone else in the band was going to deliver that." (1)

Collins: "With this album it was one story, one lyric writer. What I remember most about The Lamb Lies Down On Broadway was four of us in a big room jamming, writing and recording everything while in the other room Peter was writing lyrics to the things that were already there. Obviously, we did play some stuff all together, but it was like 'him' and 'us'." (1)

Gabriel's renowned slowness in writing lyrics meant the musicians had more time than usual, resulting in them writing a huge amount of material. Too much for a single album.

Rutherford: "I'm not sure I remember how it happened. I think we decided to do a double album to give us a bit more space. Some of the bits of music were quite short really, but we thought the 50 minutes of a single album was nothing at all and that it would constrain us. By making it much longer, it meant we could do these jams and improvisations; it gave us the chance to be a little bit freer." (1)

What's more, there were still loads of old ideas which had never been recorded that could be

Advertising the new album created by the American Atco label.

developed and used if and when needed. Banks: "*Anyway* was a piece I'd written years before. We'd always liked it and here was an opportunity to use it. So there were many pieces that came from different eras really, but most of it was written in the period after SELLING ENGLAND BY THE POUND was released." (2)

Once the outline of the project had been established, to write the album the band rented out Headley Grange, previously used by other bands such as Led Zeppelin, Bad Company and Pretty Things (the house had originally been built as a workhouse for the poor before being converted into a private home).

Rutherford: "Headley Grange had a lovely atmosphere but it was a bit of a bomb site. Musically, the ideas came very fast, I mean they just flew out, but the double-album workload for Pete, who was never a fast lyricist, meant that after a while he was up in the bedroom trying to catch up on the lyrics while we were downstairs doing the music. So there was a little bit of a divide there, which is a shame." (1)

Collins: "It was a strange period actually. I can remember driving to Headley Grange, which I think is on the Hampshire-Surrey border. I had my first wife, Andrea, with me and my daughter, Joely, and it was a bit like going into a Dickens' novel: broken windows and rats everywhere. Bad Company had used it and Led Zeppelin had recorded the *When The Levee Breaks* album there [LED ZEPPELIN IV, 1971]. But no-one had cleaned up. It was really horrible. I don't think the poor woman who owned the house knew what she was letting herself in for. You'd be walking down the corridor and two or three rats would walk past you. They wouldn't scurry away, they just walked past you and stopped to look at you. In the back garden there were these vines going up the back wall and you'd see this constant scurry of activity. And I was bringing a daughter into this and we were going to stay the night. At night, when you went to bed, you could hear this scurrying around. The place never slept. First of all we had to clear up, but we never got rid of the rats. We took over the living room to write and there was another room with a piano." (1)

Hackett: "We were working in a haunted house and the ghosts were certainly keeping me awake at night! I remember talking to Robert Plant about this, they [Led Zeppelin] had worked at Headley Grange and he said he was convinced the place was haunted. They'd recorded stuff there, the famous drum sound in the stairwell. I heard sounds at night; the place was weird. I remember on the day we were due to leave, I was just washing my hands in the sink and I stepped back and the floor gave way. Had it happened a split second earlier, I would probably have been killed. You might say it was just coincidence (it was a ramshackle house) or you could say it was haunted by a poltergeist that nearly got another rock'n'roller or maybe it was the rats scratching at night rather than the ghosts, but it was bloody hard to get to sleep at times, what with that and the geese out in the courtyard." (1)

Right in the middle of the writing sessions, in June 1974, Peter Gabriel received an unexpected proposal which put the whole future of Genesis at stake.

Gabriel: "I'd written a story, which went on the back cover of GENESIS LIVE, about a woman who

*"They didn't want to do a tee shirt...*
*they didn't want to do a tote bag...*
*they didn't want to do a watch..."*

As Genesis grows in popularity, their music grows in scope. "The Lamb Lies Down On Broadway" is two records of indescribable music. Nothing we could say or do could prepare you for Genesis' newest musical conceptions. Sorry.

**"The Lamb Lies Down On Broadway." New from Genesis on Atco Records and Tapes.**

ATCO

Mike Rutherford at Berkeley, 22 January 1975.

Phil Collins at Berkeley on 22 January 1975.

began stripping off in a tube train, taking off her clothes until all that was left was a tube of light. It was something that caught the fancy of William Friedkin, and he was Mr. Hot-and-Happening-in-Hollywood at the time because he'd just done *The Exorcist*. He wanted to use that power to try and reinvent Hollywood and bring in a whole new team of people. He invited me in as an 'ideas person', you know, to brainstorm and come up with different concepts and explore different areas. He'd actually approached Tangerine Dream to do the music and there was a guy called Philip Druillet, who was from Heavy Metal magazines [originally known in France as *Métal Hurlant*] and there was an animated designer whom he wanted to work on some of the visuals. To me it was a very exciting opportunity, not because it was Hollywood, but because I love ideas, I love brainstorming with smart people. I was suddenly going to be given a vehicle and given a chance to come to life, so I really wanted to do it. But even though Phil had always been a jobbing musician and doing other things, from Tony (and to some extent Mike) there was this feeling of "why should he have all the fun" and this sense of "no, we're not happy to make time for you to go off and piss away valuable band time when you should be committed". So it was a hot, contentious issue." (1)

With tensions running high, it took the authoritarian intervention of Tony Stratton-Smith to try and patch things up. News of the turmoil within the rock band also reached Friedkin's ears, leaving him understandably disorientated.

Gabriel: "I'd always loved film. I'd had a place at the London School of Film Technique in Shelton Street and at one point it was a toss-up over whether I was going to try and follow a career as a music person or as a would-be film director. But Friedkin didn't want to be held responsible for breaking up the band. So it all got complicated and I wasn't backing down." (1)

Rutherford: "During the album, Peter sort of left for a bit. I think Friedkin got a bit of a shock; his offer to Peter wasn't meant to do that. So, we were like, "wow, what are we gonna do now?". We needed some strong instrumental stuff, so we just carried on jamming around until he came back." (1)

Collins: "We gave him an ultimatum: Friedkin or the band. So he went. But Friedkin hadn't wanted to split the band up. His was just an idea and he didn't even know if it was going to work. My first feeling when Peter left was "OK, let's just get rid of all the vocals and do it instrumentally". That was, of course, pooh-poohed (quite rightly)." (1)

Hackett: "We started work and three days later he was back. I thought that provided we got the album done and toured with it, it would all be forgotten about." (1)

Banks: "He was persuaded to come back, I think by Tony Stratton-Smith, and so we finished off the album. But something magic had gone; it wasn't quite the 'all for one' it had been." (1)

Collins: "At that point, of course, we all knew

this could happen again at any time. When Peter came back we carried on writing and then we went to this farm in Wales to record it with John Burns using mobile recording equipment. It was great fun, it was a nicer place than Headley Grange." (1)

Banks: "We recorded the album in a sort of barn somewhere in Wales using a mobile studio. This meant we had more time to do things, but as the mobile studio wasn't perhaps quite as good as it might have been, there was a sort of buzz throughout the album. But thanks to John Burns the sound is actually very good. Doing the remixes we found that what's actually on the tape is really good and to be honest, the original mix isn't bad either; we changed a lot less on this one than on the previous records. We took out all buzzes and really had fun with the 5.1, for example with the different characters in *The Colony Of Slippermen*, we tried quite hard to make it an interesting 5.1 mix." (1)

Hackett: "The new mixes help with the fact that it's very crowded. There is a lot of detail on the album and it needs to be mixed very well. Originally it was very badly mixed. I remember I wasn't around for some of the mixes because I'd had an accident with a wine glass and I'd practically cut my thumb off. I was in hospital recovering and when I heard the album, after it was mixed, I just thought, "oh God". Listening to it now I can hear so much more detail on it than in the original mixes." (1)

Despite being back in the fold, so to speak, the lead singer was afflicted by a certain sense of detachment from his bandmates, exacerbated by problems at home.

Gabriel: "Jill (whom I was married to at the time) and I had just had our first child [Anna-Marie, born on 26 July 1974]. It was a disastrous birth. We were all set for a natural birth but Jill caught an infection from a needle which wasn't clean and so she had a fever. The umbilical cord was wrapped around the baby's neck and her lungs were full of gunk. Everything was going wrong and we didn't think she was going to survive. They carried her away like a chicken carcass wrapped up in silver paper and put her in an incubator. They wouldn't let my wife see her because they thought it would be cruel for her to bond with a baby who wasn't going to make it through. They wouldn't do that nowadays, but back then they thought they were being kind. So this became the centre of everything. The band were recording but instead of being somewhere reasonably close to where we were, in St. Mary's Hospital, Paddington, they were out in Wales, so I was making these long pilgrimages. I was based in London and whenever things looked better I'd try and zoom back to

Wales for the recording. This is something I think that the band would accept now, but back then they weren't very understanding. And I just lost it in lots of ways because this was a life and death situation and so obviously much more important than an album or anything else. There was a lot of resentment about that and I think the seeds for the beginning of the end were sown at that point. What had begun in some arguments about creative freedom and whether or not there was room to do outside projects ended with this really unsympathetic handling of my dealing with a family crisis. Relationships had effectively broken down by the end of the record." [1]

Collins: "We were all in this house even though some of us shouldn't have been because we only lived down the road. Unbeknownst to us, Jill was experiencing a very bad and difficult pregnancy." [1]

Rutherford: "We began to sense that one of our party was starting to be pulled in different directions, outside the band. We were conscious that he wasn't as committed and was starting to think about other things going on in his life. To be honest, looking back, we were so unsupportive. We were young and very into the album and what we were doing, while poor old Pete was having to deal with the terribly traumatic touch-and-go birth of his daughter. We gave him no help at all, actually. I'm sure it must have been very hard. At that stage, we didn't think outside the band very much and I think as people, as friends, there wasn't much time to consider other people's, likes, dislikes or wishes really." [1]

Hackett: "I was relatively new to the band, but Pete, Tony and Mike had been together since they were 12 or 13 years old, when they were at Char-

Advertisement in *Melody Maker*, 24 May 1975.

terhouse together. So maybe it felt like a long time in the same regiment and eventually he felt the need to depart. I know he had other pressures, which were personal and not for me to talk about. I remember it was all very difficult: my marriage was breaking up, it looked as if we only had half a singer and the level of commitment to the band seemed very shaky at that point. All this cast a shadow over proceedings and, although I think it's a very inventive album which has some great moments on it, I still feel there was this sense of claustrophobia accompanying it. The idea that we were still trying to employ the philosophy of everyone going away together and living together, cheek by jowl, you know, when there were families and children involved, wasn't a healthy kind of environment for everybody. [That Gabriel was the first person in the band to have a child is urban legend: Hackett's son, Oliver, was born on 28 February 1974 and Collins had adopted his first wife's two-year-old daughter, Joely. Evidently the singer's difficult family issues had a much bigger impact than the guitarist's and drummer's.] It was that kind of growing-up phase and we had to grow up very quickly at that point because we were going to lose our lead singer. It was a time of great uncertainty and I moved on to writing solo stuff. Meanwhile, the audiences were growing and they weren't aware of all this." (1)

## THE ALBUM

When The Lamb Lies Down On Broadway appeared in record shops the world over, the response it received from fans and journalists was very varied. Genesis had faced the winds of change blowing through both the musical world and their own personal lives with courage and intelligence. The album represented a significant break from the traditional Genesis sound. The 12-strings, although still present, were now substantially reduced to a mainly rhythmic and chordal role, with the usual dreamy arpeggios limited to a bare minimum, and Tony relied less on the orchestral sounds of his Mellotron in favour of bringing out a whole myriad of electronic sounds from his synthesizers. Meanwhile, Steve's guitar playing, maybe with the exception of a single classic solo (in *The Lamia*), engaged in experimental sounds (for example the rhythm in *Counting Out Time*) and riffs surprisingly verging on hard rock (*Lilywhite Lilith*). However, despite Steve having bought a Synthi Hi-Fli to get more effects out of his guitar, on the whole the overall instrumentation was less elaborate.

The rhythms turned out to be dry and hypnotic; Phil's drumming, now free to express itself on material leaning more towards rock, is beyond superlative and Mike pulled off a magnificent performance not only on bass, uncharacteristically hard (and often made more intense by using a fuzz box), but also as an extraordinary and untiring 12-string rhythm guitarist.

On the vocal side, Gabriel (with the help of Phil) gave his most mature performance to date.

However, one cannot fail to notice, in terms of balance within the band, that The Lamb represents a step backwards compared to the perfect equilibrium achieved on Selling England By The Pound. Musically speaking, the album is dominated by the writing of Tony and Mike, with compositional

SIDE ONE • THE LAMB LIES DOWN ON BROADWAY • FLY ON A WINDSHIELD • BROADWAY MELODY OF 1974 • CUCKOO COCOON • IN THE CAGE • THE GRAND PARADE OF LIFELESS PACKAGING • SIDE TWO BACK IN N.Y.C. • HAIRLESS HEART • COUNTING OUT TIME • THE CARPET CRAWLERS • THE CHAMBER OF 32 DOORS • SIDE THREE • LILYWHITE LILITH THE WAITING ROOM • ANYWAY • THE SUPERNATURAL ANAESTHETIST THE LAMIA • SILENT SORROW IN EMPTY BOATS • SIDE FOUR THE COLONY OF SLIPPER MEN • THE ARRIVAL • A VISIT TO THE DOKTOR • THE RAVEN • RAVINE • THE LIGHT DIES DOWN ON BROADWAY RIDING THE SCREE • IN THE RAPIDS • *IT*

contributions from the other three reduced to a mere flicker; Gabriel wrote *Counting Out Time* and *The Chamber Of 32 Doors* with a few other bits and pieces here and there, Collins provided only *Lilywhite Lilith* (and even that was actually written three years earlier), while Hackett, in the midst of a family crisis back home, limited his writing contribution to *Cuckoo Cocoon, Hairless Heart, Here Comes The Supernatural Anaesthetist* and the intro to *Colony Of Slippermen.*

Then, of course, the intricate narrative plot, written exclusively by Gabriel, is a chapter unto itself. It is, without doubt, the most complicated piece of work to emerge from the lead singer's imagination, full of extremely varied and often obscure literary and cultural references. What's more, as all too often pointed out by Banks, it was almost impossible to extract individual songs from the album due to the lyrics being almost incomprehensible when taken out of context.

Finally, the internal friction brought with it another consequence: the net division of roles. For the first time ever, Tony didn't play a single note on the guitar but stuck exclusively to keyboards, and neither he nor Mike were allowed to sing backing vocals. The vocals were also strictly divided, with Peter on lead and Phil on harmonies.

That said, on a purely artistic level, The Lamb is a monumental piece of work which only served to further enhance the band's reputation. And even though at first listen it may not be as immediate as its predecessors, it still represents a significant artistic step forward. Genesis were aware of the changing times and, more than the individual songs it contains, it is the outstanding value of the overall vision itself that shines supreme. It is an album where profoundly different atmospheres alternate: the electronic experimentation of *The Waiting Room, The Colony Of Slippermen* and *Ravine*; the dramatic emphasis of *Broadway Melody Of 1974, In The Cage, The Chamber Of 32 Doors*; the expressive hardness of *Lilywhite Lilith, Back In N.Y.C., It*, and the occasional heart-wrenching tenderness of *Carpet Crawlers* and *Cuckoo Cocoon.*

With an insight which proved to be light years ahead of their contemporaries, already slipping irreversibly into the realms of self-parody (Jethro Tull with War Child, Emerson, Lake & Palmer with their pretentious Welcome Back My Friends..., Yes with the Relayer album), Genesis showed themselves ready to embrace a new stage in their career at a historical moment in which the rock cosmos appeared to be on the lookout for new stimuli.

Meanwhile, the Prog flag was kept flying thanks to successful albums from veterans King Crimson with their Starless And Bible Black, and up-and-coming bands like Camel (Mirage) and Supertramp (Crime Of The Century), David Bowie was continuing along the path of the concept album with his Diamond Dogs and hard rock witnessed the metamorphosis of Deep Purple with Burn (the very first with David Coverdale on vocals).

In America Bob Dylan and Lou Reed were still going strong with new studio albums (respectively Planet Waves and Sally Can't Dance) and spectacular live albums (Before The Flood and Rock'n'Roll Animal), while, on the other side of America, Jackson Browne pulled the masterpiece

*Melody Maker*,
16 August 1975.

Melody Maker

Aerosmith special — Interview on page 8

AUGUST 16, 1975 — 12p weekly — USA 60 cents

GABRIEL OUT OF GENESIS?

PETER GABRIEL'S position in Genesis was uncertain this week as mounting speculation suggested he had quit the band.

Gabriel has remained incommunicado since the end of Genesis' British tour in the Spring — he has refused repeated requests for interviews and reliable sources told the Melody Maker this week that he has decided to leave the band.

The speculation comes as various members of Genesis are becoming increasingly involved in solo projects. Guitarist Steve Hackett has finished work on his first solo album and Michael Rutherford, the bass player, is also planning to record. Phil Collins, the band's drummer, has been playing with his own pub group.

Commenting on the reports of a split, the band's manager Tony Smith told the MM: "The group are being rather broody at the moment, but this happens every year when they are thinking and writing for the next LP."

And Tony Stratton-Smith, head of Genesis' record label Charisma, said: "Peter has been involved with one or two summer projects including producing a single for Charlie Drake." Both Smith and Stratton-Smith, however, denied a split in Genesis.

**Sinatra returns**

JUST six months after his sell-out concerts at London's Royal Albert Hall, Frank Sinatra will be coming back to Britain for TEN shows this autumn.

And with him will be Sarah Vaughan and the Count Basie Orchestra.

The concerts will be from November 13 to 20 at the London Palladium, his first season at the theatre since the early Fifties. The November 15 and 16 dates will both feature two shows, with early concerts at 6.15 pm.

Tickets will be available from MAM, 24/25 New Bond Street, London, on August 20. The prices will be £17.50, £15, £12.50, £10, £7.50, £5 and £3 — much less than the ticket prices for his Royal Albert Hall concerts in May.

**Instruments galore!**

12-page preview of new gear starts on page 27

PETER GABRIEL of Genesis: "The group are rather broody" says the management

Late For The Sky out of the hat.

Despite being full of great albums, 1974 still didn't seem to be a particularly innovative year, apart from the extraordinary Rock Bottom by Robert Wyatt. Even the aristocracy of rock proved to be no exception: with The Beatles firmly in his past, John Lennon released Walls And Bridges, while The Stones brought out It's Only Rock'n'Roll (the title song from which is mentioned by Gabriel in *It*).

In truth, a dark shadow was stalking the halls of rock, ready to shatter its very foundations. It wouldn't be long before punk exploded on the scene and, as bizarre as it may sound, Gabriel's Genesis played a part in bringing these changes about, starting with the leading character in their double concept: the street punk, Rael, who couldn't possibly have been further away from the elves and fairies of the stereotype prog imagery. The urban, edgy literary premise to which the band would set their soundtrack was stylistically miles away from the record released just one year earlier.

An album which has always sparked controversy, The Lamb Lies Down On Broadway stands as a unique and autonomous work in Genesis' highly fertile artistic career. The biggest regret lies in never knowing what might have happened afterwards if Gabriel hadn't decided to walk out of the door never to return.

## THE SONGS

### THE LAMB LIES DOWN ON BROADWAY

The double album opens with a memorable piano intro which, due to the unusual sequence of notes, Tony was forced to play with his hands crossed over. Very remote from the dreamy atmospheres permeating their work of just a year before, the song has a disturbing air made even more sinister by the annoying buzz created by Hackett's guitar (filtered through two fuzz boxes) and Mike Rutherford's distorted bass.

Rutherford: "The piano riff is great. Pete sets up the image, describing the New York scene. I think the lyrics really paint a picture of the album." (1)

Banks: "I always think of it as being the last

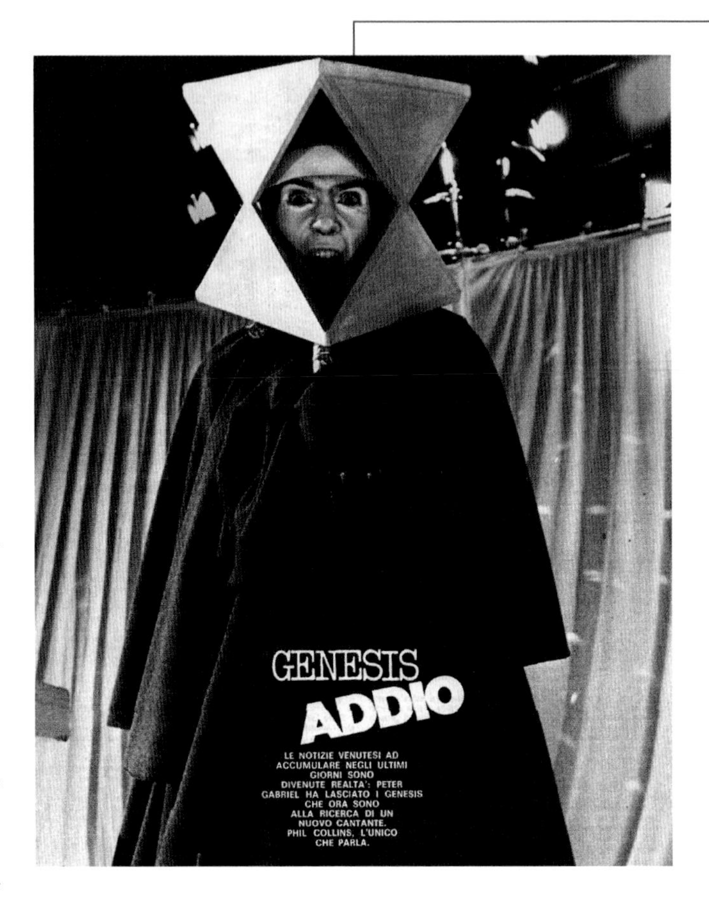


song Peter and I ever wrote together. We'd written a lot together in the early days, you know; it was a pretty good song to end on really." (1)

## FLY ON A WINDSHIELD

Collins: "We called it *Pharaohs* originally because it was like a trip down the Nile in Ancient Egypt. It was a piece of ambient music really, but with rhythm." (1)

Banks: "We were just playing fifths, you know, creating a sort of Egyptian army coming across the landscape. We had a quiet section and a loud one and we just sort of butt-joined them together. Then, combined with the lyrics, this idea of the fly coming and hitting your windshield, that moment when that first chord comes in is probably the single best moment in Genesis' history." (1)

Divided into two parts, a vocal section and the instrumental part, the song starts with Mike's 12-string guitar chords, accompanied by electric piano with some distant Mellotron (generally, the Mellotron is featured less than on previous releases, although it is still responsible for some of the album's most striking moments).

Banks: "Maybe [it was] because I'd switched to the little Mellotron [the Mellotron 400] or maybe because the album was harder-edged and needed it less. When I did use it, I often combined it with other sounds, for example, on *Fly On A Windshield* I had the strings and the RMI Electra Piano playing in unison with it all the time because Mellotrons lacked real edge. A lovely sound but a nightmare instrument to play!" (2)

The instrumental section features Steve's lead guitar playing over Banks' tidal Mellotron chords.

Hackett: "It's a lovely piece of music, where the guitar comes to the fore, rising and falling. As a guitarist, I love the parallels with Ravel's *Bolero*, the key change and the very interesting lyrics Pete wrote, with this strange parade of lost or bygone souls in the subsequent section (*Broadway Melody Of 1974*). An interesting take on America, I think that's why I like it the best, lyrically speaking." (1)

## BROADWAY MELODY OF 1974

Written by Banks, Rutherford and Gabriel and tagged on to the tail end of *Fly On A Windshield*,

*Ciao 2001* n.38, 28 September 1975.

this song exploits rhythmic bass riffs, drums and electric guitar synchronised over the original chord sequence played on the Mellotron and Peter's singing.

Hackett: "I think it was the band at its most percussively interesting. It was also harmonically adventurous. I don't think there is another song I've ever heard that sounds quite like it; a mixture of romantic and malevolent. I think we were operating on telepathy at that point." [3]

## CUCKOO COCOON

A gentle track marked by the electric guitar arpeggio played by Steve with a decisive compositional contribution from his brother, John, dating back to their younger days when they would play together at home.

Hackett: "John, my brother, had an influence as he suggested the two opening chords, but in a different rhythm. I wrote the vocal melody line and Peter wrote the lyrics. It was intended to sound sweet originally, with a harmony vocal, but I think it came out strong and quirky." [3]

The filtered voice of Peter (who also manages to find space to fit in some flute solos) is enriched by Phil who basically sings the whole song alongside the lead singer.

## IN THE CAGE

Written at home by Banks and brought into the band almost complete, this song starts on Rutherford's pulsating and distorted bass running under the organ chords and Gabriel's vocal intro. Steve's electric guitar introduces the verses with arpeggios and underlines the choruses with circular phrases, while a powerful bass riff (at 3'09") leads into Tony's fantastic synthesizer solo.

Banks: "It was exciting this one, always a climax on stage, particularly the later live version of it [starting in 1978]. Pete struggled a bit with the vocals on this one when he was doing it live. The trouble with Peter was that his voice sounded good when it was just on the edge of cracking up, but, of course, it was very difficult for him to do live, he couldn't sing it all really and in those days we couldn't really change the keys of songs very easily. Songs like this had a pretty complicated solo and so to suddenly change the key midstream would have driven me nuts." [2]

## THE GRAND PARADE OF LIFELESS PACKAGING

Banks: "Pete had a moment in his plot which needed a song and we didn't have one. I just started playing these two chords, a dopey kind of riff really … I quite like one note things, *Pigeons* [off the EP Spot The Pigeon, 1977] is a good example of that; I just keep one note going through the whole thing and just change the chords underneath it, letting it build. Then what Pete did on top was kind of wild and he didn't really make any use of the melodic content of the piece, but I think it works very well. It's always been one of my favourite songs on this record because I think it's quirky, it's very Genesis (no-one else would do a song like this) and it builds to a nice climax with a few weird chords." [2]

An atypical case, as it was written directly in the studio following the theme as outlined by Gabriel, who had already written the lyrics, this song comes in with a strange keyboard march from under which Peter's voice, filtered by some electronic wizardry worked by Brian Eno, emerges. A real surprise for a band as notoriously self-sufficient as Genesis.

Gabriel: "I was, and still am, a fan of what Brian Eno does and brings to projects. For us, this was an adventurous album and I really wanted him to come in and wave his magic wand over a few of the sound areas, which we called 'Enossification'. I think Phil then did a couple of albums for Brian. We probably didn't pay him very much (we didn't have very much in those days) and I knew he was impressed with Phil and I think that's how they ended up working together." (1)

Collins: "Eno was upstairs doing his first solo album, Taking Tiger Mountain By Strategy. I'd heard of Roxy Music but I'd never heard their music, but Peter was a fan and he asked Eno to come down and put the vocals through his ARP. After we'd finished, some deal was made and I was sent upstairs to play drums on his record. That was fine by me because I ended up getting to know him very well and playing on Another Green World, Before and After Science and Music for Films. But I felt like some kind of musical prostitute." (1)

Rutherford: "Brian Eno came with a synthesiser and put the voice through it and sort of messed around with some sounds, but I think he was mainly involved in filtering the voice. There weren't many synthesisers to choose from back then and he was always quite brave in what he did." (1)

Banks: "The Eno thing was always a bit of a red herring, people think he did more than he actually did. Sometimes I've even been asked what I was doing while he was playing all those solos! What he did was put little fiddly bits on the vocals mainly and a couple of other things but he didn't play anything. The day he was there, I think it may have been towards the end of recording the album, I wasn't in the studio. We were totally running out of time and we were doing day and night shifts. I might have been ill or something or maybe I was on the night shift the day he came to the studio." (2)

While even a whistle adds some colour to a truly bizarre piece, the marching is emphasised by Phil's drumming. Vocal inserts articulate paranoid situations which evolve in a continuous crescendo up to a kind of final, almost paroxysmal, slowing down where [at 2'23"] another deeper voice doubles Gabriel's vocals. Banks: "It's an octave divider. In those days we used whatever was available and these things only existed in studios at the time." (2)

## BACK IN N.Y.C.

Rutherford: "I love this track. It was one of our heaviest tracks actually. It doesn't sound that way so much on the record but on stage it really was, with Pete's voice just belting it out. There are some instrumental gems, like the 1 minute 30 instrumental section where we were just sort of messing around with moods." (1)

The opening is punctuated by dull tympanic beats and Mike's pulsating bass.

Rutherford: "I had a 6-string bass, a Microfret, which I'd found in America. I've never seen another one since. You could play it an octave higher. I wrote the riff with the band. I remember we did a lot of jamming and improvising and we were thinking it was a shame Pete wanted to move on because it was sounding really good musically." (1)

Banks: "It started off with a riff Mike was playing on this 6-string bass he had, which we then developed as a song. Then Pete just did this sort of shouting type vocal on it. At the time, it was quite surprising but I think it works pretty well." (1)

Intercalated with a harsh and syncopated synth riff, Gabriel's deliberately graceless voice comes in almost straight away: rough and shouted, on the very edge of intonation, it is an approach one could almost say heralds punk.

Banks: "I heard a version of this by Jeff Buckley [on the album SKETCHES FOR MY SWEETHEART THE DRUNK]. I was very surprised that he did the whole thing including the funny bits. If I'd been him I would have just stuck to the main thing. But it was fun and quite sweet really, it was kind of "why not?". Mike was playing extreme bass. We wanted to get melody out of the bass as well as the guitar. During this period Peter, Mike and I were the main writers. Phil and Steve both did the odd bit but they weren't very involved in the writing. So the main parts of this are Mike's and the bits that come later, the ones that are less good, are mine. We repeated the riff as much as we thought we could get away with, and at the time it seemed like we stayed on it for too long. It was always difficult for us to do repetition at this stage, we always liked to go somewhere else than stay with one thing. We had a lot of ideas and wanted to try and get them all in. I think Peter sings this really well. I like the build-up, the piano is quite heavily compressed and the interesting sound and the chords are suggested by the riff. But I hate the line "shave it off": shaving hair off the heart, it's a horrible concept! Then, of course, the next piece which Steve and I sat and wrote together, this rather grand and beautiful piece of music, ended up being called *Hairless Heart*. What a horrible title!" (2)

## HAIRLESS HEART

This is an intensely beautiful instrumental track dominated by Hackett's guitar playing, on both nylon and electric guitar, and Tony's Mellotron chords and organ arpeggio, with the melodic phrase provided by an ARP Pro Soloist synthesiser.

Banks: "Steve had a really nice melody so I just did the fluttery things behind it. I added this bit which I'd had around for a long time but hadn't found a home for; a kind of semi-orchestral thing, it was nice though. Because it was a double album we were able to include all these instrumental interludes." (2)

## COUNTING OUT TIME

Banks: "This is a really good song Peter had written before we started writing THE LAMB. In a different world, it might have been a hit (if we'd been in a position of having hit records at the time). I like the lyrics as well, it's cheeky." (2)

Written exclusively by Gabriel, this is a catchy song with a verse, chorus structure with variations and inventive successions of chords and rhythmic riffs, plus a truly original solo by Hackett on guitar filtered through his EMS Synthi Hi-Fli EMS, lying over a cheery rhythm guitar and dixie-jazz piano.

Banks: "The guitar solo in the middle, done on the Synthi Hi-Fli, is really good. The piano with the

Berkeley, 22 January 1975.

echo was fun to play. I was playing the piano in Dixieland style, which was pretty much in the original composition by Pete, so I can't take much credit for that." (2)

*Counting Out Time* was the first single taken from The Lamb, but it failed to make any impact at all.

Banks: "Back in the '60s I was very good at picking hits for other people, but by this time I had no idea. I knew it had to be quite simple and I thought this was quite bouncy but it didn't do anything. If a record doesn't get played on the radio, that's it, it won't be successful. Obviously, this song recalls things like *Harold The Barrel* and *Willow Farm*, which have that same kind of quirky, quite Beatleish quality about them. We always loved The Beatles and this has a McCartney kind of bounce to it." (2)

Hackett: "It was the nearest thing to a single on the album. But it was a trifle risqué and I think possibly not as strong as it could have been musically speaking. I think you need a bit more of a hook." (1)

Banks: "In any case, it's still played because it's a pop song and I think it works nicely. It's simpler compared with a lot of the other things on the album and it's all about early sexual experiences, trying to do it by the book." (1)

## CARPET CRAWLERS

Another song where, as with *The Grand Parade Of Lifeless Packaging*, Gabriel's lyrics came first and the music, written by Tony and Mike, second.

Banks: "Mike and I wrote the chord sequence really and then Pete sang on it and Phil did a bit as well. It's a funny thing with music, the listener just hears the music, the lyrics and that's the song to them. But when you are writing music, it's what you start with that is most important. If you get a good basis, you can probably write a hundred good songs on it. Like when we did *Mama* [from the album Genesis, 1983], for example, Mike played that drum box rhythm and we knew that we could write a good song on that repeated loop, no matter what we did, it was going to work. The same applies here, we could have done a hundred melodies on this and it would have sounded good. The verse melody is different every time really but it sounds good." (2)

As well as the lyrics, Peter also wrote the melody.

Gabriel: "I love the melody of *Carpet Crawlers*. I was staying with Jill's parents in Kensington and there was an old, out-of-tune piano. I spent hours and hours on it honing that melody and then the lyric." (1)

Banks: "There's a really good melody on this, very strong. It was one of those things that emerged in the rehearsal room, out of nothing really. It's nice and with the slow build-up you could always recapture the audience. It starts slowly but then with its repetition and character it's very nostalgic. The only problem really is that, out of context, the lyric is a bit weird. On the album it's fine, but if you put it out as a single (as we did) people want to know what it means. The chorus, obviously, is catchy and could work, especially with the combination of the two voices, with Phil singing the other bit. Phil always sang this beautifully. In the later days, after Peter left, this song always sounded really good. I'm not crazy

about the version we did with Trevor Horn [for the greatest hits album TURN IT ON AGAIN - THE HITS, 1999] but the vocals on it, the way it switches from Peter to Phil in the middle is really strong. We were really lucky to have two such strong singers in the group." (2)

The beginning of the song is based on a section taken from *The Lamb Lies Down On Broadway.*

Banks: "I wanted to reprise this. I don't know why, but I think the bit I'd written in the middle of the title track [starting at 2'34"] needed hearing again. It was a good bit, so I did it again and we developed it into *Carpet Crawlers.* Mike and I sat down and did a really simple sequence and Pete sang on it." (2)

After the intro, the song structure becomes extremely linear, with verse and chorus repeated four times. Without doubt this is one of the simplest chord sequences in the history of Genesis, with Gabriel's and Collins' vocals and the finishing touch provided by Hackett on lead guitar.

Hackett: "I did this melody that was designed to parallel the vocal. On the original mix it's almost inaudible, but I think you can hear it on the new version. People like it as a song, you've got interesting stuff in it: Phil's doubling himself so you've got two drummers, you've got this slowed down 12-string thing (or sped up keyboards, I can't remember). It's got that very shimmery quality thanks to Tony's arpeggios on the RMI piano and Mike on 12-string; most people today would use a pad, chords on keyboard that would just sit there and create this sort of wallpaper glue behind the whole thing. The chord work is very subtle." (1)

Banks: "It's very simple and I think that's half its charm, some things with Genesis are a bit overworked. The chorus is a little bit different and the fact that the song slowly crescendoes means it kind of just creeps into you. The other songs are a bit meandering so this one stands out like a very bright spark in the middle of the album: when we wrote it we had no idea it was going to be picked

for release as a single, we thought the single was going to be *Counting Out Time*. We did release it [in April 1975] but it wasn't a hit or anything. We've tried releasing it again, it's still never done anything, but it's one of those tracks that our own audience loves." (1)

## THE CHAMBER OF 32 DOORS

With a backdrop of Banks' beautiful Mellotron chords, Hackett's heart-wrenching guitar solo melody precedes the drum breaks and bass, emphasised with the help of tubular bells followed by the entry of Peter's and Phil's voices while a bass riff dominates over the organ base.

Banks: "It's a kind of bitty piece, mainly written by Peter, but it was arranged quite nicely. Steve and I sort of orchestrated it to get a particular sound. I think the second side is in many ways the strongest of the four. The whole album up to this point is really strong, and it would have been a really good single album if you added just a couple of pieces from the second half." (2)

## LILYWHITE LILITH

The second LP opens with an unusually hard song with distorted guitar and bass riff playing in unison over heavy drumming and a keyboard base which comes in almost at the same time as Gabriel's vocals, to which Collins' harmonies are added in the choruses. The track is a surgical operation which stitches together two fragments of songs written by the drummer shortly after he joined the band in 1970.

Banks: "When Phil first joined us he had this piece called *The Light*. We did a version on stage and it was probably one of the best songs we never recorded. It started off with this bit which we used at the beginning of *Lilywhite Lilith* (not with the same lyrics obviously) and Phil came up with a second part which became the chorus. That dramatic chord change [0'37"] came with the original song *The Light*, although that wasn't part of what Phil wrote but something that came up in the rehearsal room." (2)

This early example of the songwriting of Phil Collins is an absolute rarity, as at that time Collins was anything but a songwriter.

Banks: "He didn't have the confidence to write very much but he had this one bit that he'd had for a while, and then he came up with another piece we thought we would use as it had really nice chords. He came in with them and sat at the piano and played them for us. During *Lilywhite Lilith* you can hear a reprise of the *Broadway Mel-*

Advertisement in *Melody Maker*, 5 April 1975.

*ody* theme with different lyrics [the bit starting with "She leaves me in my darkness" at 1'45"] and a slightly simpler melody line, same chords" although played in a different key. "It's a good driving piece for a story, almost operatic. It's interesting because instead of going up it comes down and leads into *The Waiting Room*, which was another improvised piece." (2)

## THE WAITING ROOM

An experimental instrumental developed by the whole band starting with an idea put forward by Hackett. It incorporates interesting effects especially in the use of guitars and synthesizers, but also percussion, strings, bell sounds and delays.

Banks: "We tried to keep it as improvised as we could right to the end. The best version we ever did of it was the first one when we were in this rather spooky place, Headley Grange, where we wrote the album. We switched off all the lights and Steve got a glint in his eye as he likes to do that darker stuff. The first time we did it we were genuinely frightened. While we were doing it I started playing this very simple two-chord sequence, to lighten things up, and everyone joined in and it became this great piece. It was fabulous, but every time we tried to play it after that, changing from being evil to happy, it never really worked. It was still quite fun but it was never as good. If only we'd had a tape recorder at that stage, we could have taped it." (2)

Experimentation led the band to produce a whole series of really bizarre sounds, such as the sort of lamenting ghosts at 1'18". Banks: "You could get some strange sounds out of the Pro-Soloist, like the gurgly sound with echo [1'45"]. I really like the sound of the 'chk chk chk' [2'48"] played low with some vibrato on it. Mike didn't have much to do here and Pete just went off; I thought he could have done some more vocal things but he didn't. Steve and I are sort of talking to each other. Of course, we didn't have the tools at our disposal as you would today with synthesizers. Mike was trying to do something but I'm not quite sure what... When I started to play some happy chords [3'06"], Mike thought, "thank God, now I can do something!". We added the crash as a way to end it, but, on the original, it just started to come out into this bit much more spontaneously: it's very simple chords and there's a nice bit of bass and guitar and Phil can't help sort of tricksying it up a bit." (2)

Collins: "That period, between this album and the next three or four years with Brand X and Genesis, was probably the height of my playing. But there was a lot of inventive stuff from everybody. Steve, for example, was a great sound guy and Tony was getting the maximum out of what he had. Songs like *The Waiting Room* display a side of Genesis that no-one, apart from the ardent fans, really remembers. They either forget about it or have never heard it. And I think it's actually the way we would end up writing, by doing things like that. That's how songs like *I Can't Dance* and *No Son Of Mine* started. We just started playing *The Waiting Room* with the idea of changing the mood from darkness to light. We started off making noises and Steve added lots of eerie sounds and outside it was pouring with rain. Then Tony put some chords in [3'06"] and suddenly it started changing rhythm, and then there was a rainbow and it stopped raining and the sun came out. I'm not making it up; I was there and it happened and it was the most amazing thing. It was just a little golden eight- or nine-minute moment." (1)

## ANYWAY

Banks: "On The Lamb we absorbed one or two bits that had been around for a while, like *The Light*. We were kind of searching through everything we had and anything we thought was good we would use. This piece was from a long time before, even before Genesis was happening. I probably wrote it at university, at the same time as writing things like *Fountain Of Salmacis*, and we used it for the radio documentary on [the painter Michael] Jackson. I can't recall if we even had a lyric for it then." (2)

In fact, a quite different version to the one which ended up on the album, recorded for the BBC in 1970 (when Phillips and Mayhew were still in the band) would come to light in 2008 on the Genesis 1970 - 1975 box set under the title *Frustration*. The song revolves around a beautiful piano arpeggio sitting on a bass, drums and tambourine backdrop over which an intense performance by Peter reigns supreme.

Banks: "It's just a pianistic type of thing, based on a little riff with different chords underneath it. It has a strong start and then we elaborated the middle part and made it a bit grander." (2)

After the guitar riffs and an almost orchestral break, Hackett's impressive solo takes off [1'56"].

Banks: "Steve played a three-part harmony. He used to like to work out his solos very carefully; he wasn't really an improviser, which was OK with me because I wasn't either. Sometimes with guitar, you can free yourself up a little bit, without a doubt the best solo he ever did with us was on *Firth Of Fifth*; he had a structured melody somewhere but he gave himself the opportunity to just drift a little." (2)

## HERE COMES THE SUPERNATURAL ANAESTHETIST

Two chords on rhythm guitar by Mike provide the wonderfully simple base on which Peter's and Phil's voices lie as they sing together before a long instrumental section, incorporating some bizarre vocalisations from Gabriel and Collins but with Steve's lead guitar very much at the fore.

Banks: "I didn't have much to do with this one to be honest; it emerged one day when I wasn't in the studio. I don't think I played on it at all. It's a jolly and undemanding piece. Again it's Steve writing in a very structured way and you can blues it around a bit and get some ideas from that. Anyhow, it's not my favourite." (2)

## THE LAMIA

Banks: "This was again a whole piece I'd written. It didn't have a melody when I brought it to the band, but that was suggested by the various parts I already had. Pete wrote a lot of words for the

Atco label, US print.

song which I then took home (over Christmas, I think it was) and wrote a melody using his words on top of the part I'd written. It's a nice song but it's not (to me) totally successful, not like some of the ones on the album. It's not one I look back on with great pride but it has some nice parts." (2)

The song is dominated by piano with vocals mirroring the chords while the drums and bass come in to play the main hook.

Banks: "I love the part [from 1'08"], which we then, of course, reprised in *The Light Dies Down On Broadway*. I think it works much better in that song, I really like this chord sequence." (2)

The final section is a long and moving guitar solo from Steve.

Banks: "Again there was the problem with the lyric factor; "three vermilion snakes" is hardly romantic, if they had said "I love you, baby", it would have been great. I have a problem with the lyrics in what I call my three big pieces on this album: *In The Cage, The Lamia* and *The Colony Of Slippermen*... *In The Cage* just about gets away with it but *Slippermen*, you know, I had great plans for that but... I think that the one song I've written that most resembles *The Lamia* is *One For The Vine*, which is a much better song than this because I was able to write a lyric that fitted the shape of the song better." (2)

## SILENT SORROW IN EMPTY BOATS

A brief instrumental piece written by Rutherford; an almost ambient piece which insistently repeats a single phrase with an orchestral feel made up of six notes.

Banks: "This one is another improvisation, which was called *Victory At Sea*, so it starts very quietly while we were trying to recreate that kind of feeling of an ocean wave. Mike just had this one riff and it had a nice atmosphere about it, so we just improvised around it with the Mellotron sounds that I had at the time, voices and other strange things, and bits of flute and stuff which keep going up and down like waves." (2)

Collins: "It would be good if people remembered that the band which played *Silent Sorrow On Empty Boats*, which is like, you know, sailing ships, clouds and fog, is the same band that played *Hold On My Heart*. The same band, the same mentality." (1)

## THE COLONY OF SLIPPERMEN

The last side of the double album opens with a song full of extraordinary electronic effects and which is divided into three parts: *Arrival / A Visit To The Doktor / Raven*. To this, we should add an intro played on electric guitar featuring sounds with a distinctly oriental influence.

Banks: "The introduction was something we called the *Chinese Jam* which Steve was quite into. I helped out with what I could and I think it's OK. It's colour more than anything else and it doesn't really introduce the song at all. We didn't give it a title, I don't know why. We should have." (2)

Peter's voice kicks in accompanied by a joyous keyboard phrase over a happy rhythm and circling electric guitar melody.

Banks: "When I wrote this I thought it could be really good, but it's the one that got away a bit. The keyboard sequence [1'50"] could have been really powerful with the right melody and the

right lyric... it's funny because what I play on the bass line is very similar to a song by the Manic Street Preachers. I think the drums are a bit too clever, they should have been simpler. Having said that, I don't want to put it down too much. I think it works in a different way; it's still a fun piece of music but it didn't come out quite how I thought it would. I was quite right to write the triplets in 6/8 because you can change it to 6 or break it up to 3s or 2s and it changes the feel of it. The riff at 2'59" would have worked better as a piano part really. The tone of the synthesiser is slightly cheesy sometimes; I would have liked to have had a different one but..." (2)

Alternating different voices (with both Gabriel and Collins involved in interpreting the various characters woven into the lyrics) lead into a synthesizer solo.

Banks: "That was something that came separately. Again, it was Mike, Phil and I, just bluesing around. It was always a tongue-in-cheek solo; the chords were very traditional rock-like and it was a bit of a joke but ended up sounding pretty exciting. I'd done a similar sort of thing on *Apocalypse In 9/8*; there are a couple of bits where I was having a bit of a joke, but sometimes these things come out stronger than you expect. The bit I like best, however, is at 4'02" [the riffs before the beginning of *Raven*], which originally came from *The Light*, but without the melody." (2)

At 4'52" another solo kicks in which Genesis would recycle years later as part of the '80s versions of *Cinema Show*.

Banks: "One quality of the Pro-Soloist is the way the portamento works, giving it a great sound, the squelchy bass. The way we get back into the verse [6'01"] was one of our worst changes ever. It's terrible; I'd change it. But it used to be terrible to have to change between two keys." (2)

## RAVINE

Banks: "This is another of the improvised ones. Steve produced that sort of windy noise with his

*Zig Zag* n. 53, June 1975.

guitar using a fuzz box and a wah-wah pedal. Mike added a four-chord sequence on the 12-string... Nice though." (2)

## THE LIGHT DIES DOWN ON BROADWAY

The initial wind effect provided by the synthesizer is counterpointed by Steve's electric guitar playing over Mike's 12-string arpeggios. Gabriel's voice comes in with the bass and drums. There are four sung sections, two of which are mutations of other songs off the album.

Banks: "This was definitely the best thing done on this side of the album because it gives it real weight. It was made up of two previously used bits just done slightly slower. The chords in this melody gave us a chance to bring out a little more than with *The Lamb* itself, especially on the chorus part. The verse part is from *The Lamia*, which was my part, but the hook [1'22"] is from *The Lamb Lies Down On Broadway*, which Peter and I wrote together and we decided to do the arrangement a bit slower here. It often works that a slower arrangement of a faster piece can be quite exciting. Different arrangements are something we've done many times in our career and this is a good example. The harmonies on this are great." (2)

This track full of reprises gives a sense of continuity to the whole album. Banks: "Yes, that's right. Sometimes you do something and you can tell that it could be used in more than one context." (2)

This is the only song on the album where the lyrics weren't written by Gabriel.

Banks: "Peter was taking a hell of a long time to get the lyrics finished so we said, "for God's sake, just let us do one!", which saved a bit of time. So Mike and I did the lyrics on this, we were just told what action had to take place in it." (2)

## RIDING THE SCREE

Opened by a melody made up of bass and rhythm guitar (both by Mike) over Phil's amazing drumming, this song is most frequently remembered for Tony's extraordinary synth solo.

Banks: "This was a devil; the first part is ridiculous. I hate it, well I like it when I get past the first bit in 13/8 or whatever this bloody piece is in... it was a nightmare [Rutherford's riff is primarily in 9/8 but the track is highly complex, with multiple time-signature changes] Mike had this riff and I thought I'd try to do something by playing against it, so I played in 4/4, which sounds all right. There are bits where I broke it up into slabs so it would make more sense. It was quite good for the title I think." (2)

At 1'05" there is synth part which the band would reuse years later in their live shows.

Banks: "We used the melody as the peak of *The Cinema Show* in later years just because it's a nice tune and it sounds good in the other rhythm. You had to keep your head playing this sort of thing because if you got out of sync you'd be gone. There's the extra beat at the end of each section and I'd forget about it and just do my own thing, hoping they'd come back at some point." (2)

Hackett doesn't play on this track. Banks: "There were a few times that Steve didn't play at all on the album. I've said many times that Phil, Mike and I would often do some of the solos, such as in *Apocalypse In 9/8* or *Cinema Show*, on our own, just the three of us. That's why we were so happy to write

Cover of the Italian single release with an abbreviated song title and sponsorship from the Supersonic radio show which was aired on Rai, the national broadcaster.

as a trio when we got to the stage where it was just the three of us. We had done it so many times before that, we had a natural way of doing it, so it worked really well, although it was mainly instrumentals at this stage." (2)

## IN THE RAPIDS

Rutherford's chord sequence on 12-string, interspersed with arpeggio sections provide the intro to Gabriel's vocals. Later the bass, piano and electric guitar join in while the drums play softly with a touch of what sounds like cowbell.

Banks: "Mike wrote this. It's nice as far as it goes, but it doesn't go very far, it's just another filler piece. Pete was just storytelling on top, he didn't use the chords to develop a nice melody or anything. I'm doing my Floyd Cramer bits over the top [the tinkling piano at 1'19"], a bit like Ketty Lester's *Love Letters*. When we did the live CD for the first box set [Archive 1967–75], Pete had to redo most of the vocals as it was all a bit rough. The song that really sounded great with the new vocals was *In The Rapids,* I just thought it sounded fantastic. It's a fairly insubstantial piece of music but it sounded more like what he does now. It has an odd lyric, but we could never quite develop it. It was a nice beginning of something, but we could never really get it beyond that stage, so we decided to just leave it as it was. That said The Lamb was that sort of album where you could have pieces that weren't complete; we just used them as a link, so again we just did a sort of slow build." (2)

## IT

The final track on this monumental double album is driven by Rutherford's rhythm guitar after a long note played on the synthesizer. Over the propulsive rhythm section, complicated lead guitar and synth parts intertwine: as in other songs, Hackett and Banks play in harmony both in instrumental sections and under the vocal line.

Banks: "It's a nice song but it's not a final piece. We couldn't really work out what we wanted to do. Steve and I had written it and we had originally thought it would just be instrumental. Steve and I had worked out a solo on it, a tricksy kind of thing, and then, of course, Pete wanted to sing on it. We didn't know if we had enough room so it starts off with a solo as the verse, which is a bit odd. The portamento on the Pro-Soloist was very slow, which was quite fun. The basic riff is nice but it could have been better, we shouldn't really have started off with the instrumental. What Pete sings on this is good, we could have just done more of this really." (2)

Collins: "We were really pushed to get the album finished. We were at Island Studios and by this point we had a day shift and a night shift. I was on the night shift with Peter and the day shift was Tony, Mike and Steve. Me and Pete did a mix of *It* and then the other guys came in and thought we were mad and changed everything. There was a bit of friction." (1)

Banks: "We were doing day and night shifts and, in this instance, I wasn't mixing this one. I came in on the day shift, after they'd mixed this, and it was awful. They'd obviously been up all night and were completely zonked; it just sounded terrible, there was no guitar for a start and that's what it's all about, strong guitars. So that proves you can't work all through the night." (2)

## THE ALBUM ARTWORK

After three album covers created by Whitehead which were the epitome of the progressive scene, and the artwork by Swanwick, so eccentrically English, The Lamb required an album sleeve befitting of the radical change in style it represented. Consequently the band turned to the art design group Hipgnosis and used a model, named Omar, to pose as Rael.

Hackett: "For years Hipgnosis had been trying to get us to use a photographic cover. They always wanted everything to be edgy and the band always wanted something much more (to Hipgnosis' mind) airy-fairy. They were like: "Yes, you want all this romantic stuff. Why can't you have something that's contemporary, photographic, literal, perspective-driven?" I don't think this is the greatest cover ever. I think they did do some great covers, for Led Zeppelin for example, but perhaps because they were more open to some of their ideas. Like with Presence where you have a family sitting around a table staring at something in the middle and no-one really knows what it is. Everyone was sure that they didn't want their photograph on the front. No-one ever wanted their own face on the front of an album, not until Phil did Face Value, but that's another story. I didn't have any great ideas at the time, but this cover was desperately trying to be enigmatic, an attempt to be less romantic." (1)

Banks: "I think it works pretty well. It shows images from the story and has a kind of graphic novel quality about it, which I quite like because I'm a bit of a graphic novel fan. I quite like the dark side of it. It was a question of whether or not to do it bigger and cover the whole album or just use that central band. Also, the group lettering we used [for the band logo], which we came back to a few times later in our career, looks very strong. All the previous albums had been a bit more romantic whereas, here, having a stark black and white cover like that made you aware that this wasn't going to be quite as cuddly as some as our previous stuff." (1)

Gabriel: "I really liked Storm Thorgerson [from Hipgnosis], he was a wonderful character, very dry, cynical, sardonic and very talented. He was a lot of fun to interact with. He was always rude to everybody but it was great exchanging ideas with

German single label *Counting Out Time*.

him. He always had this bag of unused Hipgnosis ideas that he'd try to palm off as new and fresh. But here there was a story and some strong ideas for pictures. I had a sort of Puerto Rican figure in my head, perhaps influenced by *West Side Story* as well as *El Topo* and I remember a big search to try and find someone acceptable as Rael. I think we got pretty close but it was sort of like eight and a half out of ten." (1)

Collins: "I feel it's a little bit confused, just like the story. It's a distinct package and at least it evokes something. You know, I don't think I've actually ever read the story inside it." (1)

Gabriel: "There's this sprawling story on the inside. It's not well-written but it has some good ideas. Maybe the others were less happy with the cover because it was a visualisation of the story and I may have, you know, moved beyond the democratic process and that didn't go down well." (1)

## EPILOGUE

The Lamb Lies Down On Broadway was released in November 1974 when the band had already started the accompanying tour. It only managed to position itself at number 10 in the UK charts, seven places lower than its predecessor, while in the US the band improved its standing, reaching number 41 (Selling England only made it to number 70).

Gabriel: "Some of it does sound clumsy and awkward, but it has a character and, apart from *Supper's Ready*, which I think is more successful in creating an emotional journey, I think this is the most successful and evocative body of work we ever did, even though there are a couple of low points on it that let the steam out a little." (1)

Banks: "I suppose, looking back on it, it's something of a classic, but I didn't really enjoy writing or making it to the same extent as I did all the other albums. There's a lot of my stuff on The Lamb. A lot of bits I'd had around for a while ended up in *The Lamb* and *In The Cage*, as well as in *The Lamia* and *The Colony Of Slippermen*. We did a lot of improvising as well which created some of the most exciting bits on the album." (1)

Gabriel: "A lot of it was created in band format and quite often, when I was outside working on some of my own bits or lyrics or melodies, they would evolve new sections, but I don't think it's true to say that I featured less in the musical composition, although I probably had less to do with the jam creating process." (1)

Banks: "I like all the individual lyrics but I don't like the story. I've said many times before that it's like a Kurt Vonnegut novel but without the direction, it reminds me a bit of *Breakfast of Champions*. I don't find it moving, for me, the album doesn't really get anywhere. The 4th side could have been fantastic but the lyrics don't make it go anywhere, whereas with *Supper's Ready* you really went somewhere, it had a great shape, something this album doesn't have. My feeling about this record

German single.

is that it had lots of great individual bits, but as a whole it doesn't really work. Maybe because Peter wrote about 99% of the lyrics, it ended up being a bit one-dimensional. We all wrote lyrics and some of us wrote maybe more romantically or poetically and the contrast was quite nice." (2)

Hackett: "The album had a strange atmosphere. We were an English band singing about a Puerto Rican punk living in New York. You could even say that it was the start of punk. Even though punk bands savaged us as being part of the Establishment, quite frankly I think we gave them a leg-up." (1)

Banks: "Writing two songs because the plot needed it [*The Grand Parade Of Lifeless Packaging* and *Carpet Crawlers*] was an interesting exercise, and I think they are two of the better songs on the album; they were written very quickly and without any real effort. It taught us that we could write quite spontaneously if we wanted to, and perhaps we should do more of that, because up to this point our music had been pretty structured and complicated, particularly on SELLING ENGLAND BY THE POUND." (2)

Collins: "It wasn't an album to please the record company, we did what we wanted. That was what was wonderful about Tony Stratton-Smith, he would just try to deal with whatever we gave him. Atlantic always did their best like that too, because Ahmet [Ertegun, President of the American record label] was a big music person. He probably didn't understand anything about THE LAMB at all, but he could see that it was something adventurous and he just crossed his fingers and hoped that we weren't mad. I went to see The Musical Box [a French-Canadian Genesis tribute band famous for replicating the band's live shows] play this in its entirety and I was amazed at just how complicated it is." (1)

Banks: "I think the first two sides work the most; the music seems slightly better. There are a number of tracks I like later on, but I lose interest in the story. I'll listen to it all, but I don't like the shape of the album. For example, *IT* isn't a great ending for an album. It's a good piece but I think we could have done something slightly more epic, but it was all a bit rushed. We'd had problems obviously, with Peter going off in the middle of the album, and I think some of the spirit had gone out of both the record and the band at that point." (2)

Hackett: "I suppose I'm not really the one to ask about THE LAMB because I'm full of criticism for it. A lot of the time I was trying very hard to get my guitar through the mix, through the very dense keyboard textures, and I was always trying to do something sympathetic in the background." (1)

Collins: "The mobile studio in Wales was more like being in a rehearsal room but I still think THE LAMB sounds good. Some of those tracks sound a bit like the barn recordings of Neil Young with Crazy Horse. I think some of the best things we've ever done are on that record, the stuff where we

*The Waiting Room* live in Berkeley, January 22, 1975. The ghostly shape of Gabriel was projected behind the screens.

just improvised, like *The Waiting Room, Silent Sorrow In Empty Boats, Riding The Scree* and *In The Rapids*. Because it was a double album we had space. We had lots of improvised bits and I think that's something we've never done since. I like *The Light Dies Down On Broadway* as well. I think that's a great reprise. But there's loads of good stuff on the album: *Carpet Crawlers, Counting Out Time, The Grand Parade Of Lifeless Packaging, Back In N.Y.C., The Chamber Of 32 Doors…*" [1]

Banks: "We had too much material and some of the stuff we'd recorded in the mobile studio was a bit rough. We did a lot of the vocals at Island Studios while the lyrics were still being written, the whole thing was a nightmare. From a point of view of sheer happiness, the whole period of making the album was the lowest ebb in my whole career, it really was. And I didn't enjoy the tour at all." [2]

Rutherford: "We took a mobile studio up to this crumbling house in Wales. John Burns was the engineer. We recorded it in this room and I think that gave it more of a live feel, particularly with the drums. I think there's a good sound on this album. Also because the mics were set up more like they were when we were playing together on stage." [1]

Collins: "I felt it was our first really good sounding record. Everyone looks back at it with a lot of reverence but they didn't like it at the time. It's looked upon now in the same way that James Dean is; he only made three films but everyone thinks he's a wonderful actor." [1]

Banks: "For some people, it is a peak, I suppose the fact that it's a double concept album makes it sort of distinct, but at the time it didn't go down well with the fans. It was the only album we made that didn't do as well as its predecessor, in this case Selling England By The Pound. I think it's quite a difficult album, very dark and quite dense; it takes a bit more getting into and maybe that's why it continues to work really well for the people who like it. That's the thing about Genesis, we don't have any one album that everybody thinks is *THE* album; for example, Pink Floyd have The Dark Side Of The Moon but, with us, every album has been mentioned to me as being *THE* album (apart from perhaps From Genesis To Revelation). Sometimes the reason why an album has a significant impact depends on the point in your life when you heard it." [1]

Hackett: "I would say Selling England was more our Dark Side perhaps. Now I can listen to it [The Lamb] without any rancour, I don't remember the pain, I can just enjoy it as a piece of music. It was a clever album with lots of great keyboard work but not so many opportunities for the guitar to shine, although where it does it's interesting. I tend to think that it parallels Yes doing their double concept album Tales From Topographic Oceans. I know that often the guys have felt that maybe it would have made a great single album if we'd just kept the best stuff, but what would we have kept and what would we have thrown away?" [1]

Banks: "Although the lyrics are good, no song really stands out on its own. Take *The Lamia* for example: if you sing that out of context it makes no sense at all, being as it's about snakes and stuff and I slightly resent that aspect of it. There are two songs we used to perform quite often, *In The Cage*, which almost works (although lyrically the brother John bit in the middle doesn't make much sense) but it's a very strong piece of music, and *Carpet Crawlers*, which works because it's got a chorus

that could relate to anything. The verse lyrics are pretty strange but there's some lovely imagery in there. Looking back, it wasn't the best time of my life and it was a difficult album to make. I think it's got lots of great moments on it. As a double album its real weakness is the fourth side. Unlike today's CDs, where you put all the strong stuff up at the front, the idea back then was to build up to a big ending and I don't think this does." (1)

Hackett: "Some members of the band were trying to be romantic while others wanted to be more realistic, more cynical. Pete felt that he was trying to drag the band into the eighties. It was the start of punk rock and probably, in some ways, the death of the band's progressive rock period, although we did go on to do more of that as a four-piece. I think something was lost, dead and buried with Selling England By The Pound, and The Lamb marked a start of a new era for the band. It's not an album I feel that close to. There are some good moments in it, but it wasn't a happy time, so it wasn't a happy album. Anyone who feels it's their favourite album is coming at it from an entirely different perspective. Getting the album made was a victory of sorts, a Pyrrhic victory; ultimately we lost our singer and something of the spirit of the band was lost at that point, although we did perhaps recover some of that later on. It depends whether you think that The Lamb or The Wall are the apices of Genesis' and Pink Floyd's achievements. You've got to look at the whole of the band's history to understand what works and what nearly works." (1)

Gabriel: "It felt as if we were still living that dream of isolating ourselves and supposedly being in a nurturing, creative environment. Even though that wasn't working on lots of different levels, I still think some of our best material of that period went into The Lamb Lies Down On Broadway and looking back it's still one of the things I feel proud of. Quite often there's this irony in life; when really shitty things are going on, the creativity that comes out of it can still be strong, interesting and move people. Musically there was a confidence and an assurance about what we were doing as writers and players. I think it's a good record." (1)

Banks: "Of all the albums we made, this is the one I enjoyed making the least. I got very little pleasure out of it. A lot of it was quite a fight. I mean I like everything we've done but, coming back to it, Foxtrot and Selling England By The Pound are by far the best two albums from this period. And I prefer a lot of the later albums to this one, such as Duke and Wind & Wuthering. I like The Lamb

Single English label *Carpet Crawlers*. On the B side the band released a live version of *The Waiting Room* subtitled *Evil Jam*.

because it's adventurous. We tried a lot of things, some of which worked, having a better story would have helped a lot. It was a strange period in terms of commercial success. It didn't do as well as SELLING ENGLAND BY THE POUND, which was slightly weird. It didn't open up new territory for us and the tour didn't go down that well either. We had built up a really good following up to and including SELLING ENGLAND BY THE POUND; we had grown to a certain stature and then I felt we lost it a little bit on this whole project, although we were able to rebuild it with A TRICK OF THE TAIL. That was great for us and the fans; they were very happy with A TRICK OF THE TAIL, it was more like SELLING ENGLAND BY THE POUND. Of course, Pete went off and did something completely different himself, in some ways he became much more user-friendly. So it was a fraught time and a slightly fraught album. But it's unique and I'm very proud of it." (2)

An album, which as can quite clearly be seen was not appreciated in equal measure by everyone in the band, THE LAMB appears to be revitalised in the new 5.1 remixes by Nick Davis, released in 2008.

Rutherford: "When I heard this a few years ago, when Nick Davis remixed it, I was impressed by how much energy the album and the band as players actually had. The opening track and *Back In N.Y.C.* are really quite heavy songs. It's funny because people now regard the album as a great moment (probably because we gave ourselves space to do different stuff) but at the time it was a bit of a flop." (1)

Gabriel: "I think Nick worked very hard and did a good job of remixing THE LAMB, but at some point I wouldn't mind having a go myself, I think it's interesting to hear different interpretations of records. For example, with The Beatles, I would have loved to have heard the different band members' interpretations of their albums." (1)

Rutherford: "Nick did a great job with the remixes and Tony was there much of the time, so the early albums have definitely improved a lot. At the time they weren't recorded that well and they were mixed quickly. THE LAMB is the album that was always pretty good actually." (1)

Hackett: "The remixes that I've heard sound very good, but I think they could have been just that little bit better, they could have been a little more creative. But try working with a corporation these days... it's very hard to get a consensus when no-one is working face to face any more and you are sending each other stuff and waiting for a reply. I think the new mixes sound very considered and I like what I've heard of THE LAMB very much; there are guitar parts that I originally put down that were either left out or buried in the mix, so it's great to hear them now." (1)

# THE CONCERTS

After increasing the theatrical content of their live performances, thanks to the ever more histrionic showmanship of frontman Gabriel (who by SELLING ENGLAND BY THE POUND had perfected and extended the costumes and stage show seen in the tour to promote FOXTROT), the band was going to have to come up with something exceptional to present their double concept album.

The band, with Gabriel at the fore, intended to put on a real musical type show to help the audience get into the anything-but-simple world of Rael. With this in mind, a more intimate stage set-up was planned: the four instrumentalists were each placed on an individual platform and the lights were less invasive to create a darker scene full of black and white contrast and a focus on the rich array of slides (over 1,000). These images were projected on three screens to capture the attention of the audience who were already captivated by the now truly extravagant personality of the lead singer.

Collins: "I just have very vivid memories of record company executives coming in and heading straight for Pete. It didn't bother me that nobody said "Phil, you're great", it was the fact that the music was very rarely mentioned, and I was starting to feel that the music was being overshadowed by the visuals, which were getting a little bit out of hand. I mean, the idea of having these screens behind us was fantastic but they never worked. I think there were maybe four shows in a hundred when everything actually changed at the right moment." [1]

With the help of a carefully selected staff of well-known professionals (the original tour programme lists Alan Owen - lights; David Lawrence - projections; Jane Highfield - costume design; Peter Hart - special effects), Genesis got ready to take their latest creation out into the world.

The band had planned a dozen or so concerts in England for the end of October, aiming to set foot on American soil by 20 November. However, the high level of tension simmering within the band led to an accident involving Steve Hackett. Just a few days before the tour was about to start, the guitarist (already under strain due to the breakdown of his marriage) was at a backstage party of the Sensational Alex Harvey Band when he heard someone say, "the band is good, but they'd be nothing without Alex Harvey". Obviously projecting the Harvey comment on to the situation with Gabriel and Genesis, and with his nerves already at breaking point, Steve crushed the wine glass he was holding and severed a tendon and nerve in his thumb. Given that the injured guitarist would obviously be unable to play for a number of weeks, the first UK dates in October (29–30 in Newcastle) and November (1–2 in Manchester, 4 in London, 6–7 in Edinburgh, 8–9 in Bristol, 11–12 in Birmingham) had to be cancelled (they were then rescheduled for April–May 1975).

And so it was that the tour started in the Auditorium Theatre, Chicago, on 20 November. At that time THE LAMB LIES DOWN ON BROADWAY had yet to be released in the US, making their first concerts on American soil more than just a little bizarre.

Rutherford: "We took it live and played America before the album was out. A whole show of a new double concept album. Thinking about it, it was madness really, but actually it went down OK. That was a long tour and I got a bit tired of playing it. I remember towards the end thinking I would never do that again, you know, where you just play one era of music. It's nice to mix up different eras, different songs, different styles." [1]

In fact, Genesis, faithful to the theatrical aspect of the double album, decided to play it in its entirety, with a long 90-minute performance interrupted only by Gabriel's brief introductions before each of the first three sides. The only concession made to their faithful fans was the encore, usually *The Musical Box* (although in around one-third of the concerts, Genesis would perform a second encore with *Watcher Of The Skies*).

Collins: "We went over to America and played the album for the first time, and nobody had heard a note of it. Four sides of this new music they'd never heard with just a couple of old songs at the end. That was very brave and we had a great time doing it. Lots of good music." [1]

Banks: "The audience didn't know the album; half the time they wanted to hear *The Knife* and *Supper's Ready*. Half the songs never worked live. And I couldn't play them right because I had the wrong piano." [2]

Execution of the songs from the album did, in fact, present a few problems and timing issues. The lack of a proper piano was most noticeable in *Anyway*, played much more slowly than on the album, even though the song was, as Banks says, "pretty easy to play. I mean, there have been a few things over the years that have been bastards to play, but not this one". [2]

Apart from Banks' issues, the biggest problem was Gabriel due to the high pitch of some of the songs, but it didn't end there. Banks: "*Back In N.Y.C.* was a nightmare for Pete to sing live. A lot of the time when playing The Lamb live, the vocals were compromised because he was wearing masks and with the *Slipperman* he never got the mic anywhere near his mouth, so we were always let down by the vocals. When we came to release the live version [1998, in the Genesis Archive 1967–75 box set] a lot of the vocals weren't usable and needed redoing." [2]

If truth be told, the only mask Gabriel actually wore during this tour was the Slipperman costume, an incredible series of different sized round lumps covering the singer's entire body down to his legs to represent the disgusting warts Rael was left with from having dared to yield to the pleasures of the flesh.

Collins: "The worst thing was the Slipperman where he came out dressed in this horrible outfit with inflatable genitals. Sometimes he got a little bit stuck on the way out and other times, when he did make it out, the microphone could barely get near his mouth and when it did he was out of breath. There are a lot of words in that song and he was running around. I think the Slipperman costume was something very last minute to avoid confrontations. It was funny and it was adventurous, it was edgy and it was like nobody else. But I didn't think it was very musical." [1]

Gabriel: "It was the chance of having interesting looking visuals that would get a reaction from people. The Slipperman costume was a really ugly looking thing, and as Phil quite rightly said, it was bloody hard to sing inside there as we didn't have those little tiny mics back then. So inside this mask, I was trying to hold the microphone and was tripping up over things and I'd crawl under Tony's organ. It was just trying to explore things

JF Promociones Musicales y Gay & Co.

PRESENTAN

velódromo de S. Sebastián

en discos

fonogram s.a.

Domingo 18 Mayo - 9 de la noche

The single *The Carpet Crawlers*, Portuguese edition.

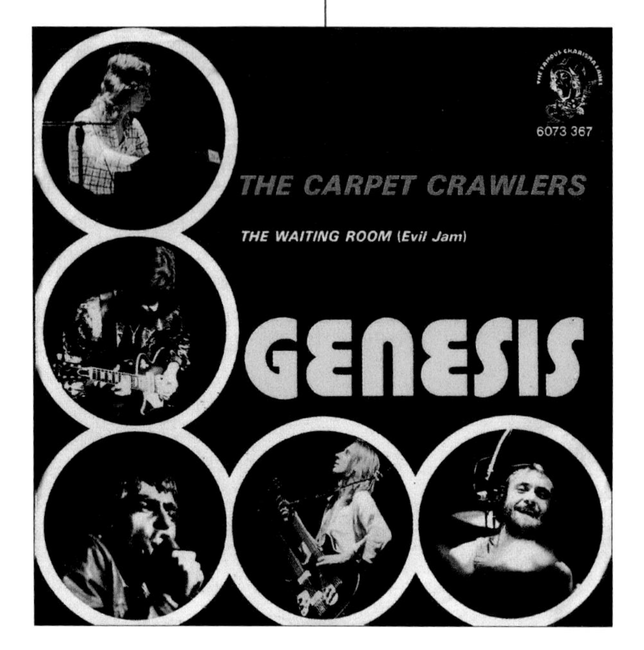


and push it a lot and have fun. But again, it was like with the lyrics, I knew that if everything went to the vote it would die a horrible death. For the visuals and screen projections I worked a lot with Geoffrey Shaw, who I think now runs an interactive arts centre in Germany. He was a good ally to have and there weren't any real problems or battles once the others felt good that there was something interesting and of quality coming." (1)

For the rest of the show, Gabriel put a great deal of energy and mobility into presenting the main character, Rael, portraying the young Porto Rican dressed in a leather jacket over a white t-shirt and jeans. During the show Peter also sang two songs bare-chested: *Cuckoo Cocoon* (during which he also played the flute lying down on one side in front of Banks' keyboards) and *In The Cage*, whereas during the instrumental *The Waiting Room* his shadow appeared behind the central screen dressed in a hat and long-fingered gloves to represent evil.

Another key theatrical moment was during *The Lamia*: dressed all in white, Peter sang from underneath a silk cone on which the female serpent figures were depicted and this would turn around him during the choruses. Collins: "Sometimes Peter's mic cable would get caught up in the scenery for *The Lamia* so he couldn't move... It was cutting edge but all very *Spinal Tap*." (1)

Finally, between the end of *In The Rapids* and the start of *IT*, an unseen roadie would carry a dummy dressed to look like Gabriel onto the stage under the cover of dry ice. From a distance it wasn't easy to tell the real Gabriel from the dummy, much to the wonder of the audience. Banks: "This was the point in the show when Rael realises that he and John are one and the same and you have them on either side of the stage lit up by strobes. That was a great effect because no-one saw the dummy go up on stage and all of a sudden you have two Peters and you didn't know which was which." (2)

Alas, less than a week into the tour the rising tension between Gabriel and the rest of the band reached a point of no return. Gabriel: "I think because we had started a tour that was getting great reactions people were hoping things would heal. But when we got to the Midwest of America it just got too much for me and I just knew that I was drowning and I had to head up for air." (1)

Collins: "We were all pleased Peter was back but

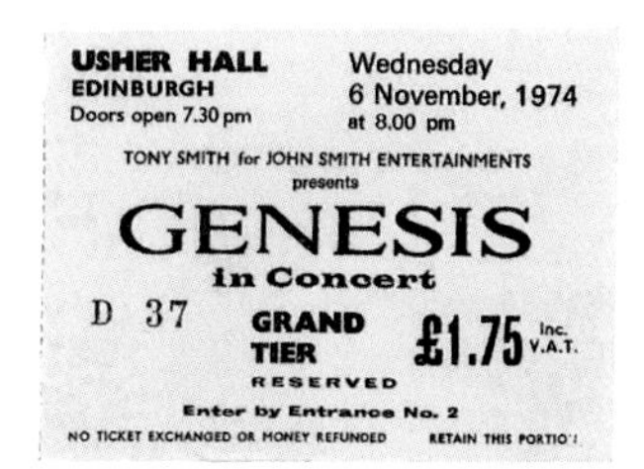


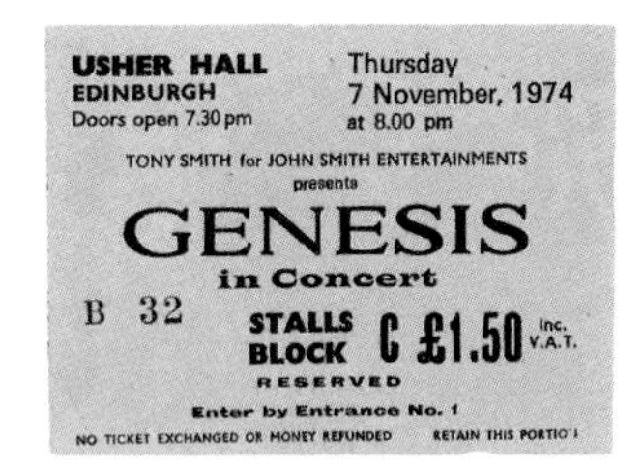


the situation was such that when he decided he was really going to leave we were kind of expecting it. Peter told Tony Smith that he was leaving when we were in Cleveland. I remember sitting in a room with Tony Smith talking about what we were going to do next... it was a bit strange to be carrying on doing gigs knowing the singer was leaving." (1)

Hackett: "I remember talking to Peter on a plane one day, I asked him if he was seriously going to leave. And he said, "yeah, 'fraid so, I've made up my mind". To start with I thought it was all part of the act, part of the show and, like the make-up, it was going to come off, but no, it was real. He had family pressures and I think that he wanted to be an active parent. At that point, it looked as if he wanted to pull out of the music business all together and do something else, but in the end he went on from strength to strength and so did the band. But it was very, very tough trying to come to terms with the fact that the star was going to leave." (1)

Banks: "Peter and I started off in the group as best friends but by then it was getting more difficult, particularly within the group, so it was a sad time. We did about a 100 shows of The Lamb Lies Down On Broadway, which wasn't a fantastic show to be honest; we were trying to do the whole album to audiences who really wanted to hear a lot of the old hits. There were one or two nights when it was great, when everything seemed to work and it sounded really good, but it wasn't so pleasurable. And in the middle of the tour Pete said he was going to leave for good so it was a strange period for us." (1)

Rutherford: "When Peter finally broke the news he was leaving it wasn't such a huge shock because we'd already had a pre-warning. We'd just managed to persuade Tony Smith to leave his business and become our manager, poor guy, and suddenly the singer leaves. I'm sure he thought, "Oh God, what have I done?". We're talking about what seemed like a long period, but it was only 5 years actually. I remember once seeing the list of gigs we did in one year and it was like 210. In one year! That's a lot of gigs. I always feel uncomfortable if someone I'm working with wants to be somewhere else. You feel you're putting your heart and soul into it and they're not really in the same space. So, in a sense, if somebody does want to leave, I've always felt it's the right thing to do. I'm sure Peter thought, "What comes next? I've written virtually all the lyrics for a double concept album, can I go back to where I was before?". But I think it would have been hard to go backwards again." (1)

With sadness in their hearts and turmoil in their minds, Genesis tackled the first leg of the US tour: 25 gigs in one month with only 4 days off. They started out from the interior states of Illinois, Missouri and Indiana before heading to the East Coast (Rhode Island, Massachusetts, New Jersey...) and then New York with two consecutive concerts at the Academy Of Music (6–7 December). At this point, Genesis were appearing in medium-sized theatres and auditoriums. Towards the end of the tour the band also set foot in neighbouring Canada, with a concert in Montréal and one in Toronto, before returning to the state of New York for the last two dates on 17 and 18 December.

Two weeks off and the band were back in the US for the second leg of the tour, again for almost

another month (10 January to 4 February). This time the focus was on the southern states. They started out in Florida (West Palm Beach and Lakeland) and then moved progressively westwards: Georgia, Louisiana, Texas, Oklahoma, all the way to California, where they played in Berkeley (22 January) and San Diego (on the 25th), with the famous concert at the Shrine Auditorium in Los Angeles in between, on the 24th. The live recording of this show would be released 23 years later in the GENESIS ARCHIVE 1967–75 box set, featuring newly recorded vocals and guitar parts. Collins: "The live show recorded at the Shrine Auditorium is probably the best version of the album, even though the studio album captured something different about us. But when we started playing it live, I mean, we were fantastic." [1]

After the happy parenthesis in California, the band went back towards the centre of the US, stopping off in Arizona on the 28th and replacing the original concert scheduled for 1 February at the Queen Elizabeth Theatre in Vancouver, Canada (simply too far away) for a geographically more feasible venue in Kansas City. The American tour came to an end with three concerts in Michigan, Indiana and Illinois.

After a two-week break, Genesis finally got to tackle Europe. The tour started in Oslo, Norway, on 19 February, and then went on to Denmark, Germany and Holland.

On the 26th the band arrived in France, a country which was very supportive of Genesis in this particular era, where they played 5 concerts up to 3 March. They then went on to play two consecutive evenings in Cascais, Portugal (6–7 March), something which was of great symbolic value as the country had just entered the Third Republic following the Carnation Revolution, less than a year earlier.

According to the European Tour Programme, after three shows in Spain, Genesis were supposed to play ten or so concerts in Italy, from 14 to 24 March. However, due to the political tensions in Italy at that time and the months of clashes instigated by the autoreduction movement, the Italian tour was all but cancelled, with the exception of a single date at the Turin Palasport on 24 March where the band played to an audience of around 12,000 (exceeding the official venue capacity) but not without the by then usual audience skirmishes with the police and between fringe extremists.

A couple of the dates originally planned for Italy were offset by concerts in France and the long German tour with 11 dates (26 March to 8 April) incorporated a detour into Switzerland (Bern) and was followed by three concerts in the Netherlands (10–12 April).

Unable to change the layout of the concept album, the band, by now showing clear signs of fatigue, started to unleash a bit of tension by making variations to the encores: after having only played *Watcher Of The Skies* on three occasions, (Paris, Badalona, Annecy), Genesis added *The Knife* for the first time in Brussels (12 April) to *The Musical Box* (something which would also occur occasionally on later dates, with them playing *The Knife* as their only encore in Liverpool on 19 April).

Halfway through April the band finally got to

*Ciao 2001* announces the only Italian Genesis concert.

play the tour dates which had been cancelled the previous October: 16 almost consecutive concerts (with just three days off) from 14 April (at the Empire Pool in Wembley with a repeat show on the following day) to 2 May with a second concert at the Birmingham Hippodrome. In between there were shows in Southampton, Liverpool (three evenings on the trot), Edinburgh (two shows), Newcastle (two) and Manchester (two).

After a couple of days off, Genesis were getting ready for the final push, with another show in Belgium and five in Germany before the grand finale in France, with a quick detour to Spain (San Sebastian, 18 May). The last gigs on French soil were chaotic. For many years it was written that the last show was played at Saint Etienne, but that's not quite how it went. The last date was supposed to be on 24 May 1975 at Parc des Expositions in Toulouse but this was cancelled due to poor ticket sales. And so the curtain fell on the Peter Gabriel era in a town of 120,000 inhabitants called Besançon, on 22 May. Collins: "The last gig, which was supposed to be Toulouse, was cancelled, so what actually became our last show was a bit of an anticlimax because there'd been no kind of build-up to it. What's incredible is that we all disagree on where the last show was. I'm convinced we ended the tour in Besançon, even if everybody else tells me we ended it in St Etienne." [1]

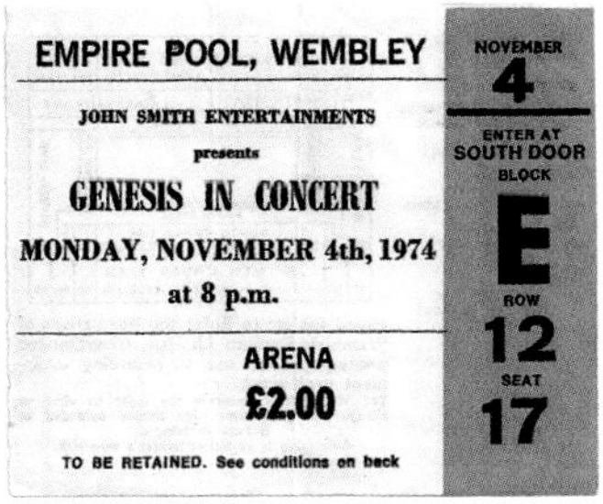

Hackett: "Besançon sounds familiar to me. But there was a cancelled show, the very last one. So it was a bit of an anti-climax because we were expecting to do one more show, so nobody realised that that was going to be Pete's last show with the band. So there was a feeling of great sadness at the end and also great relief because we were all exhausted, you know physically and emotionally." [4]

Banks: "In the middle of the tour Pete said that he was leaving and we had to carry on playing this thing and we cancelled the last show of the tour in Europe because there was no audience. We just petered out, there were some good shows in the middle of the tour but the last few were very damp. We were supposed to be doing the last show in Toulouse, but we went "oh just forget it" and so we finished a day early in Besançon... There weren't many people coming and we thought, "we can't face this anymore, just forget it"." [2]

But while the band were going through their interior torment, some of the crew thought it would be a good time for a joke, as Banks recalls, "in the final show instead of the dummy, one of the roadies got up on stage, naked, so instead of a double Peter, you had Peter and a naked roadie with the strobes flashing at the highpoint of the whole piece. I turned round and it was my roadie, Geoff. It wasn't pleasant." [2]

In August 1975, with a letter handed over to the UK press, Peter Gabriel made his divorce from Genesis official. Gabriel: "I think it was great that we went out on a good piece of work. As with any

Poster for Bern concert, 29 March 1975.

sort of divorce there were difficulties, but there was never really any bad feelings with the individuals. Most of what they wanted I was prepared to give them, including extra touring time, my tape archive and most of the equipment and stuff. They were much more successful without me so there was actually no real issue, but I think everyone had doubts and were very frustrated because we had worked a long time to get some success. We were about to get some financial rewards. So you know, then this bastard goes and sabotages the whole thing just as it gets successful, that wasn't a popular thing to do from a career point of view. Compared to some other band break-ups, where there was a lot more acrimony than in our case, I think we handled it in a fairly sort of adult way." (1)

Collins: "On and off throughout the years there have been rumours that I was either the instigator of Peter's leaving because of my apparent unhappiness at Pete's visuals or pleased that he left so that I could sing. None of that is true. I love Peter to this day. I've played on his albums. I played for him as his drummer for free at one point, when he was promoting his third album, because he couldn't afford a band. You know, I went to his wedding. He came to mine. I was very sad when he left but we had to get on with it. And I didn't want to be the singer at all because I was the drummer and, by that point, I was a very good drummer. I ended up singing because we couldn't find anybody else." (1)

Gabriel: "Some people think Phil was chomping at the bit waiting to get rid of me but it wasn't like that at all. He loved being a drummer and, although he was beginning to write songs and sing, the band didn't consider him the singer and I don't think he really considered himself as the singer for Genesis. It was clear to me that he could have a big career on his own, and I remember saying that to him because we would often be hammering out our own things, which were sounding quite different from what the band was doing. I never had the feeling that the band wanted to get rid of me at any time." (1)

For a while the singer disappeared from the scene completely. Gabriel: "I never had regrets about leaving the band, although I had some fears about working with other musicians again and trying to forge my own way, because I wanted out of the business for a couple of years. I couldn't imagine getting rid of the poison we'd accumulated in any other way. There was suddenly this sense of freedom and being able to collaborate with all sorts of wonderful musicians from all over the world and yet be able to sit in the captain's chair; when I don't like things I can stop or do them again or even throw them away." (1)

Deprived of their frontman, after asking themselves about the future, the remaining band members decided to roll up their sleeves and carry on, promoting Phil Collins to lead singer. While his ex-bandmates headed down the road towards worldwide stardom, Gabriel was in no rush to make his return, but when he did he became one of the most influential artists of his generation.

SEC. ROW SEAT
97 P 17
EAST
Retain Stub – Good Only
CONCERT BOWL
MON. 8:00 P.M. DEC. 16
Davis Printing Limited
GENESIS
PRICE-5.45+RST .55-$6.00
ADMIT ONE. Entrance by Main Door or by Church Street Door.
Maple Leaf Gardens
LIMITED
CONDITION OF SALE: Upon refunding the purchase price the man-

Gabriel: "Many people have been puzzled by how we did so well and how the hell we survived for so long when in a lot of critics' eyes the music is unlistenable. I actually think it's because our music is based on songwriters and obviously we built a very strong fan-base by playing live. If you look at, say, Crosby, Stills, Nash & Young, 10cc or other bands which are songwriter-based rather than musician-based you do see long life-spans. Maybe not all are in the same direction but it's a different sensibility. Most bands begin by playing together and then find writing, whereas we wanted to write and we found playing." (1)

(To be continued)

## NOTES

(1) Mike Kaufman's Genesis interviews, Chicago / London, October 2007, partially used in the bonus disc accompanying the 2008 remasters

(2) Mario Giammetti listens to The Lamb Lies Down On Broadway with Tony Banks, Chiddingfold, 10 May 2011

(3) Personal e-mail sent to Mario Giammetti by Steve Hackett, dated 27 April 2012

(4) Mario Giammetti's telephone interview with Steve Hackett, 7 February 2012, partially published in the article "I colori della chitarra" in Dusk, Issue no. 58, March 2008

# THE LAMB LIES DOWN ON BROADWAY TOUR

## 1974

### NOVEMBER

20 **Chicago, IL (USA)**, Auditorium Theatre - Roosevelt University
21 **Chicago, IL (USA)**, Auditorium Theatre - Roosevelt University
22 **Indianapolis, IN (USA)**, Indiana Convention Center
23 **St. Louis, MO (USA)**, Ambassador Theatre
25 **Cleveland, OH (USA)**, Music Hall
26 **Cleveland, OH (USA)**, Music Hall
27 **Columbus, OH (USA)**, Franklin County Veterans Memorial
28 **Detroit, MI (USA)**, Masonic Auditorium
29 **Fort Wayne, IN (USA)**, National Guard Armory
30 **Pittsburgh, PA (USA)**, Syria Mosque

### DECEMBER

1 **Baltimore, MD (USA)**, Lyric Theatre
4 **Richmond, VA (USA)**, Richmond Mosque
5 **Philadelphia, PA (USA)**, Philadelphia Civic Center
6 **New York, NY (USA)**, Academy of Music
7 **New York, NY (USA)**, Academy of Music
8 **Providence, RI (USA)**, Palace Concert Theater
9 **Boston, MA (USA)**, Music Hall
11 **Albany, NY (USA)**, Palace Theatre
12 **Waterbury, CT (USA)**, Palace Theatre
13 **Passaic, NJ (USA)**, Capitol Theatre
15 **Montréal, QC (CANADA)**, Forum
16 **Toronto, ON (CANADA)**, Maple Leaf Gardens
17 **Rochester, NY (USA)**, Auditorium Theatre
18 **Buffalo, NY (USA)**, Century Theatre

CAPITAL THEATRE 326 MONROE ST
JOHN SCHER PRESENTS
GENESIS
PASSAIC NEW JERSEY
7:30PM FRI DEC 13 1974
NO REFUNDS OR EXCHANGES
1213 DATE/EVENT CODE 7:30PM ENTRANCE R/C A $6.00 EST. PRICE TX 0.30 $6.30 TOTAL
ORORC R/C 104 A 104

## 1975

### JANUARY

10 **West Palm Beach, FL (USA)**, West Palm Beach Auditorium
11 **Lakeland, FL (USA)**, Lakeland Civic Center Theatre
13 **Atlanta, GA (USA)**, Municipal Auditorium
15 **New Orleans, LA (USA)**, St. Bernard Civic Auditorium
17 **Houston, TX (USA)**, Music Hall
19 **Oklahoma City, OK (USA)**, Civic Center Music Hall
22 **Berkeley, CA (USA)**, Berkeley Community Theatre - Berkeley High School
24 **Los Angeles, CA (USA)**, Shrine Auditorium
25 **San Diego, CA (USA)**, San Diego Civic Theatre
28 **Phoenix, AZ (USA)**, Assembly Hall - Phoenix Civic Plaza

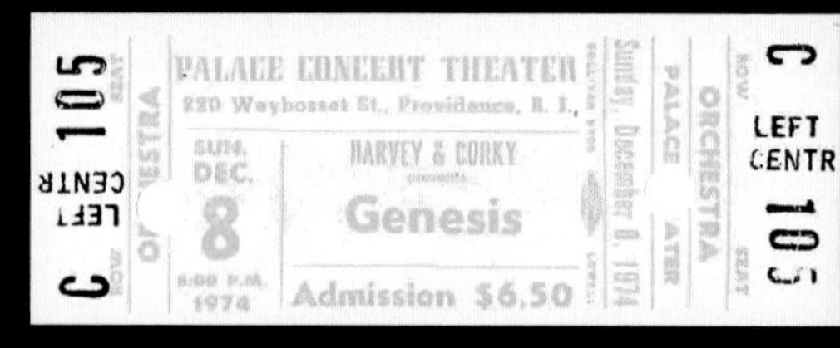


### FEBRUARY

1 **Kansas City, KS (USA)**, Memorial Hall
*Originally planned at Vancouver's Queen Elizabeth Theatre, Canada*
2 **Allendale, MI (USA)**, Fieldhouse - Grand Valley State Colleges
3 **Fort Wayne, IN (USA)**, Allen County Memorial Coliseum
4 **Chicago, IL (USA)**, Arie Crown Theater - McCormick Place
19 **Oslo (NORWAY)**, Ekeberghallen
21 **Copenhagen (DENMARK)**, Falkoner Teatret
22 **Hannover (WEST GERMANY)**, Niedersachsenhalle
23 **Berlin (WEST GERMANY)**, Eissporthalle
24 **Amsterdam (THE NETHERLANDS)**, Theater Carré
26 **Cambrai (FRANCE)**, Palais des Grottes
28 **Colmar (FRANCE)**, Parc des Expositions

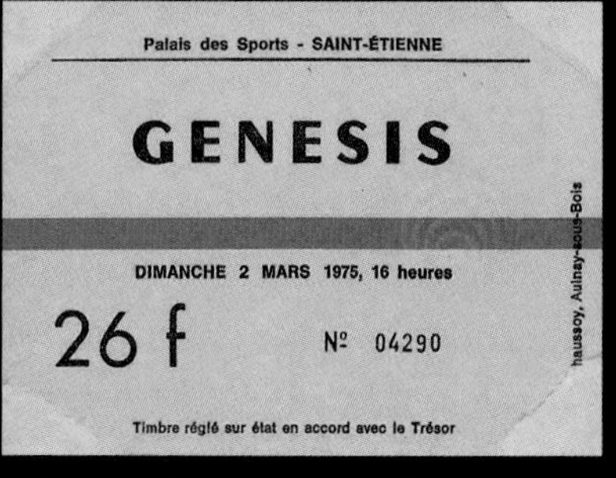

## MARCH

1 **Dijon** (**FRANCE**), Palais Des Expositions
2 **St. Etienne** (**FRANCE**), Palais des Sports
3 **Paris** (**FRANCE**), Palais des Sports
6 **Cascais** (**PORTUGAL**), Pavilhão Dos Desportos
7 **Cascais** (**PORTUGAL**), Pavilhão Dos Desportos
9 **Badalona** (**SPAIN**), Nuevo Pabellon Club Juventud
10 **Badalona** (**SPAIN**), Nuevo Pabellon Club Juventud
11 **Madrid** (**SPAIN**), Pabellon Real Madrid
17 **Paris** (**FRANCE**), Palais des Sports
22 **Annecy** (**FRANCE**), Salle d'Expositions
24 **Torino** (**ITALY**), Palasport Parco Ruffini
26 **Offenburg** (**WEST GERMANY**), Ortenauhalle
27 **Nürnberg** (**WEST GERMANY**), Messezentrum
29 **Bern** (**SWITZERLAND**), Festhalle
30 **Saarbrücken** (**WEST GERMANY**), Saarlandhalle

## APRIL

1 **Ludwigshafen** (**WEST GERMANY**), Friedrich-Ebert-Halle
2 **Stuttgart** (**WEST GERMANY**), Killesberg-Halle 14
3 **Frankfurt** (**WEST GERMANY**), Jahrhunderthalle
4 **Munich** (**WEST GERMANY**), Rudi Sedlmayer Sporthalle
5 **Heidelberg** (**WEST GERMANY**), Stadthalle
6 **Düsseldorf** (**WEST GERMANY**), Philipshalle
7 **Dortmund** (**WEST GERMANY**), Halle 3 - Westfalenhallen
8 **Hamburg** (**WEST GERMANY**), Hall 1 - Congress Centrum Hamburg
10 **Groningen** (**THE NETHERLANDS**), Martinihal-Centrum
11 **Rotterdam** (**THE NETHERLANDS**), Ahoy Sportpaleis
12 **Brussels** (**BELGIUM**), Forest National
14 **London** (**ENGLAND**), Empire Pool
15 **London** (**ENGLAND**), Empire Pool
16 **Southampton** (**ENGLAND**), Gaumont Theatre
18 **Liverpool** (**ENGLAND**), Empire Theatre
19 **Liverpool** (**ENGLAND**), Empire Theatre
20 **Liverpool** (**ENGLAND**), Empire Theatre
22 **Edinburgh** (**SCOTLAND**), Usher Hall
23 **Edinburgh** (**SCOTLAND**), Usher Hall
24 **Newcastle** (**ENGLAND**), City Hall
25 **Newcastle** (**ENGLAND**), City Hall
27 **Manchester** (**ENGLAND**), Palace Theatre
28 **Manchester** (**ENGLAND**), Palace Theatre
29 **Bristol** (**ENGLAND**), Colston Hall
30 **Bristol** (**ENGLAND**), Colston Hall

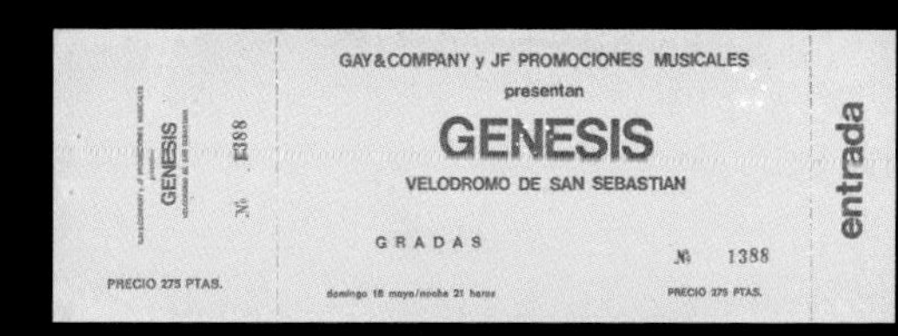


## MAY

1 **Birmingham** (**ENGLAND**), Hippodrome
2 **Birmingham** (**ENGLAND**), Hippodrome
8 **Antwerp** (**BELGIUM**), Sportpaleis Antwerpen
9 **Bremen** (**WEST GERMANY**), Stadthalle
10 **Kiel** (**WEST GERMANY**), Ostseehalle
11 **Essen** (**WEST GERMANY**), Grugahalle
13 **Münster** (**WEST GERMANY**), Halle Münsterland
14 **Wiesbaden** (**WEST GERMANY**), Rhein-Main-Hallen
15 **Reims** (**FRANCE**), Patinoire
16 **Reims** (**FRANCE**), Patinoire
18 **San Sebastian** (**SPAIN**), Velodromo Anoeta
20 **Paris** (**FRANCE**), Palais des Sports
22 **Besançon** (**FRANCE**), Palais des Sports

BANK of ENGLAND
FC 6060
THE FAMOUS CHARISMA LABEL
GENESIS
One Pound
LONDON
SELLING ENGLAND BY THE POUND
FC 6060